THE DYLAN TAPES

Friends, Players, and Lovers Talking Early Bob Dylan

ANTHONY SCADUTO
Edited by STEPHANIE TRUDEAU

University of Minnesota Press
Minneapolis
London

Published by the University of Minnesota Press
111 Third Avenue South, Suite 290
Minneapolis, MN 55401-2520
http://www.upress.umn.edu

ISBN 978-1-5179-0815-7 (hc)
ISBN 978-1-5179-0816-4 (pb)

A Cataloging-in-Publication record for this book is available from the Library of Congress.

Printed in the United States of America on acid-free paper

The University of Minnesota is an equal-opportunity educator and employer.

29 28 27 26 25 24 23 22   10 9 8 7 6 5 4 3 2 1

To Michael

CONTENTS

Introduction

ANTHONY SCADUTO'S BASEMENT TAPES

STEPHANIE TRUDEAU

ANTHONY SCADUTO WAS AN AVID READER with wide-ranging interests. He wrote poetry and short stories, but his idol was Frank Lloyd Wright. Tony wanted to become an architect. He enrolled in engineering classes at Brooklyn College, but his life took a different direction at a holiday party when a family friend suggested he forget college and architecture and take up his offer of a real job as a copyboy at the *New York Post*. Tony would make money and he could write. Within a couple of years, he had been promoted from copyboy to a police reporter covering accidents, crimes, and general mayhem in Brooklyn.

From the mid-1950s through the 1960s, the *New York Post* carried bylines by some of New York City's best writers: Pete Hamill, James Wexler, and Nora Ephron, who told the editors, "Scaduto can write. Give him feature story assignments." By the late 1950s the Mafia was becoming big news and Scaduto was asked to cover it. He told me he got the assignment because he grew up in an Italian neighborhood in Brooklyn and his last name ended with a vowel. He became the Mafia expert for the *Post* and his coverage earned him the nickname "Tough Tony."

Tony also loved music and begged to cover the rock-and-roll sensation Elvis Presley. The Mafia expert staked his claim as the *Post*'s pop music authority. At the time, pop music was broad, encompassing folk, blues, and rock and roll. The early 1960s was the era of the Beatles, the Rolling Stones, and Bob Dylan. Tony had written a paperback on the Beatles, then a hardcover publisher, Grosset & Dunlap, asked him to write a serious book on a pop music figure. The editor suggested the albino blues guitarist Johnny Winter. Tony said the only subject worth considering was Bob Dylan.

No one had written a biography of Bob Dylan, and Tony decided to take the same approach he did for the feature stories he wrote for the *New York Post*: extensive research and comprehensive interviews. He tracked down Dylan's friends from high school, including Echo Helstrom, Dylan's high school girlfriend who inspired "Girl from the North Country." Tony spoke to Dylan's second great love, Suze Rotolo, the girl described in "Boots of Spanish Leather" and who appeared with him on the cover of Dylan's second album, *The Freewheelin' Bob Dylan*. Then Tony talked to Echo's and Suze's mothers. One interview led to another. Joan Baez, Dylan's many mentors and fellow musicians, and the women who mothered the young Bobby Dylan all spoke to Scaduto. He captured their stories as well as their rhythms and colloquialisms. He gave expression to the authentic sounds and voices of subjects like Gerde's Folk City club owner, Mike Porco, who paid for Dylan's membership in the musicians' union, and the folklorist Izzy Young, who let Dylan read and learn from his huge collection of folk songs, records, and publications and who produced Dylan's first concert.

Lots of people spoke to Tony and, finally, Bob Dylan spoke to him. Dylan kept refusing to be interviewed until A. J. Weberman, a "Dylanologist" who would rummage through Dylan's garbage looking for information, told Dylan, "Scaduto is writing a real exposé on you." Dylan called Tony early one Sunday morning and asked, "What are you writing? I ain't never done nothing to be exposed about." Tony's response: "Talk to me and I'll let you see my manuscript." Dylan read the unfinished manuscript, made corrections of facts, and then sat for an interview. In the end, he said, "I like your book. That's the weird thing about it."

While Tony was interviewing sources and writing the biography, Dylan, his wife, and their children were ensconced in a brownstone he owned on MacDougal Street in Greenwich Village. Dylan's children were enrolled at the Little Red School House, a nearby progressive private school. Many of the interview subjects concurred with Tony that Dylan seemed to be in a good place. Dylan discussed his many projects with Tony, his potential books, films, and songwriting.

After more than twenty years in journalism, Tony left the *New York Post* to pursue a freelance writing career and to complete his Dylan biography. Tony published *Bob Dylan: An Intimate Biography* in 1971. It was the first serious biography of Bob Dylan—actually, the first serious book about any pop music figure.

Widely acclaimed by both critics and fans, this book is still considered one of the first authoritative biographies of Dylan. A paperback edition with updated material and an expanded discography that included unreleased recordings was published in 1973. Tony's book was translated into Italian, French, Spanish, German, Slovenian, Swedish, and Japanese. Fifty years on, new generations of readers are discovering Tony's Dylan biography, and although it is out of print in book form, it is available electronically.

I met Tony in 1972 on a blind date that worked. We fell in love. I've never been a fan of biographies. I devour detective novels. I wasn't even a big Dylan fan. My heart and soul belonged to John Lennon, but I had listened to Dylan's songs as the backdrop to both the civil rights and Vietnam War protests. I graduated from high school in 1966 and college in 1969, so Dylan's songs were the anthems of my generation. I loved Dylan's transition to rock and now there were three bad boys sharing my affections: Dylan, Lennon, and Jagger.

I wasn't dying to read Tony's book but I was in love with the guy, so I thought I should, at least, make the attempt, and I was blown away. Scaduto captured the atmosphere, the emotions, and all the craziness of the 1960s. He also illuminated the life of a giant musical artist, Bob Dylan. Reading his book, I was there again, in that time. Quite an accomplishment for a former *New York Post* police reporter and feature writer.

Scaduto captured a cultural and political era, seen through the life of Bob Dylan. He did so by using a prime journalistic technique: the interview. Scaduto's narrative skills allowed the voices of all the friends, lovers, mentors, and colleagues to tell the story of the life and accomplishments of Bob Dylan. Just before Tony died, he discovered all his interview tapes in our basement. Anthony Scaduto's "basement tapes" comprise more than thirty-six hours of conversations with Dylan, Joan Baez, Echo Helstrom, Suze Rotolo, John Hammond Sr., Phil Ochs, Izzy Young, Mike Porco, and so on. This book presents the raw material of audio files transcribed to the written word. The voices jump off the page, each person urgently revealing and talking of his or her time with Bob Dylan. They spoke directly to Anthony Scaduto and now they speak to you.

Read, listen, and enjoy.

GIRL FROM THE NORTH COUNTRY

ECHO HELSTROM

You think you're the Girl from the North Country?
Yeah, there's nobody else it could be.

ECHO AND DYLAN STARTED GOING TOGETHER while they were in the eleventh grade at Hibbing High School. They turned each other on to the music they were listening to—for Dylan, Little Richard and rhythm and blues, while Echo was tuning in at 4:00 a.m. to a Chicago station to listen to the blues and "race" music. Echo's mother, Martha, also introduced Dylan to Hank Williams, another revelation.

They considered themselves misfits and rebels in small-town Hibbing, Minnesota. Echo told Scaduto that Dylan was a "goody-goody" from the right side of town and she was from the wrong side of the tracks. He was very sexy and they made love everywhere, anyplace, on the road, in the woods. He changed the lyrics to a Little Richard song he sang to Echo at the high school talent show: "I gotta girl and her name is Echo."

They broke up in their senior year and then resumed the romance while Echo was working in Minneapolis and Dylan was a freshman at the University of Minnesota. But Dylan moved on to New York City, and Echo married and had a child.

After his first record was released, Dylan called Echo to talk about the music he was doing. He told her he was singing folk music. Echo said, "Folk music! You mean that hillbilly garbage? What the hell are you doing that stuff for?" And he said, "Well, you know it's a thing. It's a coming thing." Years later, Echo would write a song about Dylan. She called it "Boy from the North Country."

3

When we talked the other night, the other afternoon, I mentioned the word "paranoid" and you started to say, "You have to tell me the whole story sometime," you know, the whole thing? Start with that.

Oh! You mean about him being afraid of people?

Yeah.

Well, ever since I met him, if I looked like I was going to say something, or if we were out in public, you know, he'd say, "Don't do this. Don't do that." And when we went oh . . .

You mean he was afraid of being embarrassed?

Yeah. He didn't want anybody to know anything at all about him. Even, you know, before he was anybody. And now it's really bad. And like this one time . . . well, I went with him in the eleventh grade, you know? And then in the twelfth grade I didn't pay too much attention to what he was doing. But after we graduated, I went to Minneapolis and I got a job. And he was there going to college. And he got my, I guess he got my phone number from my mother where I was working, and he called me up at work there and he told me to come down and see him. And he says, "Wear something kooky, when you come to the fraternity house." He told me to meet him there, he said, "Don't tell anybody where you're from." Or anything, you know? He said, "Just keep your mouth shut." And another time . . . well, he just didn't want anybody to know what he was doing.

What fraternity, what frat house was this?

I don't even remember. But that's easy enough to find out. It was the Jewish one, I guess.

And he was saying, "Don't tell anybody where you're from"?

Well, nobody was ever supposed to know that he was from Hibbing. And he didn't want anybody to know that I was from Hibbing either.

Was he calling himself Dylan by this time?

Uhm . . . *no!* He was still Zimmerman because he was going to college.

This is what . . . he entered college in September of '59, right?

That must have been about then because he graduated in June. And when I broke up with him, always it was, you know, "Don't," you know, "Don't . . ." you know like. I gave him back his bracelet in the hallway.

What was the bracelet? How was the bracelet inscribed?

I don't remember, but it was an identification bracelet. And he had given it to me. And that was a symbol of our belonging to each other. And I gave it to him in the hallway. You know, what do I give a damn? And he says,

"What is this? What's going on?" And you know it just killed him to think that this was happening in public.

Like how? What was he saying?

He says, "What are you doing?" He used to kind of whisper and he'd just get really excited if he thought anybody was going to, you know . . . anything about what he was doing at all. (*sighs deeply*) It's gotten to be really bad now, I guess.

No! Apparently, it was bad for a while but I hear he's maturing.

Did you read the little song I wrote to him?

No, in fact, oh yeah, in "Us." Yes, yes, yes. You know what I'd like? If I could have your permission to use it in the book if it'll fit somewhere.

Yeah, except one part that's screwed up.

How should it go? What part got screwed up? Wait, I got a copy of "Us" here. Tell me, what part got screwed up? (*reads*)

> First you come around with your singing and dancing,
> Wild hair, waving and fancy prancing,
> And you want to be seen. So, the people came from miles around
> Just to see you smile and laugh and frown
> Just like a crazy clown with your hair hanging down.

Uh-huh.

> Now you've left town, don't want nobody hanging around.
> You want to hide, won't go outside, don't go outside . . .

That's where it went wrong. "You want to hide. Won't go outside. Don't make the scene. You don't want to be seen." Forget the "Don't go outside"?

You [want] won't with a "w"? And the next line with the "don't" should be stricken out?

Yeah. That's the one that me and Toby taped. [In 1969 Toby Thompson wrote a six-part piece on Dylan for the *Village Voice*. Echo was interviewed for the articles.]

Do you have a tape or can you . . . you have one of the tapes?

I have a tape, but you know, it's only one tape.

I wonder if you have any facilities for copying the tape, making another copy and send it to Bob Dylan and see what his reaction might be? Have you ever written to him?

No. I'm at the class reunion and I was so afraid he'd be mad at me because of you know, well, the article in the *Village Voice* had been out, you know?

Yeah, right.

I was a nervous wreck. I thought I was going to die of a heart attack. I think I'd had about eight screwdrivers by the time he finally showed up, you know?

Did he show up at the class reunion?!

Oh God! Yes!

When?

I got it right here, August 2nd it was.

August 2nd of this year? Of 1969? And what was he like?

He was very thin. He was a lot thinner. And he had his hair cut shorter. Real short.

You know he was telling people he cut all his hair off and he was running around the country in disguise and nobody recognized him, he said. That was that summer.

Yeah. And he had his wife around.

What was she like?

Oh she was a tiny, little, delicate creature with long brown hair. Very cute and very quiet. She just sat by his side you know, just being there.

Where was this?

It was in Hibbing, you know? The Moose Club rooms.

The Moose Club rooms? Where is the Moose Club? The Moose Lodge?

Oh, right downtown!

What street?

Howard Street. Yeah, at night he showed up and everybody was wondering if he was going to show up and there was only a few people who really knew it, and this one girl who was in charge of a lot of the things for the class reunion called me up and said, "You of all people would want to know this." But it's got to be kept a secret because, you know, a lot of people in town might report it and everything. If people found out about it, it would make him not show up at all. And I was just dying.

Tell me your reaction. What happened?

Well, I was waiting all this time, you know? And then he finally showed up. I don't think he got there till about 11:00. Toby was supposed to maybe show up. I called Toby up. I said, "Don't tell anybody else in the whole world but try to get down here," because, you know, I hadn't taken anybody at all to the class reunion for this purpose. Because everybody was bringing their husbands and girlfriends and all that garbage, you know? But I went by myself even though I called up Toby. I said, "Do everything in your power to get down here or up here because he's supposed to show up!" I was so nervous because I was so afraid Bob would be really mad at me, 'cause of the articles in the *Village Voice*.

What did he say to you? What did you say to him?

My heart was pounding so hard. I was afraid I was going to faint. It was either . . . hell, I would've died, you know, something, been hauled to the hospital! I had to talk to him before I killed myself because, you know . . . I was standing around. I was just kind of standing around waiting to see if he'd see me and see what he'd do, if he'd smile or if he'd, you know, quickly look away or frown.

Did he make sort of an entrance or what?

Well, everybody was there already, you know? And he just kind of walked down the stairs and there he was in the doorway. And everybody just crowded around him. I headed for the bar for a little support. I told my best girlfriend to walk over there with me, and I had these great big round black sunglasses. And I thought I can't go up to him like everybody else, you know, and say, "Hi, Bob," like any old ordinary person would do. I figured I gotta just do something that Bob would do himself . . . So, I put on these great big black sunglasses. Everybody was having him sign these little things that we got at the reunion. The reunion banquet booklet telling everybody where everybody was, who they were married to, and all this garbage. I put mine down for him to sign and I was going to say something like, "You probably don't remember me, but could I have your autograph?" But I didn't even have time to say that. And he says, "Hey!" and he turned around to his wife to tell her evidently that it was me.

Right.

And then he turned back around and said, "How are you?" And I say, "Just fine." You know and he says, "Where is your husband?" "Well," I said, "I'm divorced." and then he signed my . . . the back of it, the little thing and there were so many people around that we really couldn't talk. And well, I don't know if he was being polite and nice to me because he really wanted to be or, was he being polite and nice to me because of the crowd around, you know? Maybe he was being nice in spite of the fact that . . . about the article?

No mention ever made of the article?

Well, he says, "Hey, I saw that thing." I said, "Yeah." And then I got excited and I said, "Hey, I wrote this song." And he said, "Oh really? What you call it?" I says, "Boy from the North Country." And I don't know if he liked that or not but . . .

What was his reaction? What sort of a reaction did you get out of him?

Well, he started laughing a little bit, you know, kind of . . . he always kind of laughed, embarrassed, you know? There were so many people around. They were trying just to get to him. Then I just kind of said, "Well, see ya," and I wandered off and that was it. Because I didn't want to make a big thing of it because everybody, *everybody* would probably say, "Oh look at her," or, "She thinks she's going to get back with him," or something like that.

Right, right, run off to Spain with Bobby Dylan.

Well, I figured I really had to play it cool, just talk to him for a few minutes and then just leave him alone.

You didn't see him at all the rest of your trip back there in August?

No. I just wandered off, you know, to the other side of the room again and just kind of watched him.

How long did he stay?

I think about an hour and then some dum-dum, which is the usual thing in that town, tried to start a fight with him.

Was it somebody from the graduating class?

Sure. That's the way that town is, you know. But all of a sudden, he was gone.

He made no attempt to call you or anything like that?

Oh no, not anymore. I think he probably left immediately.

Did you call Toby to tell him what happened?

Yeah, and then I wrote a song . . . about that too.

Oh really?

I wrote a song about the class reunion, yeah.

Yeah! Hey, when you send me the first song, send me a copy of the second song. I'll try to find it.

(*laughs*) Hey, listen, let's start up at the top a little bit. Tell me how you first met Bob. The whole thing about how he walked into the L and B and how you talked about ["Brother"] Gatemouth Page's show from [down south] and all that?

Okay, let me tell you why we got along so well together in the first place. Well, you see, all my life, you know, I loved music and I started listening to that stuff like when I was thirteen, I think. Yeah, I was thirteen. And, you know, nobody else ever heard that stuff and I used to, like, in the summertime I'd stay up until about four o'clock in the morning just listening to the radio, tuning into Chicago after the other went off [the air], you know, and everything. And, you know, tell somebody else this stuff and they think you were out of your tree. They never heard of it. And so when he started talking to me I couldn't believe it and he couldn't believe it either. It was at the L and B. I was there with my girlfriend. I think I had on a motorcycle jacket and some blue jeans, really uncouth. And he had been standing out in front of, well, he'd been upstairs playing. He came down . . .

Upstairs, where is upstairs?

Upstairs in the Moose. The Moose was upstairs at the time, upstairs at the L and B. And he came down the stairs and he was standing on the street corner and it was kind of wintery. It was in the fall. He was standing out there and he was playing his guitar on the street corner singing, you know hollering! And I thought, "Man, what a nut!," you know? And I didn't even know him.

But you'd seen him around?

Yeah, but I thought he was a "goody-goody," you know he was from the right side of the tracks and I was from the wrong side of the tracks.

What distinguishes the right side from the wrong side in Hibbing?

Well, the rich and the poor.

Basically, that cut and dried?

Yeah, either you come from a nice home or you come from, you know, like my place, slightly decrepit, you know? And that distinguishes the good people from the bad people.

Right.

And so, let's see now. Then I walked back in. I was having a Coke, probably a chocolate cherry Coke with my girlfriend and he came wandering over and he sat down and started talking to me. We started talking about, like, B. B. King, Howling Wolf . . .

Was he trying to pick you up?

Yeah. Oh, I don't know what. I had written something or I had a piece of paper with a ditty, you know, a song or something on it and I don't remember what it was at all.

Yeah.

But he wanted to borrow it. And then he said he'd give it back to me the next day in school. And he wanted me to come to his house. He said he had some records to play for me. And so the next day after school, I was supposed to go over there. And I don't know. We just talked and stuff like that and, oh, he wanted to go up back upstairs [to the Moose] and break in and play the piano. He had an urge to play the piano. So, I had a little pocketknife and we went upstairs and opened the lock [but] I didn't dare to go in.

Right. Did Bobby go in?

Uh-huh.

Did you call him Bob or Robert or what?

Bobby.

Right, Bobby.

Bobby. He went in and played the piano. And I stood out there and talked. And I said something. I had, well, I've always been interested in people's backgrounds. Like I asked him if he was Jewish. It was again one of those things where he didn't want anybody to know anything. I usually ask people stupid stuff like that right off the bat.

Yeah, that's great! Right out front.

It was upstairs. You know, I was, we were breaking in, and I said something about it. I asked if he was Jewish. It's just very natural for me to ask things like that. Because I don't think anything of it, you know, and he got a little funny look on his face and he didn't say anything. He just looked funny, and I was very surprised because I figured people should be proud of whatever they are. Or even if they're not proud, at least learn to live with it.

Later on did this . . . did the Jewish thing ever come up? Did you ever discuss it with him again?

Never ever. And he was very funny, you know, he couldn't call . . . to this day I don't ever call colored people "Negroes." I used to call them "Negroes." And he said, "*Not* Negroes. It's 'colored people.' "

Even at that time he was saying . . .

Oh yeah. And you know to this day when I refer to anybody it's "colored people." He taught me so well.

Now tell me about how he asked you to go steady. When did you start going steady?

It was probably just more or less an understood thing. But when I first met him, I went to his house, you know, and we listened to records and he played the piano for me.

What kind of stuff was he playing?

Really wild stuff like Little Richard.

Yeah. Any Elvis stuff?

No. Little Richard. He was Little Richard then. I met him all the time and talked to him and everything for a whole month and he didn't kiss me for a whole month. And I thought, you know, "This is a great brother–sister relationship." We just had fun talking about music and going places and that was it and we were over at John's [Buckland] house one night and he finally kissed me. He finally got around to it. And then after that we just went everywhere together. Anytime he thought, you know, he'd hear anything about music, anybody who was in town that had anything to do with music or anything. I remember going upstairs to this, I don't know, maybe it was the Elk to see this other this guy playing piano. And we were up there and we all, I think John was there, and we just all sat around had a real long conversation and this guy played the piano and sang some old, dirty songs and Bob, you know, did his thing.

What was his thing at the time?
It was Little Richard.

Again, Little Richard. What was . . . when did you start going steady? Can you date it?
I don't remember. It was just kind of . . . we drifted into it. And we used to go and sit in his car. He'd get his father's car and we'd go and park, and he'd have his guitar along and we'd just sit in the car and he'd, you know, play his guitar and sing to me. And him and John used to come over and, you know, always it was the music.

Right. By this time, he was kissing you when you were parking in the car?
Oh yeah. We were doing everything.

What do you mean "everything"?
You know . . . you're not going to put that in your book?

No, of course not!
Well . . .

No, I'm just curious at how advanced he was at this stage.
Oh, he was very sexy.

Listen, we're both grown-up people. Tell me what you mean by "everything"?
Well, we were screwing.

Were you?
Oh yeah. (*sighs*) It was like, well, he used to come and see me and then, you know, he'd make love to me and he'd take off a lot of times, but you know . . .

What do you mean "take off"? Where would he take off to?
I don't know. He'd go back downtown and go home. A lot of times he wouldn't spend that much time with me.

When you said he'd come and see you and make love to you, would this be in your parents' house, your house?

Oh, anyplace. On the road. In the woods.

Right. Sounds beautiful.

And, oh, I don't know. What else can I tell you? Oh yeah, the motorcycle and . . . He tried to teach me how to ride it one day, came over and, you know I was going to drive a motorcycle! And he told me how to start it and how to stop it and everything and he put me on it. And I went about ten feet and I thought, I better practice stopping. I went to put on the brake and my legs weren't long enough. They didn't reach the ground. All of a sudden the motorcycle is on the ground and my hand had turned the throttle up so that, you know, oil and everything and smoke was just shooting out all over the place and this big noise and everybody came running and I was so scared of my father, you know, because my father, I don't know. He kind of let Bob hang around, but my father never approved of me going out with guys at all. Bob was just standing there. He didn't know what to do and I had leaped off, you know? I was okay. But it was quite an experience. And then he hit a little kid with his motorcycle. I saw him that night. I was downtown and I saw him. And we just started walking down the street towards my house. He was walking me home which is about a mile or two miles from downtown, maybe more. And we were walking down the street and we walked down the alley when he was just telling me how horrible he felt about hitting this little kid but there was nothing he could do about it because the little kid came running out from between two parked cars. And he didn't even see him until he was there, and he said he remembered this little kid's orange rolling across the street.

His what?

He had an orange with him. And he remembered the orange rolling across the street.

How badly hurt was the kid?

Not very. But it shook him up so badly that he just got rid of the motorcycle right away.

When did this happen do you recall?

It was chilly. It could have been spring. It could have been fall.

Well, like how long had you been going together?

For a long time.

Might it have been towards the end of your relationship?

Yeah. And his mother and father came riding by in a truck and asked if we wanted a ride. And he said, "No." Well, he never, I don't know. He really didn't communicate with his parents. His mother, you know, he talked to his mother a lot more. His mother was really nice to us. Like, we'd go to his house and he just kind of shied away from his father. He used to have to go down and work in the shop. And that used to make him mad.

Did he ever talk about his mother and father? Did he ever talk about breaking away from them, breaking loose from his home ties? Anything like that?

No.

How long did you go steady with him?

Oh . . . I suppose not quite a year because I broke up with him before twelfth grade started again, I think.

Before your senior year?

Uh-huh, but that whole summer, I spent the whole summer in the house practically waiting for the phone to ring, you know, and just sitting around waiting for him and I was very depressed.

Well, where was he?

He was downtown. And I remember one time I came downtown, and this was towards the end, when he didn't take me anyplace anymore. I came downtown and he found me and he took me home and dumped me off and went back downtown again!

(laughs) As if to say, stop looking for him?

I don't know. No. He just didn't . . . he didn't want me to do anything. He wanted to keep me to himself. He spent a lot of time in Minneapolis, I know.

What was he doing in Minneapolis?

I guess he was just hanging around with people, you know, singing and stuff like that.

Do you know if he went anyplace else, like California or Chicago?

Not then, no, I doubt it. I doubt it very much.

What about Kansas City?

I don't know. Well, he had this one cousin from Duluth that he used to play with. This cousin had a band. Well, Bob had these other kids when I first met him that were his band and then I don't know what happened to them and then he started singing with this cousin from Duluth. This one time we went to Superior and Bob was on a TV program.

When was this?

That summer, in the spring, I think it was.

How did he get on the TV program?

I don't know. Probably talked somebody into it. But you know it originated in Superior, Wisconsin. Well, Superior and Duluth are like right next to each other.

What did he do on the TV program?

Sang a song. I don't even remember what it was

With a guitar, with the band?

Yeah, with a guitar and this was with the old band.

What was the band like when you first met him? What kind of a sound did they have? Was Dylan the leader of the band?

Oh yeah!

What did they call themselves?

He ran everything all the time.

Was that the kind of personality he was?

He was the organizer . . .

Was he a nervous kid like he was when I first saw him here? In the Village?

Uh-huh, not as nervous but he was nervous.

Yeah, but the Chaplinesque kind of thing where he would the do jerky motions and all of that . . .

Always twitching.

Right. What was the name of the band?

I don't even remember. I don't know if they had a name.

Where did they play around town?

Well, we used to go to this one place that was closed on Sundays. We used to go in there, and it was kind of like a jam session. They used to have these jam sessions in this one restaurant called Collier's Barbeque. This one kid's father owned the joint and it was closed on Sundays.

Did they ever play professionally or semiprofessionally before audiences?

It was talent shows and stuff like that.

Was it the talent show in high school? Do you remember, was that the time he went electric in the auditorium? And the principal ran around pulling the plugs out?

He was playing the piano like Little Richard. He was standing up. And something on those little foot pedals and screaming and you know the way that he was singing, "I gotta girl and her name is Echo" and I was so nervous because I was always afraid something would go wrong because the people would boo and everything, you know, all the time and it embarrassed me. It didn't even bother him—he was just happy. I mean, like, you know, a prophet in his own hometown.

What about the kids who would listen to the [southern] station?

There weren't any!

Oh, I thought there were more than just you?

No! People didn't even know. This was Elvis Presley and what's his name, the other guy, Bill Haley, and these people were just coming out.

Well, Presley really hit it like '55. He'd already been a big star by then. By '57.

Yeah but . . .

But nobody else was really listening to the heavy . . .

Oh my God! No!

So that the kids in town were booing Bobby?

Oh yeah. It was awful.

What kind of sound did they have? Did they have a black blues kind of sound? What was the band like? Little Richard–type thing?

It was like blues only or like Jimmy Reed, you know, but it was loud.

A blues-jazz-electric mixture?

Yeah.

Tell me about the night he was singing this song to you? What were the words of the song? Is that the night the principal was pulling the plugs?

I don't even know what he was singing because I was so nervous. I didn't even hear what he was singing and you can't even understand what he sings anyway. And at this time, because all the music, all the guitars and all the amplifiers were so loud and, you know, he mumbles anyway, and I was so nervous I didn't know *what* was going on. And then somebody said, "Hey, you know he's singing to you." And he made it up as he went along. All I remember is "I got a girl and her name is Echo."

You never wrote it down? He never wrote it down?

I don't think so. He just made it up. He made it up as he was standing there.

Right, is this the first song you know of that he made up? That he did himself?

Those guys sat around and, you know, made up songs all the time.

Did they ever write them down, seriously?

No, not that I know of.

Right, okay. But they did get together and make songs up all the time?

He'd just sit around and play his guitar and make up songs.

So, your friend said, "Hey, he's singing to you"? And you listened and he sang, "I got a girl and her name is Echo"?

Yeah, except I couldn't understand what he was saying. And I remember this other time, they had a thing at the Armory Building.

Yeah.

And I don't know who had set it up. I think maybe the disc jockey over at the radio station [or] something like that set it up. It was a big, you know, big dance that night and those guys were playing. And I remember being nervous again. All the time, they just turned up those amplifiers on those guitars and it was so loud. You couldn't hear Bob. All you could hear all the time was just this huge guitar noise, you know, and I remember standing down by the stage and just telling them to turn down the amplifiers! It made me so mad. It was just a mess because you couldn't hear Bob singing.

Well, when the kids were bullying him, it wasn't necessarily because they weren't hip to the music but because Bob was messing it up at that time? I mean, to some extent?

Yeah. But they weren't hip anyways. Well, I was screaming at the other guys. Bob didn't even know. He couldn't see. He was, you know, just out there singing and I was hollering at the other guys to turn down the amplifier because it was messing up everything. And they didn't realize because they weren't out there listening. And I wanted everybody to see that he could sing. And everything always just seemed to me to go wrong. I guess he was happy. But I was always embarrassed.

Did he ever talk about some of the politics of the period that you knew him?

No.

About the nation's problems, anything like that?

I don't remember, no. Well, he never seemed to have very much money. You know, here I am a poor kid from the wrong side of the tracks and I always had more money than he had.

Why was that, do you know?

I don't think his father gave him that much money to spend.

Okay, the name Dylan. Tell me about the name Dylan.

Oh yeah. It was summertime and . . .

Not the summer that you were drifting apart? Oh, it had to be the summer you were drifting apart.

No. We were still going together and we were madly in love. Him and John came over, as usual, and he had a little blue Ford convertible.

Who did?

Bob did at that time. He finally had his own car.

How did he get the car?

I guess his dad bought it for him. His dad wasn't all that bad, you know?

And I think his dad had bought him the car. I don't think he really did anything to earn any money on his own. Except work around his father's shop. And him and John came over and he told me that he decided on a name he was going to use. He said something like, "I found a name," or, "I decided," you know, "on a name I'm going to use when I'm a singer."

Was Dylan Thomas . . .

I didn't ask him why Dylan.

Did it ever come up again? Dylan Thomas?

No, and there is no relative of his by the name of Dylan.

Did he ever talk about Dylan Thomas?

No.

Did you people ever talk about poetry in any way?

No. It was just music.

There was never discussion of books, poems, anything like that?

Oh, one thing he . . . who was this writer? That he was reading all of his books . . . *Cannery Row* and *Grapes of Wrath*.

John Steinbeck?

Yeah.

Why was he reading all of Steinbeck?

I suppose because of the people that were in the book.

Did he ever say this?

No. It's just what I supposed. He didn't really say it. But he came over and said he was reading this great book.

Which one was the great book?

Cannery Row.

Did he tell you why it was great?

I don't think so. But that summer I read all of John Steinbeck's books.

Did you two discuss it at all?

I don't think so.

What about the movie *The Grapes of Wrath*? Was that ever around in Hibbing at the time? Do you remember?

Yeah, I remember seeing it. I thought it was *Grapes of Raft,* you know, and I thought it was a bunch of grapes on a raft, going down a river. That's all I remember about that.

Did you see it with Bob?

We did go to a lot of movies, but we didn't go to that one.

You don't remember seeing it on television or anything like that?

We didn't really watch TV together. There was no place to watch TV because we were uncomfortable at his house and we couldn't go watch TV at my house, so there was no place to go.

Why were you uncomfortable at his house?

He wasn't comfortable, you know? He just didn't want to take me over there while his parents were there. He'd say, like, "We can't go over there because, my mom's home, my grandmother's home," or you know? He was just uncomfortable with his family around.

Yeah. And why couldn't you watch TV at your house?

Well, because my father didn't like guys.

Oh, that's right. He didn't like you going out with guys?

We did go to quite a few shows.

Yeah. I would think if the family owned movie houses . . .

But it was really funny because he'd go in first and then I'd come in later because he didn't want his cousin to see him coming in with me.

Why?

I don't know. He was just weird like that. Everything was like a big thing, production. You know, it had to be different. It couldn't be ordinary.

You mean he was acting like a CIA agent much of the time?

Yeah, had to be a game. Always playing games.

Was it more of a sense of a game at this stage or a feeling of paranoia that he was . . .

Maybe it was a little bit of both, huh? I don't know. I never really cared. I just did whatever he told me to do. I didn't stop to think about it. I just did it.

You both got in free?

I don't remember if I got in free or not.

Oh really? You mean maybe you had to pay after he got in?

Yeah. Quite possibly.

Do you ever remember accompanying him to the movies, you know, both of you going in together?

I think we might have gone to the State together. His cousin owned the other movie theater, so we could go to the State together. And I do remember going to one movie with him, which was really super. It was a midnight show. And it had all these really groovy people of that day in it, like, oh, Fats Domino and, you know, a few of those people. And there was hardly anybody in the theater, because people just didn't dig that. That was so important to me and him, though.

What was his reaction to it all?

Oh, he just sat there, you know, and enjoyed the whole thing immensely.

Did you talk about it in terms of his own career?

I don't remember specifically. We probably did talk about it, but it was no big thing because, you know, it was just understood. Because there was no other way.

You mean, no other way to break out of Hibbing, to break out of everything?

Well, no other course for his life to take but that one way.

Did he ever talk about Woody Guthrie at this time?

No.

He was not yet into folk at all, was he?

No. Not. At. All. The first time I knew that he was into folk music was when I was married, and I was living in Minneapolis and I was working for United Artists. And he called me up. He said, "Echo." I knew it was him. And we started talking. This was right after he made his very first album. And so, he called me up and we started talking about his music you know? And he told me he was singing folk music. I said, "Folk music! You mean that hillbilly garbage? What the hell are you doing that stuff for?" And he says, "Well, you know, it's a thing. It's a coming thing." And I says, "Oh really?" And I was very, very disappointed in him. And he said he wanted to meet me, so I told him I'd meet him in front of Penneys. And he had this album for me. And he gave me the album and he had on blue jeans, you know? And he was kind of grubby looking. He had on blue jeans and an old faded blue shirt. He looked like a farmer. And I think he had on some big old boots and his hair was kind of long and scraggly. And I remember I had on a white dress, with a full skirt and little pink flowers · on it and we looked like we didn't belong together at all. But . . .

Did he say at the time, did he make it appear like he went into folk music in order to make it?

Yeah.

Did you talk about it before he went away and got to New York? Did he talk about making it, about becoming famous, you know, rock-and-roll star or anything like that?

Well, it was just an understood thing. All along there was no other way but for him to be, you know, just up there. And I believed in him, heart and soul. And we probably would have gotten married except I couldn't, you know. He always used to tell me, you know not to get pregnant because he couldn't marry me because he had to go out and do his thing. Yeah. But

I just knew he had to, it was meant to be. You just kind of know it. The whole thing didn't surprise me at all.

Why did he come back? When he called you that time, why was he back, just to . . .

He came in to see his friends. He had some hippie friends over in Minneapolis. And I was not very happily married. I was contemplating getting a divorce.

So, he came back to town and I remember you telling someone that he invited you to parties down there.

He told me to come to this party. And I don't know if he was being polite or if he really meant it. Because when I called him up and told him I was coming, he seemed to get all shook up. You know he was afraid of having anything to do with a married woman, I suppose. I just wanted to go to the party. Because we were friends too. We were more than sweethearts all along. Even when we were going together, we were friends. And afterwards, when we broke up, we were still friends and so I just wanted to go and see him, you know, and talk to him and stuff like that. So, I went there and he was singing and playing harmonica. Everybody was happy for me. He was talking about all sorts of groovy stuff, all the things he'd done, you know.

Like what? What did he say?

Oh, this one song about East Orange? He said something about, "Howdy, East Orange"?

"Hello, East Orange" or something like that, right.

And he said it was something about some people that he was staying with, a friend of his in East Orange . . .

Did he talk about Woody Guthrie, Cisco Houston, you know, all the folk crowd?

I don't think so at that time. I don't really remember because I was running around drinking beer. But he was standing around singing and . . .

Who was at that party? Do you remember?

No. I didn't know any of those people. It was very good hippie friends, though, from Minneapolis.

Do you remember what street this was on?

No, but it was Southeast Minneapolis. And I was standing in the kitchen talking to some guy and Bob came in and he started talking to me and we went over by a stairway. He wanted me to get a divorce. And he wanted me to come and live in New York. I had a little baby. My little girl was two years old.

He wanted you to get a divorce and go to New York with him?

Uh-huh.

How did he say it?

He said he would pay for my divorce. And he just wanted me to come and live in New York. He said, "I want you to come and live in New York." I said, "What would I do in New York with a baby?" You know, "How am I going to raise a child in a big city like that?" And I said, "And *besides,* you're supposed to be in love with Joan Baez." And he said, "Just a minute." That's all he said. And he walked off and he went to a suitcase and he got her picture. He came back, waving the picture in front of me and pointing at it, and he says, "Look at that. You think I could love that?" And he was, you know, really mad. And I got so upset. I got so mad I just ran. I just took off. I ran right down the stairs. I went right out the door, and I walked all the way home.

You were living in Minneapolis at the time.

Uh-huh. It just made me so upset. I don't know why. And he came to the top of the stairs and he said, "Echo, wait! Where are you going?" He couldn't believe I was leaving. Because it didn't make any sense.

Why did you get so upset at that?

Because he was supposed to be going with her and . . . because what he was telling me didn't make any sense at all. A known fact, it was a known fact.

But this had to be in early '62?

Uh-huh.

Now, a couple of other things. What else was he listening to besides Little Richard? I mean there was Bill Haley. The Penguins, for example, the Five Satins, any of the really pop stuff?

Ugh! No. Well, I remember one song. Remember "Angel Baby"?

Yeah.

He just had to have that record. I don't know. Maybe it made him think of me.

That was the Five Satins.

I don't know. It was one of those kooky groups, but it was a good song.

Why do you think it reminded him of you?

I don't know. Just the way he acted about it. Oh, Bobby Freeman. You know "Do You Want to Dance?"

Right.

He called me up this one time and said, "Hey, me and the guys taped this song. You want to hear it?" And I said, "Sure." So, he puts it on and it's "Do You Want to Dance?" and I believed it was him. It took me, it was years later, you know before I realized that the kook been playing the record! It wasn't him at all! He pulled stuff like that on me all the time!

Listen, you told Toby something about how Bob used to work for his father. The father and uncle, were they partners in that store?

Yeah, yeah. Partners.

Yeah, and Bob used to go around repossessing miners' stuff—is that it?

Well, they repossessed people's things that they couldn't pay on. He hated sweeping up the shop, but it just killed him to go and take these people's stuff away.

What did he say about it?

Oh, he'd say, like, oh he had to go to these people's house and, you know, take their things away. I don't remember exactly how he said it, but it just killed him to do that.

Listen, when you saw him in Minneapolis, was he working in the Ten O'Clock Scholar or anyplace like that?

No. When I went down to see him, oh yeah, I was working in Minneapolis. He was at the university. I used to meet him once in a while at first and I was going with this one guy, bunch of hoodlums, you know, and I finally got so fed up with them, I called up Bob one night and I asked him to help me out, help get me out of there. And one of his friends and this other guy and this other girl and Bob all came in their car and we just grabbed all my stuff, just threw it all together and threw it in the car. And he went and got me a place in Dinkytown [the area with small shops and housing on the northern edge of the university campus in Minneapolis].

Wait a minute. You were living with this guy at the time?

Well, these guys were all staying in my apartment. One guy had gotten hauled back to the Texas penitentiary and I figured, "What the hell's the sense of letting these other guys bug the hell out of me?"

How did you get involved with these guys?

Well, I'll tell you. When I was a little girl, I used to watch movies and all the gun molls, you know, were the most glamorous people in the world and hoodlums were the sexiest guys, you know, always nice, dark-looking Italians and I'd . . .

You mean I've got to come on like a hoodlum?

Well, I used to think gangsters were really the sexiest people in the whole world.

So, you got involved with these characters?
Yeah, I thought it was a groovy thing.

But in any case, Bob came over with his friends and they grabbed all your stuff and got you out of there . . .
We went, you know, what the heck was the name of this place? The College Inn, I think it was, some real rinky-dink hotel, and Bob went in and got me a room. And we hauled all my garbage in there. And he used to come up and see me all the time. And we'd kiss and everything like that, but I'd never let him make love to me.

Why not?
I don't know. I guess I was just kind of mad at him. I figured he was taking advantage of me if I let him. But he'd still come up and see me all the time. Sometimes he'd bring these weirdos up. One was supposed to be an improvisational dancer, something like that. And here's this guy stamping on my floor. Bob told him to go ahead and show me some of his stuff, you know. And then he used to come up and see me all the time and he always wanted to spend the night. I suppose to make an impression on the guys at the fraternity.

He was living at the fraternity house at this time?
Yeah, and I always made him go home.

This would have been in 1959, when he was a freshman? Did you ever hear him singing in any of the places?
No. I remember he took me to the Ten O'Clock Scholar, and I wasn't supposed to say anything.

What do you mean you weren't supposed to say anything?
I was just supposed to keep my mouth shut.

Not let any of his friends know . . .
. . . who I was, where I was from.

And you got married in December and you lost contact with him after that?
Well, after I had the baby, he called me at home and he'd heard that I had a baby. He said he had gone up to the hospital to try to see me. But I was already gone. And he said he'd gone up there and he was going to tell them he was my husband. And I was already gone. He was such a kook. And, you know, we had a small conversation then.

What did you talk about?
Oh, he just asked me how I was and he said wanted to see my baby and stuff like that.

And then after that?

Just casual, nice stuff.

And after that did you see him again?

I didn't see him again until that party thing. It was about two years later, you know.

That was when he called you at United Artists and gave you the record all in the same day. Was that was the last time you saw him?

That is the last time I saw him until the class reunion.

He came back to Minneapolis to sing at some point?

He came back for a concert and he called me. I was working at Embassy then. Oh, must have been, like, '64? He told me that he was doing half his concert in folk and the other half in rock and roll.

Then this would be '65 even?

Yeah, probably. And he called me up and said he wanted me to come down to see his concert. And I said, "I can't because I'm going with this guy and he's very jealous of you." And he was, "Hey, I just want to see you." But it was so weird because I went home sick one day. One day out of the whole year that I worked in that office I went home and the phone rang and I picked up the phone and I knew it was Bob right away and I said, "How did you find me?" And he said, "Well, I remembered your last name." And I said, "You know, I have never gone home sick the entire time I have been working on this job. You must have put a hex on me." And he said, "Yes, I did." And I said, "When am I gonna get well?" And he said, "Oh, after a while you'll feel better." "Oh you're a witch now too," I said. "What do you do, ride around the stage on your broom, playing your guitar?" And we talked for at least an hour or two. Just about life in general. And he said he wanted to see me and said he just wanted to see what I looked like. Because he was probably married or in love or something, but he still wanted to see *me*, you know, just to see what I looked like. And I said I couldn't because I was going with this guy and he said, "Well, I'll leave tickets at the box office for both of you." And I said, "I just can't."

And you didn't see the concert?

No.

What about after that? That was the last time up to the reunion. Is that right?

Yeah. That was the last time I had contact with him at all.

You were aware of all the stories that he ran away from home when he was eight, ten, twelve, and all that, weren't you?

I think that's a bunch of garbage.

You weren't aware that he had left town or anything like that?

No. In 1960? That was after I was married and everything. I didn't know anything about what he was doing at all anymore.

Did he ever talk about meeting Woody Guthrie in California or Big Joe Williams, hopping freight [trains] with people?

No.

Meeting famous people?

No.

Okay. Did Bobby ever talk about death in any way? His own death, his father's death?

Not the way he sings. No. I don't think he ever talked about death. I remember him singing one song about . . . you remember those talk songs? Those hillbilly talk songs?

Right.

And there's a little kid. I don't know. Somebody runs over his little kid or something like that? Anyway, they're real sad, miserable songs that they used to sing, you know, and with people getting killed and it was miserably wretched. And I didn't see how they could sing that stuff.

Bob used to sing this?

Uh-huh.

But nothing specifically that he related to himself?

No. I don't think he talked about dying. Well, you know so many people say, "Oh, I'm going to die at an early age."

Did he ever say this even joking?

I don't remember, but it's such an everyday thing, you know, because everybody says that.

How about drinking?

I think I remember him having, like, one can of beer when we were going together, you know, just two or three cans of beer.

From what people tell me about him later in Minneapolis, apparently, he was a heavy drinker.

Yeah, I guess so. But never when I saw him.

What was it like growing up in Hibbing?

Well, I lived on the outskirts of town. And it's all woods and iron ore dumps. When I was a little girl, it was a very happy place to be, but as I grew up, it's like, I don't know. Did you ever have goldfish?

Yeah.

Have you had fancy goldfish or plain goldfish? Have you ever noticed how the plain goldfish will kill the pretty goldfish? That's what Hibbing is like. If you're different, they want to kill you, you know? They pick you to pieces. And I was always different. And when I went to the class reunion, this one guy said to me, "Well," he says, "Echo, times have finally caught up with *you*."

What did he mean?

I always dressed different, you know?

Oh, I follow you. And now the whole world is getting as Echo used to be.

Yeah. And it was nice of him to admit it.

What I meant is not necessarily the unbearable straightness of the people, but what it was like as a kid. Tell me something, like, about the iron ore dumps. What were they like? Where did you play? What was the whole thing like?

I used to play out, you know in the brush. I used to spend a lot of time building little houses out of bushes, and when I got older my girlfriends and I used to ride our bikes all over the country and we'd take our bikes up to the dumps. We liked to go climb on them.

Did you ever talk about what he did, liked to do as a kid?

I don't remember. One time he did something really kooky, though. He walked all the way over to my house to see me and then when he went home . . . Oh, that was my favorite night.

Why?

You can't print the bad part. Well, we didn't have any place to go because my father was home at my house and there was no place to go and it was cold outside. There was this swamp, just like little swamps. My mother handed us a sack of cookies and a jug of water and a blanket that she'd made for me and we went out in the woods behind my sister's house and parked in the woods!

Really?

And then a dog finally came along. I was telling him a story about two bears, and a doggy came along and barked at us and scared the hell out of us.

Your mother gave you the blanket and cookies and stuff? And did she know what you were going to be doing out in the woods?

I don't know. My mother was, is, a *beautiful* person. She lets me do anything. Well, maybe she didn't. She probably thought we were sweet, good, little kids out in the woods with these cookies. (*both laugh*) You can write that we were sitting in the woods eating cookies. Be "nicey nicey" about it.

Yeah, I'll make it "nicey nicey."

I went back and got some socks because our feet had gotten all wet. And

I had a blue pair and I had a pink pair. And by the time, we got out of the swamp our feet were all wet, so I gave him, you know . . . I think, one blue sock and one pink sock. And then he had to walk all the way back home. And he called me up the next day and said he'd taken a shortcut through the woods and always the wild stories, weird stories and oh, gullible me, I believed everything he told me. And he told me he'd been walking through the woods telling me how spooky it was and everything. He said there was a snake hanging out of a tree, you know. Minnesota! There are no snakes in Minnesota that climb trees. And I believed him!

Why was this the nicest day or the best day of your life?

Because we had such a groovy time out in the woods.

Yeah. A couple of other questions. Your mother was talking in one of the Toby Thompson pieces about [how] you were listening to Hank Snow, "Prisoner of Love," right?

Oh yeah.

Tell me what other things Bobby used to listen to.

Gee, I don't really remember. We used to sit around and listen to my mom's hillbilly stuff. He did hillbilly stuff.

When he was into rock pretty heavily, he was still listening to hillbilly stuff?

Oh yeah, you know.

What kind of stuff do you remember?

You know that song, oh, what is that . . . "Somewhere Over the Rainbow"? You know that song?

You mean the one Judy Garland did in that movie? That's not hillbilly.

No, but the guys used to do it in hillbilly style. It was really goofy. They'd pick on their guitars and go, "Somewhere over the rainbow," you know? In a real hillbilly style, yeah, and they did that hillbilly stuff a lot too.

You mean Bob's group?

No. Him and John [Buckland]. With the group it was all rock and stuff. When Bob and John were just sitting around with their guitars, a lot of times it was hillbilly.

Was there any hillbilly on the radio in those days?

Oh, there's always been that stuff on the radio.

Listen, that story about your being up in his room and his grandmother coming in?

Oh, yeah. That was another groovy time. I wasn't supposed to be in his room. You know, it was okay for me to go to his house. Anyway, this is what he told me. And it was a big adventure. All of a sudden it turned into a really big adventure, you know. And everything was "sneaky sneaky" and, you know, like always. And he put me in the closet. All of a sudden, he says, "Oh, my grandmother's home." And he put me in the closet. "Okay," he said, "I'm going to go tell my grandmother that I'm going to the library." He came back up and got me out of the closet and put me on this porch thing. It's like a sundeck.

Right outside his room?

Yeah. There was a door from his room leading to the sundeck and it had, like, a railing around it.

So, you got out on the sundeck . . .

He put me out on the sundeck and then he went downstairs to tell his grandmother that he was going the library! And he comes strolling out of the house with his books under his arm whistling, you know, and then he puts down his books and he told me to hang over the railing and, you know, there I am hanging over the railing by my arms and he grabbed my legs and helped me down. And we walked off! It was so silly.

Yeah. How often did you get up into his room after that?

One night—you know this is not for publication again?

Right.

But I think this was the first time I'd ever stayed away from home in my whole life with a guy. His parents went to Duluth or Minneapolis or someplace like that. I don't know where Grandma was. I think Grandma went along. He had the whole house to himself. And his parents had given him money so he could take me and John to have hamburgers and cokes and stuff and then that night I stayed at his house and . . .

In his room?

Yeah.

What did your parents say about it?

Oh, I was at my *girlfriend's* house. But we used to meet at his house—it was right down the street from the school, and we used to go over there on our lunch hour. We used to walk over to his house at noon and I'd make him some coffee and his mom would leave him some sandwiches and stuff like that. And he would play piano for me or something and then we'd go back to school. It was fun.

Tell me about Grandma? Whose mother was she?

Oh, Mrs. Stone, that was his mother's mother. They owned this Stone's Clothing Store. It was on the corner of the two main streets. I remember wondering why Bob didn't like his father very well, not that he didn't like him, but he didn't get along with him. Because every time I saw his father, his father was really nice. I remember this one time me and Bob were riding a motorcycle and we ran out of gas. And as usual he sent me after the gas. And his father came along and asked if I wanted a ride. I said, "Sure I want a ride," you know. And he says, "Where are you going?" And I said, "We ran out of gas and I'm going after some." And he said, "Well, get in." Bob was so mad. He said, "What did you do that for?"

Did the father pick up the gas with you and drive you back to Bob? What was Bob's reaction?

It killed him, you know. He was just so mad.

Well, first of all, what was his reaction on seeing his father? Did he say anything to his father?

No, he kind of mumbled, I suppose, and stuff like that, and his father says, "Well, what happened? You ran out of gas?" And, you know, just the usual conversation. And Bob carried on the conversation as best he could, but he was so upset. He was so mad, and he wanted to know why I had let his father give me a ride to get the gas! And then I got upset because I didn't know I wasn't supposed to. What the heck? It's his father!

Yeah. (laughs) Tell me, why didn't he get along with his father?

I don't really know!

Okay. The time you visited Virginia [Minnesota] to see a Negro disc jockey, tell me about that.

Well, we went up to see them twice. He had heard that there was a Negro disc jockey in Virginia. And you know . . .

How far away is Virginia?

About thirty miles.

And he said what?

He had to go up there and talk to him.

Yeah.

Because he was always sneaking off to talk to these people. And especially if they were coloreds.

Why? Did he say why?

No. Just because they're groovier, you know, than the other kind of people. And we went up there and they had a little teeny apartment upstairs in some house, and they played all these groovy records for us. They were very nice to us. And we just talked about all kinds of people and groovy stuff. We had to go and visit these people before we went to the prom.

To the prom?

The eleventh-grade prom, yeah. I have to tell you a whole thing about this. But we had to go and see these people. I suppose he had to show me off to *somebody*. And we had to go and see these people before we went to the prom. He had a suit on and I had on my formal, and we drove all the way up to Virginia and talked to this colored disc jockey. And then we went to the prom and it was miserable.

Why?

Well, because we were just totally different from all these other gung-ho, totally goody-goody people, you know? We just didn't fit in. But Bob *wore* a suit and a tie. Oh yes! We were all dressed up.

Did Bob dance?

Oh! It was horrible! He couldn't dance. We'd never danced together. And he was a lousy leader. We were just stepping all over each other's feet and he was hissing at me between his teeth, you know. "What's the matter with you? What's the matter with you? Can't you dance?" And I said, "I can't dance," and we tried and tried to dance and finally, we just said, "Let's get *out* of here," you know. And I was going up the stairs just holding my long dress up and crying and we went out to the car and we parked on some side street and fell asleep.

Did you really?

Uh-huh. It was really funny. Big-deal prom.

You know there's one thing I forgot to ask you the last time we talked—"Girl from the North Country."

Yeah.

You think you're the girl from the north country?

Yeah.

Tell me about it. Tell me your feeling about it. Why do you think you're the girl from the north country?

Well, there's nobody else it could be. He didn't go with anybody else when he went with me, you know, for such a long time. He went out with other girls, but it wasn't the same, I'm sure.

Yeah.

Because there was a lot of them, you know. But nobody really special.

You are the only one who was really special from Hibbing?

I—yeah—I think so. He went with others, but not for long, and I don't know anybody else who had long hair that he went with for any period of time. Or [that] were interested in music.

Toby quotes your mother as remembering certain songs and certain records that Bob used to listen to, some of her old hillbilly stuff that was around?

My mother remembers a lot of things me and Bob did. Because she looked at it in a different way. She remembers a lot of things I've completely forgotten.

You said something, in relationship to Bob's band and the music they were playing and the loud sound and your attempt to get them to tone it down and all that—you said something about the kids were always throwing stones at somebody different. Did Bob ever talk about that? About the other kids?

He seemed sort of oblivious to the whole fact that, you know, people just turned on you. It bothered me. But it was like he was in his own world and it didn't bother him at all. He didn't hear the booing! You know, like I did. It made me nervous. It didn't seem to bother him. He just stood there with his . . . yeah. Stood there with his head up in the air and smiled like they were clapping!

Did he ever talk about that, how everybody else was straight and square and didn't know what the world was like?

I remember him going down to Minneapolis and coming back and saying how groovy everybody was there and, you know, "everybody is really with it" and "nobody in Hibbing would even understand or begin to be able to understand what's different." And that's how we started talking in the first place. Everyone was so square and the very fact that we could communicate or be on each other's level and speak the same language was a miracle!

Did you get the feeling that Bob felt he was an outsider even among his peers, among the other high school kids?

Yeah, definitely.

You get the feeling that he knew he was different, and he was just waiting to break away?

Yeah, like, you know when school was over? Gone. And that's just what happened.

Right. You were telling me that when he came back from that concert in '64, '65, and he called you and you talked for about an hour, you said, about life in general . . . for a long time. Do you remember some of the things he talked about?

Well, I told him that I think the really happy people in life are those that are happily married, live a very ordinary life. And who really have the sense to appreciate what they *do* have.

Yeah.

And he said that, yes, he believes that's true. And we talked and he says, "Well, I certainly didn't expect to find a philosopher." You know, when he called me up. Because of the serious way we were talking.

What were some of the things he was saying about life in general at this stage?

Well, I probably did most of the talking, as usual.

Do you remember anything he said at all?

No. I guess he was lonesome. He was in his hotel room.

MARTHA HELSTROM

Echo's little girl—she's really interested in music too.

ECHO HAD SAID TO TONY, "My mother remembers a lot of things me and Bob did. Because she looked at it in a different way. She remembers a lot of things I've completely forgotten." So, of course, Tony interviewed her mother, Martha Helstrom.

Mrs. Helstrom, my name is Scaduto. I'm a writer calling from New York. I don't know whether Echo has told you about me, but I'm doing a book about Bob Dylan. And I just talked to Echo down at your other daughter's house, just hung up with her; and she suggested I give you a call and ask you a couple of questions about Bobby. Can you talk now, do you think?
Oh yeah, well, it all depends on what you're going to ask.

I just wanted to know what your impression of him was like. Mostly I want to know about the music he listened to. From what I understand, you had a lot of country and western and hillbilly kind of music. Can you tell me about some of that music he heard at your place?
Well, they were mostly those old timers, like in the '40s and '50s, those kind of records.

Do you remember the names of some of the artists?
No, I don't remember. I'm poor about remembering artists' names. I remember the songs better.

What were some of the songs?
Most of them were these sad, sad songs like that "Ohio Prison Fire," and some old cowboy songs and some in the same order of what he writes.

But I don't really all of a sudden think I couldn't remember any more than that.

Okay. Let me ask you this. What was Bob's reaction to some of this music? Did he—

Well, he seemed to be deeply interested and listened carefully to them.

Did he play it a lot?

Oh yes, he played them. Yes, he used to come here, and Echo would play the records with him, and then he'd try them out with his guitar. He was very intense at it. You could see that he really wanted to learn how to play and learn those songs, not just like some kid that had the way of playing a few chords. He was really interested in his music.

Were there ever any of his other friends around, like John Buckland?

John was the most important friend that I knew of.

And did they ever play some of the music for you? Did they ever learn it well enough to play it back for you or anything like that?

Oh yes, they played the music, yes. Bob, of course, was most interested.

Is there anything else you can remember about Bob? Did Bob ever talk about his career, about wanting to go into music?

Oh, his big dreams, yes—they used to have big dreams together about how they were going to make it good, you know. Whichever gets to be famous first would help the other one. That's what they thought. You know how teenagers are—have their big dreams.

Do you remember what some of the big dreams entailed?

Well, they were planning on being really in the limelight and get all the world's attention and stuff like that.

Did they ever talk about something like Elvis Presley or some—

Oh yes, he was a favorite in those days, and they liked him real well.

Did they talk in terms of being an Elvis Presley someday, rock-and-roll stuff?

Oh, I don't know. I suppose that was the idea, to be somebody like him, be getting that attention. They liked that kind of stuff.

Yes. Did Bob listen to any Woody Guthrie? Do you have any Woody Guthrie records?

Well, I don't believe—we might have had some of the small records that were so popular in those days. I'm sure we had some of them too—was his favorite too.

Woody Guthrie was.

Yes.

Do you remember any of the songs that—

No, I don't. They were all good sentimental pieces, but I don't remember the names. I've been so busy with the little one lately that I've forgotten a lot of those kind of things already.

Yes. Oh that's right. You have Echo's child.

She's taking accordion lessons right now, and she has always admired Bob's music.

Yes, right. Do you remember anything else about Bob and Echo being together and about some of their friends?

No, nothing special. Just that they were here a lot and they cooked and, you know how kids do at that age—they're always making something good to eat.

Yes. Do you remember what it was that Bob—

Mostly pizza and stuff like that.

Pizza, did you say?

Pizza was their favorite, yes.

Did they make it themselves?

Oh yes, it was made here at home.

How did they make pizza at home? Do you remember?

Oh, they made it from those packages, like Jeno's pizza and like that.

Oh, you mean there was frozen pizza around—

No, no, they had to make it themselves and then wait for it to get done. That's when it was really good. You fix it up yourself and put whatever you want on it then for meat. That was their favorite.

Do you remember Bob playing any rock-and-roll records in your house?

Oh yes. Oh yes. There's all kinds of them. He had those loudmouth and—what was that?—Little Richard and names like that that were so important.

What about Bill Haley and the Comets?

Yes.

The Penguins—

Yes, all kinds of records like that. I come across them once in a while when I'm looking for something special.

Bob apparently never really talked very much as I understand it. Is that your impression of him?

No, he didn't talk too much. He seemed to be careful about what he did say.

Was he a pleasant teenager?

Yes, very pleasant—we thought so, anyway.

He wasn't one of these loudmouth kids.

Oh no. No, he wasn't loud at all, or insulting, like some kids are, the kind of foolish talk. He wasn't like that at all.

Bob at one point owned a motorcycle and—

Oh yes. Echo and him went motorcycle riding, and Echo tried it on her own once and fell with it.

Tell me what happened.

Well, Echo tried it out, and Bob told her exactly what to do; and she took off and didn't go very far when she fell off the motorcycle, or the motorcycle fell, or something. I was so frightened, I hardly remember. Anyway I just thought that she had been badly hurt, but she got up, and it was just embarrassing more than anything else.

Were you afraid of their being on a motorcycle or—

No, I trusted him, because he seemed to know what he was doing. I wasn't a bit concerned when she was with him.

Did he ever talk about his own family?

No, he said very little about them. He seemed to like his mother real well. Usually kids do talk more about their mothers.

I get a feeling that he didn't seem to like his father very much.

Well, we didn't really understand what was behind it. At that age, why, fathers are so disapproving, often, about what the kids are doing, while the mothers seem to be more understanding.

Did he ever talk about going down to Minneapolis?

Oh yes, Minneapolis was the first place to go to. That was of interest to him.

What did he say about it? Do you remember?

It was mostly about music. That's all I understood about it, and he was going to school there.

This was before he went to school there.

Yes, he did go quite often to Minneapolis before he went to school, yes.

The name Bob Dylan—the name Dylan—do you remember how he chose that name?

I had the understanding that he chose it together with Echo. I remember her coming home and saying he decided on that name.

Did Echo say why that name?

Well, wasn't it an author or writer of some kind?

There was a poet. Is that—

Oh yes, that poet—I've read some of his poems even.

Yes. Was there a feeling that it was definitely after this poet that he took the name?

That's the understanding I had.

Did Bob ever talk about poetry? Was he ever writing any poetry when you knew him?

Oh, he wrote poems for Echo, too, but I don't know now where they could be. And in school he wrote some poems for her, like kids do, writing poems. But I don't know. Some things just get put away, and then you never find them anymore.

FREEWHEELIN' DINKYTOWN

GRETEL HOFFMAN

I remember we talked about that he worked at styling his language.
And that he was acting. He said he was building a character that
would sell. That was the general impression. And this was something
that was just so far from the Bobby of two years ago, who was equally
an actor, but not as self-aware of himself as an actor.

G RETEL HOFFMAN WHITAKER MET DYLAN in 1960 in the Dinkytown
neighborhood of Minneapolis. She was back in her hometown, after
leaving Bennington College where she studied dance. Greta was enrolled
in classes at the University of Minnesota and was singing and playing guitar as a member of the growing Dinkytown music scene. She met Dylan
at the Ten O'Clock Scholar, a neighborhood coffeehouse and hangout.

Dylan enjoyed playing guitar with Gretel. They both sang folk and blues,
and Gretel taught him the blues classic "House of the Rising Sun." Dylan
was aware of Woody Guthrie's life and music, but he became committed
to Guthrie's style of folk singing after Gretel's husband, David Whitaker,
gave Dylan a copy of Guthrie's autobiography, *Bound for Glory.* Gretel
said her husband David really dug Dylan, and they became good friends.

Dylan told Gretel he was an Okie and an orphan, and that he was a
piano player just starting to pick up the guitar. Gretel told Tony in their
interview that she was very aware Dylan was building a myth, a legend of
himself, but he was so interesting and so vivid that the "truth" of who he
was didn't matter. She also told Tony that when Dylan left Minneapolis
to "make it" in New York City, he was still a naive kid but with a great
propensity for storytelling and a delightful sense of humor.

How did you first meet Bobby?
This is not easy, you know. It's ten years. Okay. I met him in the early
winter of 1960. I had just come back from Longville School, or I left school
and was going to the University of Minnesota.

You were at Bennington, is that right?

Right. Let's see, that was January or February. And I was enrolled in the University of Minnesota. And at that time there was a coffee club called the Scholar, the Ten O'Clock Scholar.

The Ten O'Clock Scholar.

Mostly we just called it the Scholar. And it must be that I met Bobby there. I don't really remember the first time I met him. But I used to go there, and we hung out there and we got to be friends. And at that time, he was living in a crummy little room up above the drugstore on the corner, up above Gray's Drugs. It was on Fourteenth Avenue and Fourth Street. And it was half a block down the street from the Scholar. Very nice club.

Fourth Street. "Positively 4th Street." Was there a feeling later when he wrote "Positively 4th Street" that this was *the* Fourth Street? That it was your Fourth Street, rather than our Fourth Street here in the Village?

That's a good question and I don't know the answer. Because he lived on Fourth Street in the Village too.

And "Positively 4th Street" is a put-down of all his friends, in a sense. The old friends from the Village, here, like Phil Ochs and Tom Paxton and Dave Van Ronk are all certain it's our Fourth Street and he's putting them down. But some people in Minneapolis say it's their Fourth Street, your Fourth Street, and he's putting you down.

I don't think so. I think it's the Village Fourth Street. Kind of because [our] Fourth Street as a symbol or as an image doesn't have any power.

Not the way the Village Fourth Street does.

Right. You know, if anything, Fourteenth Avenue has more.

Positively Fourteenth Avenue.

Yeah. But it was Dinkytown. So, the street was really irrelevant. I think it was the other Fourth Street.

Your mother said he sort of dug your playing and he hung around you and was attempting to learn from you or enjoyed playing with you, in any case.

I think that's true.

Tell me about that. Let's go back. You met him in probably the Scholar, you think.

And at parties and so on.

What was he like in his early days?

He was, first of all, a great kid. He was terribly young. And I mean that in a very broad way. He was very young, emotionally. He was terribly emotional. The line he had in those days was—first of all, that he was nineteen, which he wasn't, and that he wasn't going to live to be twenty-one.

Oh really?

And it seems to me that he composed a song. I'm almost positive although I've never, you know, never seen any trace of it, and I don't think he wrote it down. And I don't know if anybody else remembers it. But I'm absolutely clear about his obsession with the fact that he was going to die before he was twenty-one.

You recall anything at all about the song?

No, I don't. And I've thought about it, since then, and wondered whether, is it my imagination? Did I turn it into a song, or did he really make up a song? Or did he add that as a refrain in some other song. And I can't tell you other than I just have a hunch.

There is a feeling that part of his "I'm going to die before I'm twenty-one" was included somewhere in a song in some way.

Yeah. At that time, he was this very emotional kid.

Did he say why he thought he was going to die before twenty-one? Did he have any notion about a childhood disease, or Woody Guthrie kind of illness, or anything like that?

He didn't know about Woody Guthrie then. As a matter of fact, it was—we were the ones who turned him on to Woody Guthrie.

Great. How?

Well, this was probably a year and a half later, after I was married. And David Whitaker, my ex-husband, is a phenomenal reader. He's read everything that anybody ever wrote, practically. And he was very much involved with Woody Guthrie as a kind of a hero. Bob had not really heard about Woody Guthrie, except as a name that sort of everybody knew—that there was a folk singer named Woody Guthrie. He didn't know very much more. And David gave him Guthrie's book to read, the autobiography.

Bound for Glory.

Bound for Glory. And I remember when he gave it to him and said, you know, "Look, you gotta read this." And Bob did that. That was when he really—he knew about Guthrie. He knew Guthrie's songs a little bit, but there was no big thing about Guthrie.

What was Bob's reaction to the Guthrie book, first of all?

He was ecstatic over it. That's a characteristic Bob had at that time. That's something I really wanted to stress, and I can think of two or three other occasions when he was capable of this incredible enthusiasm. Another occasion when he got tremendously enthusiastic was he was with a group of Israeli singers who came to Minneapolis to perform there. And they came at exactly the same time the Clancy Brothers were there. It's a little bit confused in my mind about the whole time sequence, but I can remember that after the Israeli performance, we took these people to the Scholar with us and they played and sang some more. I remember Bobby sort of hugging me and jumping up and down just out of sheer excitement for this great music.

The Clancy Brothers, were they along too?

I think the Clancy Brothers were there, too, but I'm not sure. It may be that that was a different time a little bit later. Or that I've really condensed two different things in time.

Is it your feeling that Bob did meet the Clancys in Minneapolis?

Oh yeah. Oh, I'm sure he did.

It is strange in a way. Because I was talking to Pat Clancy and one of the other brothers a couple of nights ago.

And they didn't remember that?

Well, they remember meeting him in the Village.

I'm reasonably sure they had some very slight contact with him before that. But they probably don't remember it because he was just one of lots of other people. I don't think he played for them or anything like that. And I can remember Odetta was around then too.

You mean Bob may have met Odetta back in those days?

Oh, of course he did. But let me put it this way. During that time between 1960 and 1961, '62, Odetta was in Minneapolis a couple of times. The Clancy Brothers were there. Bob must have had contact with all of those people. I can't pick any one specific except that we were all around.

Back to Woody. His great enthusiasm over the Woody book.

That happened sometime before he left for New York. As a matter of fact, I think that was one of the motivations that got him going.

People were telling me that in the period when he got into Woody Guthrie, he practically became Woody Guthrie. His enthusiasm was so great he practically became the man. Tell me about some of that. I mean, what was he like? Was he doing Guthrie stuff primarily?

Almost exclusively for a while.

One other thing. Excuse me. Going back to the Guthrie book. I've since discovered that, back up in Hibbing, Bobby had gotten very heavily into John Steinbeck. The whole Okie thing from the John Steinbeck angle. Was there any discussion of Steinbeck in relationship to Guthrie?

When I first met Bobby, he claimed he was an Okie. That's the other thing

I'm sure you know. It's this incredible imagination that sometimes you really didn't know—and I think he didn't know—what was truth anymore, and what was his own involvement with it. And so, the whole initial set of stories when I first met him was that he was an Okie, that he was an orphan, and that he'd been on the road for years as a piano player. This big thing was that he was a piano player and just starting to play the guitar. That he lived in California.

You knew him as Dylan—Bobby Dylan?

Always, yes.

When did you learn about the name Zimmerman?

Oh, I suppose I learned about Zimmerman within a few weeks of the time that I first met him.

And yet he continued to say he was—

What he said was that Dylan was his mother's name.

What about the uncle who was a Las Vegas car dealer or something?

Yeah. There were a hundred stories. And after a while it dawned on us all that they were really all stories. But it kind of didn't matter, you know?

Why didn't it matter?

Because he was so vivid and so interesting and so much fun. I think I came to the conclusion after a while that I didn't care about the quote, unquote, "truth" of what he was. That it was sort of irrelevant.

Practically the exact same words that Dave Van Ronk used.

Really?

Yeah, when I asked him his reaction to the Dylan legend and the myth that Bobby built around himself.

Of course, one of the very interesting things—here, I feel a little bit hesitant about—I don't think I want to be directly quoted at this point. But it was very interesting to watch Bob build the myth, the legend of himself. And he did it, I think, very consciously and very deliberately. Because I can remember having a conversation with him—it was he and David and I, after he had come back to New York with success. Was that '63, already?

No, it was probably earlier. I think he returned—

Sixty-two. It was right after the first—

The first album is released in March of '62.

Oh, this was before that. It was before the album was released, but I think he [had] already cut it. And he had had a couple of snippets. He was back in Minneapolis, briefly, for a visit. I think, you know, he came back several times. Once again, I'm confused about what happened at which period of time. But I know that when he came back after he had already had a good amount of success, we had a conversation about this character that he was creating. And this was a very explicit story about creating such a character.

In what way? Do you remember what he said and how the conversation went?

No, I really don't. I don't think I can give you any single direct quote at all. I remember we talked about that he worked at styling his language. And that he was acting. He said he was building a character that would sell. That was the general impression. And this was something that was just so far from the Bobby of two years ago, who was equally an actor, but not as self-aware of himself as an actor.

What happened in between? You have any idea?

Well, he spent that hard winter in New York. I think that had a big effect.

Plus, the fact that that hard winter did include rubbing shoulders with a lot of professionals, here in New York.

Yeah, exactly. I would attribute it partly just to simply he was very intelligent.

He did apparently have a drive, a need to become a star in some way.

Oh, absolutely. And he had a terrible need to be the center of attention or a star, back in Minneapolis, at the Scholar, or at a party. And he was terribly—oh, I can remember. I just remembered a party where Bobby was playing by request. Everybody played guitars and you'd get in an empty room and you sat and played the guitar, and Bob would play. And people were listening, and then after a while some people drifted in and began talking. And then there was a lot of messing around and more talking. And pretty soon he realized people weren't listening closely to him and I'm quite sure he threw down the guitar and really stomped off in great anger.

A lot of people recognized this need of his for recognition. When he was just a kid here in New York when he first arrived, they felt Bobby was the kind of kid who needed recognition, and everybody worked hard to build up his ego. Was there any of that at that time, back in Minneapolis?

I don't know how—

Was there a feeling that Bobby was one of those who could possibly make it?

I don't think so.

What did people think? Bobby, I assume, to some extent talked with his friends, at least, about going professional.

Oh yeah.

What was the feeling at that time among his friends?

In one sense, you believed Bobby when he said he was going to go and do it. "I'm going to go to New York and I'm going to make it." There was something kind of believable about him saying that. But on the other hand, I don't think any of us took it terribly seriously. I don't think any of us believed he would be able to make it because New York was so tough. It wasn't that we didn't think he was good. But there were a lot of good people. And you see at that point he was with very, very little of his own composing. He was mostly singing other people's songs.

But he was—you are aware that he was doing his own composing at the time. One song I have heard about is something called "Black Jack Blues." Are you aware of that?

You know that rings a faint bell. I know there were some songs he certainly played along with. And that's why I said I think that he added—he either composed a song word for word or added words. But it may be that he completely composed that whole song. I guess, yeah, we knew he was doing something of that. But I didn't realize when he left for New York that he was in any way really intending to become a writer. He was singing Woody Guthrie songs, but he hadn't—and he was identifying with them but not to the point where he was, himself, you know, writing and doing all of his own stuff. That came later.

Going back to the early months, the first months that you knew Bobby, this was January/February of 1960. Was he going to school at that time?

I think he had quit school. I think he quit that winter quarter. I'm pretty sure.

Just the one quarter.

Yeah. Either he quit in the winter quarter or the spring quarter.

Did he talk about quitting and why he quit and what he wanted to do?

A little bit, yeah. He was just completely dissatisfied with the university. He said he wasn't getting anything out of it. His classes were uninteresting to him, and it was all very fake. There was nothing in it. I'm quite sure that he quit just about the time I met him.

He talked a lot about meeting some very famous people, about being from California and doing a lot of things. Apparently, he did play a honky-tonk piano in Central City, Colorado, for one thing. He did meet Big Joe Williams, somewhere. Did he ever talk about any of these heroes of his?

He certainly talked about Big Joe Williams.

What did he say about him, do you recall?

No, I don't remember. Other than there was always a lot of storytelling about great people. But I can't tell you what he said specifically.

Did he ever say that he met Big Joe Williams hopping a freight? Hopped a freight with him and he went down to Mexico with him on a freight car?

Yes, yes, yes, he did. Sure, he did.

Did any of the Dinkytown crowd ever go to Chicago to catch some of the acts?

I think once in a while but not very often.

You know if Bob ever did?

I rather doubt it.

In those first months that you met him, where was he living?

That's when he was living above Gray's Drugs in one room.

By himself?

Yeah, all by himself. It was a horrible room.

What about money? How was he supporting—did you know he came from Hibbing? When did you learn that?

Sometime during that early time I learned that. And I sort of assumed he was being supported, at least partially, by his parents.

Did he have money? At least, spending money and money for the rent?

He had a little money. He didn't have very much.

Did Bobby play professionally around town? Play for money, that is, around town?

Yes, he started to. He started playing at the Scholar for coffee.

Really?

I'm not absolutely positive, but I have this image of being there one day and we both didn't have any money, and he wanted some coffee and some pastries. Bob said, "Well, if I play, will you give some to us?"

Bobby, by this time, was already making plans to leave for New York. What did he say about coming to New York? Was it primarily to see Woody, at first?

Yes. I think initially he was going to make the trip and find Woody. I have a postcard from him telling about when he did get in to see him.

Getting back to Hibbing. Did he talk about his parents, his folks up in Hibbing?

No. Never.

Never talked about how his father was rough on him, he couldn't stand his father, or anything like that?

No, no. Never talked about his parents at all. And then much later, when he was successful and he came back, he sort of admitted very shyly, I thought, that he was really going to go up to Hibbing to see his mother, and that he was going to bring her a present. And that's sort of the very first time he had really mentioned his parents.

When did this happen?

This must have been '62, already.

When you first met him, what kind of music was he into? Was there rock in his background? Did he talk about rock and roll at all?

Yeah. Let's see. What was he doing? You know, he was doing a lot of the—I think there was rock in his background but I'm really unsure. And I would feel nervous just to say anything about it because I'm not sure. I remember he was singing some blues. As a matter of fact, I taught him "The House of the Rising Sun."

Oh really?

Yeah. He was singing a lot of blues. A lot of the stuff that was around in 1960 and '61.

But basically, it was folk.

Oh yes, yes.

Getting back to Guthrie again. Now, you said you and David turned him on to Guthrie.

Right.

Records too? I mean, besides the book. David gave him the book, right?

Yeah. We didn't have any records.

There were no Guthrie records available?

No, I don't mean there weren't any Guthrie records available, but we didn't have any. I'm sure, of course, he must have heard them.

Yeah. In talking about his being an Okie, at the very beginning, again, getting back to John Steinbeck, was there any discussion of Steinbeck?

I don't think so. That is, I certainly don't recall having a discussion about Steinbeck. One of the things about Bob, at that point, which I think really stands in very stark contrast to what he was a little bit later, is that in this particular, he was very nonintellectual.

He was attempting to give the image of an American primitive. And he couldn't be a well-read man and still be an American primitive was the basic feeling we were getting down here in the Village.

Right, yeah, yeah. And I'm really sure he never talked about Steinbeck. This was one side of his character.

That's right. And to talk about him might blow the cover, blow that fact that he picked it up from a book somewhere.

But he did keep growing, you know. It didn't take very long to figure out because he was several different people. He was sort of never—

It was hard to keep the balls juggled up in the air.

Exactly.

Ellen [Baker] says that when she first met Bobby, she thought he was very boyish and kind of shy. A little-boy helplessness that made people want to do things for him.

Absolutely. Yeah. That's a great characterization.

Tell me about some of your feelings about this. Any anecdotes that would highlight it?

First of all, he was very different in appearance. Some people don't change very much as they get older, and Bob is someone who changed incredibly as he got older. It was partly because he lost huge amounts of weight. When I knew him, when he was nineteen, he was a little pudgy. Sort of pleasantly plump.

Really?

He was very round-faced and [had] curly hair and he looked like a little kid. And he acted like he needed somebody to take care of him. He didn't eat properly if somebody didn't feed him.

Did people feed him? Did you and David have him over, for example?

Oh yeah. Oh yes, a great deal.

What about others? Are there any others who were close to him at that time that I may not have heard? John Koerner, for example, I haven't called Spider John yet. Did he have any great contact with Bobby?

Oh, sure. He had some, certainly. How much contact, I'm not sure.

Was there any hillbilly—getting back to what Bobby was into at the time—real hillbilly? True hillbilly stuff?

I don't think so. I doubt it. Not at that point.

When he finally went off to New York, did he say goodbye? I'm told that he and Hugh Brown and whoever else they were rooming with, Dirty Max, slipped away from their place without paying the rent.

Oh, I'm sure that's probably true.

When was the last time you saw Bobby?

I think the last time I saw him was the summer of '62. In that spring, a few months before that, David and I went to New York for a few days and we stayed with my sister, but we spent quite a bit of time with Bobby. And I remember that he gave a—he was part of a hootenanny at Carnegie

Hall, with a lot of other people on this program. And that when he walked onto the stage and there was this incredible roar of, you know, this sort of hysterical roar that I associated with Johnnie Ray. I was just—I couldn't believe my ears. It was incredible that this was for Bob. And at that time, he was living down on Fourth Street.

This was at Carnegie Hall? A hootenanny at Carnegie Hall?

Yes. Pete Seeger was on the program. As a matter of fact, Pete Seeger was running it.

I'll be talking to Pete Seeger next week, so I'll ask him about it. I wasn't aware that Bobby was involved. I know he did a couple of individual concerts, solo concerts, at Carnegie Hall.

Well, this was a group thing and he only did a couple of songs. And it was sold out.

I don't remember that one.

And at that point he was living down on Fourth Street right above this store.

Oh, the Door Store.

It was very strange to see him there in really very much the same—his physical situation was identical to what it had been in Minnesota. It was sort of this crummy little apartment. The refrigerator was filled with mold and a couple of cans of beer and that's all. And that's how it had been back—

Just as it was on Fourteenth Street.

Yeah.

How much time did you and David spend with him? How long were you in town?

We were just there a few days. We spent a lot of time with him and he was very high. I don't think he was high on anything. Oh, yes, he was shooting mescaline.

Was he really? That early?

Yeah, I think so. Yeah, I'm sure he was. Of course, he was. Because then later on in the same year we went San Francisco and the people were shooting it a lot there too.

Made aware of it by Bobby.

Right.

I wasn't aware he was using anything that early. I know he smoked pot but I wasn't aware he was—

Oh, he was smoking pot long before then.

Was there much pot back in Minneapolis?

Oh, sure. Certainly there was pot around.

Was Bobby into it?

I think so. I would be very surprised if he wasn't. Oh, he had to have been, I'm sure.

It was the thing to do.

Yeah. Everybody was.

Going back, again, to the early days—you met him in early 1960. Did he have any close friends who may have known him before then? From 1959 on? From the beginning of the fall term? I'm trying to find somebody who met him when he first got down to Minneapolis.

I don't think so. He was really a loner in a funny, artistic kind of way. You might be able to find somebody who knew him earlier than I knew him, but I doubt it. Now, he had a room in a fraternity house. And it might be that there is somebody—I forget even which fraternity it was. It might be that there was somebody back then that he knew, but I couldn't help you.

Did he have a room in the fraternity house before he moved into Fourteenth Street?

Yes.

That would have been then in late '59. The beginning of that fall term.

Right. But when I knew him he was already out of there. He just spent one quarter there.

What else can you tell me about how other people reacted to Bobby? What was the general feeling? How did David react to Bobby?

Well, David really dug Bobby. The two of them got to be good friends. It started out on a negative footing because David came back from Israel in February. So, I met him just a couple of weeks after he'd gotten back. I really wasn't Bobby's girlfriend in any sense, but that's how it seemed to be, that I was considered his girl. And I started going with David and then I very quickly got married. It was unexpected, very quick. And when I told—we saw Bob just a couple of days later and said, "Hey, you know, I just got married," he reacted very, very badly.

Kind of understandable, I would think.

But you see, I thought of our relationship as really platonic and kind of—if I had thought it was anything other than that, I never would have done it that way. I was sensitive to things then. I can remember standing in the middle of the street with my mouth open at his reaction and being really,

really shocked. And I can remember that he shouted at me, "Well, if you get divorced, let me know," and stomped off down the street.

(*laughing*) Did he know David at this time?

No. David hadn't been around very much. But then very quickly after that, he got to know David, probably just around and about at the Scholar and at other places. And they got to be friends. And then what happened really was that at the time they got to be better friends than I was with Bob.

I understand later on David came to New York and either worked for Bob or was a companion in some way. You know anything about that?

I don't know anything about that. There is this critical period in Bob's life—this is before he moved to New York—and David and Bobby were really good friends.

Is there anything else you can think of that we may not have covered?

Well, one other point. We sort of covered this, but I'll say [something] again that gets lost a little bit about Bob—was this incredibly rapid professionalization.

Yeah, yeah. This is something that's very hard to understand. You get a kid coming down from Hibbing in the fall of '59 and ending up in New York in the beginning of '61, totally accepted by the Dave Van Ronks and all the other professionals here.

Because when he left Minneapolis, he was still a kid. He was very, very much just a naive kid, with a great propensity for storytelling, and an exciting musician. He was an exciting musician.

Was he really?

Yeah. I found him to be, always. There's always been some very compelling quality about his singing.

Even back in those days.

Mm-hmm.

Did he have the little Chaplinesque mannerisms that went over so big in Gerde's later?

Yes, yes he did. He was delightful. He really had a delightful sense of humor. And he was very delightful but not deliberately or consciously that way. And he learned very quickly more and more to capitalize on that.

It's quite clear that this kid was capable of absorbing much from people around him and swirling it around in his head and coming up with something unique and original and doing it rather quickly.

Very quickly. Incredibly quickly, really.

Apparently, he was learning all the time. This is the one thing that is quite clear

about Bobby. Who were some of the people he was picking things up from? I mean, were you capable of teaching anything in those early days? How professional or how into it were you?

Well, I'd come back from Bennington, which was—there was a lot going on there. I'd picked up a lot of songs already by that time. And so, yeah, I think I—I can't pinpoint anything, except that I think I did have influence and I think I wasn't as into it as he was.

What kind of an influence, what sense? Specifically, did he ask you to teach him certain songs? Were you collecting songs? Was he borrowing some of your material, that kind of thing?

The folk songs he was singing at that point were really—when I first met him, seems they were very much around in 1960, '59, and even the Kingston Trio kind of crap.

You mean the pop folk nonsense?

Yeah, yeah. Besides "House of the Rising Sun" and maybe, what else? Some other blues. He was just beginning to pick up on that. It's very hard to recall specifics, but I have the feeling that when I met him—I don't have any image that he had any style at all. He was just sort of—he was learning how to sing anything that came in his path. It seems to me that we had some conversations about blues.

Do you remember what the conversations about blues may have been?

Not really, no. No I don't, not really. Oh, I find it so annoying. I'm so angry with myself not being able to—

Well, it's possible our talk today may jog your memory and over the coming days and weeks you might—if you do, in fact, remember things, please jot them down so when we talk again you'll have them.

There's a reason why I never saw Bob after that. That is—no reason in the sense that something big happened. Nothing big ever happened. There was just a feeling like, well, we were pretty small time, now.

Yeah, right. In fact, even, you know, people we would consider big time, like Dave Van Ronk and Eric Andersen, their feeling, again, is they're small time now. Bobby is the king.

I was going to ask you. I was going to say, before you hang up, tell me what he's doing now.

Apparently, he's becoming a very mature man approaching thirty. He's got four kids.

Four.

Yeah.

Wow.

And he's come back from Woodstock and apparently he's out of that entire secrecy, great need for privacy kind of thing and he's back looking up old friends, realizing that he missed a lot by cutting out of the city and moving up to Woodstock and isolating himself. He appears to be kind of lonely and he appears to be at a loss [as to] what to do next in his career.

That's what I was going to ask you.

Also, he's running around telling people that *Nashville Skyline* is the best thing he ever did and that's where his head is at. But this was, like, six months ago. He's also saying he's writing a Broadway musical.

(*laughs*) Wouldn't that be a groove? He probably is.

I believe it. What about the poetry?

The poetry and *Tarantula* and all the other books he is supposed to have been doing. Apparently, he's discarded them all. That's not where his head is at.

My goodness. I'd love to see him sometime.

If you come to New York, I'll tell you where he lives.

I'm scared to go.

And I don't find that too strange. I hear stories from—who tells me? David Cohen, another part of the folk crowd. Last time Paul McCartney came into town, right, big Beatle, right? Biggest man in the world. Comes into town and he wants to see Bobby Dylan. He calls up somebody and says, "Hey, this is Paul McCartney. I'm in town. Do you think it'd be all right if I called Bob Dylan?"

Yeah, that's weird. That's just weird.

DAVID WHITAKER

*There's a tape of his first song, and I don't know what happened to it,
but that was done in my house. It was called "Bobby Dylan's Blues."
I still remember the day we recorded it. He put the microphone over
the light shade, and he played this, and it was his first song.*

DAVID WHITAKER, a self-described "resident radical" of the Dinkytown
scene, lived down the street from the Ten O'Clock Scholar music club,
near Dylan. Whitaker played guitar, but his influence on Dylan was in
the social-intellectual realm. Dylan admired Whitaker's freewheeling rad-
icalism. Whitaker gave Dylan a copy of Woody Guthrie's autobiography,
Bound for Glory—a turning point in Dylan's social-political awareness.

How did you first meet Bobby?
I think it was around the Dinkytown scene, in 1960, '61.
Was it after you married Gretel?
Almost simultaneously. I think it was slightly before. I had come back
from Europe and he was there playing at the Scholar. And there was
maybe a handful, you know, of folks in the scene.
In any case, you first met Bobby around the Scholar.
Right. He was playing there first for a few dollars a night.
He was getting paid?
Yeah. A little. And he and Johnny Koerner were alternating nights there, I
think. And Dave Ray was a drummer who showed up many times.
Tony Glover was a little younger, wasn't he?
Dave Ray was in college. And I think Glover was maybe a few years
younger, but he was an expert in blues. He grew up around it.
Were you into it even semiprofessionally at that point? Were you playing at all?
No, I'd just go out and hang out. We had an apartment just down the

street from the Scholar and I'd go there. It was Koerner's old apartment, in fact.

Where was the apartment?

Down near the Scholar.

What was your impression of Dylan when you first met him?

Well, he didn't really, like, talk to people, at first. He always had a guitar in his hand. And he'd be playing, and he'd sit and just be pickin'. He played almost constantly, from the time he woke up to the time he went to sleep. This is before he picked up on Guthrie.

Yeah. Let me ask you about that right now, as long as you brought it up. Gretel says that you were the one who laid the Guthrie book on Dylan.

Yeah, *Bound for Glory*.

Tell me about that.

I had talked to him about Guthrie. We had a couple of records and we listened. And then I started talking about Guthrie's book, *Bound for Glory*, which I had read, and I had never met anybody who had. It came out in the early '40s, I think. In those days, Dylan hadn't even read. That was probably the only book that he read that year.

He had been aware to some extent of Guthrie's music, had he not?

Yeah, right. We had some records, *Dust Bowl Ballads*, stuff like that. And then I remember him—the first one he learned was Guthrie's "Tom Joad." You know the song?

Yeah.

And this is, like, half an hour long. He played it over and over. It was really fantastic.

And getting into Guthrie's writing, into the book, did Dylan in any way talk about John Steinbeck?

No. I don't think he read—

Apparently, back in high school, talking to kids in high school, Steinbeck blew his mind and that's when he became an Okie. Dylan became an Okie, like, in early '59.

He got his accent a little bit later than this time. I would say about six months. He would disappear from time to time, then come back.

Where would he go? Do you have any idea?

Well, he'd say that he was in Oklahoma, but I think he went up to Hibbing. I don't remember exactly what made me realize that he was in Hibbing.

Did he ever talk about going to California, playing in Central City, Colorado, with piano in a strip tease joint in Central City?

Well, there used to be—you mean, earlier than this?

Right, or even around the time when he was disappearing.

Yeah, he went to Denver for a while. This was a little bit later. And played—

The Gilded Garter or something?

I can't remember now. It was one of the few in the country.

Oh, in Denver, right, right.

And I think during that this black folk singer had written a song called "The Klan." And this became one of his favorite songs.

Did he ever talk about Big Joe Williams?

No. Glover knew Williams. Yeah, from Chicago.

Could Bobby have met Williams through Glover?

I don't think so. I remember once when I was—it was very important for Dylan to see Josh White, who was playing in a club in Minneapolis, and we were both nineteen. We tried to get in and they threw us out. And we stood in the snow for hours and tried to talk to Josh. I remember this as a really traumatic experience.

When did this happen? Do you recall?

About '61 or so. During the Scholar days.

Did you ever get to Josh?

He said he did the next day. But I never talked to him.

Could you tell me a little bit more about his reaction to Guthrie's book? Did you talk about it after he read it?

I just remember him carrying it around for quite a time. Just after that, he began to write. And after that he was entirely dedicated to Guthrie. I think that's all he played at that time, until the first time he left Minneapolis for New York.

But he did begin to write some of his own stuff at that time?

Yeah, right. There's a tape of his first song, and I don't know what happened to it, but that was done in my house. It was called "Bobby Dylan's Blues." I still remember the day we recorded it. He put the microphone over the light shade, and he played this, and it was his first song.

The first song you know of that he wrote?

Right. I can't remember any of the words or anything.

"Bobby Dylan's Blues." You don't remember any of it? Or the sentiment even? What was his blues about?

I can't remember. It was so long ago.

But he began to write around the time that you gave him the Guthrie book and he was digging into the Guthrie work.

Right, almost simultaneously.

You said that his Okie thing, the accent and all, came a little later. Gretel seemed to recall that when she first met him he already had an Okie accent. He was already an Okie.

No, no. There may have been a slight accent, but it came out in its full flower later.

But she remembers that he told her he was from Oklahoma, at the very beginning.

No, I remember Hibbing and all that. I talked to his mother once on the phone very shortly after knowing him. And when he left for New York for the first time, too, I still remember a very intense scene. There was a heavy snowfall. It had been snowing all that night. We were sitting there and so he decided to call Woody on the telephone. Woody was, of course, at Greystone, I think, a mental hospital in New Jersey.

How did Bobby find out some of the details of Woody's life?

He went to see him. That night after trying to talk to him on the phone.

How did he know he was in Greystone [Park Psychiatric Hospital]?

It was around. I knew it. Maybe from *Sing Out!* or something. I had certain connections with the left bent. I would generally hear those things.

Certain connections with whom?

With very left-wing circles and the papers. *Sing Out!* and the other papers. We were very much involved in that too. And an older-generation Communist Party then. But, anyway, so we got as close [as] a psychiatrist on his ward. He said, "No, Woody can't come to the phone. He can't move," and so on. Dylan said, "Well, I'm going to see him." And he left for New York that night. And I didn't hear from him for two months.

Do you remember when this was?

'61.

No, in '61 he was already. He cut his first record in—

Oh yeah. Then it was '60, I guess.

This would be the winter of '60.

Right. And then about three months later I got a card from him saying— with a picture of Woody on the back. The Woody Guthrie Children's Fund. And on it just, "I saw Woody! I saw Woody! He likes my stuff." And it ended [with], "This card kills the Fascists." So then about a month later I got the same card from him but further information, that he's playing in Cafe Wha? And people really dig him and they like him and so on. The same card, all with Woody on it, that he sent that winter. And then he reappeared and was already starting to be somewhat of a success. He had graduated from the Cafe Wha?, playing for donations, to Gerde's, I think. And came back and what's his name had discovered him? John Hammond.

John Hammond Senior. Right.

I remember him saying, Hammond says that one day you're going to be more famous than—than—who was it? "Blue Suede Shoes," the rock-and-roll singer who is still famous?

Elvis.

Than Elvis, yeah. "Hammond says I'm going to be more famous than Elvis," he said. Then his first record came out, and then his second. And the Minneapolis side of *Great White Wonder* was recorded at my house, I think. In one of these sessions. Somewhere on it he shouts "Whitaker, Whitaker," and this was recorded—we recorded that on a trip he made then—the last one before he took off.

When was that? Can you date any of these trips that he came back?

Not really. '62? The last trip was after the second record.

That's when those cuts were made? At your place.

Yeah. With Glover.

Glover taped them?

Yeah. We just had tape recorders and a mic set up. Everybody sat around and played stuff.

Let me throw a couple of things out. Gretel [Hoffman] remembers that after Bobby went to New York the first time and was beginning to make it, he came back and he was talking about the character he was deliberately creating. He was working on styling a language, working on a personality, working it into a character that would sell. Do you recall any of that?

Yeah, that was obviously happening, but I'm not sure how really conscious it was. He left Minneapolis a guy more, like, plump than skinny. And he came back tremendously thin. He'd hardly ever speak other than singing, before. And by the time he came back the second time, he'd become a fantastic kind of conversationalist. A great kind of humorist. You'd say that he'd probably not only make it as a singer but as a stand-up kind of comedian, as well.

Oh, really?

And he had a really ironic and humorist view of all the things that were happening around him, the whole show business things that go on. I remember thinking he was using a great deal of speed, but there was nothing said about it.

Well, I know that as soon as he got here he was getting into it because I know everybody he had contact with, like the Van Ronks and all, he definitely was into it. You made a trip to New York with Gretel in '62. Saw him at Carnegie Hall at a hootenanny Seeger put together apparently. Can you tell me what was he like at that point?

Well, he was living over the Door shop, on—

With Suze? Was Suze around?

No, she had just split.

She had just gone to Italy?

Right. I think we stayed there for a week or so. He took us around to all the clubs like the Gaslight, Gerde's, and so on. Then we went one more time, later, just after the March on Washington. I saw him there.

Did you go to the March on Washington with him?

No, I met him there.

What was his reaction to you by then?

Oh, then he was still very friendly. There hadn't been any kind of craziness yet. Because after that I went up to New York and stayed for a while at his place on Fourth Street again.

Same place?

The same place. But by this time I guess he had got gotten far more famous than I imagined. He talked about people mobbing him in the streets and so on. I never took it seriously. You know, to me it was still Bob Dylan. I remember him saying, "I can't go on the streets." This is just after the second record.

Was he pretty paranoid about his lack of privacy?

Oh yeah, entirely. But he'd always been generally into things going on even back in Minneapolis.

In what way?

Enemies and so on. Well, the campus police picked on us because we represented what there was of the hip community of 1961.

Right. And we had just come out of the Eisenhower era.

Right, right. Hardly out. Hardly out. It was, like, thirty thousand students at the University of Minnesota and less than a handful that was all, ten, fifteen people that were involved in this particular group, where we'd drink at the Holland Bar, Triangle Bar, Dobb . . . I just remember we were in the house and them being dragged in and being accused of all sorts of stuff that Bobby took very, very seriously and almost having a scene at a police station. It was a long time ago.

And Bobby was paranoid about things like campus cops. Anything else? For example, well, you knew about his parents in Hibbing. Was he paranoid about people digging into his background?

Oh yeah. They would just find out something about him by accident and he had this whole mythology about himself being like Bobby Vee and his history of working carnivals and all of that. He would talk about it, but you'd never know. You were always pretty skeptical of the stories but accepted them pretty much at face value.

What did he say about working carnivals?

He just said he used to do it. At the time I was skeptical. But I know he plays the piano and I didn't know it then. I never heard him play the piano.

Yeah, I've discovered that a lot of the stories he told in the early days that people put him down for lying about, I've discovered in my research are true.

Like the Bobby Vee thing?

The Bobby Vee thing—obviously, the Bobby Vee thing is natural. But things like hopping a freight with Big Joe Williams and going into Mexico.

I don't know.

Big Joe Williams was around and said it was true, without Bobby prompting him. Dave Van Ronk said he just fell off the seat because Big Joe said, "Oh, Bobby, remember those days we spent on a freight." It just knocked everybody out. The March on Washington. What was Bobby like at the time? By this time, he's really famous. He's in the college crowd and on the campuses. What about his privacy thing down there?

Well, there he could just go to an open party with Joan Baez at the time, who was very close. I remember him saying to me, "I can't even go on the streets. They attack me." I said, "Why? Do they think you're Bobby Darin?" And that was a great laugh. Then I went up to New York and all the—Suze Rotolo moved all of the furniture out. There was, like, two mattresses and a card table. By this time, I don't know, I guess they had broken up or something.

They broke up a few times.

I suddenly realized that he was quite wealthy after being poverty stricken for years. Nevertheless, he had nothing in his large apartment but two mattresses, a card table, four chairs, and a refrigerator that you couldn't open because it had stuff growing in it. I remember he said, "Don't open that refrigerator. There's stuff growing in it." He was always a guy who seemed to have a great deal of difficulty taking care of personal things, like remembering to eat and doing anything that had a schedule. He just would fall asleep in his clothes kind of thing.

When was this trip to New York that the Fourth Street place looked like that?

It was immediately after the March on Washington. It was amazing. You go there, and I realize that something really heavy was happening to him. Peter, Paul and Mary were singing "Blowin' in the Wind" for two hundred thousand people. He was singing his ["Only a Pawn in Their Game," about the death of Medgar Evers] for the same enormous crowd and so on. But then, yet, you went to New York City and here it was still the same. So, it was a funny time.

Getting back a little bit closer to the beginning about some of the songs he was writing. Do you recall anything called "Blackjack Blues"? People around seem to vaguely recall that this was one of the first things he wrote. Do you recall anything like that?

And so it could well be, you know, "Blackjack Blues," if it's the same blues I'm thinking of.

You mean the "Bobby Dylan's Blues" that you were talking about.

Yeah, right. It could be. Because I remember he came over and he said, "I've just written a song and I want to record it."

Was this, wow, his first song he wrote?

Something like that. And so, we put it on and he started with that and ended up with about three hours sitting there. The man has a fantastic memory. He could hear a song once and immediately have it down.

And you did, at the time, put much of his stuff on tape?

I did that one and other things. A bunch of bootleg records. And then there's a debate with Glover and the editor of the *Little Sandy Review*. You ever heard of that? On the local underground Minneapolis station. They put on a review of the second record, really bringing it down for using electrical guitars and so on. And so they got into this extended discussion freaking about this thing which just happened to record it. If that still exists that could be amazing.

You mean the taped debate?

Yeah. If somebody still has it.

Possibly Dylan has it.

I doubt it. Because he just left with the clothes he had on his back, the way he came. It wasn't until later that he realized the price of fame. Martin, have you come across Dave Martin? He was very close to Dylan, maybe still is. He's around Minneapolis, more or less. I think he's become kind of the guru of the psychedelic set, in Minneapolis. He had a jug band called the Jook Savages. Because he was staying at my house totally while Dylan was here. They were working on this version of his of "House of the Rising Sun." I still remember Martin mimicking him, Dylan, line for line, the two of them. Like, they're dying over these guitars, singing "House of the Rising Sun."

Gretel tells me that at one stage, there, in the last month before Bobby came to New York, you and Bobby were very, very close. Very tight. Tell me something about what Bobby was like personally.

Well, I think that up to that I had always dismissed him intellectually. But I began to understand far closer what he was trying to do, and what this particular kind of mind which he had was. And so was on the same kind of wavelength in that we had a similar sense of humor, as well. And a very kind of combined and kind of a radical view of the world around us, with a sense of humor about it.

A sense that it was all a big shuck.

Yeah, exactly. But it began to seem at the time to us more and more humorous, which we spent a great deal of time rapping about and laughing about it. I know one time when he came back, he wanted me to go out and be his road manager, but I didn't.

Why not?

It just wasn't for me.

Before coming to New York—when he came to New York for the first time, was he coming primarily to look up Woody Guthrie, or was there a sense that he was going to break into the Village scene?

No, he knew nothing about the whole Village scene. I think what little he knew was what I had told him, because [of] my experience from the Village. I had spent far more time before that around North Beach in the beatnik days. And back in '58 to, yeah, 1958. I was just sixteen when I was around North Beach and had been around the Village too.

So, your feeling basically is that he was coming to New York the first time to see Woody and not quite clear exactly what was happening, from there.

Yeah, right. His first job in New York wasn't playing the guitar, but it was shoveling snow off the docks.

Tell me something about that. What do you know about that?

That's what he talked about it. And then playing at the Cafe Wha?

For basket money?

Yeah.

Did he ever talk to anyone, as far as you know about turning pro? For example, Rolf Cahn?

When Cahn was there, it was before I was. I heard about the trip Cahn made and how he picked Dylan out from the rest and—

What trip is this?

Well, Cahn came to Minneapolis in 1960. And I think that put an effect on local guitar players, like Koerner.

How much weight did Cahn have at that point? Because, frankly, back here in the East he's not that heavy at all.

No, I think it was more because he knew some guitar-playing techniques that no one else did at the time. Like the flamenco and so on.

And he did have some effect on Bobby?

Maybe. I think it wasn't until he got to New York, though, that people actually had that sort of—and the whole Gaslight [Cafe] group, [Hugh] Romney [a.k.a. Wavy Gravy] and Van Ronk.

Dave Van Ronk, right. Apparently, Bobby was learning. Back in those days, your basic feeling is that Bobby may [have] been seriously thinking of turning pro. Am I right?

He wasn't really thinking of doing anything else. I mean, I don't think at this stage he was thinking of taking up a career and working on the side, or any of that. I think he knew pretty much that one way or another he would be playing the guitar and singing for the rest of his life.

Apparently, he was learning all the time and absorbing all the time. Did he ever talk to you about what he was doing, what he was picking up on?

Not at first. Eventually, though. I don't think it was all that conscious with him, at first. It was just a natural kind of response to this world.

Getting back to the Guthrie book, did you discuss it much?

You know, it's difficult to remember. Of course, what now is of interest to biographers and historians and so on, to us it just seemed like a perfectly ordinary way of going through one's day. Or just actually remembering what seemed normal.

Obviously. I was just hoping to, you know, possibly jog your memory a little bit. When was the last time you saw Bobby?

New York, after the—

After that second album.

Yeah.

Or after the March on Washington?

Right.

Why didn't you see him after that? Anything happen between you or . . . ?

I don't know. We just separated. It probably had become impossible to see the man after that. I don't know.

You mean, he's much too big for us, now, kind of thing.

Right.

Couple of other things. Hammond Junior was out in Minneapolis occasionally, wasn't he?

I didn't meet him until New York.

Until later, okay. Gretel seems to remember also that Bobby was going through one stage of "He's nineteen and he's not going to live until he's twenty-one." You recall that?

I think that's something he probably kept for girls.

Yeah, I think maybe we all did. (*laughs*) There's a basic feeling from the people I talk to that Bobby was kind of young, emotionally, at that time, even for a nineteen-year-old. What's your basic feeling about it?

Well, I don't know. I'm sure that's something that can be said about any young poet, whatever. You know, young, emotionally still needs to be developed. Oh, Jack Elliott was very close to him at this period. Elliott was just around the corner. Just across Washington Square, in fact, from him.

And Elliott and a number of people who were close to him in the Village—

I remember the first time he came back he had this review from Bob Shelton from the *New York Times*. It was the first public record of Dylan. Did you ever see that?

Right, the great review from Gerde's, yeah.

He used to carry this around until it was falling to pieces and show it to people. Yeah, wow ["Bob Dylan: A Distinctive Folk-Song Stylist; 20-Year-Old Singer Is Bright New Face at Gerde's Club"], by Robert Shelton.

And he was really high about it, huh?

Oh indeed.

Remember what he said? The kind of reaction he had to it?

No, just enthusiasm, the fact he was just being recognized.

Listen, one quick question. Was there any rock and roll? Were you aware of Bobby's rock-and-roll background?

No.

SPIDER JOHN KOERNER

I think it was divided. There were a number of people that thought he was a no-talent bum, and there were some people that thought he was really great, you know? So, I'm sure some people thought that—well, I know people thought he was really talented and could make it.

"**S**PIDER" JOHN KOERNER was a part of the Minneapolis folk scene, playing guitar in Dinkytown coffeehouses. He met Dylan at the Ten O'Clock Scholar in late 1959. They became drinking and guitar-playing buddies, learning and honing their skills and technique.

How did you first meet Bobby?
Let's see. I first met him in—there's a coffeehouse named the Ten O'Clock Scholar in Dinkytown and I first met him in that place. That was—oh, shit—1960, probably.

Were you playing there at the time?
I think so, kind of in and out, you know? I don't remember exactly if I was playing at the time I met him, but at least shortly after.

Were you going to university?
I'd just gotten out of the Marine Corps.

Of all things.
Yeah, right. (*laughs*) I'd done eight months and then managed to get out. It was during the summer. I came back in August, I think.

1960?
Yeah. Well, August of '59, I guess, or fall of '59. And the first time I heard him play, we somehow wound up getting together with a friend of ours named Len Duriseau.

Len D-u-r-s-i?
I don't know how to spell it. It's French, you know? The name is French.

But anyway, we went on to the university. We went in back of the chemical engineering building or something. We had some wine and sat around and playing in the middle of the night. From then on it was just a lot of hanging around with various experiences and all that kind of stuff for quite some time.

Were you getting paid at the Scholar?

Yeah, we used to get something. I don't remember how much it was, but it was probably in the three or four dollars a night area.

And Bobby was getting paid also at that period?

Yeah, right.

This would be somewhere in early '60, I would guess.

Right.

Spring of '60 or something like that?

Yeah, and there was another place we played, too, called the Purple Onion, run by Bill Daniels.

What was Bobby's professionalism at that time? How competent was he with his guitar? What was he playing?

It was strumming, mostly—chords and like that. And the singing was a little different. It seemed a little smoother than it did after, you know, when he first started making records.

Was he singing more the melody line than he did after he started making records? I get a feeling he was kind of bending the melody a lot more.

Yeah, I think so, actually with folk songs and stuff like that—although he did write some of his own at the time, too.

That's one of the questions I wanted to toss at you. What are some of the things that he—Dave Whitaker tells me he remembers taping some of Bobby's stuff— you and Dave on occasion putting some of Bobby's stuff down on tape. Do you recall any of that?

I don't remember any tapes, actually. I can't remember, really, any of the songs either. I just have impressions of some things that he did.

The reason I was asking you about his professional quality at that time—maybe Lynn [Kastner] said it—that you had taught Bobby to some extent. You apparently were a hell of a lot better at the guitar than he was at that point and were giving him a great number of tips on how to handle himself. Is that so?

Well, I never actually taught him much of anything, I don't think, but we all played around, you know? I'm sure he picked up from some people there, but I don't actually remember having taught him very much.

Right. The same thing apparently goes at least with Lynn's memory, and also

Dave and Gretel—that Tony Glover was giving him tips on harmonica. Do you recall any of that?

Not very well. I don't know.

Do you know where Glover is now? Do you have a number for him? Is he back in Minneapolis?

Yeah, he is in Minneapolis. Oh boy.

But getting back to Bobby, Gretel described Bobby as being terribly young at that time—young and emotional. Do you remember what Bobby was like personally—your impressions of him when you first met him?

Well, kind of, yeah. There were a lot of things that were different about him, you know? He wasn't so skinny, for one thing, and he still had a nervous temperament, it looked like. I don't mean nervous in that it bothered him; it's just that he didn't sit around in one place too often. We were all kind of—there was a whole bunch of us who were all kind of emotionally adrift at that time. I don't know. I don't remember him as having anything specific that happened to him, you know. But some of the impressions are hard to recall.

There was also somebody who told me something about Bobby having a run-in with campus police at some point, which made him kind of uptight and almost paranoid. Do you recall any of that?

Jeez. Yeah, there was something. It had something to do with the house he was in or something.

It was, like, a raid on a house for some reason.

Yeah, that's really vague.

You don't recall it?

No, not really.

Or another incident that got Bobby uptight—four young guys from up in Hibbing apparently came down and wanted to beat him up, or even rub him out, according to Gretel Whitaker.

(laughs) Jesus Christ.

Do you recall anything like that?

No.

This is like Bobby saying, "Oh, they're coming down to kill me"—that kind of thing.

Yeah. Sounds like him, you know, some of the time.

Did he ever talk about his background, about being from Hibbing? What did you know about Bobby in the beginning?

Actually, he was kind of secretive about a lot of things, you know? We all knew he was from Hibbing, and we all knew his name was Zimmerman, although he kind of shied away from talking about it. But anything outside of that, I don't know. We were just, I don't know, drinking all the time.

So, drinking and playing. Apparently, you guys were really doing a lot of playing at that point.

Sure, at clubs and just sitting around and doing it too.

Gretel tells me that she got the—her memory is that at the point where she met him, he had the beginnings of the hobo thing, even at that point—you know, the vagabond from the Southwest, the kind of thing that he really became later, in the early days here in New York. Do you recall that?

I'll tell you, I kind of recall sort of a turning point, actually. I can remember one time that he was—well, he was playing a lot of different things, sort of, and writing different styles. He was like Odetta, for instance, quite a bit at one time. It seems to me there was a time when—well, I think he heard Jesse Fuller and Woody Guthrie back then—around that time.

Was this on records, or did he ever meet Jesse Fuller personally that you know of?

Not at that time, I don't think. Anyway, I don't remember him saying he met Jesse Fuller. Then he started going off with the Woody Guthrie thing. There was a time when a direction kind of sprang up.

What spurred that? Do you have any idea?

Oh, I don't know. I think he just liked the music.

Did he talk—you started saying he was pretty mysterious about his background. Did he ever try to leave the impression that he was an orphan, really from the Southwest, or any jazz like that?

I don't know. I never got that kind of thing anyway. It was just more or less getting into whatever he got into. Although I'm sure there were people who were thinking about that, but I never bothered to think about it.

What effect did Rolf Cahn have on you people—on all of you? I understand that he came into town at a certain point and did have some effect. Do you recall that at all?

Yeah. One thing—the only guitar lesson I ever took was from him, and it might be the only one that Bobby Dylan ever took.

Did Bobby take lessons from him as such?

He took one lesson.

What kind of lesson? Were you there?

Yes.

What was the session like?

Well, it was kind of funny, because Bobby wanted to learn some songs that Cahn had, and Cahn was trying to teach him guitar work. And Bobby—you know, he played along with it, but it seemed like he was more interested in getting these songs down, rather than some basic stuff—is what I remember. But Cahn was kind of impressive at the time, because he could play pretty well and sang some really interesting songs.

Yeah, I mean, he had been a professional too at that point.

Right. Did you hear David Prass's name?

No, that's new. Who's David Prass?

He was a fellow who—he's still there now, but he used to have parties up at his place that a lot of us got together. Dylan, you know, was at quite a few of them. It was kind of a special occasion, going over to those parties, singing some new songs, drinking wine and [audio dropout].

What was Prass's role? Was he part of the university scene? Was he in the university?

He was in theater at the time. He went off to become an actor, but now he's back in Minneapolis, running his father's bar.

What's the name of the bar?

The Golden Horse, I think.

Somewhere along the line, I'm told that both you and Bobby discussed at great length with Rolf Cahn what it takes to break into the New York scene, into the whole folk circuit and become professional. Is that so?

I don't know. (*laughs*) I don't know. I wouldn't be able to remember a conversation from back then, I don't think, to save my life.

At that point, at the point just before Bobby came to New York, was he discussing going professional? Why did he come to New York?

I don't know. I may not have been there at the time he left for New York. I remember him saying he was going—you know, that he wanted to go—saying the Guthrie thing had interested him.

He wanted to go see Woody?

Well, I don't know if he wanted to do that, but he wanted to get into a situation where something that Guthrie was doing could develop, you know? It's kind of hard to get that happening in Minneapolis, in a way.

Yeah. At the point that he's talking about coming to New York—well, did you have a feeling that he wanted to turn professional eventually? Was music his thing? He had dropped out of school. The only thing he was doing, apparently, was hanging around a lot, drinking, going to parties, and playing constantly.

Yeah.

Did you have the feeling that music was his thing, that he would indeed be going professional?

Oh yeah. I don't know about professional. None of us really thought about that, but it seemed that he was—you know, that he wanted really to get into it somehow and be professional eventually, but I don't know if he had any designs on what he wanted to be. But it's kind of obvious that he wanted to get serious about it.

Right. Did any of you have the feeling that he could possibly do it, that he had enough confidence or enough ability to pick up quickly enough to do it eventually?

I think it was divided. There were a number of people that thought he was a no-talent bum, and there were some people that thought he was really great, you know? So, I'm sure some people thought that—well, I know people thought he was really talented and could make it.

In the summer of '60, he had played at the Gilded Garter in Central City. Did you know him by that time, the summer of '60? Or you met him a little later?

No, I met him before then.

Before then? You met him when you first—you got out in '59, you said?

Yeah.

Okay. You knew about the Gilded Garter thing?

Right. He said that he had a job somewhere, that somebody had come to give him this job. I don't know who it was, but all I remember is he came back and said, "Jesus, what a job"—because apparently it had strippers and all that kind of stuff. He said he had to play in between some weird people.

Dylan seems to have, from what I hear from back in those days—that he was learning all the time and picking up things like blues, like country, like—

Oh yeah, right.

There seems to me to have been a very incredibly rapid [professionalization] of this guy—that as a kid from Minneapolis who apparently wasn't really that professional or that good, according to some of the people that I know, turned out to be what he became. Can you figure what Bob had in him in order to achieve something like this?

Oh Jesus.

I know, it's a rough—you know, it's a rhetorical question.

I don't know. It was kind of a feeling about what he was doing, you know? It seemed to—I don't know exactly what to call it. It's just almost like confidence, you know. Or maybe even sometimes a touch of arrogance.

I mean, real confidence, basically. Is that it?

Yeah. I mean, I think he felt when he was doing it right that it was quite awesome. You know, I felt he was getting it off somehow, you know? And I think he was confident in that way.

Did you see Dylan in the early days, when he first got to New York?

Yeah, a couple times.

What was he like here in New York, before that first album came out?

Oh jeez. I don't know, I saw him probably around the time the first album came out. It was, I don't know, just obvious that he'd go. He was friendly and all that, but it was obvious he was into something much stronger than we'd gotten into, you know?

Right, right. Did you get the feeling that he was growing away from you, or growing beyond everyone?

Kind of, yeah. Sure. You could see it. It was forceful, you know. Something was really coming off.

BLOWIN' IN THE WIND

MIKE PORCO

In the beginning people liked him more than I did, [but] I didn't realize he had a lot of talent until I find out that a lot of the numbers he was doing he wrote himself. Then I started to realize that there's some that sound very good. And I said, to write it himself, he can't be stupid. The kid must have some talent.

I T BEGAN AS GERDE'S, a jazz venue in the Village at 11 West Fourth Street, owned by Mike Porco, a soft-spoken, old-fashioned guy. Sometime in 1960, folklorist Izzy Young convinced Porco to turn his place into a folk club. By the summer of 1960, Porco renamed his club Gerde's Folk City, and it soon became the most important folk club in the nation.

Monday nights were slow and Porco, trying to figure out how to make Mondays pay off, decided to try an amateur night, a talent night. Robert Shelton, music critic at the *New York Times,* suggested he call it a hootenanny. Porco had never heard the word before, so Shelton wrote it out for him, and Porco thought the word had a little bit more tone than "amateur night." Gerde's Monday night hoots were born, providing some of the finest young folk and blues artists a venue to showcase their talents. Many of the hoot night performances were by younger professionals such as Dave Van Ronk, Judy Collins, Tom Paxton, Jack Elliott, Paul Clayton, occasionally Cisco Houston—and, in 1961, Bob Dylan.

Porco mentored the young folk singer and offered him his first gig. He gave Dylan the money to join the musicians' union. Dylan was forever grateful and referred to Porco as his "father."

Well, when I spoke to Dylan, he said that he didn't know nothing about it. He said, "I don't think anybody is doing a book on me. I didn't sign the papers for nobody that they can do a book on me." That's what he told me. **Well, I could still do a book, and the thing is I've already started—**

77

You would do a book without the authorization?

Oh sure. He's a public figure. The only thing I couldn't use would be his songs. I mean, could I do a magazine story about Bobby Dylan without his permission? Of course.

You could?

Sure. The only permission I would need would be for his songs.

I think Bob Shelton, he told me was going to interview Dylan—tell his life story. But then it never came through. This is about four or five years ago.

Yeah, a couple of things happened to Bob Shelton. Grossman wouldn't give him permission to use any of the songs. Grossman wants $1,000 a song, and Shelton was totally tied up. I think I could do it without using any of the songs, if I never get permission. [Albert Grossman had been Dylan's manager since August 1962.]

Secondly, Shelton was so close to Dylan that he doesn't know how to handle him, whereas I was never close to Bobby. I've always been at a distance, and I can write about some of these things. I don't want to hurt Dylan, but I could write about some of these things without having to worry that I might destroy a friendship, because I don't have a friendship, whereas Shelton and Al Aronowitz, it's the same thing. He can't write about Dylan because he's too close to him. This is one of the big hang-ups Shelton has, but you can write a book without permission, sure.

I didn't know that.

I've got to people who were close to him. I'm staying away from Grossman, but I'm trying to get to Dylan.

See, I'll tell you, he's a good kid. He's a good kid, believe me.

In any case, I don't need any permission. Grossman is very much disliked by a lot of people in the industry. I mean, he's a good manager, but apparently, he's a manipulator and tends to get people to dislike him.

In some way or the other I think maybe—that's what my opinion of it is, because Grossman comes from Chicago.

Yeah, he used to manage acts out there or something.

But I think he did some—he stepped on somebody's foot, from what I understand. I think it was one of the Mafia.

Really?

Yeah, and he came to New York, but I think he's still a manager over there.

Then he started putting together Peter, Paul and Mary.

I don't know if he still has them. And he had Ian and Sylvia.

He also had Joan Baez at the very beginning, and then Joan had a fight with him and left him.

That I wouldn't know.

The Cafe Wha? back in the days of when Dylan first started coming around—who owned it back at that time? Do you remember? You know, in '61?

I never had anything to do with the Cafe Wha? I was the only—the people from the Gaslight, they come in and ask me. See, I was running the hootenanny when nobody was in it, like I told you before. Then that started to do so well, and those people were starving. They had maybe two customers in the place. Mine was so full I had to stop the show. Even so I didn't know how to take advantage, as I said before.

People from the Gaslight come in and they want to do hootenannies on Tuesdays. And they say, "You're the one that started [it]." They didn't know if I had to copyright the name or something, you know? They said we would like to use it without it being offensive. I said, why not? They don't want to create hard feeling. Then Weintraub come in also—Fred comes in and asks me.

Fred Weintraub?

Yes. From the Bitter End.

The Bitter End, right.

He comes in and asks me. He says, "Mike, you know, you're doing Monday and I want to do Tuesday. I don't want to do it if you mind." So, I told him. I said, "No, not at all." And they did also. I don't know if somebody else was doing it, but we all got along fine. Art D'Lugoff from the Village Gate. I mean, we were all really able to develop one another.

So, you started with the hootenannies—for the new people.

I had all these pictures of all those people—every one of them. I took pictures. Anybody that performed at Gerde's. In the beginning, nobody had any pictures. I used to get a friend of mine, a photographer, who used to come in and take the pictures, in order that I could use them.

Who was the photographer?

What was his name? I'm not going to remember his name. Goorin, I think was his name—Howard Goorin. G-o-o-r-i-n. Anyway, I've got his number—telephone number and everything.

Listen, one other thing. Back in the early days, somewhere after Dylan first started to make it, he began to project the feeling that people in New York were trying to screw him, were trying to take advantage of him. Did you ever get this kind of feeling from him? Did he ever talk about it?

No. I never got that feeling, because it was before he got popular. But I can't see what advantage they could take.

Somewhere along the line, he apparently worked in a coffeehouse for a dollar a night.

Maybe they were a little jealous of the trade, because something—I think Joe Turner was one of them. I think Van Ronk was another one. A few people started recognizing his songs, and when they saw the songs, they started singing them also. They would use them. A lot of people were using Bobby Dylan before he was known, before he copyrighted them, but they were using him. And I think some of them were jealous of the trade, of the song—that they would never sing one of his songs. They were a little jealous.

But some of them were singing his songs?

Oh yeah.

Dave was, and Gil was.

Yeah, Gil, Dave, and—

Well, Paxton was doing a lot of his own writing.

Yeah, Paxton was doing a lot of his own also, but I think Paxton—

But you think some of the other guys were using his songs?

Well, you could tell when they didn't use them. Not in the beginning because in the beginning, when the guy's not known, they don't know if he's going to be a bum—if he's going to be a good musician or a good songwriter.

But even from the very beginning, you say Dave Van Ronk was using his songs?

Dave Van Ronk and Gil Turner. I think they started—

They really began to feel that Bobby had something?

Yeah, they liked it. To my knowledge, I think Gil was the first one, because he worked with us maybe about a year. He would do the MC and stay in the place all the time, and he liked Bobby a lot too. And he came in and told me that once in a while he takes parts in movies. Now he tells me that maybe they were supposed to make a movie about Woody Guthrie and he was supposed to take a part in it.

And who was going to play Woody Guthrie?

You know, I heard about it, Fred Ireland, the guy from the Weavers.

Fred [Hellerman], yeah.

Do you know him?

Yeah.

Yeah, I think they would try to pick him out or something. I don't know what really came out of that, but Gil Turner was telling me about it, that they were trying to make a picture. His kid, Arlo Guthrie, sang with Cisco Houston when he was fourteen years old. But I didn't know him.

Mrs. Guthrie and Mrs. McKenzie were telling me. Mrs. McKenzie was a woman on Twenty-Eighth Street that Dylan was living with for a little while. She was telling me that Arlo, Mrs. Guthrie, Peter McKenzie, and Mrs. McKenzie came down to see Cisco Houston.

I must've noticed this. I didn't know this Mrs. McKenzie.

When they first met Bob Dylan, but he wasn't singing yet. He was just there that night.

I tell you the truth, someone should have written about Cisco.

He was totally submerged by Woody Guthrie. You know, he was in Woody Guthrie's shadow all the time. That was the big problem with Cisco. Then the end came. No, he didn't have time to develop himself.

He wrote a couple songs—one was "A Dollar Down and a Dollar a Week." That one could've been picked up if they pushed it right.

I think the problem with Cisco Houston was that he was so tied up with Woody Guthrie and that he only had a few years before his own death between the time Woody Guthrie stopped working and Cisco died. He only had a couple years, and there just wasn't enough time.

Nobody ever tried to help him. Maybe Harold Leventhal. He did try a little, but not enough. He had a little time away. He wrote some. He could've been more popular, because he was very, very good. Out of all those people out in Hollywood, people that were in show business, I don't think I felt from anybody the way I did feel for Cisco Houston. He came to me [before] the last engagement I gave him and he said, "In this show we're going to make money." I said, "Why are you worrying about making money? Make a living." He says, "I'll tell you why. You got to listen to me. I have a few friends, and I want you to advertise this is the last appearance ever of Cisco Houston." I said, "What makes you say that?" And he said, "You know I'm sick. This is going to be my last. You watch, this is going to be my last."

Do you remember when this was?

I have the date somewhere.

Did he advertise it that way?

No. I told him, "Cisco, three months from now, you'll do another show."

Did he have a wife? Kids? Anything like that?

I must know this McKenzie woman if she used to come to—

She only came once or twice, she said. But Cisco Houston is an interesting story.
And sure enough, it was his last appearance, and he put on the best show
he ever put on in his life. He went over there and sang thirty-five, maybe
forty, minutes and really gave the best. I swear every time I think, it makes
me sick. I wish I'd never hired him, because when he told me that, he
said, "You should put that on paper. We're going to make money." I said,
"Cisco, three months from now you're going to come in and we're going to
do another show." He said, "My doctor told me if I get a certain symptom,
he says to forget about it—to not even go to him." In fact, me, my brother,
and another fellow that used to like Cisco very much—he used to come in
and listen to him. We wanted to find another doctor for him and he said,
"Mike, you don't know how I appreciate this." To me he was superior. A
great guy.

Listen, suppose I came to you and said, "Look, I want to write a book on Cisco
Houston. Who should I see? Who would have the most information on Cisco
Houston right now?"
Harold Leventhal would know enough, but I think somebody that would
know more than him and really from the heart is the guy from the Weav-
ers, Lee.

Hellerman?
No. No, the old man, the big guy. He used to remind me of Lionel Bar-
rymore.

I know who you mean.
Lee Hays. Lee Hays would know about Cisco more than anybody, and
even Pete Seeger would know something. Of course, maybe Bob Shelton
would know a little.

Now, when I do the book on Dylan, I want to do something on Cisco in the book.
Well, that's a good idea. Cisco to me was one of the greatest.

Did Woody Guthrie ever show up at Gerde's at all, or was he too sick by then?
No. He was too sick by then. I saw his wife not too long ago. I know his
wife for a while, [Marjorie].

Yeah, I talked with her a little while back.
Oh yeah? [Marjorie] I know, and Arlo. Arlo is another kid I had dealings
[with]. He wanted to come in and do a couple of weeks. And I said no
because I had too many other engagements. He said, "Mike, I'll do it for
nothing because this place is special to me. And I know Leventhal very
well. I mean, he's very nice to me." When I can, I give Arlo an engagement.

Bob, Cisco, Dave Van Ronk, Paxton, Arlo. Listen, that's a lot of people who appeared at Gerde's.

I have a book with all the names of the people that have been appearing in our shows. Some of them today—they've become very well known. Yes, we started in 1959, I said. And then I started different things. Then I started a little jazz. I had some jazz groups that played.

Well, a lot of them today like marijuana or pot. It's very popular. At that time it was a little dangerous. They used to penalize the restaurant owner for those things, but today they don't penalize much the restaurant. If you smoke pot in [a pipe] now, and a cop will come in, very seldom will you hear they penalize the place.

Right. In those days they were very uptight about it. Now they can't do it because everybody's smoking.

Pot or reefer. Yes, they used to be very thin ones, and they used to charge thirty-five, forty cents at that time. This was before they became popular like today. And I said to myself, one day or the other I'm going to get in trouble with these people if they catch someone that smoked in here that gets locked up. I said, I better stop. So, I stopped smoking in the club.

Let me ask you something. What happened to this book with all the names?

I have the book at home.

And you have the dates of the gigs?

The dates, the number of times for engagements—

I spoke with Victoria Spivey. You know, Dylan made a couple of records for her.

Yes, well, because she owned some kind of record company.

It's called Spivey Records now, Spivey Records. And Big Joe Williams—

Big Joe Williams, yes. They all played in my place.

Let me start an interview. When did you first meet Dylan? How did you first—

You have the tape open.

Yes, your first recollection of Bob Dylan—not the first time he played; but when do you first remember him?

I remember in '61 he came in.

He started on a hoot night the first time.

He wanted to start. The very first time I think I didn't make him play, because he didn't have the proof of age, and he looked too young, but he was eighteen.

Actually, he was nineteen. Did he bring in proof of his age?

Yes. He had some kind of proof of age.

So, you thought he was too young. What did you tell him?

I said, "You've got to have proof of age to play in here." Then when I come in the next weekend, he says, "Let me try." Anyhow he come in the following week. From then on, he used to come in every Monday.

I have, even, his card. I give him the money to go and get his card.

So, before he gets the union card, the first night that he played—what was he like?

To me it was nothing impressive really, but look, it was good enough that he could come back. See, if people were really bad, I might tell them you couldn't go on tonight because I got too many on. In the beginning people liked him more than I did, [but] I didn't realize he had a lot of talent until I find out that a lot of the numbers he was doing he wrote himself. Then I started to realize that there's some that sound very good. And I said, to write it himself, he can't be stupid. The kid must have some talent.

And the first chance I had, I even spoke to Bob Shelton, and he said, "The kid is good, Mikey. Listen. Are you going to give him a couple weeks?" I said, "Well, I'm booked for about two months, but my first opening I'll give him an engagement."

I said, "Bobby, I will give you two weeks." He said, "Really, Mike?" And I said, "I'll give you two weeks, but you've got to do me a favor. Number one, you've got to cut your hair." See, now it's all long hair, but at that time it didn't used to look okay.

Was his hair that long?

He had pretty long hair, and I said, "And you'll dress yourself proper." He says, "Mike, I haven't got no money. You know I'd dress better, but I haven't got no money." I used to give him a sandwich.

You fed him?

Yes, every time they come in I tell them stay in the kitchen and we give them a sandwich. I can't refuse a guy that needs something to eat.

And then I give him a job, and I know he didn't have any clothes, so I went home and got clothes from my children—they're much bigger than him in size. And I think I got some shirts, and I got a couple pairs of pants. I brought some down, and I said, "Do me a favor. Change and put on a clean shirt." And he come in one day, the first day that he was singing. He had [on] all my children's clothes.

Bob was wearing—the first time he went on, he was wearing your kids' clothes.

Yes.

Tell me.

I had all these pictures of all those people—every one of them. I took pictures. Anybody that performed at Gerde's. In the beginning, nobody had any pictures. I used to get a friend of mine, a photographer, who used to come in and take the pictures in order that I could use them. I have also a magazine with a write-up, *Newsweek* in 1962.

The one where they told his real name, said his real name was Bobby Zimmerman—

Well, no, I remember. I think it was even before his name was revealed, that it was Zimmerman. I had his name from the first day he worked with me.

Oh, you had his real name.

He had to have a cabaret card years ago.

So, you knew his real name when he first started work. Mike, let's get back to the beginning, when you bought him his union card. Tell me about that.

As I said, he was working at the hootenanny, and finally I made a decision to hire him for a couple weeks.

Why did you make the decision to have him a couple of weeks?

It sounded to me like he was good for the hootenanny.

Was there an audience interested in him?

Oh yes. The audience liked him maybe more than I did.

Who was the lead on the bill that night?

I think John Lee Hooker—I think he plays second to John Lee Hooker. I'll tell you the truth. I like him better when he was singing then than the way he sings after.

You liked him better at the beginning.

Yes, I like him better. I like better the numbers.

When he was singing like Woody Guthrie?

Oh yes, he sang a lot of Woody Guthrie. It's the only stuff he'd sing. Then his own stuff. "Don't Think Twice"—every show he made, "Don't Think Twice" he would sing. "Blowin' in the Wind."

Anyway, how did you come to buy him his union card?

I made the decision I was going to hire him because people liked him, and I would say I liked him myself but I wasn't really crazy about him, but I figured, this kid, sooner or later, will make it, because he used to sing a lot of his own stuff. An expert, which I'm not—I mean, I have a little knowledge but I'm not an expert. I can't say, oh gee, this guy has got it—you appreciate more if people sing a popular song, something you've heard all the time. Then if you do a good job, right away you say, Jesus, you did a good job out of that song. But when it's a new song—I don't know—

It takes awhile before it means something to you.

That's right. But anyhow, I made a decision that I'd give him the two weeks to work there, and I told him, "You will work with John Lee Hooker." And he was very happy, because he liked John Lee Hooker. Besides, he figured John Lee Hooker would bring people, and he did. So then I told him. I said, "Bobby, you've got to belong to the union." So he says, "Mike, you know I haven't got nothing." I said, "Look, I'll give you the money for the union."

How much was the money at that time?

I think he had to put down $46. But actually, it probably cost $90 or $100 a week. I don't know if I paid him $110 or more. I said, "We'll go to the union and I'll pay for it, and then whatever you want me to take out from your pay." "Hey, yes, Mike, if you do that I can be in the union." He said to me, "Mike, you're so good to me. Why don't you manage me? You're like my second father."

I said, "Look, buddy, I would be unfair to you, because I've got to take care of the place. If I take care of the place, I can't spare any time to call up people, see if I could get you more jobs."

Do you know how rich you would be today if you had decided to manage him?

I called up Marty Erlichman—that's Barbra Streisand's manager—and I said, "Take a look on Bobby Dylan. I think that kid is going to make it." Marty come in, and he thinks he wouldn't make it. He says, "You've got to spend a lot of money with this kid before you do anything." He says, "I've got Barbra, and she's out of this world." At the time she wasn't that famous.

Yes, I know. She was still nothing.

I didn't want her to sing at my place, because she wasn't a folk singer.

Anyway, how did Bobby—

So, I took him to the union, and we go see the president of the union. I knew him. Max Arons. And Max started asking Bob questions. He says, "All right, you want to join the union." He read the contract, and Arons says, "I can't okay this here." He says, "Tomorrow, you come in with your father, because he's got to sign for you if you're under twenty-one." Bobby says, "I haven't got a father." Arons says, "That's all right. Then come in with your mother." Bobby looked at him. He's kind of shy, you know. And he says, "I'm sorry, Mr. Arons, but I haven't got no mother either." Arons looks at me and he says, "Mike, how about you? Do you want to sign as a guardian?" I said, "Why not?" So, I went and signed his contract, his first contract with the union.

But he had a father and a mother. You signed as a guardian.

I signed, and I give him the money, $46. Then you've got to take a test to take you in the union. They make you play guitar. We went downstairs, and within about ten minutes they give him his card. He's so happy.

I said, "Bobby, now we've got to have the cabaret license. They'll finger-print you. You'll need two pictures." And he says, "I haven't got no pictures." We stopped on West Fourth Street. They had one of those machines like a telephone booth. You put in a quarter, and you'll get four. I said, "Bobby, I'll tell you what you do. Comb your hair a little." He goes in his pocket, and he says, "I haven't got no comb." I said, "There, use my comb." He combs his hair and I said, "Well, anyhow, now it looks better." I gave him $2.50. And another $2. I said, "You go around the corner, go someplace, and cut your hair. He hesitated. He didn't want to tell me, "I don't want to cut my hair," but anyhow, I give him the $2. "Okay. Thanks, Mike."

So, we're having our shows on Tuesday. He comes on Tuesday, and the hair is cut, but very, very little. He says to me, "You know, Mike, I had a friend cut my hair. I think it's okay." And not too long later he asked if I manage him.

And then Terri came along. Terri Van Ronk was managing him a little bit, wasn't she?

Not too much. Then he was with Grossman.

He was already with Grossman.

Yes.

In September, that September gig that Bobby Shelton wrote about—back when Bobby, in his first gig or maybe even the second one in September too, Carla [Rotolo] tells me—at the beginning, Bobby was almost afraid of his audience. He wasn't really sure of himself, and the girls like Suze and Carla and a couple of the other friends used to have to bolster his ego, give him wine, tell him, "Bobby, how great you are. Go on up and perform"—remember any of that?

Yes, he was a little nervous up here when he started. Even so, when he did the hootenanny, he appeared very loose. But when he came in to perform and he was getting paid, it was a kind of nerves; because he's thinking now, who knows, maybe they won't like him; maybe we won't keep him here. He was really anxious to become something.

He says, "Mike, you know that some of these days I'm going to be very big, just like that." Then he'd repeat the same words when I was in Paris—I'm very big.

But was that what he was saying back in '61? I want you to manage me because someday I'm going to be big?

"Because some of these days I'm going to be big, Mike," he says. "Why don't you manage me?"

Did he ever talk about how big he was going to be? Did he ever talk about Elvis Presley or anything, like he was going to be really big?

No. Only time was when I met him in Paris, he says to me, "And now I'm big. I'm much bigger than maybe you think."

You met him in Paris.

Yes, I met him in Paris, because I was there, stopping just for a couple days. But you know we walked on [the] main street in Paris. I think it's Champs-Élysées. On the walk there's a big poster there. They advertised him very big in Paris, much more than New York. Really great poster. And underneath the poster was written, "Someone of us must know him." That's what was on there.

Really, on the poster?

Yes—yes, underneath, that's all.

Did it have his name on the picture?

Oh yes, Bobby Dylan—he was appearing at the Olympia and was the sole act. I called my wife over and said, "Did you see this here? Bobby Dylan. He must be appearing somewhere here. We've got to find out where he stays." We asked a girl from the hotel if she would call and find out from the Olympia Theater where he was staying. She says, "We're not sure, but I think they took him to [George V]." We call up [that hotel], and he is there. We were only two blocks away from where he was. While I'm walking—I'm on the other side of the Champs-Élysées—I meet Grossman. I didn't recognize him. I hadn't seen him [in] over a year, and he's got the long hair.

Yes, he changed.

So, anyhow, as soon as I seen him, I said, "Where's Bobby?" He says, "Oh, there are so many people, newspaper guys and everything. So, they took him out from the hotel. They took him somewhere."

Anyhow, to make it short, I didn't like the way he told me. When we call, they say Bobby was there. It was only five minutes before. I said, "We'll go there." I asked him if Bob would go out for a drink or a cup of coffee. He says, "No, no, we've got to go some places with my friend, and we'll come back." So, I go to the hotel. I told the hotel I wanted to see Bobby Dylan. They took me up, and I go to the door, and one of his musicians comes in, I said, "I'd like to see Bobby Dylan."

He says, "Well, Bobby Dylan is not here." I said, "Don't tell me he's not here. I can hear him from here. He's rehearsing back there. Just tell him Mike Porco's here." [Bobby] comes to the door, and he hugs me and my wife. He didn't know. He was crying, the kid. He had tears. So I told him the truth: "I saw your poster there, and I inquired, and Grossman told me you were somewhere else, but I didn't take his word. I decided to see for myself." He laughed.

Right away he calls up the bellhop and says, "See [to] whatever they need, whatever they want." This is in front of all the guys that were in there in the band. He says, "This is my father. And by the way, call up the Olympia and make a reservation for two more people, because tonight I'm performing over there." I said, "Wait a minute, don't let him call. I made a reservation to leave for Switzerland tonight. I'm going to Geneva tonight, and I wish I knew before, but I just saw the poster. If I knew before, I would have stayed an extra day to come to the concert, but we already made reservations for tonight." "No, no, no. You've got to come. We have six or eight seats onstage. You can sit on the stage." I said, "Don't worry about the seat. I feel more sorry than you do, because I really would have liked to stay."

What was he like at this time? Was he—

Well, I'll tell you the truth. When I saw him in Paris, to me it looked like he had lost a little weight.

You interrupted a rehearsal. Was he really into the rehearsal?

I think he had a record in there, and I think he was trying to copy or something, the record.

Which band was this, incidentally? Was it the Band?

I don't know. It was the people that would back him up when he would do the concert.

Was Sara—was he married by then? '66.

No, his wife was not with him. He was going to leave the following day to go to England. Anyhow, we stayed there over an hour. We had already ate, but we had a little something to eat with him. We had a drink. He didn't know what to do. Really. He says, "Mike, if you need any help, I want to let you know that—I don't have no obligations, almost, to nobody, but with you, in some way or the other, I feel obligated, because you give me the first start. You never refused me nothing. And now, I don't know if you know this, but I'm big. I'm much bigger than, you know," he said, just like that.

Did you know at that time? Of course, you must have.

Oh yes, I knew when I saw him. But he says, "The only thing I want to tell you: If you ever need me, I want to give you one full day. If you feel that your business is a little quiet, he says, don't speak to my manager either. You call me personally. If you need a day, you find a place that will hold a certain amount of people, that you feel you can make money. The only thing is, you've got to take care of the taxes. You must take care of what they want to collect, but outside of that, whatever you make—"

Even a venue like Yankee Stadium—

Yes, at that time—in fact, he was going to make an appearance in Shea Stadium in August.

But then he had the accident, and they—

Yes, they canceled.

So, you saw him before the accident. This was before July.

Before the accident, yes. I saw him in May.

What else happened in Paris? Is that about it?

Before we left, he says, "Come here, Mike. I want to show you something." We looked out the windows, and there were at least about fifty people there, all with cameras, movie, I think television. He says, "And they want me to go out. How am I going to go out? Look, all those people—they're going to mob me. Maybe they're going to kill me."

It's amazing that you got in so easily, that you got up to his hotel room.

Well, I told them I wanted to see him and I didn't look like a bum. At the time I had a tie on.

You didn't look like a newspaperman, either, right, that they were trying to keep out.

So anyhow he says, "I'm going to call you, and I'm going to give you some tickets for Shea Stadium." I said, "Okay." We wished each other luck, and I tell him that we'll see each other in New York. The following day, when I [was in] Geneva, I tried to buy an American paper. The review was terrible. I think in one line it said it took three-quarters of the night to finish a song or something.

Well, he was heavily into drugs at the time. He was using a lot of drugs at the time.

Yes. Well—

I know when he was in Europe that time, he was very heavily into drugs; very, very heavily into drugs.

But the write-ups in Europe—they were terrible.

Yes. The only people who dug him in Europe were people like the Beatles and the Rolling Stones and all the other artists.

The write-up was bad in Italy too. Because I read it in the Italian newspaper. It was no good either.

You said you saw him six months ago.

I think it was.

He came down to the club.

Yes, he came down there to say hello. The last time he was there I think it was with Grossman. I wasn't there. My brother was there and told me.

What was Bob like?

He looked good now.

He looked good, calm—somebody described him as being—

Yes, very calm. When I first met him, he always looked at the ground?

He was shy. He looked away. Like a shy little boy does. But somebody described him now as a father and a suburbanite and a calm guy who knows who he is.

I don't want to give you that description; but he looked good, and he looked much more at ease, relaxing. He don't look like before.

He's living on MacDougal Street now, right? He's right down the street from you.

If he lives there, I'm going to go over, see him. I'll tell him, forget the concert you promised, because I never ask him anymore. I'll tell him, once in a while come over to the club, and give hello to some people that come in, that's all. I guarantee people see him a few times, people that come in, I get business.

But, going back to the gig—the September gig that was his first. In early September you had Victoria Spivey and Big Joe Williams on the bill, and then Bobby followed them with the Greenbriar singers, and Bobby was second on the bill. This was in September.

But on one show, maybe for one weekend, he was working with the Greenbriar Boys.

Right, but that September gig that Bobby did when he was with the Greenbriar Boys—a couple weeks before that, Victoria Spivey and Big Joe Williams were—

Big Joe was there. You remember Big Joe?

Yes, very well.

Okay. Bobby used to tell everybody that, back in the early days, he used to hop a freight with Big Joe, that he rode the rails with Big Joe, went into Mexico or New Mexico, and nobody believed him. And then that night at Gerde's, when Big Joe first opened up—tell me what happened that night.

Well, as far as I know, that night they all were talking, and they were very close friends. Then when he went to do a set, Joe probably had an extra drink, and Bobby went in there and played with him, and Bobby took over. They—I don't know how many numbers. They played all night the one night in there.

Did you know that Bobby made a record with Big Joe for Victoria?

No, I didn't.

Do you remember, did Big Joe ever talk about knowing Bobby back when he was a kid?

No, he never said nothing to me. Really, I never asked him.

Did he say how or where he knew him? Like knowing him from Chicago?

He might could have, but I'll be honest, I don't want to say something that I don't remember.

Did he ever talk about being in Chicago?

No, I don't think I had a conversation about that.

Did you know that Bobby played behind Belafonte on a record too? Did he ever talk about that?

No.

He made a record with Belafonte. He played harmonica behind one of the Belafonte albums. Nobody knows that except me.

Bob Shelton—he had told me he was writing a book on Dylan. And I had the same interview talking with Bob. He knew them all and he asked for a lot of things that skip out of my mind. When I was talking to Bobby, when I was in Paris, I said to Bobby—this is the truth—I said, "You told me you haven't got no obligations with nobody. But I will say that you have an obligation, more than you do with me, with Bob Shelton."

DAVE VAN RONK

I once thought the biggest I could ever hope to get was like Van Ronk.
—*Bob Dylan*

BOB DYLAN HAD BEEN IN NEW YORK less than three months, and he had moved at a remarkable pace there in such a short time. He had been befriended, fussed over, mothered and smothered, and fathered and bothered, and he had been helped in his craft by some of the most talented folk and blues musicians around.

Dave Van Ronk, a big bear of a guy who was then one of the best liked of the young urban blues singers sparking a revolution in folk music, was one of the early "citybillies." He provided great comradeship and mentoring to the young Bob Dylan. Van Ronk turned Dylan on to poetry, leftist politics, and a vast amount of different musical styles and genres. He also unwittingly aided and abetted Dylan's breakout blues performance of "House of the Rising Sun." Dave played his new arrangement for Dylan, who then recorded it before Dave had a chance to get into the recording studio. Dylan made it his own. It created a rift that took a long time to heal.

What are your first recollections of Dylan?
"Poor" is the way to describe his look that winter. He dressed in army surplus, cheap work-style clothes. He needed a haircut and because haircuts cost money, the whole mystique of long hair was conspicuous "unconsumption."
When were you first aware of Dylan?
When he came down into the Gaslight, that winter of '61, '62.
Your impressions? What you remember?

He was pretty much the same as everybody else in the scene. In a month or two I discovered he was a pathological liar—too many inconsistencies in his yarns. How could he be from Taos, New Mexico, on the one hand, and from the Midwest, on the other? He told all kinds of phantom stories. He told me one time he had run away from home—and run into Big Joe Williams in a boxcar—he talked about always moving, to be free. I figure here's some more Dylan bullshit.

We knew he took his name from Dylan Thomas, and we knew he was a Jew. Here was another middle-class Jewish kid with an identity crisis. Here was a fantastically talented cat who was a pathological liar with an identity crisis. We accepted him not because of the things he said he had done but because we respected him as a performer.

So, Big Joe Williams and all the other stories . . .

Dylan said he went down to Mexico with Big Joe in a boxcar. We figured, "Sure." Big Joe turns up at Gerde's Folk City—we knew of Big Joe but had never met him. Big Joe was in and Bobby shows up. Joe throws his arms around Bobby, like a class reunion. I was thrown—I figured it was just another one of Bobby's stories—and Big Joe says, "Don't you know me and him travel down to Mexico in a boxcar?"

Mikki Isaacson told me, "My place was a hotel for Bob. The Van Ronks gave him a home." How long did Dylan live with you?

He slept on our couch. Maybe I'd say he lived with us for a while, off and on, in our apartment on West Fifteenth Street.

You're just a couple of years older than Bob. Would you say you became one of his teachers?

More his friend. We let him sleep on our couch, he met our friends.

Dave, you're one of the more talented blues guitarists. Did you show him stuff?

I turned him on to new material and musical ideas. Not formally teaching, not lessons. At that time Bob was learning from everyone around him. I wouldn't say I officially taught Bob Dylan, but he picked up songs, approaches, and picking techniques.

Dylan has acknowledged you gave him a good deal of support during the early years.

I read a lot—politics, poetry. I got Dylan into the French symbolist poets, particularly Rimbaud, and into Villiers and Bertolt Brecht. We had long sessions of arguing.

Jack Elliott told me, "Dylan never talked much, but Dave could actually get him

to start arguing. Long hours, mostly with Dave, about politics and the world
and everything."

You see, being a hayseed, that was part of Bob's image or what he considered his image at the time. Like, I once asked him, "Do you know the
French symbolists?" And he said, "Huh?" The stupidest "Huh?" you can
imagine. And later, when he had a place of his own, I went up there and
on the bookshelf was a volume of French poets from Nerval almost to the
present. I think it ended with Apollinaire, and it included Rimbaud, and it
was all well thumbed with passages underlined and notes in the margins.
The man wanted to be a primitive, a natural kind of genius. He never
talked about somebody like Rimbaud. But he knew Rimbaud all right. You
see that in his later songs."

Elliott said you were "both like bulls, locking horns for hours."

Good way to describe it. Long nights of arguing.

**It seems Dylan didn't pay much attention to radical thought in Minneapolis,
but do you think that changed in New York. Do you think he just capitalized on
social issues to "make it"?**

He was no opportunist. He really believed it all. I was there. He absorbed
what was around him, believed it, but he didn't really understand it. He
only absorbed the superficialities. It's entirely possible he fell into the
broadside bag not knowing what those songs could do, but he believed.
He meant it. Basically, he still believes it, but he's in another bag now. He
does happen to be a genius entitled to a certain amount of nonsense.

**Dylan was part of your circle of, some would say, "active radical friends." Would
you say they helped shape Dylan's thinking about politics and the deficiencies
of the country?**

Well, I did tell him to forget the Guthrie thirties idolization and get on with
the business of the sixties. I mean, Guthrie's dying, and his generation is
dead. That's what I said during our wine-drinking nights of arguing. I told
Bob, "You can't keep rewriting the songs they wrote. Do your own songs.
Their songs are for the history books. You're just going to be a history
book writer if you do those things. An anachronism."

There was Guthrie and Cisco Houston, who was also dying.

Bobby worshipped those old cats, no question about it. There was something courageous about the way Cisco took the fact that he had cancer and
it was terminal. Cisco never stopped, never copped out, never showed the
white feather.

Besides Guthrie, who were his other musical influences? Lord Buckley?

Oh, yeah, he was into Buckley. I know he loved Buckley, but Dylan never talked about his influences, except Guthrie. One reason was his pride. Another was Bobby really does believe he's better than anybody else and I think he has a good case.

What did you think about "Blowin' in the Wind"?

I said, "Hey, man, you're really getting into something with those songs. Welcome to the twentieth century."

I heard you guys had some great poker games.

Yeah, we played poker a lot—penny ante. Bob was a pretty bad poker player. We used to play in a back room above the Gaslight that they had set up with a table and a loudspeaker and in his first game with the boys he was fleeced of the couple of pennies he had set aside for poker. Sam Hood, who ran the Gaslight, announced a new game, Indian poker, and when Bobby asked how to play it, he was told that everyone holds his cards up to his forehead so that he could see all the other hands but not his own. Everyone else cheated, and Bobby lost his shirt, all ten cents of it. He never caught on that we all cheated, but later Bobby became a fairly good poker player.

Dylan had all these stories about his background, meeting Guthrie in California, being part American Indian. What were some of the ones he told you?

Yeah, he said he had an "uncle who's a Sioux." He claimed his Jewish nose was due to his Sioux Indian ancestry. I studied American Indian lore and I remember one night Dylan was solemnly doing things he claimed was Plains Indian sign language, using signs to try and tell me he had seen, I don't know how many buffalo, and his sign for buffalo was the sign for teepee.

But we didn't mind his poses. We accepted him not because of the things he said he had done but because we respected him as a performer. The attitude of the community was that it was all right, it was cool. He gets onstage and delivers, and that's fine. His pose didn't bother us. Nobody was turned off by it. Whatever he said offstage, onstage he told the truth as best he knew it.

What was he like onstage in the early days?

He was obviously no virgin on a stage when I first saw him at the Wha?, backing up Freddy Neil. He had been around. And he was something of a natural—a cat who seems to know all the rules and systematically breaks them. He gave the appearance of not knowing anything, but you could just feel he knew what it was all about, and he was deliberately breaking the rules and making it work. But in the beginning, nobody would hire Dylan. He was a freak.

Back to his "background." He wasn't American Indian, but you knew he was Jewish?

One night we were all at the Gaslight, Bob and me and a few other musicians. We're talking about Jack Elliott. As far as Bobby knew, Elliott was good coin goyishe cowboy. In the course of the conversation, it came out somehow that he was Elliot Adnopoz, a Jewish cat from Ocean Parkway, and Bobby fell off his chair. He rolled under the table, laughing like a madman. It was a good thing we were privileged characters in the Gaslight, or we would have been thrown out. We had all suspected Bobby was Jewish, and that proved it. He'd be laying under the table and just recovering from his fit and every once in a while, Barry or somebody would stick his head under the table and yell 'Adnopoz' and that would start him off roaring again."

Tell me about "House of the Rising Sun"—your arrangement and Dylan's recording on his first album. I was told that you helped him with it and that you said he could use your arrangement.

We had a terrible falling-out about "House of the Rising Sun." He was always a sponge, picking up whatever was around him, and he copied my arrangement of the song. Before going into the studio, he asked, "Hey, Dave, mind if I record your version of 'Rising Sun' "? I said, "Well, Bobby, I'm going into the studio soon and I'd like to record it." And later he asked me again and I told him I wanted to record it myself, and he said, "Oops, I already recorded it and can't do anything about it because Columbia wants it." For a period of maybe two months we didn't speak to each other. He never apologized and I gave him credit for it.

Some people thought he was mean, even vicious. Definitely single-minded.

You could say Dylan was always vicious from time to time. This was no lollipop singer, you know. The only trouble about his viciousness, until he became famous, he couldn't get away with it.

How was he with other singers? I heard stories about Bob and Phil Ochs and some other guys.

I remember sessions at the Kettle of Fish, where Dylan was especially obnoxious to Ochs, [Eric] Andersen, and Dave Cohen [David Blue]. And I realized something: Bobby came over like that because he knew something about those guys, he was into them—they wanted to get rich. They were hungry, scuffling cats looking to grab the brass ring. I felt it. I saw how hungry they were. They wanted to be honest, but they suddenly realized they could say what they wanted to say and make a million dollars. Dylan was a terrible influence, not through any fault of his own, but he tickled everybody's opportunism. None of us were poor, exactly, but then wham! Two hundred and fifty billion dollars and an infinity of chicks to play with, and they reached out and grabbed for that brass ring.

It was especially bad for Ochs, Andersen, and Cohen; Paxton was never bothered by it, and neither was I. Our attitude when Bobby was being foolish was a shrug of the shoulder. I remember one time at the Kettle of Fish he tried some of his line on me: "Dave, what you really gotta do is this, that, and the other thing." And I said, "Bobby, if you're so rich, why ain't you smart?"

A lot of it was about "making it" and who was going to "make it."

The big thing to keep in mind is that Bobby wanted to be a superstar. When he discovered the reality of being a superstar, he freaked out.

When did he start to get the sense of "superstar freakiness"?

I remember at the festival, some of the crowd came and charged after him.

Which festival?

The 1963 Monterey Folk Festival. The crowd was running after Bobby and we were running away from them. We got in a damn station wagon and got away from them. I was sitting on the tailgate and Bobby was inside, and he said, "Get used to it, Dave. Next year it'll be you." It terrified him. He was paranoid to start. All of a sudden five million people were pulling at his coat and picking his brain, and he couldn't take it when just five people were doing that. His feeling, basically, was that the audience is a lynch mob. What he said was, "Look out, they'll kill you." He never trusted anything or anybody in his life. At the same time, the man has some notion of the basic dignity of a human being. If you are a brilliant person, the wages of your brilliance are not to have your clothes torn off or your mind invaded. And that's what they started doing to Bobby.

Obviously, there's a lot of changes in Bob. Things have happened, the motorcycle accident and—

Retreating to Woodstock. I think Bobby has returned to being the middle-class Jewish kid. He's now looking for safety because he's scared—not scared of America and its monstrosities; that poor kid is scared of himself. You know, like Rimbaud, who also backed off after a few years of shaking things up. Rimbaud stuck up critically for the divine disorder of his mind, which is what makes a poet and a visionary out of ordinary men. It was too frightening for him.

And for Bobby?

Basic human dignity. He didn't want his mind invaded.

TERRI THAL

ERRI THAL, former wife and manager of Dave Van Ronk, was Dylan's
first manager. My sense is that her relationship to Dylan was more
mentor than mother hen. She is sharp, a good thinker, and an excellent
writer, and Terri definitely moves to her own drumbeat. I am happy we
are friends who enjoy the theater, great food, and good conversation. The
first part of the interview was conducted by Tony Scaduto in 1970, and the
second part took place during the winter of 2019 in Terri's home in upstate
New York. We talked, shared chicken and sweet potatoes she roasted, and
then I foolishly drove off into a blizzard to get home to feed my cat.

————————

Summer of 1961, Dylan was living with you and Dave.
Bobby was spending a lot of time at our apartment on West Fifteenth
Street, sleeping on our couch, practically living with us. He stayed with us
after the McKenzies, pretty much on and off during the summer of '61. I
didn't mind. It was being a hostess, which I apparently enjoyed.
What did you think of his singing, his performing?
He was just great. A lot of folksingers believed he was a genius. He was
very nervous, with a funny knee twitch. He didn't talk much, just sat for
hours listening to people, and then he'd open up and he'd be hilariously
funny. He didn't relate to people too much. I think he was afraid to let
anyone get to know him too well. I mean, if you're going to chuck your
past every couple of years you're not building on solid ground. I think Bob
was afraid of people, a little shy and afraid to have his pose discovered.

Suze and David didn't know he was Jewish. They felt it but didn't know the details.

Everybody believed he was a genius. I'm not sure why. It wasn't about his writing because he wasn't writing much in the beginning.

How was he funny? Tell me about that.

He had that Chaplinesque thing, which was weird. He had a funny pathetic little boy style about him. And a sense of comedy. I remember one hoot night he was on stage for forty minutes, and he kept falling off the stage and it was so funny. We had been drinking a little and Bobby couldn't hold his liquor—his beer or wine, really because he couldn't afford liquor—and we all thought he was drunk. It took us a long time to figure out that when he fell off the stage it was timed, a planned thing, he was falling off within the context of the song, and it was hilarious.

What about his stories? Riding the rails with Big Joe Williams?

Bob said he ran away from home, maybe twice. Once when he was ten or twelve years old, he said he went to Mexico with Big Joe Williams and Joe confirmed it. He said they first met in Chicago. Big Joe was a hero to Bob. And I think his carnival stories have some truth to them. Bob's songs have carny language, a carny sound.

So, when did you start managing Bob?

I started managing Dave that spring.

Spring 1961?

Yes, Dave and I decided his manager wasn't doing anything to promote him, and he asked me to manage him. By summer I decided to "become a grown-up manager" and started handling some of the singers in our circle who needed managers: Van Ronk, Tom Paxton, Mark Spoelstra, and Bob. Later I managed the Holy Modal Rounders, Maggie and Terre Roche, Mark Ross, and some other people.

You got Dylan bookings?

I got Bob his first out-of-town gig, which was huge because there were very few clubs around outside the Village that would book folk singers. There literally was no place to get a singer up on a stage outside of New York. I called Lena Spencer, an actress who ran a place up in Saratoga Springs called Caffè Lena, and asked her to book Dylan. She didn't want Bobby.

But you got him a gig there.

For a whole year, whenever she needed an act, I would find her someone at the last minute. She'd call me and I'd go around to Spring Street, where a lot of people were hanging out, and get her a performer. Finally, I told her that for a whole year every time she needed a favor, I'd come through and now I needed a favor. So, she booked Bobby for the weekend.

And what happened after that?
After Bob's gig, she called me and said not to ask her to book him again. Dylan's two-night stand at Caffè Lena was not an overwhelming success.

What happened after that gig?
I couldn't get him many other gigs. The Club 47 in Cambridge refused to hire him because he was too much of a freak for the folk crowd. The owner of the Second Fret in Philadelphia heard a tape of some of Dylan's early Guthrie interpretations and told me, "Why should I hire a Jack Elliott imitation when I can get Jack Elliott for nothing?" Elliott had just filled in at Second Fret for no pay for a benefit.

I spoke to an executive at Vanguard Records who said he wasn't interested in Dylan, "that he wouldn't go over at all."

So, you were trying to get him gigs. What happened that he went to Grossman?
I was up in New England trying to get work for Bobby and Dave at the folk clubs, and there wasn't anything doing. When I got back Bob told me that he had signed with Grossman. I was both hurt and pleased for him. It was a very intelligent thing for Bobby to do. My managing Bobby was minimal; there wasn't that much managing for anybody to do in those days, and Grossman was one of the few really commercial managers around.

As his first manager, tell me about some of the songs. "Blowin in the Wind" . . .
A day or so after he wrote "Blowin' in the Wind," Bob asked me to stop by and get the words, and either he or Suze wrote them out for me. He went around singing it for everybody, and everybody was knocked out by it. Yeah, I was knocked out by it.

I asked Dave, "But what do think about the early topical songs?"
Like "Talkin' Bear Mountain Picnic Massacre Blues?"

Among others, yes. What do you remember about that song or how he wrote it?
Bob read the newspapers. I think someone told him the story about the picnic at Bear Mountain and the boat accident. We thought the song was hilariously funny at the time. Now it's not so funny, but it was then. The thing is, though, that he was beginning to think about and talk about people who were being trod upon. Not in any class sense, but just that he hated people who were taking advantage of people. He did read the newspapers, and that's what came through in "Talkin' Bear Mountain."

Any other songs?
I remember everyone thought he should record "I Will Not Go Down

Under the Ground" because we all thought it was one of his better topical songs. He was going to record it on the *Freewheelin'* album, but he decided to cut it. I don't know why, but I thought he should have kept it.

His influences?

Bob worshipped Guthrie. He had a thing about Jack Elliott, partly because of Jack's relationship with Guthrie.

I know Bob and Suze hung out with you and Dave. Tell me about their relationship with Suze's family.

Carla and Suze's mother weren't crazy about Bob. I mean, in comes this scruffy, dirty, slightly strange, and totally poverty-stricken little boy of nineteen and your daughter falls in love with him. You can't be too ecstatic about that.

What were they like together? What happened?

They were young and crazy about each other. And Bob really needed Suze. Suze was seventeen and a half years old when they met, and Bob asked me how they could live together since Suze wasn't eighteen yet. I told him to wait six months.

To everyone else, on the surface, he was the ultimate cool person. But with Suze he would break down, shouting and screaming and crying, overwhelming her. She couldn't help but get swallowed up in it. She was unable to work or paint when Dylan was around. She was her normal self when he was away, but she couldn't work when they were together. Bobby wanted approval. Really wanted it desperately. You could smell it, feel it, taste it—it just emanated from him.

Did Suze talk about it with you?

She talked about leaving him. When Suze decided to break off with Bobby, she didn't know what to do. She ran around for a month asking whether she should go to Italy for a while. I gave her some advice that just about ended my friendship with Bob. I told her that if she went, she shouldn't expect Bob to wait the summer for her, and if she didn't go she might completely regret it. I told her to make up her own mind. I know Bob would have wanted me to tell her to stay, but I wouldn't do that, and we had a falling-out.

Tell me about when it started to get crazy for Bob. Dave told me about girls screaming after Bob. Do you remember that?

Oh, certainly. The Carnegie Hall concert.

When was that?

In 1963. Something had happened. It was very strange, like the precursor to Beatlemania. Bobby's first big skyrocketing was right there in that Carnegie Hall gig.

Girls screaming and chasing Bob?

Yes. When it was over and we were all backstage, Bob's friends began to plot the getaway from all these little girls who were screaming outside. Suze and I were delegated to go outside and act as decoys. So, we went out the stage door and started walking up the street in the opposite direction from where the car was parked, and a whole bunch of kids began to follow us. Suze got a little panicky and she began to tell them to go back, that Bobby was still inside, and after a while they finally believed her, and they all ran back. And Bobby came out, flanked by Geno [Foreman] on one side and [Victor] Maymudes on the other, and we all pushed our way to the car.

So, you didn't really do the decoy thing.

No, Suze was frightened. It was scary. Bobby was terrified of mobs, and that was a mob. It was something I had never seen before, little girls hanging on top of the car and policemen pulling them away so Bobby could get out of there safely. I can understand the panic that performers go through, after seeing that.

Bob went with Grossman as his manager, he and Suze split up, and a few years later you and Dave split up. You weren't involved with Bob so much.

Our lives went separate ways, and Bob was really making it. And other stuff happened for him and for us. I didn't see him for a while. After he became well known, he cut himself off from the past. This is normal. Most people move on and leave friends behind, but with Bobby, it was even more exaggerated.

After he came back to the Village after Woodstock, he came by to see you?

He came to my apartment on Waverly Place. I think he was looking for a piece of his past. That's the feeling I got in the four hours we talked. When he became famous, he disappeared, went to Woodstock, and cut himself off. Now he seemed to be looking to find out what he'd been missing in the music world. The music, plus actually looking to catch up with his past. How far back, I don't know.

What did you talk about?

He seemed stressed. He said he was uptight, told me he had all this money and didn't know what to do with it, had not the foggiest notion what to do with all his money. He said he couldn't perform anymore, that he doesn't like performing in front of big audiences, but he's going to perform again because he doesn't have anything else to do.

Did he talk about music?

When he came, he looked around the apartment. He looked at his old corduroy cap, which I still had. He had given it to me before then. He said he wanted to see it. I held it and he looked at it and he said, "Wow, what a great cap." I asked him, "Would you like to hold it, take it?" and he said, "No, I don't want it." He just wouldn't touch it. There's also this poster by Eric Von Schmidt that Bobby gave to me and he wanted to take it back, but I wouldn't let him. He asked, "You got any other old stuff has anything to do with me?" I showed him a coloring book that I still have. I bought it the day David and I had the blood tests we needed to get married, and we all colored in it, including Bobby, and he looked at it like he was looking into the old times.

Terri Thal Interview with Stephanie Trudeau, 2019

Mikki Isaacson said her place was like a hotel for him and then she said, "The Van Ronks gave him a home. Dave, one of the more talented blues guitarists and singers of the day turned him on to a wide variety of new material and musical ideas." According to her he lived with you guys for a while.

No, he didn't live with us. He was around a lot. I don't remember exactly how much, but a lot, really a lot. And yes, we turned him on to a lot of music he hadn't heard. We listened to classical music. We listened to seventeenth-century music. We listened to twentieth-century music. We listened to Charles Ives. We listened to Ravel. We listened to fourteenth-century music. We listened to the Bulgarian Koutev choir.

Very eclectic . . .

Fairly eclectic. I was in love with Penderecki. Most people in the "folk music" world didn't step out of that world. But Dave had a jazz background, and even then we listened to a lot of jazz and we both listened to classical music. At that point if you sat down with most folk singers and the people they associated with, they listened to folk music almost exclusively. They might be concerned with some current event, and that was kind of like the end of it.

Maybe a little blues?

Well, the blues is part of the folk music world . . .

Part of the folk scene. Okay. I guess I think of it leaning more towards jazz than folk but that's just . . .

At that time people were listening to country blues.

Ah. Okay.

This really even predated listening to Chicago blues.

Yeah, I was going to say . . .

The blues bands were not around New York yet. You didn't hear them. So, it wasn't even that. You heard country blues.

Right. Country blues, meaning more like, well, more like the southern black rather than the urban.

Yes.

Black blues?

Yes.

Because I think of Chicago blues as more like an urban black blues.

Paul Butterfield Blues. We all knew Muddy Waters. He played at Cafe Au Go Go. I remember the first time I heard him, I came home and said to Dave, "My God, I just listened to a greased cock!" That's what it was like. It was incredible. I don't know whether he was alone or had a group behind him. Those clubs paid shit.

I know I was going to say: how could you even have a band behind you, because how could you pay them? Even if you fill the place you still weren't going to make any money.

That's interesting because when the Blues Project started it was as a group.

Well, I think back then, the money . . .

It was a little later. And that was a bit later.

And at that point then it was, like, "Did you get a recording contract?" And if you had a recording contract that's where you had money. So . . .

You didn't get money from recording.

Well . . .

There was very little money from recording. The advances in folk music sucked when there were any; and you never collected royalty checks— never, never, *never*. A little check might float in five years after you made a record. (*laughs*) But remember, your advance, whatever it was, the piddling little bit you ever got was an advance from royalties.

Right. Yeah, and somewhere in there they were covering the expenses to actually make the recording.

Yes, and royalties weren't that big. The place where the money was—and this came just a little bit later—was in songwriting and publishing.

Right.

Publishing was where you made money. David and Dick Weissman had copywritten a song which was a rearrangement of a public domain song:

"Bamboo." "You take a stick of water, you take a . . . River come down, bamboo." Peter, Paul and Mary put it on their first album. Dave and Dick Weissman split the writer's royalty on that and then of course the publishers got the publisher's royalty. We banked enough money just from Dave's share of the writer's royalty to start the Hudson Dusters. We funded the group out of that. I took those checks and put them in the bank and said, "That money doesn't exist." That was PP&M's first album and it was a hit. That song wasn't, but the album was. So . . .

So, you got money from . . . publishing.

And it was one lousy song on one hit album.

That's why publishing was where you were making the money?

Before Dave and I broke up, we were doing all these crazy things to try not to break up, and one of the things we did was decide that perhaps I shouldn't manage him. I said, "Maybe I shouldn't be your manager. Maybe it's too . . . whatever." So, he found a new manager. It was a dreadful mistake. Not leaving me but the particular person he chose was a dreadful, dreadful mistake. Dave wrote songs occasionally, and his new manager wanted the publishing rights to his songwriting. Less than a year after we separated, he came to me and he said, "I want to backdate a publishing contract with you. So I can honestly tell them you're my publisher, and I have a contract, and I can't break it." They wanted whatever he wrote.

Yeah, so this was his way of holding on to his material?

Yeah.

Quoting from Tony's book and Eric Von Schmidt saying about Bob, "I think his attitude towards me and Van Ronk and anybody who knew a little bit more in terms of chords was that he wanted to pick up on it. He wasn't really looking for ideas, he was looking for instrumental chops. Dave Van Ronk and I represented a coming together of black expression and that's what Bob wanted at that time. I felt this later from time to time about Bob. It was Van Ronk's and my connection with [the] black funky thing that he wanted."

That's Eric's perspective. I don't know.

There was maybe one other thing and then—oh! David saying that he remembers "sessions at the Kettle of Fish, where Dylan was especially obnoxious to Ochs, Andersen, and Dave Cohen [David Blue]" and talking about their . . . that there was a real . . . he doesn't say competition. He says, "They were hungry, scuffling cats looking to grab the brass ring. I felt it. I saw how hungry they were." and he said that he feels that was the bone of contention between Dylan and them. Dylan was becoming . . .

That was when Bob started recording. When he was picked up by Albert and he was recording for Columbia, suddenly here was this guy who was very successful. Nobody knew quite what was going to happen. Yeah. They were hungry.

And Dylan took the big step.

Yeah, yeah. He made it.

And they didn't. Do you remember what you thought about, like, "Positively 4th Street"? That whole thing about everybody was wondering who it was written about?

Yeah, I remember but . . . I'd have to go back and look at it to remember it, frankly.

(laughs) Okay.

Honestly. Really. Maybe I'll do that. You know there's so much . . . Stephanie, there is so much that I have to go back and look at to remember.

It was a long time ago. This is what, like, fifty, sixty years ago? It's fifty years ago, I guess. 1960. And we're almost in 2020. Oh my God! Yeah, it's more than fifty years.

Yes.

It's a lifetime ago.

And everybody says to me, "Oh you should write your story." I remember a lot . . . I'm not Peter Stampfel. Peter Stampfel remembers everything. (laughs) I may get to it, though.

Well, one thing I thought was interesting when you were talking about the music that you and David listened to is there was sophistication. There's a worldliness there. I don't know how much older . . . What's the age difference between David . . .

Very little . . .

It's not a lot.

David is three years older, *was* three years older than me. I am two years older than Bob.

Bob is seventy-five. So . . .

I think he's seventy-seven. I'm seventy-nine.

Yeah, so you're two years older than him.

It's not an awful lot now.

No, you're right. It's not a lot. And David was, like, five years older than him?

Yeah.

It's not a lot, but it can be a big difference between, let's say, somebody who's twenty-five and someone who's twenty.

And by then Dave was living with me and then we got married. We had an apartment. We had broader interests. And Dave was an extraordinarily smart guy. Well read, well rounded.

Yeah. What was Dylan's music background? What did you guys glean from it? Was his background mostly rock and roll?

A lot of it was. I saw a lot of country music.

I was wondering about that?

I saw a lot of country music and I saw a lot of blues. There was blues in there.

I mean, I guess that would have been from the Dinkytown days, when he was going down to Minneapolis when he was eighteen or seventeen?

Yes.

Thinking about the Midwest, there must have been country-western and . . .

The rock part was the part that he never talked about then. He did later. And we really didn't pay that much attention to anyone's background. Where did Tom Paxton's background come into play? . . . Nobody paid any attention to that. It was what you had, not where you were from.

So, you weren't asking, "Where did you graduate from college?" It wasn't anything like that?

No. I mean, there was all this stuff that just . . . everybody talks about now and nobody talked about them then. It was irrelevant.

Yeah, really.

We spent a lot of time together socially, and when he met Suze . . . Suze and I liked each other enormously. Suze was young. But she wasn't that young. I was probably twenty-one and she was sixteen. But that's a big age difference.

Five years.

But it's a *huge* difference. When you're younger, it is. And Bob didn't live with us, but he spent a lot of time on our couch. He spent a lot of time on other people's couches. And the four of us spent a lot of time together.

Did you know Suze before Dylan?

No.

So, you met Suze through Dylan?

Yes. No. No. I knew Carla [Suze's older sister]. I don't remember when we met Carla. We probably already knew Carla, but I don't remember.

Was it through political stuff?

No. Carla and I became fairly good friends, to the extent that she was good friends with anybody. There was a period when Carla and Naomi Fein (who then lived with Barry Kornfeld, who lived downstairs) and I spent a lot of time together. This was later. Dave was traveling. Carla lived around the corner. But I don't know whether we met her before we met Suze.

If you met Carla before?

I think we met Carla through Mikki Isaacson, but I'm not sure of that.

How did you meet Suze? Dylan just came over and said, "This is my new girl-friend" or . . . ?

I don't know what he said. She was just there. (*laughs*)

(*laughs*) Okay.

There she was. And we spent a lot of time together. There weren't that many other couples. Phil and Alice, some of the older musicians. I don't know when Bob and Suze got together. You know, I have no idea.

HEY, HEY WOODY GUTHRIE

SID AND BOB GLEASON

SID: But I do know that the time he got his first paying job—
now, Bobby himself would have to tell you what club he played in.
It was the first job he got that he wasn't paid, you know, with just
passing the hat or whatever they do in the Village. He didn't have
anything to wear. [Marjorie Guthrie] will kill me, but I gave him
a complete outfit of Woody's, and he wore Woody's clothes just
exactly like it was tailored for him.

BOB AND SID [SIDSEL] GLEASON had been Woody Guthrie fans since the thirties. After visiting Guthrie at Greystone Hospital in New Jersey, they got permission from the doctors to take him to their East Orange, New Jersey, apartment to spend weekends with them. Guthrie did so for two years, and the Gleason home became a center of folk activity filled with a loose crowd who came to spend time with the greatest figure in modern folk music. Pete Seeger and his wife, Toshi, came with their children; Peter La Farge, Jack Elliott, Cisco Houston, and of course the new kid on the block, nineteen-year-old Bob Dylan, also visited. Sitting at Woody's bedside, Dylan talked to Guthrie and absorbed the swirling conversations while listening to the Gleasons' extensive record collection of blues and folk music, as well as tapes of Woody's record collection.

Basically, let's start with Woody Guthrie. How did you get involved with Woody?
SID: What was the radio program that we were listening to the night they played that record?
BOB: "Bound for Glory"?
SID: "Bound for Glory." He played "Bound for Glory" on his program. And then he announced that Woody was out at Greystone Hospital and asked people to write him. Well, I had met Woody once years and years before out in California. And we were living on the Colorado River when the Parker Dam was being finished. And the people were

coming from Oklahoma and Arkansas and Texas and places like that, trying to find work out there. And one time Woody came through and he sang for the people on the riverbank. But before that, I had heard him. He had his own radio program out on the West Coast, KRKD, I believe. Anyway, I rode out to Greystone. Mother's Day we went out to see Woody.

I want to know what year it was.

SID: '58, '59. Anyway, we went out to visit him at the hospital. They allowed us to take him out. His speech at that time was a bit guttural, explosive. His faculties—I think he was very alert, except for the fact that he just had trouble expressing [himself] because of the speech problem. And we stopped and got him coffee and bought cigarettes and so forth, and Bob said, "How would you like to come and visit us if we can get permission." "Fine," he said. And I asked him, "Can you go up four flights of steps?" He said, "I can go up faster than you can." The doctor told Bob, yes, that we could come out and get him and bring him to our home. [But] he had to be back in the hospital by 10:30 or 11:00 p.m. And on special occasions we could keep him out longer than that. But not overnight because of the medication he was taking at that time. The next weekend we got him.

BOB: In two years we missed two weekends.

SID: And I started answering his mail then. And we really never knew him before, had just really heard his songs.

BOB: No, I knew him also back prior to the war, when I was working in New York City. I used to read "Woody Sez" in the *Daily Worker*.

1959 you first took him out.

SID: Yes, it was Mother's Day, May '59.

When was the last time you—

BOB: Just before they moved him to Brooklyn. That was right after, just about the time Cisco died, wasn't it? March of '61.

What I'm primarily interested in is the younger folk singers like Jack Elliott and Bob Dylan who would come out. Let's start with Dylan. When did Dylan first show up? Dylan didn't show up actually until possibly January or February of '61. Is that right?

SID: Now, Jack Elliott—see, Cisco was one of the ones that we knew, who had traveled with Woody, and Woody writes about that in his book. Now I don't think he had met Jack when he wrote the book. Tell you something funny, though. Jack was probably, what, seventeen? Sixteen, seventeen years old? Maybe he was older than that. I don't know. But anyway, they traveled all over the United States. Everywhere. And Jack, well, his father's a very well-known doctor. And I know he wanted him to go to college. But Jack, I'm not sure now, where he met up with Woody. New York City? They did all kinds of things together. And it just seemed as though—he copied him so completely, that one of the first times his father saw him in a performance, he said, "Jack, it's perfectly all right for you to copy someone, because in copying them that shows your admiration for the person. But must you imitate his mannerisms that show his disease as well?"

Is that what he was doing at the time?

SID: He didn't realize he was doing it. And it took him years to get undone what he had learned to do. Woody had a funny way of twisting one arm. It was one of the spasmodic things that he couldn't help. Well, Jack was picking all these things up. He's a tremendous mimic. Apparently Woody heard about it, and he asked Jack to go with him to the West Coast. He was very, very ill, and he sent Jack to the coast. Anyway, when Jack got back to New York, Woody was gone.

Really?

SID: And it took, I don't know, months that Jack tried to find him. And he couldn't. And then when he did find him, Woody wrote him a card, a postcard. And he says, "Dear Jack, Fuck you." And that was all that was on it. And Jack was so terribly hurt that this man [who] had been his everything, his father, his brother, his everything, would do that. But he didn't realize until many years afterwards . . .

BOB: It was the way Woody weaned him.

When did this happen?

SID: Well, just before Woody went to Greystone. Do you know how he got in there?

He was arrested, as a vagrant.

SID: He was deliberately arrested as a vagrant. He knew he would be. He had cased Greystone. He knew the whole way up. He knew the wooded areas and everything. He didn't like Brooklyn State, because there was no place to sit under trees, he couldn't lay on the grass. So, he goes out there and he gets himself arrested, puts on the most beautiful show on God's earth. And they have a psychiatrist for him because they think he's crazy and they ask him if he ever heard voices. And he said yes. He knew what he was after. And he was committed there, you see. But there was nothing insane about the man.

He was committed by the court.

BOB: It relieved the responsibility from his family. See, they didn't have to pay anything. He knew they couldn't afford—

That sounds like Woody because that's the humane kind of thing to do for your family, sure.

SID: One of the funniest things I think I've ever heard is he was going across into Mexico and he wore the Jesus Christ shoes, you know. He was the original hippie, I'm telling you.

BOB: Kerouac could have taken lessons from Woody.

SID: His hair was long like this, and he had a long beard and he was carrying this big mandolin and he was kind of seedy looking. He was on this bus and the guy at the checkpoint said, "You look like a Communist." So, they put him in jail. Pete Seeger at that time was about seventeen, eighteen years old. Pete went down busking on the streets and made enough money to get Woody out of jail. That's one of the funny stories.

Was Pete out there often?

SID: Quite frequently.

I'm interested primarily in the younger people who were influenced by Woody. So, since Dylan is the most famous, let's start with him. How did he first get out here?

SID: He hitchhiked.

BOB: He wanted to meet Woody.

Did he knock on your door? Was he at the hospital first? What do you recall about it?

SID: No, no. He never made a visit to the hospital. You see, our place was halfway out. They could come out from New York very easy, much easier from New York to our place than it was out to Brooklyn State Hospital. Or to Greystone.

And do you recall the first day Dylan got here? Was he alone, how he got here, who he was with, did he hitchhike? Did he take the New Jersey PATH tubes and then hitchhike?

SID: He hitchhiked. He came out through the Lincoln Tunnel. I said I didn't know it could be done and he said it can. That's all I know.

What did he do? He showed up and knocked on your door?

SID: He just showed up. As far as I remember.

BOB: I'm pretty sure he came alone.

SID: And that was a traumatic thing for him to do.

In what way?

SID: Well, he was almost as blind as a bat. He still is. And meeting people has always been very hard for him, I think. Bobby came, and he looked like an archangel, a choirboy, we'll say. A little round face with—he's got these beautiful eyes. And his hair was, in those days, blond.

But not high and frizzy as he wore it a couple years later.

SID: Oh, no, no, no. It was long. It was curly. Very curly. And he wore a little tiny—what did he call these, little caps with a little donut on it. Little boys wear it.

BOB: Like an Eton cap.

SID: And he had a pair of shoes to slip on, but they were about two sizes too big for him. Everything that child had was either too small or too big. He was quiet. He said little. He was just like an ink blotter, just absorbed everything. He listened to the records and tapes we had. We had maybe ninety percent of Woody's record collection. Bobby would start in the morning and listen all day to Woody's records. Carter Family, Big Bill Broonzy, everything. He'd listen and after a couple of times Bobby would have the words and the chord progressions. I had a girl that was living with us at the time who was seven years old. I was taking care of her. Her mother was gone. And Bobby used to sit and play and sing to her.

What was her name?

SID: Kathy. And she adored him. And Bobby used to go and sit on the edge of the bed and he'd sing to Kathy. He'd get her to go to sleep.

What would he sing for her?

SID: Folk songs. A lot of Woody's stuff. He used to sing one. She loved "Jesse James," and you know the song that Woody wrote to the tune of "Jesse James."

Yeah.

SID: "Jesus Christ"? And he'd sing "Jesus Christ," and she'd get so mad at him. She'd say, "You know that's not the right words. You're just kidding." And things like that. Anyway, I couldn't begin to tell you how many times Bobby was at the house and how many times he stayed. But I do know that the time he got his first paying job—now, Bobby himself would have to tell you what club he played in. It was the first job he got that he wasn't paid, you know, with just passing the hat or whatever they do in the Village. He didn't have anything to wear. [Marjorie Guthrie] will kill me, but I gave him a complete outfit of Woody's, and he wore Woody's clothes just exactly like [they were] tailored for him.

That would be April. Did you still have contact with Bob after Woody left?

SID: No.

Woody was here through May, I think you said.

SID: Bobby was—I know I gave him the clothes. Now whether he was, yes, he was working at Gerde's. It was March or maybe April. Because we went in and saw him.

Yeah, his first paid gig was Gerde's in April.

SID: Uh-huh. And Jack Elliott had a concert. We went to the concert. And I think that's the way it worked. But we saw Bobby and that was the night that the other woman and her husband . . .

BOB: McKenzie.

SID: McKenzie. She's a real doll. She was there that night. And Jack Elliott, I think, was there. Bobby asked if we could bring Woody to his gig at Gerde's. He said he'd love him to be there.

BOB: Woody was on all kinds of medication that wouldn't mix with liquor. [Drinking] could kill him. We said we could bring Woody if they close the bar down. Bobby said he didn't think they could do that.

SID: Like I said, I gave Bobby the clothes to wear for that because he didn't have a decent rag to his name. Anyway, as I say, Bobby didn't say much. He came out and he learned a lot.

Did he have his guitar with him the first time out?

SID: Probably, yes. But then after that, I don't think he brought it, because he used to come out and play the twelve-string that we have. And there was one thing about that child that I loved. If there was snow to be shoveled, he'd shovel snow. If there were dishes to be washed, he'd wash dishes. Bobby didn't bum.

Really? That's not what people said later, at least.

SID: No, Bobby didn't bum. I helped Bobby. Yes, Bob and I gave him money occasionally. But he used to shovel snow. And he would do things like that. He wasn't lazy. Bobby was not lazy.

He found these things to do without anybody mentioning it to him? He'd seek out the work and stuff?

SID: He had to live. He couldn't make it on what he was getting, just people throwing nickels and dimes. He wasn't lazy, as I say.

In New York he shoveled snow to make money?

SID: Yeah. In the winter because he didn't have any money. You know, they weren't paying him to work in these clubs. He didn't have anyplace to stay. And sometimes he stayed with Dave Van Ronk and sometimes he stayed here and sometimes he'd stay there. I don't know where all he stayed. In fact, he stayed in flophouses in New York some of the time.

Did he tell you he stayed in flophouses?

SID: Yeah. This is what they call it. But anyway, Bobby, as I say, he wasn't a lazy boy. And he didn't expect people to pay his way. He wasn't that type of a person. Because Bobby—for instance, he's worked all his life as far as I know. He made pretty good money before he ever got into show business by being other's people's backup man. You see, he was backup on rock- and-roll records because he is a fantastic performer. He can play piano almost as well as Jerry Lee Lewis, and I think Jerry Lee Lewis is one of our best, well, what would you call, hard-rockin' piano players.

Did he ever tell you about playing the piano in a burlesque house or a strip tease place in Colorado City?

SID: Yes.

BOB: Uh-huh.

You must have had some wonderful weekends.

SID: Fantastic. But anyway, as I say, Bobby was not a lazy boy. When he'd come out to stay with us, if I didn't feel good, he'd get the vacuum cleaner and he'd do the floors. And you know, things like that. They always helped. They all helped.

Somewhere along the line I heard that you people wanted to adopt Bobby.

SID: Oh no.

Did you know that he had parents back in Minnesota?

SID: The story Bobby told us is, many times—I mean many, many times—is so different from the stories we have heard about Bobby. He told us he had been in a number of foster homes, that he did have parents but he'd been in foster homes all over. Now, we never questioned him. What Bobby wanted to tell us, or what anyone wanted to tell us, is what they told us. We didn't ask questions, because it was none of our business.

Bobby told you that he did have parents but he had lived with several foster parents.

SID: He told us he had parents but that he'd been in many foster homes.

And he said he just couldn't be tied down. He'd just stay there awhile and leave. Period. And that's all he'd tell me.

BOB: I think he came up to us from a tour of the South, where he was hanging around with some of the southern street singers.

Do you recall what he said about it?

BOB: Vaguely. I remember him saying that he had been with a couple of them. I don't remember who they were now.

SID: That's where his interest in blues originated.

What about Big Joe Williams? Did he ever talk about Big Joe Williams?

SID: Big Joe, yes. The jazz singer. Yeah. He probably knew not so many people like that. He went through some albums that we had once, and he and my daughter were talking about it. And he said, "Oh, I played for that one and that one and that one. Played the piano on that one and the guitar on this one" and, you know, like that. And then she said, "Honest, are you kidding?" "No," he said. "Why should I kid you? I'm not. I've even played for Elvis Presley. I played piano on some of his recordings."

Did you believe him?

SID: Yes.

Well, how did you feel when he was telling you the story about his foster homes? Did you believe that also?

SID: I didn't have any reason not to believe it.

BOB: People come here, and we take them at face value. We're not here to judge people. If he wants to lie to us, that's his problem. We weren't asking him questions. "What did you do here? What did you do there?" It's just spontaneous from him. He volunteered the information.

Did Bobby ever stay the night? Where did he sleep?

BOB: He slept on this couch.

SID: They all did when they would come. Jack Elliott and Cisco Houston, and Woody used to—every Sunday he'd stretch out and have a little nap on there. All of the fellows that stayed overnight slept on that. And it was mostly boys, you know, mostly men. There were very few girls that came out.

No girl folk singers that you—

BOB: Most of the people who showed up were old friends of Woody.

SID: Bobby would talk to Woody when no one was around. Woody couldn't talk that much. He would sit at Woody's feet and talk to him very quietly.

Did Dylan ever come out with a girlfriend?

SID: No.

Do you remember any of his friends? I mean, kids his age?

SID: No, I don't know. I never met any of his friends. He would come out and he'd spend hours going through the tapes. Spent hours, literally, for days.

Going through your recordings and tapes and listening to—what kind of stuff was he listening to?

BOB: Woody's VD [venereal disease] songs.

SID: Woody wrote the VD songs, you know, the government paid him to write those. Bob copied them off of the old paper[-backed] tapes. And they're not very good. But he learned them, and I said, "Well, what are you spending all your time doing?" And I said, "Tell you what, I dare you to sing them in one of the clubs."

Did he?

SID: He did. And he called me up and he says, "You know, Mom, I don't think they knew what I was talking about."

When was this?

SID: Was it the Gaslight? He sang some of the VD songs, a couple of them that were complete.

What was the last time you had contact with Dylan?

SID: Oh, one of the last times I saw him, I guess, was when he worked at Gerde's, I really got to talking to him. But he used to call me occasionally.

That first gig at Gerde's?

SID: Probably. He never was out to our place, really, after he made his first recording for Columbia, or is it Capitol?

BOB: It was before he made that recording was [the] last time he was here.

SID: Because we saw him high at Gerde's, I think. I don't remember for sure. But anyway, I suspected he was on pot, and I don't believe in that.

I didn't think he was on pot that early.

SID: I suspected.

Did Dave Van Ronk ever come out?

SID: No. I'll tell you why. Woody didn't like him because he bragged he could play guitar like Lead Belly, and Woody said Lead Belly could have taken Dave's head and crushed it with one hand.

Oh really? How often did Marjorie and Arlo come out? Marjorie would come out with the kids?

BOB: Three kids, yeah. We took Woody there a number of times.

SID: Howard Beach.

Did [Dylan] ever talk about his ambitions, about what he wanted to do with himself?

SID: Yes, he wanted to be in show business. He wanted to be a musical—

Did he ever talk about how high he could possibly go or what—

SID: He had no idea what he could do.

Do you recall what he said about it?

SID: He was looking for a style. I think he pulled the biggest hoax in the history of music.

In what way?

SID: He sang southern mountain style, and he didn't sing southern mountain style. And he almost ruined his voice doing it. It was just an absolute pure hoax. And when I try to tell people that doesn't sound like Bobby Dylan, [they say] "Are you kidding? That's Dylan."

Did he sing more natural when he sang for you here?

BOB: Oh yeah. Guthrie used to say that Bobby had a voice. He'd say Pete Seeger was a singer of folk songs, not a folk singer. Bobby Dylan is a folk singer. Woody would ask people he liked to come back. He was always saying, "When is the boy coming back? Is the boy coming this weekend?"

Because I've heard tapes, at the McKenzies', for example, and they've got him both natural, like he sounds on his last couple of records, or the last record at least—

SID: And one night Bobby was saying how his guitar broke. So, he picked up a mandolin and his string broke on that. Jack [Elliott] walked in. Jack played guitar, but he was second liner—I forget the headliner—and they kept applauding and applauding and applauding.

When was this—do you recall? That first gig probably?

SID: Probably.

Let me ask you something again. Why did you bring Woody to your home every weekend? What impelled you to do this? There must have been a lot of people around who knew who Woody was.

SID: He just needed somebody.

Did Jack Elliott bring any other friends out?

BOB: Girlfriends occasionally.

When was the last time you heard from Dylan?

SID: I tried to tell you. As I said, I started suspecting that he was on pot. And as I say, I don't believe in that stuff. I asked Peter [La Farge] to keep an eye on him. So he did. And the last time Bob called me he said, "Mom, I promise—"

He calls you "Mom"?

SID: Yeah.

What does he call you?

SID: He calls him Bob.

I'm sorry, go ahead.

SID: Bobby says, "I promise, I won't do anything like that again. Just keep him off my back." You see, a lot of people were afraid of La Farge.

How do you think Dylan found out he was being watched?

SID: Because he knew Pete, he knew me, and he knew what I do.

BOB: Every place Bob was, Pete would show up.

What made Dylan think to call you to ask you to call him off his back?

SID: He knew me.

BOB: They called her Den Mother. I think Pete Seeger started that.

[Music playing] Which recording is this? Is Woody in it?

SID: It's Cisco Houston singing Woody's song "The Biggest Thing That Man Has Ever Done." That's another person Bobby learned from. There was another thing that Bobby learned from Woody, I'm pretty sure. Because Woody preached that if you have a song to sing, sing it, and let people hear the words. If you have a message, they must. You know, Pete Seeger told us once that he wanted to learn to play the mandolin. So Woody just ran through it and said, "You know, this is how you do it."

BOB: Don't fuss about it, do it.

SID: Now you do it. And Pete learned to play the mandolin in an afternoon.

Was there a feeling around that this kid was going to make it? Were people treating him like somebody special? Because apparently, later, in the Village they were.

BOB: We weren't.

What about when he was sitting around singing these songs? I mean, I'm sure Woody was around when this was being taped.

SID: He wasn't, no. In fact, he didn't perform in front of Woody.

Really? He wouldn't perform with Woody or with Cisco, say? Or Jack Elliott?

SID: It was hard to get Bobby to play. He'd say, "Why should I play when these guys are, you know . . ."

Were you aware of his "Song to Woody"? "Hey, hey Woody Guthrie, I wrote you this song."

SID: I think I've got the original.

Did you play it for Woody here?

BOB: I remember the head of our service department was married to a woman who is a concert artist and she was giving Bobby some tips on voice control.

Oh really?

SID: And I'll tell another thing. He had one of the largest repertoires of—he knows more songs, the old songs, I think, than anybody.

BOB: He's just a gold mine of this stuff.

SID: That's why I say he was literally a sponge.

SID: This is the original of the song to Woody. He said, "Here, Mom," and he gave it to me.

BOB: He wrote this in Mill's bar. Remember Dave Collins was telling us how they used to hang out in Mill's bar and Dylan would be dashing off songs and throwing sheets of paper out of it? Yeah. Mill's bar on Bleecker Street. It was the only nonhippie bar—

SID: This is the original.

MR. TAMBOURINE MAN

THE CLANCY BROTHERS

(Pat and Tom Clancy)

TOM: *After we'd do a set, Bobby would be down chatting away with Liam about different songs and about chords and about music when Paddy and I would be up having a beer, you know. But Liam and Bobby Dylan usually stayed on after each set. And they swapped songs and things and we got to like Bobby very much. I like him very much. He was a strong personality. Young, ambitious, strong. . . . He had something to say and he was goddamned well going to say it, you know.*

AMONG THE GREENWICH VILLAGE FOLK SCENE were Irish folk artists the Clancy Brothers—Tom, Pat, and Liam, alongside others like Phil Ochs and Ramblin' Jack Elliott. By 1962 Dylan was the center of this group that made music, sometimes together, at Gerde's Folk City, the Limelight, and Caffè Lena in Saratoga Springs, upstate New York. They hung out drinking—Dave Van Ronk, Tom Paxton, Bob Dylan, and the Clancy Brothers—at bars like the Lion's Head and the Kettle of Fish. Tom and Pat (Paddy) were singers and Liam was a guitarist, so he and Dylan forged a musical relationship.

When and where did you first meet Dylan? You remember?

PAT: Over at Gerde's Folk City.

When was that?

PAT: I'd have to guess? Uh . . . '56, '57 . . . '56 . . . late '56, I suppose, either '56 or '57, around there.

It had to be later than that, wouldn't it? Bob Dylan, I don't think showed up until about '60. And was he appearing at Gerde's?

PAT: I was there the first night that he went up on the amateur night. It was on Monday nights.

Right. Right. The hootenanny night.

PAT: And he had a harmonica, I think, and his cap and the bit you know?

Right. And what kind of stuff did he do?

PAT: He did his own kind of stuff! Eh . . . you know it . . . stuff that he'd written himself.

Oh really? What about some of the Woody Guthrie stuff?

PAT: Yes, he did some Woody Guthrie stuff also.

And you say this was the first night he showed up?

PAT: It was on a Monday night, yes. Yeah, that's the first time as far as I know that he played in Folk City because it was on the amateur night, you know.

And did you get a chance to talk to him later?

PAT: Yeah. We chatted around a bit and he talked about Woody Guthrie, and I gathered he got his name from Dylan Thomas, you know, and . . .

What do you mean you gathered? Did he say in any way?

PAT: He didn't, no, and I didn't . . . you don't like to question a person about their own name, you know, in that sense.

Right.

PAT: But I remember the first, how he got to Columbia Records, I remember quite well. There was a girl I'd recorded called Carolyn Hester. I was involved with Tradition Records at that time. I was running a company called Tradition Records. She was married to, eh . . .

Richie Fariña.

PAT: Yeah, Dick Fariña, yeah. And from that recording she went to Columbia. A fellow called Bob Morgan was the A&R man and he liked her. She asked Dylan to go up and accompany her on one harmonica number. And while they were up there and Dylan was fooling around with the harmonica and playing the piano, there was this man up there . . . what's his name now? He was first A&R man.

John Hammond.

PAT: John Hammond. Signed him up right there!

Do you remember Dylan coming back and talking about it? Was he excited about it? Do you remember what he said about it?

PAT: Oh yeah, he was. He was very excited about it, you know.

Do you recall what he said about it?

PAT: No. I don't.

Do you remember him talking about bumming around the country with some of the folk singers or Negro bluesmen or anything like that?

PAT: There was this one man down South, a Negro singer from down south that he was very interested in. No, it wasn't a Negro singer. It was an old folk singer from down south. I can't remember his name now . . .

Not a black man? What about Big Joe Williams, for example?

PAT: I never heard of him, no—no, I don't know if there's any involvement with that.

Did you ever play with Dylan or did Dylan ever play with you anywhere? Either professionally or as an amateur or anything like that or, you know, jamming together in somebody's apartment—anything like that?

PAT: I can't remember, no. We were often at the same parties and we might have been up at the stage the same night in Gerde's, you know, but I can't remember anything specific like that.

What about some of the people? Where was he living at the time, for example? How close to him did you get?

PAT: My brother Liam was closer to him than I was. Liam and he were quite close. They were nearer in ages than we were, you know?

Right, right. And Liam's not around?

PAT: He's not. He's up in Ottawa. He's at the Skyline Hotel in Ottawa if you want to give him a call.

Yeah. I'll try that. Tell me, can you remember anything else about Dylan? When was the last time you saw him, for example? Maybe that'll . . .

PAT: About a year ago. We were doing a concert up in Westchester.

Yeah . . .

PAT: And Dylan drove down with his family.

Did he really?

PAT: He came to the concert and came backstage.

Where did he sit while you were performing?

PAT: I don't know! He just came back afterwards. We had a message and, you know, he was down to see us and he came in, brought his wife and family, and it was very nice [of him] to drive down and show up, you know.

Nobody recognized him? How did he get away with . . .

PAT: Well, he was very sort of clean shaved and fairly normally dressed and he had his family with him.

What do you mean his family?

PAT: He had his wife and a couple of children.

Oh really? Where was the concert?

PAT: Can you hold on? Jerry would remember . . . we were just talking, and I'll find out . . .

Before we get into the facts of it, what did Dylan say when he came backstage?

PAT: He said, "It's nice to see you again" and, uh, "After all we've both been through . . ." and, you know, that kind of thing. He was very kind, very nice about it. I mean he was kind of anxious to renew an old sort of acquaintance, you know?

Yeah. You got a feeling he was looking for some of the people he knew back in the early days?

PAT: Something like that, maybe, and I know he was kind of being genuine, you know, and saying hello and "although I've been through all this thing it's . . . ," you know.

Yeah.

PAT: There was something quite . . . quite nice and genuine about it.

Right. Did he introduce his wife?

PAT: Oh yes! He brought her and the kids in, and we talked for a long time and he said he'd like to come to Ireland and was going to try and come, you know, and . . .

This was before the Isle of Wight concert?

PAT: Just a few months before he went there. That's right.

Did he make any attempt to reach you when he did get over to Ireland?

PAT: Not that I know of, no, no . . . because he was moving fast, you know.

I know that was a big hassle over on the Isle of Wight, sure. Do you recall anything else you talked about? How long did he spend with you backstage there?

PAT: Oh maybe half an hour, you know, and then he had to drive all the way back up to—

Woodstock.

PAT: Woodstock. Yeah.

Did he say anything else? Can you recall anything else you talked about?

PAT: I can't at the moment, except that he'd like to come to Ireland. He was hoping to. He was asking me all about farming and that he wanted to . . . I have a farm in Ireland and he was hoping to come and stay there, you know.

I understand he had been asking Paul McCartney about a farm in Wales. He was talking seriously about looking around?

PAT: Yes. he was very serious that night.

Yeah. Can you ask Jerry when and where your concert was?

PAT: Yeah. Can you hold on just a minute? Do you want to talk to Tom? He might remember some things that'd be . . .

I'd love to if he's available.

PAT: Yeah, he's here somewhere . . . if you hold on just a minute . . . Jerry says the concert was at the White Plains Community Center last April. Not April, it was a year ago St. Patrick's Day, that's right!

The Isle of Wight concert was in August, so it would be about five months before the Isle of Wight concert.

PAT: That's right. Yeah.

Did you see Dylan during the years that he was really getting famous?

PAT: Met him a couple of times, yes.

Like when? Do you recall any of it?

PAT: No. I didn't meet him, you know. I didn't get a chance to talk much. He was always surrounded by people, you know? He was being chaperoned by Al Grossman and uh . . .

You mean all the bodyguards and the mindguards that were around?

PAT: That kind of thing. You know, you felt you were barging into something, so we just sort of said hello and went on by. But he came back, went out of his way to come see us at that thing, which I thought was quite nice.

Yeah!

PAT: Because, I mean, I could understand his position at the time. We didn't want to bug him and step on anybody else's toes . . . so we just let it go, you know?

And he actually did come all the way from Woodstock to see you.

PAT: He did and to say hello, you know?

And you had no idea he was coming?

PAT: No, no, absolutely not. At various times in England and Ireland and when he was on television or radio, he mentioned us and gave us a plug, you know, even at the height of his fame and everything.

You mean he seemed to be deliberately giving you a plug?

PAT: Yeah. Especially when he had an interview in Britain and in Ireland, you know, he mentioned us.

That's a real sweet thing to do.

PAT: I thought so, yeah. I always thought he was a genuine kind of a guy myself.

If you think of anything else . . . If I can, I'll tell Jerry Campbell. It's a thing kind off the top of my head, it's hard to, eh . . .

PAT: One of the things is, first time Al Grossman came to town, I got a letter of introduction for him to cruise him around and show him who the folk singers were.

Oh really? Who was the letter of intro from?

PAT: From Noel Behn, who later wrote a book called *The Kremlin Letter*.

What was Noel doing at the time?

PAT: Noel was involved with us in theater and he called me and said, "A friend of my family from Chicago is coming to town and he wants to know about folk music, so I'm going to send him to you. Is it all right to take him around?" Which I did. And that was Al Grossman. He was dressed like a Madison Avenue businessman.

Yeah. I remember when I first saw him that's how he was dressing.

PAT: Right. Tom's here. I'm going to go off.

Thanks so much. I'll see you later. Bye.

TOM: Hi.

Yeah, hello, Tom. Did Pat tell you I'm doing a book on Bob Dylan?

TOM: Yeah, I heard about it.

And I'm trying to talk to everybody from back in the early days, including you and Phil Ochs. I talked to Dave Van Ronk and his wife and all that. Can you tell me when you first met Dylan? When you first saw him?

TOM: Gerde's Folk City. I think we all met about the same time. Now, I couldn't say whether I met Bob over at the Limelight or whether I met him at Folk City, but we were all kind of swingin' around together at the same time there. But I think it was probably Folk City where we met, at Gerde's.

Right. And you had been in the business quite a while?

TOM: Well, I was in the theater for a long time.

You'd been pretty much established, where Dylan was just a kid.

TOM: Oh yeah.

How did he impress you at the time? What were his reactions to you as someone who was established?

TOM: Well, you can ask Bob this himself, but I'll tell you he wanted to talk about it. He wanted to talk to us because we had been in it, you know, and he and Liam were more together because they were talking mostly music and songs and Liam playing the guitar and Bobby playing the guitar. It was downstairs at Gerde's among the old cats that they used to have down there. After we'd do a set, Bobby would be down chatting away with Liam about different songs and about chords and about music when Paddy and I would be up having a beer, you know? But Liam and Bobby Dylan usually stayed on after each set. And they swapped songs and things and we got to like Bobby very much. I like him very much. He was a very strong personality. Young, ambitious, strong.

How ambitious? He struck you as ambitious in what way?

TOM: Well, he had something to say and he was goddamned well going to say it, you know.

You mean he had the drive to . . .

TOM: He did, yeah. I knew he had enough to bring him along. I knew he was going to ride the thing out to the very end.

Did he ever talk specifically about making it?

TOM: No he was a very kind of aesthetic man, and it was always "man," you know, in between each sentence. "Man, you guys, man, you know I love this. I love listening to you guys, man," you know?

Right.

TOM: And he was always kind of bouncing on the balls of his feet when he talked to you, you know, always sooo enthusiastic about talking to people . . . he just loved people. And I think he loved us a good deal. Even recently he came to see us again when we were playing up in Westchester or someplace up there.

When you were playing in White Plains. I heard about that. Tell me about that. What did he talk about when he got backstage to see you?

TOM: I asked him, "Jeez, where did you come from, Bobby?" He said, "I've driven a hundred and something miles. I just wanted to see you. I just wanted to be with you." I think he wanted to be back with us for a while and he had a beer with us backstage and he was exactly the same as if he'd gone through the whole mill . . .

. . . and came out the other side.

TOM: And came out back again to us! To say, "Man, I just drove here maybe two hundred miles, just to be with you." And he came back after the show and he had to drive back all the way home again, but he seemed changed. He seemed different from when I met him at times in the Village, you know, in the Lion's Head. He was communicating much more. He was back there where we all began.

Was he really?

TOM: Very much so. *Very* much so. His hair was cut. That means something to me, because I had longer hair than he did. The thing is that he was coming very much across as a guy who has gone through the mill, coming back to himself, very sensible, looking for a way to begin again, and he seemed at ease!

Like a man back where his head belonged.

TOM: Back to where he *really* belonged because he made much more sense this last time I saw him than he made at other times when I met him in the Village.

Well, what kind of sense did he make this time?

TOM: He was able, quite ready and willing and able to converse about, you know, songs and the road and things and himself and his family.

Do you recall what he said about himself and his family?

TOM: He said, "You know, man, I'm happy now. I'm happy. I'm at ease, man. I just love to come and hear you play the thing and I don't mind driving two hundred miles."

Yeah. And you said this was different from other times you'd seen him in the Village? What was it like the other times?

TOM: Well, at the times when I met him in the Village, we ate at the same places, in the Lion's Head, you know, and he was kind of vague about things. Vague.

Was this during the height of his popularity when he . . .

TOM: [The] very height, yeah.

Yeah. When he was going through a really freaky stage?

TOM: That's about it.

What was he like then? What was your view at that time?

TOM: Well, I'll tell you now. I didn't have much communication with him at that time.

He didn't seem to have much communication with anybody at that time.

TOM: He didn't, no. He didn't with me, but the last time we met him, up again in White Plains, he was back again to the Bobby Dylan I knew, the guy who was always bouncing, saying, "Man, this is great!" You know?

Some of that refreshing kid had returned?

TOM: Oh, he was such a pleasure to talk to, you know?

Do you recall anything? What did he say about being on the road? Did he talk about having cut his hair to be in disguise so he could travel around the country, that kind of thing?

TOM: No, no he didn't. I tell you, we were doing a show as a matter of fact and he came back before we went on, and then he came back after the show but there wasn't much time. There were so many people there, you know. I mean our fans were there and went looking for autographs and the rest of it, so really there wasn't much time for talk, but all I'm giving you is my impression, my feeling about him.

He actually sat in the audience and watched you guys perform?

TOM: Oh yeah!

What about the whole fame bit, the whole bit about kids screaming for Bobby Dylan? Nobody bothered him?

TOM: No. He looked like a normal guy. His hair was cut. He looked like a young Bobby Dylan again.

You mean it's possible nobody recognized him?

TOM: They *did* recognize him! A lot of people did, but our fans are not screaming kids.

That's right. That's right, your fans—you don't get the teenage kids who are going nuts screaming.

TOM: No. We get people with families and so on. We have kind of a different audience.

Bobby was with his wife, with Sara. Did he introduce Sara to everybody?

TOM: Yeah sure.

And he had a couple of kids with him. Which kids do you recall?

TOM: I don't recall, but I think there were two kids with him.

This was a night concert, an evening concert?

TOM: Yeah.

And apparently the kids were old enough to stay up that late?

TOM: Well, he wanted to bring them to see us, I guess.

Yeah. That's groovy. Gee, that sounds like he's really coming back.

TOM: I think so. I really think so.

PHIL OCHS

I mean, just an endless series of great conversations. I don't remember
what they were about—what was said—it was just real rapid talk.
It was speed trips, huge speed trips. I mean, we were running up
to—I forget what was it there? Arthur's discotheque, laughing at
all the people there and meeting Marlon Brando one night in some
apartment uptown. Always the singing—singing all the time and
starting to travel around the country, getting to England . . . and
writing all the time. Everybody was very, totally creative. I mean,
Bob Dylan came up to the house and he said, "I want you to hear my
new song." And he sat down and sang "Mr. Tambourine Man," you
know, in an empty living room.

I N 1961, IN THE WEST VILLAGE, Phil Ochs, a journalism student from the
University of Ohio, discovered folk songs and joined the crowd made up
of Tom Paxton, Pete La Farge, Dave Van Ronk, and, of course, Bob Dylan.
They hung out at the *Broadside* office and sang their latest songs to each
other. Ochs and Dylan were friends, fellow songwriters and competitors,
verbally sparring to see who could get off the fastest, sharpest, meanest
quips.

When did you first blow into town?
Oh, I guess . . . I think it was September 1961.
How did you first meet Bob? Where?
Funny, I first directly met him at some Chinese restaurant in Chinatown,
New York City, with John Herald and Gil Turner and a bunch of people
going down to dinner. We all had dinner together.
By this time Bobby was already at Gerde's?
Yeah. I don't remember the exact dates. He was just around.
**What was your reaction to him? What was his reaction to you? How did it go
down?**

I don't—I don't know what . . .

First couple of meetings?

I don't know what his reaction was to me at first. As soon as I heard him
sing . . . I mean, I heard his first album before I came there.

The first album wasn't released until like March of '62.

Oh no, really?

**Yeah, he went into the studio in November of '61—all right, the dating is not
important I can always work that out.**

Whoa, that doesn't make sense, does it? Maybe it was September '61,
when I wrote my first song? I don't know . . . I had heard his album in
Ohio before I met him, and it was just like hearing another folk singer's
album. It made no impression. I mean sort of like a Jack Elliott, you know,
a record and it's all a vague memory now. I was just running into him at
various parties and at various clubs and we'd be sitting around. There were
a lot of times at the Kettle of Fish bar, spent a lot of time sitting there. We
used to come there every night for a long time actually.

In those early days? '61, '62?

Well, that . . . I think a little later than that, and that period, too, but [more]
like '63, '64.

I want to explore some of the things you talked to Mike Thomas about in that
Time **magazine article. You remember that?**

Yeah.

**Thomas quotes you in that interview as saying that after Bob started making it
he became, "super hostile"** (*Ochs laughs*) **around the Village, arrogant, attack-
ing all of you. It quotes you as saying, "He was really obnoxious, really insulting
to a lot of people." Was that an accurate description?**

Pretty much. Pretty much.

What was it like?

Well, he just got sort of speeded up and sort of arrogant, you know, and,
but whatever. That's not all, I mean, sometimes he was great too.

**Yeah. I realize that was just a small part of the whole scene and I don't need to
dwell on the whole thing . . .**

Yeah, it's not a blanket statement. I didn't say it was like that. I mean, that
was just a characteristic that was definitely developing.

Right.

A general sort of feeling like that. He used to be . . . I mean at times in the
Village he was very friendly. He came over for dinner one night with Suze

Rotolo and was very nice. But it just seemed as he got more . . . bigger . . . and he, of course, he always seemed to say he didn't put any value at all on fame or whatever. He said things like that.

But that lamé suit that you were wearing out there was basically where his head was at most of that time, I think.

Maybe and that's conjecture. That's quite possible, but he was also afraid of fame. I think he basically was a very human person and wanted to keep human relationships going and I think he felt that slipping away because of his fame and the way people reacted to him, you know. I mean, he was so sensitive anyway and people . . .

Yeah.

You imagine someone that sensitive sitting at a bar and somebody walking up to you and saying, "Hey, aren't you Bob Dylan?" It would just drive him crazy, and it would bring on that kind of essentially huge defense system he was building up.

Was that basically your explanation of it? It was a defense system, the walls of privacy?

That definitely was one part of it as far as I can see.

Like Dave Blue said that he was he was, like, building a wall around himself to protect his need for inner privacy.

Right. He definitely was doing that, yeah, which is natural.

How does this explain the fact that he was kind of "super hostile," the words you used, as everyone has kind of confirmed. How does it explain the fact that he was like this to the other professionals around? That the fortress might be against outsiders, but why would he be hostile to you, to Eric Andersen, to Dave Blue [Dave Cohen]?

I don't know, but it wasn't always like that. He also invited—there was also sort of like a mutual ribbing. I mean, it might sound like it leans a little too much that way, but, I mean, *anybody,* engineers get together, they'll sit around and put each other down on a certain level. That's another unequal aspect of this same operation here, you know, and his friend Bobby Neuwirth, who also hung around with him and was his right-hand man and assassin, you know?

Neuwirth was apparently, from what I gather, responsible for some of getting Dylan to be mean.

I don't know . . . maybe. But at the time they both got completely into it. They were a team and sitting at the table doing it, and "hostile" isn't exactly the right word either because it was really a matter of assumed arrogance and high nervousness, sitting around and sort of just . . . bantering, you know, like cubs bantering in a sense, too, and if you were tough enough and smart enough, you might just get involved with it and just do it and then it wouldn't be hostility in the way you might read it in that [*Time*] article.

I realize that article was overwritten.

And that's why I'm sensitive to it. Yeah, it's not hatred. It was very clever and very witty, barbed, you know, and very stimulating too.

In what way was it stimulating?

Well, I mean, you had to be really on your toes, like walking into a thrashing machine. If you were a regular guy and naive or open, you'd get torn to pieces. But if you could banter back and forth, you'd be okay, and it was just a high-energy situation. That's what it boils down to, and it was a high-energy time. There was lots of talent around. Bob was the greatest talent and he knew it, and then again maybe insecurity was another part of it. Getting to a place like that at that point could have led to a lot of insecurity and stuff which would lead to the defense mechanism, which would lead to the hostility, you know?

Ben Rahm said that part of this was the fact that Bobby wasn't able to take it when there were like five people tugging at his coats and then suddenly there were like five million tugging at his coats.

Right.

Would this be basically your feeling?

Yeah.

Eric Andersen said that he thinks part of the explanation for this was that Dylan was under great pressure. He was forced into being this kind of hip hero that he didn't really want to be. He didn't really dig it. It made him feel kind of negative and was one of the reasons he lashed out. Would this be your assessment of it?

Yeah it's—it's so large and complex, and all these things are true.

Any other positive complexities you've thought about, or did you kick around with Mike Thomas that he never got?

Hmm, let's see . . . Oh, it's jumbled up. I want to sit down and write about it myself sometime if I can recall it. I wish I'd kept notes at the time. I could have had the most extraordinary notes on those few years. Agh! Incredible what went down.

Big problem is, they were people that were living something and didn't have the sense of potential history and . . .

Yeah. And thinking that might have hurt it a little bit, take away from the naturalness of it.

Eric told me that during this "super hostile" period there was a great feeling that nobody was able to say anything to Dylan . . . you were all in awe of him. You couldn't criticize him. You couldn't tell him to lay off. Eric remembers that Dylan attacked you in some way and Eric said, "Hey, lay off!" and Dylan turned around and started yelling at Eric, "What do you want me to talk about? I buy you wine. I try to be your friend. You want me to talk about the rats in the river, the sunrise over the Hudson? What else is there to talk about?" Something like that. Do you remember that?

Vaguely. Yeah. I remember statements like that. That's funny.

Anything else you can add to this whole picture.

No, just certain things. There was one time when I was able to block his outrage at everything. One day he walked in and sat down. He was real drunk. He said, "I tell you what. Recite me about three of your latest songs, 'cause that's definitely what one of my songs is worth, so give me about three of your songs and I'll give you one of mine," his being "Visions of Johanna" at that point, which he was totally in love with as one of his greatest works. So he sang to me or recited to me "Visions of Johanna" and luckily I'd just come back from England and had just written "The Crucifixion."

So, at first, I said, "The Flower Lady," and he said, normally he would have said, "Oh, that's bullshit" and this and that and then he sort of pulled back and all that. Then he said, "Well, that's the right idea, that's the right direction." And then I did some regular song and he said that was nice and then I did "Crucifixion" and he was, I think it sort of really got to him and I mean he just couldn't say anything and the attack was totally played out. Luckily for me. I don't know. It was a great time and it's a . . . I hope no negative feeling came out of the Michael Thomas article because it wasn't meant that way. Man, it was a much more thrilling and exciting and energetic time than just that aspect, which is what it sort of became toward the end when the arrogance and the defensive thing came so much into play.

That arrogance and defensive thing, this was just before the real split to Woodstock?

Yeah. Right before the accident was the high point of it, yeah. I mean, he got especially more into that.

What was some of this high-energy thing like, some of the better memories you have of . . . some of the more positive . . . ?

I don't even remember. I mean, just an endless series of great conversations. I don't remember what they were about—what was said—it was just real rapid talk. It was speed trips, huge speed trips. I mean, we were running up to—I forget what was it there? Arthur's discotheque, laughing at all the people there and meeting Marlon Brando one night in some apartment uptown. Always the singing—singing all the time and starting to travel around the country, getting to England . . . and writing all the time. Everybody was very, totally creative . . . I mean, Bob Dylan came up to the house and he said, "I want you to hear my new song." And he sat down and sang "Mr. Tambourine Man," you know, in an empty living room.

Yeah, where were you living then?

On Bleecker Street. I mean, what can you do? What can you say? It's so outrageous to have something like that happen.

Did he talk about "Tambourine Man"?

No. He just . . . sang it. I sat down when he made his third album, I listened to him. It was the final version in which he really softened up on the "Hattie Carroll" song. "That's the one I really like," he said. I played him my first record on Elektra—[*All the News That's Fit to Sing*]—and he sat down and he said, "I like the Woody Guthrie song best." He thought the record was too cluttered with guitar work, you know . . . I mean, just a lot of things . . .

Getting back to Bob Neuwirth, I want to explore a little bit what effect, what influence he may have had on Dylan?

It's hard to say. I can't say much about it because I didn't know him directly. A lot of people knew him directly before in Boston, but I didn't, so I can't tell about what he was like before I met him. I just knew him when he was, like, Dylan's road manager and buddy and guy he hung out with. He was . . . they were like twins almost in terms of personality, and Bob Neuwirth was a very clever, very funny man, as was Dylan, so it's hard to say who was doing what.

Right.

And in the very old days Dylan was more open to people in general, but that was before he was hit by the deluge, you know . . .

This was the folk rock before the electric . . .

Even before that even, before the "folk" fame happened when he was just a guy, sort of known but not really. I mean, at first he was not as threatened by people and wasn't as pressured by people, and I'm sure with every passing day the pressure built.

Right. Neuwirth has been described to me as being a guy with a "very negative attitude, an attitude filled with pride and ego," who said, "Don't take shit, man."

Yeah.

"You gotta be on top, man," that kind of thing.

Yeah that's probably . . .

He was affecting Dylan with it.

Like I said, I didn't know him that well to say he was affecting Dylan. That's quite possible. Quite possible. But he was also very, very clever and very funny and some form of frustrated artist, and there's no reason why he couldn't have been writing songs better than most of the songwriters.

Really?

Yeah. He was a very bright guy.

Why wasn't he? You have any idea?

I don't know. I mean, I assume in back of [it] all is a super huge insecurity problem in both guys, but sitting there at the table you wouldn't . . . Neuwirth could conceivably have been every bit as good a writer as Dylan was, just by the way they were talking. He was as fast [as] or faster than Dylan was, you know, and, I mean, when he was on, he was invulnerable.

Right.

Just invulnerable. He was the court wit. He really was.

Do you remember any of it?

Nope. No, not one. (*laughs*)

But he was the court wit?

Yeah, he really was.

More than Bobby was?

Yeah. Bobby was the king. Bobby was the king and Neuwirth was the court wit.

There was also a bit I want to talk about, the whole freaky scene with Neuwirth and Joan Baez and Dylan.

I don't know about that at all. You tell *me*. What was it?

Well, I can't even use it in the book but it was just something I wanted to explore, just so I have it in the back of my head what the thing was like. God, it seems it was a wild, sexy whole crowd. It involved Fariña.

Yeah, I vaguely heard stuff like that, yeah.

And that Bobby, that Joan was a lesbian . . . this whole . . . and that after the accident he apparently felt that everybody had taken advantage of him, that everybody fucked him up badly. Much of it is stuff I won't use.

Yeah.

Somebody said that part of this "hip mean"—

What kind of a book is this going to be?

A critical biography, which sounds rather pretentious, especially since Al Gross-man won't let me quote the lyrics. Basically, a biography—a good solid job. I want to explain who the man is, how he got that way.

Did you ever meet him?

No! I'm working on that end of the story. [I'll] get to Bobby and Grossman last after I talk to everyone around.

Are there a lot of books being thought of now or . . . ?

I know of people writing books, but I'm the only one with a contract, money up front.

Yeah. Do you have any kind of background in this kind of stuff?

I've been into rock all my life.

Yeah.

Basically that's it.

Yeah.

And I'm a professional writer and someone said, "Hey, how about a book on Bobby Dylan?"

Yeah.

Uh, "Positively 4th Street"—what significance does that have for you?

I don't know. Everybody wondered who it was about, you know, right when it came out. I was . . . I mean, at that point I think I started to take a very musical and commercial view of Dylan. After "Like a Rolling Stone," I thought—and on an even deeper [level]—not only is this one of the greatest writers that ever lived and everything I always thought from the beginning . . . First time I heard his two songs, I knew at that second—at some party or someplace he sang a couple of songs which I don't think he recorded—I said, "This guy, he's it—he's the best writer, the best singer, I've ever heard." I just wondered what the future had in store for him, you know? Extraordinary.

Was there a feeling that this was the guy that was really going to make it?

Yes and no. That, and there was a very widespread feeling that he couldn't possibly because he was too crazy, and his voice was too raspy that the public would never buy that kind of voice. Period. The middle class here would never go for that.

Getting back to [a] somewhat earlier period, talk about the meetings in the *Broadside* office. How you'd all come in [and] swap songs with each other. Tell me about some of it. What was it like?

Well, we'd be just sitting, about fifteen people sitting in a room about this size on couches and Gordon serving coffee and doughnuts and just going around and 'round singing songs. Everybody would sing about two or three new songs they had, and I forget what Dylan sang. I think it was, like, "Masters of War" or something. I forget.

What was the reaction to Dylan's stuff?

Well, he was one of the boys there, you know.

Nothing special at that point?

Well, I mean, everybody knew he was special.

Yeah but . . .

No big applause or anything like that.

What about his reaction to your stuff, for example, or other people's material? What was he like?

He was sort of noncommittal to my stuff. I don't know. He never said much about my stuff. I mean he'd laugh at some of the political satire stuff in the old days. I mean there was one show, way back when, where Seeger and Dylan and myself all sang, and he did "Hard Rain's A-Gonna Fall" and I did "Talking Cuban Crisis," which he really liked—I mean, he walked up and said it was a really funny song and it's hard to say. I sang "Changes" to him, which was one of my best songs. I sang to him and Neuwirth in my room on Bleecker Street, and he just sort of sneered and said, "Everybody wants to be a poet." And Neuwirth laughed and kind of walked out. You know, that kind of thing

Really?

Yeah.

Did he ever talk about the stuff he was writing instead of just playing it, even in those early days?

No, no. Didn't ever talk about what he wrote. Hated to talk about his work, hated to have his work discussed, I mean, like, analyzed, hated that.

Still does.

Still does, yeah. Always resented it.

Did he make a habit of putting down other people's work?

No. That was only at a couple of drunken evenings. He didn't spend his time doing that. I mean, that just came out, and they sort [of] sensationalized him a bit.

Those early protest songs, those early topical protest songs, he told an interviewer—it may have been Nat Hentoff—that he didn't really mean any of them, that it was just his way of getting in or getting published at *Broadside*, although you have said he really was political. Dave Van Ronk said, "Bullshit, he did mean it."

Oh yeah, definitely. He meant it as far as I can tell. Obviously meant it.

There was this whole big leftist political scene there with Terri and Dave and the whole crowd and Bobby really fit into this?

Well, I don't know if he really fit—

Or not fit in, but his head was there at that point?

At one point he definitely was, yeah, a left-winger, believe me.

. . . "man to man rapping left winger who would never show up in court as such" . . . I hate that phrase. It was all done by those headline writers that I hate to even use it.

Yeah but, I mean, he was, yeah; he was a radical. Of course he was, for a while.

You're also quoted as saying that it was very difficult to be a writer after Dylan. "You'd have to literally be forged in his mold because he was so striking," is the way Thomas quoted you.

After Dylan, if you were like twelve years old or something or fifteen years old . . .

What—you said Dave Blue got trapped into this.

Yeah. Some people who weren't really writers or thought about being writers were completely overwhelmed—Dylan's personality was so strong it completely captivated them, and it's become very difficult to shake off. There's a lot of people like that today. I mean, a lot of people.

What you're basically talking about is the kids who came along after, like Dave Blue, like Eric Andersen.

Yeah.

You're not talking about yourself or Dave Van Ronk or Tom Paxton?

Right. Except we were all caught in it anyway, but we were lucky to have started out forming our creative processes in such a way as to not be a slave to it.

Right. You said also that you were obsessed with him for three years because he was a genius . . . that his songwriting was pure genius, that you felt at one point it was really Shakespearean.

Yeah.

Talk about some of that. What was the feeling?

Well, from the beginning I thought he was great and with every succeeding album up to *Highway 61,* I'd get his new album—with an increasing amount of sort of secret fear, you know—saying, "My god, what's he going to do next? Can't possible top that," you know, and *Highway 61* was just the end of it all. I put that record on and listened to it once and I just laughed. "That's just ridiculous." I just walked away and didn't listen to it again.

Why ridiculous?

It was just so good. The writing was so rich. I just couldn't believe it.

What's your assessment of after that?

Well, after that on a straight literary level I don't care for his writings much. I mean, other things happened. It became more pleasant. He tried to sing more on a straight musical level and stuff and the country thing and everything, which is all fine, but it's not why I stood in awe of Bob Dylan—because he was a good country singer. There's lots of good country singers. I mean, at that point, which is the point, right before *Blonde on Blonde,* right before the accident when he was—but I didn't finish my train of thought: I started to look at Dylan, at that one early period after "Like a Rolling Stone," as doing popular music, as doing what he was doing lyrically. I thought it was exciting and good music, you know, and I thought there's no end to what he can do now. I thought then that he would become Elvis Presley. I mean on that level of having made this incredible contribution of lyrics, I thought he could now become Elvis Presley. Meaning he would essentially and physically be able to sum up young America and rural America and put out fifteen gold records in a row. Meaning fifteen produced, musical, exciting, hit singles all with great lyrics and thereby revolutionize the music business. That was my vision. My first reaction when "Positively 4th Street" came out was total disappointment. I said, "Oh no, that's not a single at all! What are you trying to do? You're trying to blow it." It was a hit anyway, but I thought it was a disastrous thing to do and then they put out "Please Crawl Out Your Window" and stuff like that and they literally took him off the air. He went from having achieved total air play and that possible Elvis niche—he just completely—he threw it all away.

What happened?

I don't know what happened. I have no idea what happened.

You said, the last time you saw him . . .

The last time I saw him he was having his picture taken by that photographer—I forget his name.

Dan Kramer.

No, Dave . . . you know . . .

Oh! I know who you mean.

And Dave and I and Dylan were there and he was taking these pictures and he was really excited about—

Dave Cohen?

Yeah, and he was real excited about this new single, you know, which was "Sooner or Later One of Us Must Know," before *Blonde on Blonde* came out, and he was saying to David, "Well, this is the one I've been waiting to make for years" and "This is the record," you know, and so he played it and said, "What do you think?" And I said, "Well, it's okay," you know, and he said, "*What?* What do you mean?" He said, "I'll play it again." He played it again, said, "What do you think?" I said, "Well, the sacrilege thing, that's okay, but it's not going to be a hit," which was sacrilegious to say to him at that point, really stepping on it, you know? And he said, "What do you mean it's not going to be a hit? That's crazy, it's a great song." This and that, you know, and then we all got in the limousine, and he said, "Get out. Get out of here."

You mean, get out of the car?

Literally, yeah. Because he wasn't used to being criticized.

Yeah.

And I said it's on the level I was thinking, which was, Dylan was Elvis.

You think he could have pulled that off?

I think he definitely could have pulled it off.

Well, what happened? You have any idea?

I don't know. I have no idea what the circumstances—

Grossman? Columbia? His own head? Any idea?

Any one of those or combinations thereof, you know, and if he ever talks about it, he might say at that point it wasn't important or that it never even occurred to him it or he didn't want that.

Well, did you get the feeling he did want that?

My feeling was at the time was, yes, he did want that.

Yeah, it's the feeling of everyone I've talked to.

Yeah. That one flash, that one moment he suddenly could've done something on a whole other level higher than . . .

Was there ever a feeling that the Beatles got in his way?

I don't know about got in his way. I mean, that's what happened. Dylan wrote the lyrics and the Beatles captured that mass music, but there was no reason why Dylan, with a straighter head, couldn't have done an equivalent thing to the Beatles, musically. He could have done something, too, to have matched it. But he just . . . it was thrown away. It was silly. Maybe . . . but it's too late now.

Oh, you were going to say something?

I was going to say maybe he could do it now but it's not important if he does it now. It's just like that was the moment—that rare moment that won't ever happen again at that level.

Yeah.

I think actually it was "Help" that was number one and "Like a Rolling Stone" that was number two. I think "Help" actually stopped it from becoming number one but then it all fell apart anyway.

You mean the accident and the whole . . . ?

Everything. Everything just collapsed.

What were some of the factors that made it all fall apart?

I don't know.

And you've had no contact with him since then?

I haven't seen him since then. Except I hear he's very friendly. He's seen David and Eric and he said some very nice things about me and . . .

Yeah, he's back around town looking to connect . . .

He's back around town, very friendly and warm. He said to David and Eric, "Well, it's Ochs's thing now. He can have it now if he wants it."

He said what?

He said, "Ochs can have it now if he wants it."

Was there any period where there was a feeling of competition between the two of you?

Maybe a little bit. The one time he came closest to it was when he made his fourth album and stopped being political. I was then becoming super political and we were both at Newport in 1964 and I got a huge reaction there and there was a lot of good talk about me for that period of time right before rock and roll became . . . and then there were articles in *Broadside* saying, "Dylan is a sellout and Ochs is the future," is what they were saying. At which point I wrote some articles defending Dylan, saying that the main thing was that Dylan's level of writing keeps improving, which it was.

Yeah, the articles in *Broadside* or was it *Sing Out!* that . . . Did *Sing Out!* have any articles or was it *Broadside* mostly?

It was mostly *Broadside*. *Sing Out!* had more general stuff, but there were a couple of articles in *Broadside* that were all about that kind of stuff. And that was a slight general feeling on the political level. That was right before rock and right before drugs.

Yeah. There's another major theme that comes in here. At least, Eric brought it up. Back in October '66, you were reported as saying you didn't know if "Dylan could get on the stage a year from now" because "he's gotten inside so many people's heads and so many screwed-up people in America and death is such a part of the American scene . . ."

Right.

The Kennedy assassination is a big part of the story. What effect did the assassination have on Dylan?

I don't know.

Right after the assassination Dylan moved away from the protest song. Eric seems to feel that the assassination, the reality of what Johnson was doing, really was beginning to sink in. Things had started getting really weird, and Dylan began to get the feeling, maybe down in his gut, maybe subconsciously, that he was out front, and it was possible he was next.

That's quite possible.

Did you get any of this feeling at that point?

Oh yeah. I was all done with it. Yeah, that feeling was everywhere. I was almost destroyed by that very same feeling.

Tell me about some of it? Can you?

Well, it just robbed your spirit when you're sticking your neck out like that and you're a very public figure and you're political and obviously the bad guys are on the loose and they're going to kill anybody that gets too close to the seat of power. It's only common sense, you know?

Right. Did Bob ever talk about this?

He never talked about it. But that's good conjecture on the part of Eric. It's logical.

Right afterwards was Bob's speech before the Emergency Civil Liberties Committee in which he was accused of saying, "Oswald did a great thing for counterculture." Right?

Yeah.

Did Bob talk about that at all? As part of this whole feeling of freaking out that was going down.

No. Not to me.

Oh, one other thing. What was Bob's reaction out front, on the surface, to the charge that he had sold out?

Cynical jokes . . .

Like what?

I couldn't remember them but all just cynical jokes.

Eric said he was heading for rock even before the Beatles came along, that he wanted to get out there like Presley, that he was moving in this direction.

That's my assumption about everybody. I mean, he wouldn't say that to us. That's a good guess.

RAMBLIN' JACK ELLIOTT

Bobby was very erratic. Very uneven, very erratic. A great thing about Bobby that was so exciting is that he's singing his own songs, and he's doing a thing like he's sounding like he knows what he's talking about, and the words that he used to make the images that he used for poetry and the musical ideas and all that combined to make a fabric of something which was, even though it was very rough, was like a diamond in the rough.

A RAMBLING INTERVIEW WITH RAMBLIN' JACK ELLIOTT. At the time of the interview Jack lived in California but was in New York for a performance—at the Gaslight, a club in Greenwich Village.

He was born Elliot Adnopoz, the son of a successful doctor, and like Dylan, couldn't see himself taking on the "family business." Jack Elliott became Woody Guthrie's protégé in 1951, knocking around the country with him, playing music wherever people wanted to hear the Okie folk singer/songwriter. He imitated Guthrie's music and style and became known as the son of Woody Guthrie. And in his first few months in New York, playing with Elliott at folk clubs, Dylan began to absorb some of Elliott's tricks and mannerisms. Folkies began describing Dylan as the son of Jack Elliott and the grandson of Woody Guthrie.

Bob dug [Hank Williams] back in high school. Did you ever talk about [him]?
I've known that he dug Hank Williams. I've never even dug Hank Williams. I thought Hank Williams was a commercial, insincere-sounding person. [Dylan] was, when I met him, doing a completely roughshod Woody Guthrie–style thing, and I was out of it. I wasn't wearing dirty Levi's anymore. I was wearing, like, clean, neatly pressed, black Western pants and my Frank Sinatra shirt, I used to call it, which was like a striped kind of jazzy shirt. And I'd wear cowboy shirts and I wore a cowboy hat

because it was part of my style, but I wasn't sure whether I should really keep on. I could have thrown away the cowboy hat and start wearing a neat suit, and there were so-called folk singers around [who] were doing it that way. And it was the Kingston Trio that were, like, totally, completely commercial—nothing like a real folk artist at all. Total shits. I met them later, and they're really nice guys.

Yeah, but you know, musically, like, I know—

Here's these guys can't even play a fucking thing on a guitar, and they're making millions of dollars doing this travesty. I hated that. Here I'm stumbling along at a hundred a week, you know, singing the good stuff. These very poor people were really, really smart people who know where it's at.

Bobby was working along these lines. I mean, Bobby was taking whatever came his way.

Yeah, well, he didn't have those fans who saw Woody—say. I met a lot of people that remembered Woody and knew what he stood for. Woody's songs meant something to those people, and I appreciated the importance of that. You know, I didn't grow up in those days, but I'd met enough people who lived through the Dust Bowl days, to feel that experience and those people. And I liked what Woody had to say. I didn't imagine that somebody would come along like Bob Dylan and take Woody's style and write stuff about today. And I thought, well, here I was with Woody. I had all the opportunity in the world to learn anything I wanted to learn from him. And last night—Bobby composed [a song] that was based on a song he made up the other night on stage at the Gaslight.

It's not on paper, but he got it on tape. I'm gratified to have recognition and—but it doesn't thrill me at all to get reviews in the paper. But this song is the greatest kind of recognition or badge anybody ever did or wrote about me or for me, and Kris Kristofferson wrote a song about me, and Johnny Cash wrote a song about me.

Oh really?

The Cash song is "Ramblin' Jack, Ramblin' Jack, when are you ever goin' to get to ramblin' back. Your little lady's in a family way, you better ramble on back today." Sounded cute.

That's great. (*laughs*) What's the thing that Neuwirth did for you?

Neuwirth did an epic poem. It's, like, an hour long, man. And it tells my whole life story, and it says things I never knew were true. But it's all true and it's all poetic and it's all crazy and it's all wonderful and it's done with such a great feeling and he did it live onstage and I was running frantically around looking for a tape recorder. And it's the same way with me. To this day, I can't sit down at a typewriter or write a song. But I've made up songs in front of audiences, on my feet, lots of times. Hundreds of them, and forgotten, and there was no tape recorder. I've made up millions of dollars' worth of songs and thrown them up in the air. I should have somebody with me every minute with a tape recorder. Three or four of them going at all times and, like, have twenty-five blank tapes, ready to use.

But anyway, you were aware that Bobby was writing about you at this time, back in '61. Like, songs of Woody. Did he play this for Woody at the places you've been to?

I don't remember if I ever was present when he sang to him personally. And I was also a little bit burned because this was just the same god-damned song that I could have and should have wrote, you know?

I stopped playing the harmonica because I didn't want to clash with him and make it seem competitive—well, he's playing exactly—a lot of Jack Elliott harmonica. It was a lot of Woody Guthrie and it was a lot of other things too. But he's gotten so good at it that I don't think I could touch him on harmonica now.

Everything he did, like things that I thought were square and corny and he just dug everything that I was doing and he saw the beauty of it, and he just latched on to it and magnified it. Glamorized it. He, like, wore dirty Levi's, dirty old work shirt for two years. And then he started going off into really beautiful clothes and started a whole style himself. Where I was just wearing Western clothes all the time.

Were you still close to him those few years later as he started to make it? What did happen to your relationship?

He went away to Europe, man. Then he came back, and I bumped into him on the street and I saw him, and he was wearing high-heeled shoes.

Yeah, the high-heeled boots.

Yeah, high-heeled boots, the Spanish thing; And I didn't recognize him because he was taller, and I walked up to him, looked at him, "Yeah. Hi. Hey, Bob—I didn't recognize you with them boots on. How you doing?" And he said, "I just back from France, man," and says, "I met a singer over in Paris, man. He's the greatest singer in the world. His name is Charles Aznavour, and boy, he's great, man." And then I heard him and I thought he was good, but I wasn't flipped out by it. They were going to a recording session that day, and I fell in a car with him and we drove uptown.

What album were they making? Any idea what the session was?

I know that it was before the album which had "Tambourine Man" on it. I think it was only his second or third album. *Another Side of Bob Dylan.* And it might have been that album.

Right after that was *Bringing It All Back Home.*

Or it might have been *Bringing It All Back Home*—yeah, it must have been *Bringing It All Back Home,* but he was going to do "Tambourine Man," and he asked me to do it with him. He just said, "Hey, Jack, come here. Sing a song with me." And I jumped up, and he was doing a lot of songs that he'd just written the night before, it seemed. And they were all on these typewritten sheets of paper, and he just had them propped up on a music stand and was reading them, you know. And, you know, he didn't seem like he rehearsed them.

Really?

He was just, bang, just reading them cold. And that was it. I said okay, "What song you want to do here?" He says, "It's 'Tambourine Man.'" Oh, "Tambourine Man." Well, a girlfriend of mine was nuts about this song, because she knew Bobby and she was very fond of him and, like, crazy about that song. And she wrote the words out for me even, and I never learned them, right? Just lazy. I had the words for like three or four months. And I never learned them. I ask, "You got the words?" He says, "No. I know this one." Oh, yeah, goddamn. I didn't know it actually. I was embarrassed then because I could have known it. "Well, that's okay," he says. "Just fake around with it. See what you can do with it." I said, "Okay, let's go." So we started it off and I knew the first verse and then we got to the second or third verse and I started fucking up. I didn't know the words anymore. I was just humming.

Oh, that's too bad. You would have fit on that album, with that groove. Jesus.

Yeah, it would have been great, man. I would have loved it. But that's where I was. I was just too lazy to learn the song and so serves me right. Anyway, they couldn't use it, because it didn't sound very good. But they didn't throw it away. Oh no. A friend of mine out in California got hold of that tape and he taught it to a group that he was managing, an unknown group called the Byrds. And they learned it off of that tape. Made a million dollars off it.

Yeah. (*laughs*) Boy, did they. They also helped make Bobby a little bit more.

Yeah. And that's my version. (*laughs*)

What was your relationship—I mean, back when he was recording?

It was, "Hey Jack, come here and sing a song with me." And we're still kind of pals. I was just there, carrying in some bottles of wine, [to] help make him feel groovy. I was like one of two or three other friends that were there in the room. Victor Maymudes was there. He was his road manager. I wasn't getting along too good with Victor because he'd run off with my wife at one point there. And I was pissed off at him for about a year or so. And this was the first time that Victor and I were together since he went off with my wife. There was no big hostility thing going on. We were, like, tolerating each other. And after a little while he stopped hanging out with Patty and was hanging out all the time with Dylan. And he ended up just leaving her and traveling all around the world with Dylan. He was a very good road manager. He takes care of business.

I met some guy who was on one of the road trips. He said he was stoned all the time—

Oh, he was. He was one of the most stoned people I've ever met, man.

He just messed up a lot. In fact he, they, had to cancel a Los Angeles gig for Dylan because they got there a day late. They just didn't show up.

Is that right? At one point, Victor was a big fan of mine. He liked to hang out with me before Dylan ever was around. I met Victor in Topanga, when I went out there with Woody back in '53. He was trying to learn how to play the guitar, but he couldn't play the guitar worth a fuck and he got no sense of rhythm, and he has no voice and no sense of tone. He'd say, "I'm not musical." But he liked to be around the folk scene. He was always after me to show him how to play some things on the guitar. I never bothered to do it very much because I didn't think he had any talent, right?

You were saying—

That's why some of the best road managers are this type of person who is a guy who was a frustrated, would-be musician, but hasn't got the ability or the talent to do it, but wants to be close to it and be with somebody that's doing it. I've got a guy now I've known for a couple of years, and he's like sort of in the same bag, and he's just become a record executive or a record producer. He really wanted to be the producer of my record and get his name on it too. But all he'd do is light cigarettes and hang around.

If he's got a tin ear, how can he produce the record?

Well, this guy hasn't got a tin ear. He's much more musical than Victor. But he's not a singer. He's not an entertainer, he's an agent, and he's been doing the agent-type things and getting me gigs. But he's stoned all the time, like Victor, and he fucks up. Every time he promises to be some-where sometime, he's never there. But he's a good cat, and he, like, loves me and he's always like a loyal friend.

Good guy to have around.

He keeps calling me up now, with gigs for me.

What does kind of help for Bobby—to carry the wine and to get him in the mood, like that?

As a matter of fact, the carrying-the-wine thing wasn't my idea of my function there, but that was something that was described in that story in the *New Yorker*—

Was that the Hentoff piece?

Yeah. I felt pretty pissed off with Nat Hentoff, because he painted the thing like I was just one of the hulking lackeys that came in to carry wine. That's all I knew how to do, that's all I was.

That's right. I remember that now.

And I go, "You son of a bitch, Nat Hentoff." I thought he knew me better than that.

Well, he should have.

He wrote me a letter one time. He was writing a story about Alan Lomax, and he wanted to interview or get people's opinions of—any anecdotes about Alan Lomax. And I wrote him a letter and I sent him some anec-dotes. Everything I could think of that would be of use to him in his article. Because I was a good friend of Alan Lomax. But I never have actually met Hentoff face-to-face. I always used to think Nat Hentoff was hipper than that, though. But I really enjoyed hanging out with old-time Dylan, and I'm his biggest fan, man, and I'll be his groupie.

The thing that you all were doing was setting him up in a mood to a great extent.

Sure. All artists are great audiences, and the best actors I've known are always the best audience too.

Do you find you need your friends around to put you in the mood for making records?

Yes. We all need that.

The other night when I saw you with some of the others it was—the feeling is that they helped bring more out of you if there are friends—

Well, I felt absolutely dead at the beginning of that evening. This last gig at the Gaslight, I really have enjoyed it. It's one of the best gigs I've ever done.

Why was it so great?

Because that was the most satisfying love trip I've ever had for singing in a club. Because in spite of having no sleep, I believe in being professional, to treat my body like an athlete. Get a lot of sleep, and I like to eat steak sometimes, you know. And I like to be in a good mood before I go on, and I don't like to talk to anybody backstage before I go on sometimes.

Get yourself set to perform.

I've got to really get in the mood and be in shape to go onstage. And I have my own little way about doing it and I'm very serious about it, what I do to get in the mood to go onstage. So, onstage, it looks very loose and looks like I'm totally unprepared to go on the stage, and sometimes, I almost am.

It's kind of risky and right on the edge. It's what makes it real. One of the no-no's is that I won't be so wasted, but Dylan and cats like him—and he picked it up from all these folk singers and all these guys like, say, Kristofferson—being wasted is part of it. Sometimes you do your best singing when you're really wasted. Some of the best singing I've ever done is, like, after a long trip, when you've been driving for days and days, you're all wasted, worn out, exhausted, you know? And you finally get where you're going and get to this friend's house and it's about three o'clock in the morning and you're sitting around with coffee, you're sitting around a kitchen, and it's coffee and cigarette butts everywhere, and you're singing. Picking. And that's when your voice really gets groovy, you know?

But some of the best performances I've ever done were unplanned and they were accidents, and they were just happenings with people. But it's unprofessional and sort of unreliable to count on something like that. And it means there's going to be—law of averages—there's going to be a night coming up where you're going to be really bad. And Shelton used to put me down for being that way. He used to come in and he'd always catch me on a bad night, when I wasn't good. Or he'd come in right after I did a fantastically good set on some evening, and then that crowd had left and then did another set and it wasn't very good.

He rarely ever saw me when I was really good. And so, a lot of times when he'd write about me he'd say, "Elliott is capable of being very good at times, and he's also very bad at times, and is a very up and down performer." He'd always mention that. And that is true, but I don't think it's very tactful of him. And then he'd sing Bobby's praises to the fucking world about his great talent . . .

But Bobby was also very uneven at that time.

Bobby was very erratic. Very uneven, very erratic. A great thing about Bobby that was so exciting is that he's singing his own songs, and he's doing a thing like he's sounding like he knows what he's talking about, and the words that he used to make the images that he used for poetry and the musical ideas and all that combined to make a fabric of something which was, even though it was very rough, was like a diamond in the rough. And you know that this kid has got a fantastic brain, you know? To be able to think and know that way. And here we are, we're seeing it in the flesh. So, that was the thing that excited me and I just knew this cat is going to be a matinee idol in about, I don't know, four or five years. He's going to be like Elvis Presley.

Yeah.

And I thought, make it, baby. Because I didn't dig Elvis Presley at all, you know? Why should a guy like Elvis Presley make a million dollars when you can have guys like Bob Dylan making a million dollars, and it's much more real?

Did Dylan ever talk about making it that big? Or making it big at all? Did he ever talk about his goals in any way?

As a matter of fact, he talked about it, but right offhand I can think of one conversation where he talked about the subject of himself as a career. And this was perhaps a lot of phony signifying, but that's cool, too, you know, because I knew that maybe it was because he felt guilty he was starting to make it, and I was still struggling along, the main guy he learned from. I think only his first record was out, and I met him on the street corner one day in front of O. Henry's. And I bumped into him on the street and he says, "I'm going to leave town. I'm going to move up to Woodstock and just paint. I'm going to give up this folk music. I've got to get out of this folk music business. It's phony, it's a drag. I don't want to be a folk singer. Terrible people. I don't dig it. I'm going to live out in the country and I'm going to paint."

(*laughs*) What was your reaction to that?

I said, "Okay, groovy. I'd like to see what kind of paint that's coming out." (*laughs*) I don't remember what I said, but, you know, that's what I thought, like, what's the matter? You get scared? Don't chicken out now. You're starting to make it.

Did you say this to him?

No. I don't think it's necessary to say anything because whatever is going to happen is going to happen anyway. He's more like stepping on my shoulders and pushing me down to get on top and all that stuff. Then he's saying, like, "Oh shit, this is a rat race, and I don't like it, I'm not even going to do it."

Was there any feeling of that, on his part, that he was—

See, all along, I think he's a little bit too paranoid about me. But he's a very paranoid kid, and I understand that, and I know it, because I've seen him be that way all along. I thought, you know, he's got it. It's in the bag—but I'm the same way, too, really. When you look at it from the inside out, all you see is a lot of greedy people are after you.

Yeah.

And he had a lot of friends that later on, they'd come to him and say, "Hey." You know, "Hi, remember me? You stayed at my place. I helped you out. I fed you. Remember that? I helped you," you know. So many people are always doing that, man, and come rushing at you with their eyes all aglitter.

They were grabbing at—

Yeah. And they don't mean any harm. They're not bad people, they're just normal, everyday people.

But they're a real scary kind of thing.

But anybody that's just a regular person. They were just trying to be decent, but now it's fame, hotels, and now they say, "Hi, remember me?"

How would you assess your influence on Bobby? How did you affect him?

Well, he probably saw, like, where not to fuck up and, you know—first of all, he probably dug me like a hero when he didn't know me personally. He just knew my records and my reputation and my story. I was a cat that lived with Woody and I traveled with Woody and I was in Europe, bumming around, doing all that stuff. So, I was the king; I was the legend, and he was following in my footsteps a little bit. But he had more freedom than I had, to be crazy or be different or be new. Like, I was locked into my old character—I was already set—well, you're never locked in. You're always free. But I didn't know that then. Yeah. And he—I learned a lot from him. I still am. And I would like to see him very much. I've always been very much wanting to get together with him if he would like to get together.

One of the last times—

Like I went over to his house a few days ago, and I wouldn't have even had the nerve to do that, but you know, last couple of years I've seen him, I never quite know for sure if he really likes me or if he's just being polite because, you know . . . I saw him when he was on his way to Australia. And he was very strange toward me, but he was being kind of strange at that time anyway. He was very, very nervous.

Yeah, he was also very high. I'm told he was on speed, as were all [the] people that were with him at the time.

Mm-hmm. So, I understood. It might have just been the speed. We had a conversation that lasted about one minute. "How you doing?" "I'm just fine, you know. Just played a gig at the Ash Grove. I'm playing some places around." He says, "Want a cookie?" We're in the kitchen. Somebody was eating a delicious ham sandwich. I could smell it from across the kitchen. Icebox-raid moment. He had a cookie, box of cookies. Ginger snaps. So, he gave me a cookie. Says, "Have a cookie." Said, "Are you hungry?" I said yeah. All right, he said, "Are you hungry?" I said yeah. He says, "Have a cookie." I had a cookie. Good cookie. He says, "Are you very hungry?" I said yeah. He says, "Have two cookies." And he gave me two cookies.

(laughs) Some conversation.

Fantastic sense of humor always. Never lets up.

Last time you saw him?

That was the whole conversation. Then he dove out of there. I said, "Where are you going now?" He says, "We're going to Hawaii." Hawaii. Great, man. Wow. I always wanted to go to Hawaii. When are you coming back? Then he says, "I'm going to Australia." Australia. Australia's the first place I ever wanted to go outside of America.

Really?

I read two geography books about Australia when I was a kid. I wanted to go see it because it was like the old West.

And is this the last time you saw Bobby?

No, that's not the last time.

He was married to Sara then.

Mm-hmm. I saw him right after they got married. I said, "Hi, congratulations." He says, "What for?" I said, "I heard you got married." He says, "I didn't get married." I said, "Oh, wow, I thought you got married." I was embarrassed. I said, "You didn't get married?" Oh. "No," he says. "I didn't get married." Oh. He says, "If I got married, you'd be the first person I'd tell." Always joking around that way, you know.

What happened when you knocked on the door the other day?

Oh, he wasn't home. The maid was there. So, she was a little bit freaked out by these two guys with cowboy hats on, you know. I said, "Just tell him Jack Elliott came by and said hello." And then we left.

What—how did fame affect Bobby? You know, as he really began to make it, he changed where, apparently, he began to get pretty mean around that time.

Oh, yeah, he was very quick, sarcastic and fast, and he dealt with people like a boxer, you know. Parrying their blows and their remarks and always skipping out in a hurry.

Yeah.

Which is good. I admired his style and learned a bit from it, although I haven't had to copy it, because my style works for me too. I've always been more open and just plain old straight with people. Which always ends up a drag and regrettable and I think, no, I should do it more like Dylan. You know, a lot of these people, they just want to hang on to you and bore you to fucking smithereens, man. It's just an energy drain. They think just because they own a record of yours, or that they clapped when they came to see you—they think they own you, body and soul. Fans and groupies are—can be—destructive if you let them. So, you just have to learn how to handle them. They're drunk. The excitement of seeing you. So, you know, you can't blame people for doing it, and if you lead them on, or if you're open at all, they're going to come in the door, so you got to learn how to keep your hand on the door. You have to have security measures. The bigger you get, the more protection you need. Then knowing Dylan now, how paranoid he is, too, that he needed it more than I did, not just because of his bigness but because of his paranoia.

How did you get involved with Neuwirth?

I met Bob Neuwirth way, way back in Boston when he was just a young kid—in Cambridge, And I saw one movie he made; it was the worst movie I've ever seen in my life. It was so sloppy and messy, and I couldn't understand a lot of it, and I wondered if he really knew what he was trying to say and do.

The reason I ask how you got involved with Neuwirth is that he was part of Bob's entourage for at least a year or so. Back when he was a kind of road manager. He was also part of the whole entourage here in the Village and—

The thing about Neuwirth is, opposed to other road managers, guys like Victor, Victor is more, I think, more like a valet and buddy to Bobby, or was—I think Bobby learned and picked up things from Neuwirth that he couldn't from Victor—that I wouldn't have even bothered to want to do, but—

Like what?

I saw a thing where Bobby's speech pattern was affected by Victor, just his—his style of talking is one of the most way-out, far-out style of talking, that it's affected a lot of other people. Including myself, too, and I've picked up a lot from Dylan's speech pattern, and some of that was originally from Victor.

Yeah.

Victor has some very original—he's got a way of speaking which is purely him. And Bobby must have dug it and he picked up on it, you know, things like saying "Hey." That's Victor. "Hey."

Yeah.

Dylan picked up all kinds of tricks, man.

How did Bobby's growing fame and popularity affect your relationship between you and Bobby?

Well, when he moved to Woodstock, I didn't see much of him except when I went to Woodstock. And even then, I would only see him for moments. Like we'd ride bikes together or something, or we'd hang around the fireplace and sing songs. Was alone a lot of the time too. He always spends a lot of time alone, writing. I thought it's such a good deal to be able to have a setup like that, where—just simply because you've got all this immense talent. And he's, like, free to come and go as he pleases and write songs. He's got a typewriter in there. A bunch of books. And it was great for him.

At any point, as he was making it, did you feel any sort of a strain on your relationship? Was there anything that Bobby did in any way that put you down?

No.

I know he did it to Dave and Rob to some extent. He was putting down Phil Ochs and Eric Andersen and he was being kind of mean and a little, you know, I made it fellows, and you guys are down there kind of thing. Did you get any of this feeling?

He once said something about Woody that sounded slightly like a put-down. I was a little shocked by it, but not totally, and like the whole song "Hey, Woody Guthrie, I wrote you this song," was kind of a necessary stage in his career thing. That's why I'd hadn't written no song to Woody Guthrie—I didn't have to. Everybody knows about my relationship with Woody. I don't have to talk about it.

Right. Well, actually, Dylan has no real relationship with Woody.

Yeah. In the song, he's making a tribute to Woody and it's not phony in any way. It's true and selfless and I could have written a song like that and my song could have been even, you know, better.

How did he put Woody down?

Well, I was saying, "Boy, you really are carrying on in Woody's footsteps," or I might have said some remark like that. Like, "You're really doing what Woody was doing, carrying on like you're the Woody of today," something like that. He said, "Well, I've gone way far beyond Woody. Woody was good in his time, you know. He served a purpose, and he was the best in his time, but I'm much better." And it was true.

Woody limited himself to the rules of the language, which doesn't mean he didn't have the freedom, didn't have the hipness. Just at that stage in the game, he was as hip a man as he could possibly be, with the knowledge he had and the information he had and the life he lived. And his background. But Bobby had a lot more information available to him, for the time he was growing up, years later as a college student. And he could see things from an even more sophisticated light.

And you know, see, he adopted Woody's roughshod Oklahoma way and sometimes naive kind of country words and phrases and stuff like that. Coupled with all kinds of words that are right out of Freudian psychology. But you can't say this is a real hobo song if it's got words in it like hoboes don't know.

And Bobby was not afraid to put that stuff in. And I thought, wow, it's kind of ugly or phony in a way, but it's ballsy too. And I was toying with the same kind of thinking and writing in my head, too, because I was thinking that way, but I didn't actually come out with it and I never wrote it down, you know? I was starting to think that way. I was starting to have all these kinds of Bob Dylan songs in my head, and I didn't have the nerve to write them, because, like, I was afraid it would be rejected and had to be just truly like a Woody Guthrie song, you know, carrying on in the same tradition.

I'd been wearing cowboy clothes so long, and identifying myself with authentic cowboys for so long, that I was influenced by some of their squareness—I had picked up and adopted a lot of their square, old-time, rigid, narrow-minded, conformist things. Like, I didn't want to do anything to break the cowboy mold. Cowboys themselves, they don't always go around in cowboy clothes. (*laughs*)

They don't even like it, man. And people that know more about the West than I'll ever know aren't always wearing cowboy boots and all that stuff. Then they went to the city and they're intellectuals and stuff and artists and whatever. I was trying to re-create and just hang on to that beautiful mold and all that's pure in its purity, you know?

Let me ask you something: Bobby came out of the Midwest as a kid who was barely able to play a guitar and didn't really know a hell of a lot, and in a pretty short period of time, there was a great speed of, great deal of professionalization in this kid.

Oh, he knew who he liked, and he went to the sources and got it.

Like, how did he become so damn professional so fast?

I watched him pick up on a lot of stunts and tricks of mine that make you look and appear more professional onstage. Because he was a very shy kid and very nervous to be onstage and to this day doesn't speak a word hardly on stage, you know, and just is never loose. Like I'm not afraid to be totally loose. But Bob, the ways of his standing and moving and stuff like that. He took it and he made it his own style so it wasn't just a dead ringer of me. You know, he's got a way of standing and a way of moving and things that are definitely Bob Dylan.

Hey, there was one story I heard that I want you—

He's now such a good singer I don't even try to copy what he does. He came out with a record, "Corrina," and that was the first time he started really singing. I remember digging that record so much. I'm still trying to answer that question about what was it about Bobby that made him professional.

Yeah, not only professional as a musician.

I know he rubbed people the wrong way, everywhere he went. He's a very rude and brash kid, and he said what he thought. Or, like, some of them thought, well, Bob's just imitating Jack Elliott, you know?

Is this the time when he went over [to England] with Dick Fariña and Eric von Schmidt.

All I know was that he was on television over there and he was sort of doing this television play, in which he was playing a guitar and walking around playing. And somebody said they didn't dig it at all, but—

Yeah, the reviews were bad. I saw a couple of reviews from over there.

I read they really dug the way Dylan walked around so casual and loose and everything like that.

(laughs) You started to mention Rory McEwen.

Well, Rory told me that he took Bobby over to meet Robert Graves one time, and Bobby was very rude to Robert Graves, and I think Graves didn't dig it.

How was he rude? Do you remember what Rory said about it? What happened?
Oh, I think he wanted to read his poetry to Robert Graves. And he wanted to, you know, get his approval or something. And maybe just came on a little too strong.

Also, I would imagine a guy like Graves has got the same kind of problem—all the kids coming around saying, "Read my poetry. Am I any good?"
People have been telling me for fucking years and years and years and years that I should write, that I could write, and I can write, because of the way I rap. It's part of my name, Ramblin' Jack Elliott. I rap, you know. I've been rapping for a long time. Woody could sit right down at a typewriter and write a song in a minute. Woody Guthrie told me that, when he was in the army, he was put behind a typewriter. They wouldn't let him play the guitar in the army.

Oh, he was in—I thought he was a merchant marine.
He was a merchant marine. He would have liked to have been in the special services as an entertainer, go around and sing a song.

They put him on a typewriter instead.
And he said he was branded prematurely antifascist. That was the name they gave him, prematurely antifascist.

Let's get back to Bobby, what you thought about his music and him and—
I just about worshipped him. I think he's the greatest cat in the world. I really think he's great. Last time I saw him was at a Woody Guthrie concert. He played my guitar for two hours backstage. And I was playing on his guitar. We were just farting around. We weren't playing Bob Dylan songs. We weren't even playing old American folk songs. We were just making up shit, just like when we used to be together. We were just like two kids just messing. We were playing together.

Did you do much talking?
Hardly any talking—we just played a lot of music and sang a few things together.

Before the concert—was this the afternoon?
Yes, in the afternoon. He was a lot more grown up than before, and he had on kind of a shiny blue-gray silk suit. His hair was cut, and he had a slight beard. Yes, he was more settled, more calm. Because the last time I saw him before that was when he was going to Australia. He says, "Then we're

going to Europe. India, and then Europe." I said, "You're going around the world. He says, "Yes, guess so." I said, "Hey, can I carry your guitar case? Give me a job carrying your guitar case, man." And I kissed him goodbye, and they all split. And then as he grew, he got to a bigger place as far as money and numbers of people and everything. Whenever you meet somebody, you learn something from them, osmosis, vibes. You don't even have to talk. Well, it was the way that he had of treating people in a public place. And so, he had kind of a crazy, silly way of dealing with it so that people couldn't latch on to him. It's like mercury. People can't pin you down or get you down.

Did Bobby ever talk about his own background, about being a Zimmerman from Hibbing?

No. I never asked him that, what it was like or—I never met his folks even. I never asked him a lot of questions. Whatever he felt like talking about—something from his past—I was glad to hear about it.

Did he ever talk about bumming on the road as a kid, running away from—

We once swam across a big lake, about a mile and a quarter, out to an island in the middle of this lake, and back. We called it "Lake Dylliott."

Where was this?

In New Jersey, I think, somewhere. It was a very pretty area with a lot of lakes, northern New Jersey.

How did you end up swimming in the lake?

Well, we were passing by this lake. We thought it would be fun to stop and have a swim. It was a hot summer day. It was a beautiful lake. We just stopped, and the girls sat around on a rock, and we just dove in the water. We had swimsuits, and we swam across, all the way over to this island, about a mile and a quarter over and back—took us hours.

Did Bobby ever talk about bumming around as a kid, hitting the freights, bumming his way around the West?

He talked about it. I don't remember any details.

Specifically, did he ever talk about meeting Big Joe Williams on a freight or hopping a freight with Big Joe?

Really? No, he might have. I don't recall.

The Gleasons were telling me a story about, [at] one point Bobby, maybe at one of the hoots, was up there doing his bit, and a guitar string breaks. And he picks up a banjo, and a string on the banjo breaks. And he goes and starts pounding on a piano, which is never done in a folk place, and you got up and accompanied him on the guitar.

Where did they say—

Maybe at Gerde's. Yes.

Could have happened. I don't know because all kinds of wonderful goddam things have happened. I don't recall, because to me it was just another happening. To the people who saw it, maybe a big deal.

Especially the outsiders—

People who dug it, man, that was like history being made. They're seeing it all—you lifted your left hand, and you put it on Dylan's shoulder, and you patted him on the back. I'll never forget it. Memorable, sacred shit, man. I don't know. I've probably patted him on the back a million times. I don't know—never sucked his cock or nothing like that, but we were friends. We were liable to bump into each other a million times onstage. Both of us were runaways, but I've never asked him about how he felt about his parents. I've never known exactly how he feels about his parents and why he ran away and what he was running away from, how he deals with them. But I know that he's been nice to them, very good stories.

Well, Bobby apparently had some of this with his father. So, when was it that he sent that letter?

Oh, that was—

Last year, you said.

Yes. Dig this. He says, "What are you doing." I said, "I'm just trying to make a record. I've got twenty-seven bad records out, and I want to make one good one." And he said, "Oh no, Jack. I like every one of them re-cords." He was my biggest fan. So that was the last time I talked to him, and I don't know.

Who is Bob tight with now? Does he have any close friends now?

I think he's a loner. I think he just hangs out with his family, and that's it. And I even heard that he broke up with Al Grossman. I can understand why he has to be this way, now especially, because he was sort of that way all along anyway. But now that he's really sitting on top of the world, you have to—I guess you have to have a quiet hiding place. He must be really plagued by people always trying to get to him, get at him. I've just had a little wee taste of what that's like, and I don't have too many people bugging me every day. Even what little I get, I want to go hide out.

BOOTS OF SPANISH LEATHER

SUZE ROTOLO

Tony: Did he ever talk in terms of the forces that were driving him to write?
Suze: You can't put that kind of thing into words, really.

S UZE IS THE GIRL walking arm in arm with Bob Dylan on the album
cover of *The Freewheelin' Bob Dylan*. She was seventeen years old
when she met twenty-year-old Bob Dylan. Fair with long-flowing hair the
color of wheat, she had been described as "kind of like a Botticelli woman."
She was highly intelligent, artistic; one of the brightest young women in
the Village folk scene. Although happily married and clearly having moved
on from Bob Dylan, Suze's responses during the interview are guarded.
Many years later she told Tony that it wasn't that she didn't trust him. She
just didn't want to rehash the memories and hurts.

———————

You can answer a couple of questions. Don't duck me completely.
But what I've already told—I mean, you've got everything. I don't know
what I can possibly—
But you don't know about all the other things that I want to talk about.
Like what?
**Like, at one point, Dave Van Ronk was telling me that he asked Bobby, "Do you
know the French symbolists?" And Bobby said, "Huh? What do you mean?
What's that?" You know, playing completely dumb and then later he's up at
your place, you know, West Fourth Street, and he sees a couple of books, well
thumbed, with notes in the margin, of the French symbolists. Basically I want
to know, like, what was he reading at that point, you know, when you first were
with him.**
As I said, he was open to everything. You know, and he would, if somebody

would mention something, like Van Ronk mentioning a poet, then Bobby would later go look it up.

Oh really? What kind? Do you remember any of the books that were around in West Fourth Street?

No, I had a lot of books.

The kind of stuff that he was reading, do you remember anything specific? Again, how about the I Ching?

No, I don't think he—no.

You know the Chinese book of changes?

Yeah, yeah.

Because at some point, some interview later, you know, like around '64, he talks about it with some interviewer. Do you recall it at all?

No, we didn't have it. So, he might have eventually gotten in touch with it.

Could have been later, yeah.

Could have been later.

You got him into Brecht, according to Carla. You know, apparently you were into Brecht.

Yeah, well, I was working on a play, *Brecht on Brecht,* at Sheridan Square. That's the Sheridan Playhouse. He used to come to rehearsals.

What were you doing working on it?

Scenery, props, and general—it was a small cast. You know, reciting Brecht's stuff, his poetry and his writings. So, Bobby used to come and— and Brecht's songs. He used to come listen.

And what was Bobby's reaction?

Very, very impressed. It was the first contact with Brecht he'd had, I believe.

What about his first contact with the theater in any way? Which that must have been also.

Oh, by then he'd gone to opera, off-Broadway plays, et cetera. He was most impressed with the songs, I think.

Do you remember anything he said about them? Or which ones of the songs impressed him specifically?

One might have been—I think the ship, "The Black Freighter," that one, as I remember. That was an impressive song.

Was he into anything else, like Genet, at that point, or was it too early?

That's hard to individuate, honestly. I'm not faking memory here, but that's hard to place. I know I had, as far as the poetry goes, I had an awful lot of poetry collections, and Rimbaud [was] one of them in those years.

I know, if I had that book, then he would have looked it up, hearing the name, and he'd begin reading it.

Do you remember which collection you had that had Rimbaud in it? Was it a collection of Rimbaud.

A collection of Rimbaud. One of the ones with one page in French, one in English.

Pete Seeger went on trial in March of '61. You didn't meet Bobby till August. But did Bob talk in any way about that Seeger trial?

Not that I recall.

Lord Buckley. Mikki Isaacson was telling me Bob used to have her copy a lot of things, notes and things he had in his guitar case and in his pockets, and she remembers that one of the things she was copying was something off a Lord Buckley album. The rap on the—the death of a black man, that apparently Bobby turned into the thing about Hezekiah Jones? Do you remember that?

I know somebody was doing—Steve Israel of the Living Theater was doing Buckley at the Gaslight. So was Bill Cosby. He was doing a few Buckley things.

Oh, was he really?

Uh-huh. I know it was around then. Yup.

Do you remember Bob talking about it in any way?

Specifically, no, but I know he was interested in—I think Hugh Romney was doing Buckley.

Did he talk about Buckley that you can recall?

I'm sure he did, but I can't give you any quotes. I don't know. But I know he was interested in him.

Let me see. When he got the chance to play on Carolyn's record. You knew him by then certainly, because that was like the beginning of September, end of August.

Uh-huh.

In fact, Carolyn seems to recall that it may have been at Carla's apartment at, maybe on Perry Street, that she and Bob first got together to start working out a couple of songs that Bob would back her on. Were you there at the time? Do you recall that?

Well, I did see them at Gerde's when they would play together. He would play harmonica for her.

Right. Do you remember, was Bob excited about playing on Carolyn's record, backing Carolyn?

I'm sure he was.

I mean, do you recall?

Yeah.

What about recording for Victoria Spivey? Are you aware that he backed Joe Williams on the Spivey label?

Yes, yes. I remember that vaguely.

Just vaguely?

Uh-huh.

Okay. The understanding everybody has is that Al Grossman came along after Bob Shelton wrote that review. But a number of people told me that Grossman actually was managing Bob before then but kind of keeping it quiet for Grossman's own little things. Do you recall?

No. I know he was around. And he might have gotten him a few gigs or something. But nothing official. Grossman didn't officially manage until much later.

What do you mean by much later? After the first album.

He didn't become his official manager until later.

Do you remember when Bob signed?

No, I think I was in Europe then.

But apparently Grossman was around in some unofficial way. As far as you know, he was pushing Bob. Because Izzy Young seems to remember that Grossman was pushing Bob long before Grossman was an official manager. Is that your feeling too?

I don't know.

That Shelton review, do you recall Bob's reaction to it?

I'm sure he was pleased.

But you don't remember details.

No, I don't. I told you that before. I'm lousy on details.

I'm trying. You know, somewhere along the line you'll remember something. "The Black Freighter" you remembered, right?

Uh-huh.

Okay. So that's a big help. What about when Bob signed the contract. Mikki Isaacson again recalls Bob running into her place and waving a piece of paper and [saying], "I got it, I got it, Columbia signed me," that kind of thing. Do you remember any details like that? Do you remember Bob's reaction to the signing?

Oh, he was very glad about it. Columbia's a good company. And that was a big step because at that time folk music was nowhere.

Yeah, no one else had any kind of contracts around at that point.

No. Except with, you know, the lower labels like Vanguard and Elektra because they were smaller labels and folk—It was the first major label, so it was a good sign.

Do you recall, you know, what Bob's reaction was [to] the contract? I mean, anything specific. Can you think back and remember where you were when you heard it and how he told you about it?

No, I can't.

A lot of the interviews that I showed you [have] Mikki talking about how much Bob needed you and how you—oh, I think there's one quote in there from Mikki on how Bob wouldn't go to sleep until—

I don't remember any of that.

Okay. Was it your feeling that Bob needed you? As a person? In those early stages at least?

I wouldn't say that. I mean, both of us were just going together at that time.

Not only Mikki but a lot of others had a feeling that he had a need for you. But it's quite possible you couldn't see it from your angle. Let's see. Some other questions . . . Oh, Johnny Cash. Was he around at the time? Did Bob talk about Cash? John Hammond Senior tells me that Cash was around and was pushing Bob at Columbia and there was a stage where Columbia decided after that first album that maybe they wouldn't renew Bob's contract and Cash was running around saying they had to renew it, things like that.

Yeah, because I guess they met eventually after the first record.

And do you recall Cash and Bob being around—what the relationship was, how tight they were? Did they play together?

Not yet. No, that was later.

How much later?

Oh, it was later. I can't tell you the date.

Well, after the first record, second, third, I mean roughly.

I don't know.

Okay. On the first album, he used Van Ronk's arrangement of "House of the Rising Son," and Dave tells me that there was a big argument between them about it, that Dave was totally pissed at him because he did use it. Do you recall Bob's reaction to that? You know, Dave said he didn't talk to Bob for, like, a month or so.

Yeah, they had kind of a falling out about that. Yeah.

Do you recall Bob's reaction?

Well, he felt he made it his own. But I think he should have given credit. I think Dave thinks it's valid to give credit, that it was Van Ronk's arrangement.

Well, he did give credit on the album, on the liner notes.

Yeah, he did. But he recorded it first or something like that.

Yeah. You mean Bob's feeling was that he made it his own? I mean his unique style and interpretation of it?

Yeah.

Bob wasn't completely upset about Dave being mad at him?

Well, I'm sure he wasn't pleased.

Okay. I think I may have asked you this, but let me throw it out again. On the poems on that third album, he talks about Woody Guthrie, quote, "shattering even himself," close quote, as an idol. Did I ask you whether you remember any specific incident where Guthrie may have—

Yeah, you did ask that.

Did we talk about that? Your reaction was you didn't remember, right?

As usual.

Yeah, let me see. Oh, the trip to Italy. I basically have it right that in leaving Bob it wasn't a question of leaving Bob but it was a question of picking up on your plans that had been broken up the year before. Is that basically accurate, that you were torn between going and between staying here with Bob?

Yeah, that's right.

Okay. There was one song that you said, no, it wasn't written for you, as we went through my notes. "It Ain't Me, Babe," right? And a couple of others. That it was written for women in a general kind of thing.

I don't know. Specifically, I don't know.

You said, "Oh no, no, that wasn't written for me." You mean you're not sure right now?

I didn't think so at the time anyway. Just sort of a statement at the end, there's no more hassles. I don't remember which one it was.

Okay, it's my basic feeling—

Oh, yeah, yeah, I remember it. It's like somebody that—at the end of a heavy affair, you know, that song sounds as if I can't, I don't want any more.

Right.

You know, just something light and easy. It sounds—I don't know. That's how—

My basic feeling is that even those songs that were not specifically written for

you in that period when you were gone were written under the impetus of what he was feeling about you. Which you might agree is kind of accurate.

Yeah.

I asked you about Robert Graves. Did he talk about visiting Robert Graves in London?

Yes, he did visit him, yeah. He was impressed by him.

Did he say how he got to Robert Graves?

No, I don't recall.

Somebody tells me a story that the meeting didn't come off too well, that Bob felt that Graves was an old man more interested in his own stuff and wasn't about to listen to a young kid. Do you recall Bob talking about anything along those lines?

No, I can't say I do. I remember him saying he was surprised to see this old guy. He was just a little old guy, that's all he was.

You mean he wasn't a giant.

Yeah. You know—

Oh sure. Of course, of course. While I'm on poets like that, Pete Karman tells me that they stopped off to visit Carl Sandburg on that trip across country. When Bob got back, did he talk at all about the Sandburg visit?

I remember Pete telling me about it, more than I remember Bobby telling me about it.

Did Bob ever talk—somewhere along the line he's told a couple of people that he has to write in order to keep from going insane, is the way he put it a couple of times. Did he ever talk in terms of the forces that were driving him to write?

You can't put that kind of thing into words, really.

Yeah, but do you remember if he ever put it into words in any way, even if you don't remember the exact words, even the gist of it?

That's just it. I think that quote's very good. That covers it.

Were you around when he was going to go on *The Ed Sullivan Show*, but CBS refused to let him use "The John Birch Society Blues"?

Yeah.

What was his reaction to that whole thing? You know, that he was being censored and then he couldn't make the Sullivan show.

Bad. That was bad, I remember that.

Do you remember how bad?

No.

Bob took off somewhere because he was so upset about not being able to— you don't recall that?

No.

"Don't Think Twice." Apparently, the tune was swiped from something that [Paul] Clayton had discovered on one of his travels down South, and eventually, there was a falling out between Clayton and Bob on the melody. Do you remember that?

No, that was written while I was in Europe too.

Yeah, but later—

Yeah, there was something about Paul going to sue him or something. I never knew what the outcome of that was.

Do you recall Bob's reaction to Clayton's feeling that he should have been cut in on it?

It was crazy to sue. I remember that. Because he didn't feel it was actually stolen from anything. It was public domain. I'm very vague on it, but it was kind of that's insane, taking a step like that.

Do you know if Paul ever did sue?

No. I said I don't remember the outcome. I think maybe he did begin because I remember Bobby was surprised.

Well, you know, he's always—

Borrowed from.

At least later on, when he felt he had achieved stardom, unquote, and he felt more secure, he admitted that most of the early tunes were public domain.

Right. Not stolen.

But Bob talked about tunes and you know, stuff that he stole. Victoria Spivey and a couple of people told me that Bob refused to sing for benefits—but secretly contributed money to various causes.

I don't know anything about that.

Okay. In May of '63, you were back from Italy by then. Bob went out to Chicago, did a couple of nights at the Bear in Chicago and an interview with Studs Terkel.

Yeah.

Did you go out to Chicago with him?

No.

The Newport Folk Festival, in July of '63, where Bob first sang to the big folk crowd. Can you recall what your feelings were at the time? The impression I got is that you were beginning to realize that Bob was going to make it and that it might change things.

No, that was already evident.

In other words, you had those feelings back when he was making that first album. That that's liable to change things.

Uh-huh.

What were your feelings at the time? Do you remember what you were feeling?

I don't remember. I was bored a lot of times. I do get bored.

Oh sure.

A lot of people, not just me, but a lot of people get bored waiting backstage and waiting, people waiting to go on, people ambling around.

Right. Was that the festival at which he was fooling around with that bullwhip for those couple of days.

I don't remember.

Or the fans beginning to chase him and he's starting to get paranoid about it?

There was a lot of that.

Yeah. Do you remember any of it? Do you remember what he said about the fans?

No. I just remember that the town hall, the Carnegie Hall, was it.

Carnegie Hall. That was October of '63.

Yeah.

That's the one where Terri said you and she ran up the block and you were getting a little panicky and telling the crowd to go back.

Oh, that was a horror show. God.

In what way? Tell me about—

To have all these people chasing you up the block. That's when I first, that really sent it home, that anybody around Dylan was really, was in as much danger as he was.

But this, did this affect your feelings or just reinforce what you had already come to suspect?

Like what? Reinforce what feelings?

Well, come to suspect that you were not going to be able to live as a human being for yourself if you got trapped in this kind of world.

I don't even think I had any thoughts like that.

You wrote them in the letter way back in—

Yeah, that's one letter. But that doesn't mean—

Well, what do you recall that your thoughts were when you realized—

A lot of times I just wanted out, period. For no other reason that it was, this isn't working. It was too, we weren't getting on and—sometimes. And when we were it was all right. Then we weren't, I wanted out.

I see, okay. Later on, you know, after that Carnegie Hall thing and just a little bit after that, is when the people started, you know, fans started almost making him a Christ, almost deifying him, or, you know, like the biggest God substitute

around in the folk field at least. Did he realize that people were doing this? That people were actually feeling this way about him?

I'm sure he did.

Did he talk about it?

I don't remember.

Did he express fears, any feelings about the freakiness?

I don't remember.

Yeah, okay. A couple of people have described Grossman as almost a substitute father, you know. What's your feeling about that? You know, what was their relationship?

He was his manager and Bobby was his client. If there are other heavy feelings alongside of it, I don't know. Let other people speculate. I never speculated on that.

But other people did get a feeling that Bobbly relied on Grossman a little more heavily than as a manager, that, you know, there could have been this father feeling.

Maybe. They were very close.

Yeah. But you're not aware of any—

No. I said I don't speculate on anything.

Okay. Allen Ginsberg, Gregory Corso, Ed Sanders, you know, the East Side Poets, so-called, were they around at any period that you were still with Bobby?

Uh-huh.

What was Bobby's feeling about them? You know, the intellectual relationship?

Oh, he was very interested in them.

In what they were doing in the poetry and the whole bit? Is that what he was interested in?

He was interested in them.

In them.

Uh-huh. And "them" means what they were. And everything they were into.

Yeah, okay. Everything.

Oh, hey, come on. Put it the way you want to. I'm just saying it, huh?

Well, I'm not quoting you. But, you know, the fact is that his relationships with certain people are very important, and if the relationship that I believe took place with certain people did take place, it's important, although I'm not going to mention it. But I want to know about it, even though I'm not going to write about it. At least I want to know where his head was at as I'm writing. Understand?

Yeah. Yeah.

In other words, if I say something about him being extraordinarily close to Allen Ginsberg, that could imply that there may have been even a homosexual relationship. And if I—

If that's what you want to imply, put it that way.

Well, no, I don't want to imply anything—

There were a lot of rumors. There were an awful lot of rumors about everything you can name. I don't know if you want to feed those rumors or if you want to—or you want to be tasteful. I don't know, because that's up to Bobby. As far as I'm concerned, I get upset from how you imply from me. But for him, I don't know. Everything's been said and speculated and deduced and—

No, the thing is that—

I know he was, when he met them he was excited about them, about Allen Ginsberg, his poetry, the kind of a guy he was, et cetera. If it went to a homosexual thing, personally, factually I don't know.

I don't want to imply it. If I'm going to mention it at all, I'm going to say it outright. What I'm trying to avoid is implying it through ignorance.

No, I really can't help you because there are too many rumors that I wouldn't know. Because that's normal. And you wouldn't tell the girl you're going with that you're having an affair with a man, right?

Right, right.

So, if we were even going together at that time, I don't even remember.

I knew the rumors were around. I mean I heard them back at that time.

Oh, there were fantastic ones. You can do what you want with them. Honesty is nice.

Honesty is nice?

Yeah. If you want to feed rumors or speculation, but if you've got facts, okay then. Do what you want with it.

Do you remember when he met Ginsberg? Were you around when he met Ginsberg?

I don't know the date. No, but I was around, yeah.

Can you place it? Between the first and second breakup?

We were still seeing each other. But I don't know what period it was.

The Western trip that Pete told me about that he went on, both Carla and Pete tell me that your basic feeling when he left was somewhat of relief, that he would be gone, that you could begin to breathe a little. Is that about accurate? That you were getting some breathing space?

Yeah, yeah.

The Kennedy murder. Carla tells me that you sat around watching TV much of the weekend, drinking a little wine, put a requiem on the record player. Remember that?

Yeah.

Do you remember Bobby's reaction to the whole weekend? You know, like we were all stunned, but do you remember Bobby saying anything?

No.

Doing anything?

Watching. Totally absorbed in what the TV had on for about ten days, I think that was.

The Civil Liberties Committee, or Emergency Civil Liberties Union, Tom Paine Dinner Award, were you around at the time? Or were you in Italy?

I was around. I didn't go, though.

Do you remember his reaction to being booed off?

I remember him thinking it was all funny for some reason. They were all very out of it when they went.

Who went with Bob, do you know?

I think Albert Maher and Geno [Foreman].

Anyone else?

I don't remember anybody else.

But his reaction afterwards, it was that these old bald people didn't understand what he was trying to say?

Yeah.

Oh, did I talk to you about Bobby talking about history in some way, as if he had all the answers, where actually he never read anything about it.

Yeah, yeah, we talked about it.

Do you remember? Is that basically accurate?

I remember it.

Can you tell me the incident from your viewpoint?

I didn't remember specifically what he was talking about. But he was doing his usual know-it-all thing or something.

Yeah, did he do that often?

Oh yeah.

You remember any other incidents that he did that?

No.

Okay. Oh, *Tarantula*, the book he was writing.

What?

Tarantula. **His autobiography or whatever it was. What did he say about that? Do you remember it at all?**

Yeah. I remember he took on something bigger than—he never finished it.

Yeah. But why? Do you remember?

No. That was later too. I don't think we were going together anymore.

Did he ever talk about wanting to be bigger than Presley?

I don't think—I don't remember him competing with Presley, no. But maybe he was.

Because at least around the time that you first began going with him, he had been telling people this. And I'm wondering if in fact even—you remember that John Hammond said that, wow, he's going to be bigger than Presley. It seems he was still talking in those terms after you started living with him.

Probably. Because I'm sure Hammond would say things like that. You know, pushing the client and—

Yeah, yeah. But—

I'm sure they lined up *The Catcher in the Rye.* They were going to line up—

Yeah, tell me about *The Catcher in the Rye.* You remember?

That's it. I just told you. They were going to line it up for him. You know, all these things that, you know, what we're going to do for you, kid, and all that.

Or do you recall how it came about?

No. I remember hearing it through Hammond.

I mean, was your feeling, like, Hammond was pushing Bobby or bolstering his ego and, you know, that kind of thing?

No, did it sound like that?

No? What did it sound like?

Just the way I said it. If it sounded like that, there's nothing more I can say.

Right, okay. Boy, Suze, you're being difficult.

No. I get this feeling that you're wanting this to fall into a line of what you already have. If it doesn't, then you turn it.

No. Well, the thing is, [you] have the feeling that I'm trying to fit you into a pattern. But what I'm really trying to do is get information. And if what you tell me conflicts with what other people have told me, then I've got to do some more legwork. I'm not trying to force you into a mold.

I'm the least dependable because I have the worst memory of everybody. Even Pete told you that.

Yeah, but you also are the closest. And if I can jog your memory on just one little item, you know, it might be helpful. And I'm willing to give you a hard time for an hour.

To get a hard time in return.

I know, but that's okay. I've been doing this for too many years to worry about it anymore. But you know, don't get the impression I'm trying to fit you into a mold. I can only ask you a question based on the way I see it now.

Yeah.

And if you don't see it that way, I wish you'd tell me you don't see it that way. Don't say, "Well, if you want to take that way, take it that way." If you don't see it, disagree with me. That'll be more helpful than your saying, "Sure, if that's what you want, that's what you get."

Uh-huh.

Let's get back to the *Catcher in the Rye* thing.

Yeah, that's what I remember.

Okay, you remember it the way you said it before I asked the question a different way.

Are you taping this?

Yeah.

Oh, you could have said that before.

I told you I was going to tape it. You know, at some point when we talked. I'll let you have the tape. If you want it.

No, that's okay.

You will see everything before it gets printed.

Fine.

And again, don't think I'm trying to twist anything that anybody says to fit into preconceived patterns. I had no preconceived notions about anything when I started writing the book. Except that Bob was a hero type and I wanted to dig down below the surface and find the truth. Except now I think I know a lot of things based on what so many people have told me about him that if I ask a question from a certain viewpoint, it's because it's the viewpoint of the people who've talked to me.

Right.

All right?

Okay.

CARLA ROTOLO

When he was a kid, he wasn't being that mean. As he got older, he
started getting very nasty. But when he was first in the city, he was
a very sweet kid. Just not too articulate. But I think that's probably
why he did hang on to Suze, for that sweetness. Because as things got
worse and worse for him, in terms of the demands made on him. . . .
I think Suze's character was a balance for him, because she is a sweet
girl.

CARLA WAS SUZE ROTOLO'S OLDER SISTER. She was dark with glossy black hair, while Suze was fair with long flowing hair the color of wheat. Carla worked for folk music collector Alan Lomax, and both Carla and Suze knew most of the artists from the West Village scene. Suze and Dylan shared Carla's apartment for a time. Carla is infamously the subject of Dylan's "Ballad in Plain D."

When did Bob take the West Fourth Street place?
Sometime in, I'd say, November of '60.
'61.
'61, yeah. Somewhere around there.
And when did Suze move in with him?
She moved in with him sometime after that.
She was living with Bob on West Fourth Street before the trip to Italy?
Yeah, I believe so. Right.
And when did she return from Italy?
She came back in December, just before Christmas of '62.
And returned to West Fourth Street.
Yeah, in January. That's when she was staying with me. He was still in Europe.
And then the oven thing [Suze's suicide attempt]. When was that?
That would be August of '63.

Right. And then she went to live with you over at Avenue B.

Yeah. First on Perry Street, then over to Avenue B.

And then the final break was in—

March.

March of '64.

Right.

And then after that they had very little contact.

Right.

Okay. Those are the basic dates. Tell me about when Suze and Bob were both living with you.

That whole situation was so absurd. Because I wasn't getting any advice. I realized that it was just going to have to play itself out. But I was stuck in the middle of this thing living there. And in absolutely no position to go out and find another place to live at that point. Because as far as I was concerned, that's why I didn't give a shit what happens to him.

Why did he make you out to be such a bitch in "Ballad in Plain D"?

Because he felt I was responsible for it. Who knew?

The parasite stuff.

The song, such an absolute screech. I was going to sue the pants off him. I decided—my lawyer said, don't even bother, don't even, you know, really. Because parasite, the parasite is someone who feeds off somebody. And I was the only person who was working at that time. Fucking Bobby, of course, he makes me the parasite when I was working. A couple of times. He came looking for me. Later on.

Did he offer you any apology?

Oh yeah. He came looking around and he said, "Hey, I'm really sorry about that and I didn't even mean it. I just—"

The song, he meant?

Yeah. "I really had to do that. I mean that's not, you know—" I said okay. That's a petty way to get, you know, to work out your own. It wasn't a nice thing to do, particularly when it was all made up out of whole cloth. And the Limelight thing. I used to hang out there until four in the morning because I didn't want to go home.

Just to stay out of their way.

Stay out. Because you'd come in, you'd see them sitting in the living room, maybe with the TV set someone had given me, sitting like zombies with all these people around or something. There was no privacy. Absolutely none. I felt that I was some kind of freak. I began to think I was crazy because he had a way of telling me, "You're full of shit" and you're this and you're that. And he didn't like it that I was around. You know, at one point I thought I was—I had my own little nervous breakdown.

Really?

Oh, at one point I got bitchy and I said, "Hey, man, let me take your place and we can all play 'switchy housies,' and you know, everybody will be happy." And I think a good part of his guilt was he couldn't be real. I mean, I know it was. And he couldn't sort things out himself at that point, because of where his career was going. Just couldn't get himself out of himself.

I got a feeling from talking to lots of people that part of the problem between Bobby and Suze was that Suze really didn't know how to break off with him— didn't know, in fact, if she wanted to break off with him.

Yup. Bobby had this magnetism that overwhelmed people.

What about Bob Neuwirth's influence in all this? Was he around by this period? In other words, were there outside forces that were acting on Bob and Suze?

The whole Grossman group of people. And Grossman's house up in Woodstock. His house and that whole drug scene.

By now the whole Woodstock thing had started?

Grossman had a house up there.

When did Bobby start moving up to Woodstock. Getting involved in Woodstock? Did he still have contact with Suze?

He got his house later.

No, I don't mean his own house. But getting involved—

It must have been at some point because I remember they went up there to Woodstock. Again, see, these are things that I had no contact [with].

What about Bob Neuwirth —what role he may have played in any of this?

I can't say because I just didn't have any contact with that scene. I haven't seen him in a long time. See, the only person who was around, you could talk to, is Pete Karman. But he broke off at some point as Bobby was doing the whole mean scene. He can give you some kind of story if he wants to talk about it. Because I gather it was a very bad thing for him because Dylan at that time was very vicious towards everybody.

Yeah, I've heard.

Bayonets on everybody.

Yeah, I've heard a lot from Van Ronk, of course, and Dave Blue.

Dave Cohen.

Yes, Dave Cohen.

Dave Cohen really hasn't got much to say. Because that kid wasn't into anything at that time.

No, but at the point where Dylan was using the bayonet on everybody, Cohen was there. You know, the whole Kettle of Fish thing. You know, hanging out and stabbing each other. Cohen was part of it.

I get the impression from what he said that Dylan needed victims, you know what I mean? But at that time, I had no contact.

Tell me something about the relationship between Bob and Suze in the very early days. For example, a number of people have said that Suze had the ability to draw some sweetness out of Bob whereas he wandered around like a nasty, mean kind of guy. But when Suze was around—

I don't know. When he was a kid, he wasn't being that mean. As he got older, he started getting very nasty. But when he was first in the city, he was a very sweet kid. Just not too articulate. But I think that's probably why he did hang on to Suze, for that sweetness. Because as things got worse and worse for him, in terms of the demands made on him, he got tighter and tighter and nastier and nastier, and he was going to show everybody everything, tell—he had the truth. And that's where that whole bayonet-y thing comes in. Telling the truth about everything. He decided he would pick out your weakness and then suddenly grab it and use it on you. Which is what he did with everybody. Find their vulnerable spot and that was it. So, I think Suze's character was a balance for him, because she is a sweet girl.

What do you know about his wife, about Sara?

Nothing. Never met her. My contact has been, besides seeing him once, when he came looking for me, is I've had no contact at all.

When he did come looking for you, was it just to say, "I'm sorry"? Was there any other context? Where did he find you?

In one of the theaters I was working in. And then I saw him later, I think, at the Limelight. I said, "Meet me at the Limelight later," and he said, "This is my phone number and you have to do lights for me sometime," or something. You know, anything to smooth it over. "You want a car, I'll get you a car." Some stupid thing like that, because that was his jittery way of trying to smooth it over.

And he hasn't come looking for you since then or anything like that.

Well, I don't know. Somebody said that he was trying to see me. In this whole period when he went to Terri to get his hat back. Or look at his hat. But I don't feel one way or another about him now. I certainly know much more of what's happened to him since, and I can appreciate what his changes were.

There was some talk, in the very beginning, when he was first getting the gigs at Gerde's, that he was afraid to go on much of the time, and then Suze had to bolster his ego, give him a drink, tell him how great he was.

That's probably possible.

And you. And a couple of times being there, getting him to go on.

Could be. Because I know he was drinking a lot. He needed some of that to go on and perform.

Do you recall Suze's role in this? Were you around much at that point?

I suppose I was, but I don't remember. I really don't.

Victoria Spivey, for example, you know, the old black blues singer, said that—the little contact she had with him, she got the feeling that Suze was bolstering this kid and that she helped him a lot in those first months. Like what? Like how?

I suppose just by being with him. You know, being a good influence on him. That's all I can think of. I do remember there was this whole thing, we had this project at one time to get Bobby, Jack Elliott, and who else—I guess, Dave Van Ronk, to put some kind of a record or tape together and sell it to Columbia.

This is before Bob got the contract?

Yeah. And he wrote a letter to John Hammond and he made some trip to Philadelphia, I think, to organize the whole thing.

Why Philadelphia?

Dave was playing down there. So, we all went down. I don't think it was organized very much, but we crashed and partied.

There was a feeling around that Bobby was going to make it, and Bobby was the kid that had to be pushed.

It was very important, yeah. Everybody did go through a mothering thing at that time. That's true. Get him onstage, make sure he was there and sober, you know, get him to do his thing. And Suze was part of that also.

Why did everybody do this? Was it a feeling that here's a kid who needed help in some way?

And I think just because he was important, that he should be heard, and we argued with Mike Porco at Gerde's to give him a gig there. And he was so young and scruffy that people wanted to help him

Whereas the folkies themselves, that is, the Van Ronks or the younger folk singers, realized that he was important.

And they were just coming along themselves. Don't forget, Tom Paxton wasn't anybody then. Eric Andersen wasn't even in town. All these people. They weren't there. So really the predominant scene was Gerde's and then as Bobby got to do more at Gerde's, there developed two factions. They either hated him or they loved him. And that was it.

Who were the haters?

Let's see. There were several. A couple of music business people that I remember. Some record person. I think it was the guy from Vanguard.

Who, Mo Escher?

No, the guy from Vanguard was Maynard Solomon. He didn't like Bobby. Oh, also the guy from Elektra. Jac—

Jac Holzman?

Right. Couldn't stand Bobby.

Really?

Thought he was terrible. Awful. Sat at the bar putting him down. Bobby was the first new thing, and Jac Holzman thought he stunk. I remember him sitting in a striped sweater and saying, "Ugh, just awful, terrible. Worst thing I've ever heard in my life. Guthrie imitator."

Did he really say that about Bob?

Yeah. Originally, he sounded just like Guthrie. Then he began to change a bit. Then he started doing his own thing. The very first time he played at Gerde's, he did just Guthrie songs, mostly.

At a hoot night?

No, when he had his own paying gig there. And it was—he was terrible. He wasn't good. Then, when he started to do his own stuff, he was very, very hot. I used to bring people in to hear him because he was so unique. You know, there were those who loved him, and again, those who couldn't stand him at all.

Who else was around who was involved in that period?

Let's see, Carolyn Hester was, because they rehearsed for a record. Her first record on Columbia was rehearsed partly at my apartment.

And Hammond . . .

Well, there's a whole confusion about that. About Hammond signing Bob. About Hammond hearing Bob. About the time Carolyn's record was being made, I think he just heard him play backup.

Well, Hammond is also saying that at the time his son was saying, "You've got to go listen to Dylan," so he was getting it from several sources. And then he finally decided to listen to Dylan.

He didn't really hear Bob play, as far as I know. He had never seen him perform.

He said he saw him at Gerde's.

I think he saw him after.

No, no. The story I heard is that the Gerde's gig, the gig Bob Shelton wrote about, John Hammond was there, and he was raving at how great the kid was.

I somehow thought he hadn't ever heard him. He was supposed to come down and he didn't, though it's possible he did. So, what else do you want to talk about?

Bobby at this point is growing more and more paranoid about his fame, about people clutching at him.

That's the key point.

And I get from some of the people around him, like Eric Andersen and Dave Blue that after the Kennedy assassination, Bob got out of the protesting because the Kennedy assassination made him physically feel that he was a target for so many freaks in this country.

Well, Bobby was completely paranoid anyway at that point. It's hard to know. I remember the day Kennedy was killed. We were all there watching television.

Who's "we all"?

The three of us. Watching television and listening to the radio. And I remember him saying once about his "Masters of War" song, for example, saying it's just a whole big put-on, a whole crock of shit. That's what they wanted.

That was one of the shittier protest songs he had written.

Right. But this was what he said all of them wanted. There was a point, back when Bobby was going to make his first record, he was still not sure what songs to record and he going over the list of what he's going to put in the record and also what to sing at his upcoming first concert.

At Carnegie Hall, or Town Hall?

Town Hall Annex. A little place with—

Carnegie Hall Annex? Town Hall Annex?

It was Town Hall. But it wasn't the Town Hall. It was a little room. Anyway, everyone was getting into it, like, do this song or don't do this song, you know, supervising the whole thing. And then talking about it one night, rapping about something, and I suddenly got the feeling, this is a guy—now remember, mind you, everyone, everybody was into getting him recorded, getting him well known, getting him gigs, everyone who could do anything for him. Terri, all these people. And I got the feeling, just from talking that night, that this is someone who knew. He wasn't befuddled and a confused little kid that he came on as. This is somebody who knew exactly where he was going. And he was using that befuddled act as a weapon, because it worked. And from then on, I never said anything again about do this song or, you know, get a gig here, stuff like that. Because I knew that he knew. He knew where he was going to end up.

Do you think it was a put-on or was it just his style, an act he didn't even know he was doing?

I think it was a bit of both.

Did he ever talk about making it?

Sometimes, yeah.

Making it big as a folkie was not the same as making it big as Elvis Presley. Do you recall any, you know, talk like that?

He used to say he'd like to do movies and things like that. Stuff like that. Like have a big house. Be on the radio, have a Top Ten hit, things like that.

But not like he'd like to be another Elvis or—

I don't remember him ever even talking about Elvis. He used to talk instead about some others, like Buddy Holly and things like that. Everly Brothers and those people. He used to sing a lot of those songs. Country and western stuff.

What about—did he ever equate himself with Woody? You know—beyond the stage—

That was his beginning and then that dropped off.

Getting back to the Kennedy assassination. What was his reaction? We cried a lot in those days. Did he cry?

I think he was just more mad. Or very quiet about it. We were all pretty quiet. Just like shock. And that's the most that I can remember, that we were just dead quiet, and then we played Berlioz's Requiem, and nobody talked very much.

What about in the days that followed? The funeral, the killing of Oswald, any of that? Do you recall any of that, his reaction?

I think he was just—I remember just staring at the television set and nobody talking very much. Just staring.

Later, some months later, I guess it was early '64, the Emergency Civil Liberties Committee thing, in which he made some remarks.

A family friend of ours was there. She happened to be there, because it was just before Christmas. I think she was at our house, my mother's, for Christmas dinner. It was Bobby and we were all there. I remember they were talking about it.

Yeah, right. I've run out of questions basically. I mean, you know, this is basically on their relationship. I may not have known exactly when they broke up and what her thinking was, but I think much of what I had are some of the wild rumors that have been going down, I dismissed way back.

Which is that she was spirited off in the middle of the night—no, no. Originally the idea was to have her go for a year or something like that.

And she didn't return till Labor Day and it was clear that she was staying on her own.

Yeah. Nobody was making her stay at all. And then the telephone call saying, "Come home." Look, people don't—some people, I'm sure, don't know about it.

I didn't.

Maybe they do. He told her he missed her, calling once a week. "Come home, come home, come home." As you can imagine what it was like in [a] small, very poor city. This American girl getting all these phone calls, right?

Yeah, Jesus.

It made her freak immediately.

What about pictures of Bobby and Suze?

I don't have any. It was so many years ago and that was that time. Gerde's. That was that time.

PETE KARMAN

We wanted to see the old man [Carl Sandburg], and we went up to
the guy's farm. He had a goat farm. We knocked on the door and he
came out. He answered the door, complete in his beard. He's a little
old man, wrinkled up. And Bobby said, "I'm a poet, like you."
And Sandburg said he hadn't heard of him.

PETE KARMAN, a young writer who worked for the *New York Daily Mir-*
ror, took two of his friends, Carla and Suze Rotolo, to the Riverside Folk
Festival Radio Show in 1960. The two sisters, longtime family friends of
Pete, met Bob Dylan at the show. Pete drove Bob, Carla, and Suze home at
four in the morning, and shortly later Bob and Suze were going together.

――――――――

Where was the festival?
It was up at WRVR, in Riverside Church. It was an all-day folk festival.
This was 1960, '61. I don't remember the exact date. Dylan was up there.
He had just come into town. Right around that period. And I didn't really
know him. But somehow or other we got to talking and we all came back
down in the Village in my car, with Carla and Suze.
Carla and Suze already had met Dylan.
No, they hadn't. In fact, he ended up in my car, with Carla and Suze. That
was the first time he met Suze. Then I didn't see him again for—
Oh, because Carla's recollection was that you actually took Suze to Gerde's or
to one of the clubs and Bob was there. But then she said, "I'm really not sure.
Talk to Pete." Tell me about the thing up at Riverside Church. The first time you
saw him, what was he like? What was your impression?
Totally raw. He was just a kid from the country. I talked to him and he told
me he was from Gallup, New Mexico. A young new voice from Gallup,
New Mexico, sang with grittiness, or something like that. Then there were
a couple occasions right around there where I was going to Gerde's with

Suze and I knew a lot of people in the folk thing. As I recall, the first time she saw him was up at Riverside Church. Or the first time she spoke to him. She may have seen him, previously. We all came back to the Village, and off the record, it seems to me at the time Dylan was more interested in Carla.

Carla said for the first couple of weeks, at least, he was into her.

So, then I didn't see him again for a while. I don't know, a week, two weeks. That's when Suze was living at 1 Sheraton Square, I believe. Suze and Carla and her mother. And I went up there a few times. I'm a very old friend of that whole family. No one especially thought anything of him. He was sort of a drifter, you know.

I'm finding now, though, everybody—at least, the professionals—say now that they knew this kid had it.

I didn't have that feeling.

Carla didn't have that feeling. The McKenzies, with whom he lived for a while, didn't have that feeling at this point. He was just a little kid that they were try-ing to help.

He was just a little kid who drifted in and had a guitar, like forty thousand other kids. I didn't think much of him at the time. He was just another run-of-the-mill kid with a guitar. Suze and Bobby started going out. A couple of months after that they were fairly serious.

Was Suze living with him by that time?

I'm trying to remember. Yeah, yeah. She was living in about three places at once because her mother was in the hospital. And then she was living with Carla for a while.

Carla was on Perry Street at that time?

Right. Suze was more or less around Fourth Street a couple of months after they met where they were living together. And that's when the whole series of the arguments started with Carla and whatnot because they seemed to be hanging out over at Carla's house a lot.

What was their relationship like?

Impetuous. Well, she was seventeen. Both of them were, like, really green behind the ears. The relationship was extremely intense. And they didn't know how to handle it. I mean, it would go from love to total hatred in five minutes and then back again.

Do you remember what would drive it from one to the other? Specific incidents?

Both were really unprepared. I think it was Suze's first real thing with a guy, you know.

Suze apparently was going over to Italy. She was going to school there. Then Bobby comes along and kind of sweeps her off her feet. She's now apparently in a stage of conflict. She doesn't know if she still wants to go to Italy. Do you remember any of this?

She finally did go. They split up and she went. I guess it was a year later or something like that. And stayed for a while. Came back again, to him. The first time she went to Italy she met the guy who is now her husband, Enzo.

How close did you get to Dylan in the early days? Did he talk anymore about his background? His plans? Was he going to make it? That kind of thing.

His plans were—yeah, he was interested in making it. He was.

You were working at the *Mirror* at the time.

Yeah.

Did he attempt to use you in any way? Never made any attempt to grab some publicity or anything?

Never, never.

Do you remember him at Gerde's?

Yeah.

Tell me something about what he was like working, say?

At Gerde's he was very nervous. He sang a lot of Guthrie stuff. He used to sing that Bear Mountain thing. That went over very good. It was the kind of thing where there was a whole scene, you know. He would do a set and then there were always five or six people around, Suze and a few others. Then he'd come off and chat and whatnot and then go back.

I was told by some people that Suze was so great for Bob because she bolstered his ego. That he needed somebody to push him up onto that stage, to give him confidence.

Very much so, yeah. She's a very soft, gentle sort of person. Ask me specifics.

Start with the New Orleans trip.

That I know. In February, this was '64, he was going on a concert tour and then decided to go by car. And I was invited along, along with Paul Clayton, this guy, Victor and Bobby.

Victor Maymudes.

Maymudes, right.

Apparently, Paul was in love with Bobby, which again is off the record and not attributed to you. What was Paul like?

Paul was—had an adoring attitude towards Dylan. Very obvious. He was a real pillhead. That whole trip he was stoned, from coast to coast, on everything.

Tell me about the trip. When did it get started?

It was February second or February third, 1964.

Whose car was it, do you recall?

Dylan bought a big blue Ford station wagon.

Who was driving?

We all drove.

What kind of equipment did Dylan have?

He had his guitar and he had a typewriter.

No amp? He hadn't gone electric yet.

Hadn't gone. That was right when the third record came out.

That was '64, right, okay.

There's a lot of nice anecdotes about that trip. We left New York. The first concert date was in Atlanta, at Emory University. But on the way down we stopped in Harlan County, Kentucky. And we had brought this whole load of clothes that Dave Van Ronk and some other people gave us that we had gathered for—the miners were on strike, and Dylan, you know, he was in his protest period and very involved with that. So, first stop was Emory. There were a lot of groupies, a lot of pot, and all sorts of shit. From there, we went to Mississippi and he did just a short sort of off-the-cuff couple of songs at a school down there, a black school. It's not a college. I'll think of it. From there, we went to New Orleans, which he wrote about on the back of, I think, his fourth or fifth album. This guy, Joe B. Stewart, that he met on the street. A southern white poet. And we all five or six of us palled around together, running in and out of—this was Mardi Gras time and we were stoned.

Tell me about some of it.

It was right out of that scene in *Easy Rider,* exactly. We were all totally stoned, and we were running in and out of gin mills and saloons. We got over in the black neighborhood and got thrown out of the bars of five or six places.

Why were you thrown out?

Because they were black places.

Did Bobby groove on getting into the black places.

He did, very, very much. Not on getting thrown out but on getting into them. And he was sort of like a pied piper, you know. The crowd got larger and larger. I mean, more and more people were following him. And there was one cute thing where he sang on the street. There was a street singer with a guitar, a young white kid. And he asked to borrow his guitar and he sang a song. And the kids said something like, "You sound just like Bob Dylan." And we left him wondering, you know. So, it was the whole Mardi Gras. It was three days. We were only able to get one room. There were four of us in one motel room.

Did he have a date in New Orleans?

No. Just wanted to see Mardi Gras. From there, we went up to—the next date was Denver, but we spent so much time in New Orleans, he was almost late. We drove up through Dallas and we stopped at the place where, you know, Dealey Plaza.

What did Bobby say about that?

He was very quiet.

There's a basic feeling—Eric Andersen has a basic feeling that one of the things that turned Dylan away from the protest movement, among a lot of other things, is the fear that went down after Jack Kennedy got shot. That Dylan might have been a target himself.

I don't think he ever expressed that. While we were right around Dallas, he was writing a song. He used to write in the back of the car. He was writing this song called "The Chimes of Freedom."

He was writing at that time?

Right. That came out on his fourth album. Oh, I almost forgot. We stopped at Carl Sandburg's house.

Where was Sandburg living?

He had a place in Flat Rock, North Carolina [near Hendersonville]. And we went into the town. We asked around for it and—

Whose idea was it? Bobby's?

Yeah. We wanted to see the old man, and we went up to the guy's farm. He had a goat farm. We knocked on the door and he came out. He answered the door, complete in his beard. He's a little old man, wrinkled up. And Bobby said, "I'm a poet, like you." And Sandberg said he hadn't heard of him.

He wasn't aware of Dylan, but Sandburg had been putting together a book of folk songs around that time.

At that time, he was not aware of Dylan. And he was very nice and we talked on his porch for about ten minutes. It was very pleasant. Nothing serious. Bobby left him some albums, and then we were off down the road again.

Was Bobby hurt that Sandburg had never heard of him?

He was, yeah. I mean, he didn't show it. But it was obvious because after that he was very like cool. He was like cool for a while. And then I had an argument with him in New Orleans about his music, you know.

What about?

He was getting into a very freaky period, and I was in favor of the social protest music. It was sort of philosophical. It was like, you know, if there weren't people out there growing the pot in Mexico, you wouldn't have any.

Tell me more.

I don't remember what the hell. We were arguing about a chair. That's when he got into his whole thing about even the birds are chained in the sky—it's in one of his songs. Oh, oh yeah. "The birds are unfree because they're chained to the sky." And he started rapping this stuff at me, you know, and I said, like, "C'mon, it's all a lot of shit. You're saying that because you're stoned."

What kind of stuff were you using?

Grass, mainly. There were some pills, you know, but mainly grass. Grossman was sending it to us in parcel post. We'd go to general post office box so and so, and it would be there. It's very hard to remember because we were literally stoned.

Getting back to Sandburg, do you recall what they rapped about, the pleasantries? Anybody else come out on the porch?

There was a little old woman who came out. I think it was his wife. But she didn't say anything.

Did Bobby ask Sandburg about any of his writings, about any of his work, anything about his songs.

No, no. Bobby was trying to promote himself, you know. He wasn't interested in Sandburg. He was interested that Sandburg was interested in him and knew him. And he told him, you know, "I'm a poet and I've written some songs."

He called himself a poet?

Yeah, yeah. He said that, "I'm a poet, like you." And Sandburg smiled, you know. But it was all like very light pleasantry. Nothing really serious. You know, "I like your work and I've read you," and you know, this and that. But in the sort of a way that "you should recognize me too. I recognize you. But I'm Bob Dylan and I'm the new Carl Sandburg and you ought to know who I am." Then when we got to Dallas, we were all moved by that situation.

Yeah, this is only four months after.

We hung around Dealey Plaza and walked all around. We were trying to figure out how the shot came and what is possible. Because it looks like a weird shot. The place was empty. This was February. It was cold.

Did anything freaky happen as a result of this walking around? Did the cops in any way give you a hard time?

No. The craziest thing that happened was we asked a lot of people where Dealey Plaza was on the way there and no one knew. None of the people from Dallas. And finally, about the fifth person we asked, he said, "Oh, you mean where they shot that bastard Kennedy."

What was Bobby's reaction to that?

Well, we were riding through the South and we were, like, putting everyone down, you know. But at the same time, we were scared shit[less] because we were in Mississippi and Louisiana and Texas and we got a shitload of dope in the car. And everybody was stoned and if we had gotten busted, you know, forget about it. We'd still be cracking rock down there. When I thought about it later, I was scared to death. And we got involved with civil rights people in Mississippi.

Who were they?

They were the guys from the Freedom Singers, Cordell Reagon. Bobby was very close to him.

This is well after Chaney and Schwerner and the other guys were killed down there, right?

Right. No, it wasn't after. But, you know, I mean, you were in Mississippi. You were hanging around with black civil rights activists and you had a lot of dope.

What was Bobby's reaction to potential danger? Did you talk about the fear?

We talked about the fear in Alabama because we went into a joint to eat and they had all these signs on the walls, flags up. "If you're a nigger, Jew bastard, Communist from New York, keep out." You know. Things that said, like, "This place is for Americans only. No blacks" and with the flags up and all that. So, we were uptight about the whole thing, you know. And when we got into this college. I'm trying to think of the name. It's a name like Tuscaloosa, but it isn't.

In Mississippi.

Yeah.

All-black college.

All-black, yeah. And we got into this college and we were very upset because, like, cops tailed us from Jackson. The college is right outside of Jackson. Any New York plate gets tailed.

And you had stuff in the car.

We had stuff in a jar that we bought in Kentucky. And it was one of these joke jars that said "Marijuana" on it.

Oh shit. (laughs)

And we had put it up on the dashboard.

Oh Christ. You were really stoned.

Yeah, and at that time, like, we were scared but not really. Thinking back, it was lunatic. It was absolutely lunatic and especially to get involved with civil rights people. If there was a bust on that campus, you know, it would have been bad.

Bob performed at the college.

Yeah, but not formally. He sang a couple of songs in a room.

Let's get back to Dallas. I want to explore the thing that Eric Andersen tells me. Was it your feeling in any way that Bobby was grossly upset over the assassination? Did it affect him personally?

Not grossly, no. We were all upset. Plus, the fact that it was so recent. But it was more a curiosity than a really uptight sort of thing.

I want to explore this a little further. Do you remember anything at all that Bobby said about the whole set-up—Dealey Plaza, itself, the assassination, the reaction to this guy saying, "That's where they killed that bastard Kennedy"?

You know, we were yelling something out the window at the people on the street in Texas, in Dallas, but I forgot what. Something nasty, you know. Like "Killers" or "Murderers" or something, but it was a little hipper than that, you know. Like we were passing through Dallas and we went out of our way to see the spot, you know, and we stopped there for maybe half an hour. Just walked around that little plaza.

This is not the kind of thing Bobby might verbalize.

He was very closemouthed, you know. He didn't really talk about his feelings that much. He left that to his songs.

Did he talk about his songs much?

No. Very secretive.

How did he work? Did he write the thing out on a typewriter and then work out the chords later? Or did he work out the chords and work out words and work out chords?

I don't really know. Because I never saw the actual music-making process.

In other words, he was writing lyrics at the time.

He was writing poetry.

Or he already had it in his head as he wrote them.

But the main thing, I mean, when I saw him, time and time again, was over the typewriter. Punching them out.

That he may be a poet who was putting it down to music later.

Exactly.

That is the feeling you got. That he was writing poetry and he just happened to be a singer.

Definitely, definitely. I want to tell you about something that happened outside Denver. He had a concert in Denver, and we went to look up Judy Collins. But she wasn't around and we left and then we were heading west, again. Victor was driving and it was mountainous, and we came to a funeral procession, which you're not supposed to pass.

Victor decided to pass it. In fact, I was driving, and I didn't want to pass it because I was aware of the law. Victor—we didn't even stop the car. Victor jumped over the back. He slipped in next to me, shoved me over and said, "I'm going to pass it." So he did some beautiful driving, right, on these mountain roads, and we pass one car with the lights on, and two, and when he finally got in front of the hearse, and right in front of the hearse is this big state police car.

And we've still got all this stuff in the car. The guy pulls us over, and I was sure we were at least going to be taken into town and given a ticket. And he asked for the registration of the car. It was registered to Ashes & Sand, which was his holding company.

So, the guy looks in the car and there's, like, four freaky-looking people in the car. It was a brand-new Ford. It was the biggest, fanciest station wagon they make. And he looks at the New York registration, Ashes & Sand, and, you know, "What are you people doing a stunt like that?"

And the cop let us go. You know, when the cop starts to force us over, we were hiding the stash in the back seat or somewhere.

What was Dylan's reaction while you were hiding it?

Scared shit[less]. He did very little driving. He was always nervous in the car. It seemed to me he was always nervous about going too fast and going too slow or doing this or that. But it was a situation like you were constantly stoned. Right out of Kerouac, you know. [Victor's] driving a hundred miles an hour and stoned.

Did he talk about having been in these places before?

Yeah. In Denver there's a place called Central City that he had sung in before he came to New York. He sang in some joint—coffeehouse or something—in Central City, which is sort of like a small Disneyland. It's an old Western town that's been restored up in the Rockies. So, we stopped there, and he told us about when he sang there.

He played the piano. He didn't play the guitar then.

Right. He said that he played a rinky-dinky—

On the liner notes he's talking about how he played guitar in the place in Central City and the girls would come on and do their strip and then he would play and the guys would try to boo him off and he finally got fired because nobody wanted to hear a guitar player or something like that. Did he talk in any way about that?

No.

Apparently, that's bullshit. Apparently, he was playing the piano.

Right. I remember him saying that.

Did he ever talk about his name, where it came from?

No, never. Very uptight about it. We knew, I knew that he was Zimmerman.

Oh, by then everybody knew he was Zimmerman. When did you first learn he was Zimmerman?

Suze told me right around the beginning. But it was a thing like it just wasn't mentioned. I'll tell you about the rest of the trip. So, we stayed overnight in Grand Junction, Colorado. They had these steam pools out in the open, thermal water, you know, pure. And we swam and it's freezing out, like twenty below. You ran out of the building into this pool and you were covered by the steam. Didn't have any clothes on. That's one of the times that I got some weird feeling about him and Paul playing around. At this point I was very disillusioned. My mind was blown. Bob, he's a very strange character.

How was your mind blown? How was he a strange character?

Well, his notion of reality was like nowhere near mine, you know. I consider myself pretty hip, but I'm a fairly straight person, you know. I sort of got this idea that, you know, I was crazy. He's really a nut and Victor is really, you know, a freaky nut, you know. And you live in a situation when you're constantly with people and traveling in a car most of the time, or in a motel room or a greasy spoon, you know, and I had this feeling like I had to break away, soon.

What was his notion of reality?

It's all very strange. It was all philosophical, you know. You know, people always involved in mysticism and stuff.

Was he into mysticism?

Yeah. And he was saying very mystical things, constantly. Like the thing about the birds. Everybody's chained up and no one is free, and everybody is putting pressure on you, constantly.

Was he doing any reading at the time on the trip?

No, no reading at all. He would talk about that French poet all the time.

Rimbaud?

Yeah.

What'd he say? Do you remember?

That he liked him and that he really knew where it was at and things like that. He never said anything profound. In the whole period that I knew him he never said anything profound. He wrote some profound things. It was always like, "Where you at?" Like this whole trip was more feelings than words, you know. And all he would say was, "Where you at? What's happening? Oh, wow." You know, useless shit. (*chuckles*)

Then after Texas—this is backtracking. We stopped in a chili joint somewhere on the Texas/New Mexico border. Dumas, Texas. The waitress was a real country bumpkin and she wouldn't believe we were from New York. She said she never met anybody from New York before in her life. And he tells her not only is he from New York—and he showed her the license plate on the car out the window—but he made records. And that blew her mind. And he gave her a record, you know. She was, like, hugging it when we left. I'm sure it's still the biggest thing that ever happened in her life. Dumas, Texas.

What was Dylan's feeling, you know, reaction to all of this? He was grooving on it, I would assume.

He was grooving on the people and he was grooving on the road. He was grooving on talking to farmers and gas station—

Does Woody Guthrie ever come up as you're going along?

Right. That was the whole idea of the trip—that he was going to do a Guthrie-esque thing in traveling around.

Did he say this?

Yeah, yeah.

He was picking up the bill for all of this?

And we all had some sort of phony title in order to justify it on his taxes. Victor was the road manager.

Getting back to the whole Guthrie thing, did you go through Oklahoma?

No. We didn't go through Oklahoma. We had a weird route because we went down to New Orleans and we came up through Texas and through a corner of New Mexico and then to Colorado.

Dylan ever talk about Oklahoma, where Woody was from, or anything like that as you were going along?

No. He didn't really say anything about Woody.

Okay, continue your travels.

All right. Then we went to Reno and played a lot of blackjack, where I went broke. I blew, like, every dime I had, and I was very uptight. Of course, he wasn't. He was kidding around with the waitresses and all.

He was not the famous Bob Dylan as you're going through these places.

No, no. He was recognized in only one place, in Charlottesville, at the start of the trip. We went into a record shop. His third album was not out yet. And it was interesting—he was carrying a lot of albums with him, and he'd give them to people.

A promotion thing.

So we went into a record shop in Charlottesville, and they had his third album. For some reason, they had it. And he bought every one in the store, at list price, just so he could hand them out. And he was recognized in the store. It sort of blew people's minds to see Dylan in the store buying a Dylan album. And they started following him down the street, and he got into his usual uptight feeling—he was always afraid of a crowd.

Tell me about that.

Well, there was always a specific thing after a concert. It was like a bank job, you know, with the car parked in the back and it was always set up beforehand, you know, so he could shoot right out. And then we'd go off to the motel at a hundred miles an hour to make sure the teenyboppers weren't following him or anything.

But his uptightness about crowds . . .

He would run. He would feel like there's a lot of people here, let's leave. Like people were closing in on him, and he'd run off down the street or to the car. This happened at every stop. From Reno, we went to San Francisco and he had a big date—

From Reno to Frisco. Any stop in between?

No.

No attempt to look up Jack Elliott, who I guess was living out there by then?

No attempt whatsoever. In fact, we were going to be late for the concert. It was a big concert at Berkeley at the college in their big hall.

Was Baez at the concert?

Yeah. Baez came up onstage. It was a great concert. Because, you know, the audience was with it and they had been waiting for it. In Denver, you know, they came because they were interested, or they heard the name, but they weren't really Dylan people. But here they really were. That's about as far as I went because at that point we got into a big argument, and I said, "You're all crazy."

How did you get into an argument?

It was over something very small. I had some friends in San Francisco and I went to see them one night, alone, and it was just two people. I asked Victor for a couple of tickets for this concert and he started hassling about that. Then Dylan came in, you know, and Dylan accused me of using him, more or less, because I was asking for the tickets, and that was that. Dylan had a very funny attitude towards me. Because on the one hand he was trying to put me in a thing, like, that I was using him, which was a thing about almost everybody. He really felt people were out to manipulate him.

Were there people trying to use him? Do you have a feeling that Grossman, for example, was using him?

Yeah, yeah. Oh sure.

Like how?

He was a very young kid at that time. There were certain mechanical things that had to be done, you know, certain arrangements, financial arrangements and things like that that had to be made that he didn't really understand. I think he was very, very uptight about that whole scene, you know, about the mechanics of it. Because Victor was supposedly along to make sure that he reached each place and he got onstage, which Victor did very badly because he was a freak himself, you know. (*chuckles*) In fact, they blew one concert in LA. After San Francisco. There was a concert scheduled in LA and they got there the day after. I split in San Francisco. I said, "Screw you people. You're all crazy."

Tell me some more about that.

I said to him, "I'm beginning to think I'm crazy." And, "You're the people that are really crazy. Not me." I had friends also in Denver. I went to see my friends and all of a sudden, I was feeling like straight people. It blew my mind, right? And the same thing in San Francisco. And then when I got back, I went to see Suze right away. She was very uptight about the trip. Of course, she figured—

This was before she tried to commit suicide?

I think so.

Because that may have happened like in March, right after he got back.

Right, exactly. That's when the really bad stuff started. I mean, like really fierce, violent arguments.

Do you have any idea what was stirring some of this?

It was about lifestyle, more or less. Suze, at that time, was living at Carla's house on Avenue B. And Carla resented having him around all the time.

I'm trying to place the attempted suicide in relationship to the trip. Was it before you went away or after you came back?

I think it was after. Where did it happen?

They were living on Avenue B. On Fourth Street.

Right. You're right.

There's a feeling I get from a lot of other people who knew them that Suze had a basic feeling of her own worth and was not the kind who could devote herself to Dylan and his career and his lifestyle.

Exactly.

And, you know, just being his slave, in effect.

Exactly. Well, she had been talking about being an artist and she was doing a lot of drawing and painting. And he was the sort of personality that when he was in the room, he had to completely dominate the situation. He was running her ragged, in a way, with his fantastically overpowering and intense feelings and intense emotions that he had with her and that he had with no one else. Because with everyone else he had a cool facade, you know. But with her he would really break down to a little kid, you know, yelling and screaming and crying constantly. And then I would see Suze alone or Carla alone and they would say what was happening.

Carla was very uptight because of Dylan being around. Tell me about that.

Carla got the apartment. Then she invited Suze to stay there. And Suze came to stay, and Dylan was constantly around Carla's place, twenty-four hours a day, day after day after day. And it was grating on her. They were fighting, they were arguing, they were making love, you know. It was like a madhouse. It was like living in a loony bin. And the only other thing that I remember about then is when they had the big fight, the big split-up.

Carla said it was a nervous breakdown.

Suze really flipped out. I was around then. I was around the next day. I don't know what the argument was. The feeling I got was they were too young to really have a relationship. That they really weren't able to cope. And after that Suze saw him maybe a couple of times.

Was Bobby still attempting to get her back?

There was a period of a couple of months after that split-up where he was trying to reconstitute the affair, but she turned it down. And she was very uptight about seeing him.

What was Dylan's relationship with Baez at that point? Had he had a relationship with her before?

There were rumors. I recall one time in the fall of '63 we were sitting around—Dylan, myself, Suze—and Geno Foreman rapped on the door. And Dylan had just done something with Baez, a concert or had been out to visit her or something. Geno comes in—in Carla's place. And Suze is in the other room and Geno comes in and Bobby answers the door. And Geno puts his arm on him and says, "I hear you're getting into Baez's pants now," really loud. "Was it any good?" or something like that. And Suze turns a little, you know. And we're all kind of embarrassed.

Back to Berkeley. What was the relationship between Bob and Baez at that time? You were there for the concert.

I was there for the concert and I was there at the party after the concert. It was very, very close. It was very huggy and falling all over each other.

Had Bob ever talked about Baez before?

Yeah, it was the whole—the king and queen.

Yeah, but how did Bob talk about it? The king and queen is the public bit.

He talked about it. I mean, he had that image himself.

As the king and queen?

Right, right. And I think he was worried about Suze because he knew Suze was a little uptight about that. In fact, earlier in that trip he was calling her every night. And then as the trip got on, you know, like every other night or once a week. And towards the end he wasn't calling her at all. So, I saw her the first thing when I came back. I think the same night I got into the city and she was quite upset because she hadn't heard from him and she didn't know what was happening.

POSITIVELY FOURTH STREET

MIKKI ISAACSON

*How did he exist? By living with Mama Mikki, who scrambled his
eggs and took out what he didn't want. . . . You felt he was
somebody in terrible need and you wanted to help.*

M IKKI ISAACSON, combination mother hen and folk collector, had an
apartment on Sheridan Square in Greenwich Village that was an
around-the-clock open house for folk singers and hangers-on. She was
among the substitute mothers who fed Dylan and put him up when
he needed a couch to crash on. Eve McKenzie was his uptown yiddishe
mama, and Mikki filled the role downtown. She also typed out ideas and
song lyrics from the scraps of paper she gathered from his guitar case.
Mikki said, "I was a fan of Bobby's before Bobby had fans."

Did he mention Suze?
Well, I'm trying to remember. It seems to me at one point he did say, "I
don't think Suze's ever coming back," something to that effect.
Did he kind of explain why?
I'm not sure, yeah, because her mother had taken her [to Italy], and she
was to come back sooner but she ended up staying longer than she was
supposed to.
**She stayed through October or something. Instead of coming home Labor Day,
she stayed another month and a half . . .**
And so, he was convinced that it was all over. And I don't know what
happened in the mail between the two of them, maybe nothing.
Did Suze write to you at the time?
No. She was extremely confiding in me when she was around in person,

but she never wrote to me. But if we'd meet on the street and they were having any kind of trouble, she immediately unloaded on Mama Mikki.

It's hard to think in these terms now because we're well beyond that. These were two teenage kids . . . basically, it was a teenage love affair kind of thing.

Yes.

Terri (Thal Van Ronk) described it as a very pretty thing.

It was and everybody knew how Suze could make him jump through hoops. So, when it became time for him to perform, they would always push her and say, "Go on, Suze. Go put Bobby in a good mood so he can give us a decent performance." Because in those days you never knew what kind of a performance you were going to get out of the guy. Another thing was, in the first song or two if you applauded hard enough and acted enthusiastic enough it would give him encouragement to get better, just like Jack . . .

Jack Elliott?

Yes. And if he felt that he had fans in the room he would really become responsive. If he felt people weren't paying any attention, he would become absolutely doleful.

Were you at the [Caffè] Lena gig? Were you in the audience?

Yeah.

I understand it was a bunch of girls from Skidmore who weren't paying attention, who were talking through the act and the owner of the place had to get up and bawl them out . . . tell them to be quiet.

Do you know, I have no memory for that at all?

By the time your relationship with these people ended it was early '62. Would that be right?

It didn't really ever end. It was just that I was in the hospital.

When you left the scene . . .

I went to the hospital in November of '61.

And Lena's was sometime after New Year's, a couple of months after that apparently?

Bobby's gig at Lena's, I think, was in the early spring.

Right.

And I have never forgotten that bear hug he gave me. And another thing is that he once hinted when I asked him to come see me at the hospital, he said he had had an experience in a hospital himself and he wasn't the least bit interested in having another one. And that was one of the few confidences I ever heard from him.

Did he tell you what experience or . . . ?

No, but I think that when he wrote "The Walls of Red Wing," he must have been talking about that institution. You put things together, you know, years later.

You were telling me earlier, at the very beginning, about Suze. How at the time Bob was flopping at your place, Suze was living upstairs with her mother?

She wasn't living there. She was really living with Carla supposedly. But because the hour would be so late by the time we got Bobby off to sleep, she'd end up sleeping at her mother's.

At this time she was, like, seventeen. Why wasn't she staying with Mama?

'Cause Carla had a place of her own and she was staying with Carla.

And she wanted to stay with Carla?

Apparently. Except that she wasn't really staying with Carla. Half the night she'd be with us and the other half, she'd be up in the penthouse.

Right.

And it was a beautiful thing to see. Bobby lit up like a Christmas tree whenever she was around. He was so sweet, and sweetness was really not part of his personality. And compassion. But you didn't ever see it, except when Suze came into the picture. And Suze is such a beautiful thing.

You remember any anecdote that would illustrate this feeling that Suze got out of Bob?

I guess later on in life when he felt uptight, he'd get snotty towards people. He'd get wise aleck. He was never a wise aleck when Suze was around. He was gentle and sweet and loving, and so was she when they were together. They almost always were hand in hand. Everything they did, they did together, like when they'd look at a magazine. They split it between their two laps and read it together.

When did they take the place on West Fourth Street? Were you still around at the time?

Oh yeah. You see I kept coming home for leaves, and I kept my apartment and I'd still throw the parties during the time I was in the hospital, especially towards the end. I don't remember. I think it was after the Columbia contract and he couldn't quite believe it was happening to him, that's what he said.

Tell me something about his reaction?

He came in waving a piece of paper and yelling . . . with glee. He announced to everybody in the room . . .

Who was in the room? Do you recall?

No. I don't recall. No. I don't. You see, when Bobby was around—it was very much the same way with Jack or Dave even—when they were in the room, you forgot everybody else. And if Bobby ran in yelling you forgot everything. Their personalities were so dynamic that everybody else faded in comparison. I might have told you this on the telephone . . . someone said I was a fan of Bobby's before Bobby had fans.

You said, "He came in running, waving the contract . . ."

I don't know what he was waving. He wouldn't let anybody see it, but he was waving something, and he said, "I've got it! I've got it!" And we all looked blank and we said, "What have you got?" and he said, "A contract with Columbia." And nobody believed him.

Really?

Absolutely nobody believed him. And for a long time after that, he acted as though he was the same Bobby Dylan and then something happened. Nobody really knows what happened. It must have happened with the end of the Suze relationship.

When was this now?

Oh, quite a while later. Because after his first record for Columbia, he did a second record with a picture of Suze and him on the front in Greenwich Village in the cold.

Yeah, walking along West Fourth.

Which is a delicious picture.

The McKenzies. Is the name McKenzie familiar to you at all? Bob apparently stayed at the Mackenzies', and every time the name came up Bobby would shudder. Why?

Apparently this woman was mothering him to death, smothering him to death, and the man was fathering him to death and he had already had enough of that at home and he wanted no further part of it. He had gotten out of their house in the nick of time as far as he was concerned. They were laying claim to owning him practically, and all he could do was shudder and say, "Keep them away from me. I don't want any part of them."

What made people so maternal and paternal towards the kid at that time?

Well, a perfect example is the kind of thing I told you he did when it was time to go to sleep. He couldn't sleep unless he had Suze's arms around him.

Did he ever act this way before Suze came along?

No.

He was trying to break away from the McKenzies where he was tired of that

smothering kind of thing and yet he still needed someone like Suze to help put him to sleep?

And someone like me. To be the mother figure. I'll never forget one time, this is not answering your question, but I'll never forget he had a gig at, I think it was Gerde's, and he was chafing at the bit and he kept saying, "A week long is always enough. Two weeks is ridiculous. I can't hang in there for two weeks. I can't stand it. I want to cut loose and go. And I can't sit still for two weeks. It's just more than I can bear."

You mean he was saying he couldn't take performing two weeks at one place?

Yeah, because of the jerks in the audience.

Oh, and yet at the same time he was trying his best to—

To make a name for himself.

Did he ever talk about making it? Ever talk about fame or money?

Never. He was so closemouthed. Even about the McKenzies or whoever it was that he was trying to get away from. And yet he would drop so many little hints. You know, you just get a glimmering of what he was up to and then he'd cut it off and you couldn't get another word out of him.

Right.

And he didn't like to be pumped, so I did whatever he allowed me to do and I didn't overstep those bounds. If I saw he was turning off, I let it drop. And if you tried to pump him, he'd leave. He'd just get up and go.

Yeah. . . . Anyone else around at this time that you can remember?

The Van Ronks. Jack Elliott. Jack and Bob used to get on the stage together in those days and perform things together.

At the hootenannies?

Even at the performances, at the gigs.

Well, how many paid gigs did Bob have at that period?

Not too damn many.

Any idea? My impression was he had a couple at Gerde's.

That's right.

Maybe one at the Gaslight, one up at Saratoga.

Yeah.

And one out in East Orange that I'm trying to track down.

I don't remember that one. Although that doesn't mean it didn't exist.

But the Gleasons lived in East Orange, and it may not have been a gig. It may have been a trip to their house or something . . . the family that knew Woody Guthrie. In any case he apparently didn't have too many paid gigs during that period.

And all of a sudden Albert Grossman came along and he was flyin' high.

Right. What do you know about how Albert Grossman came into it?

Absolutely nothing. Bobby said he went to his office. He sat down. They talked for a few minutes. Then he shoved a piece of paper at him and Bobby signed and that was it for the next five years.

Five years, that would be in '67 it was up.

Five, yeah.

Now, at this point he only had a few paid gigs. He apparently had no money. I mean, he didn't take straight jobs?

Absolutely not.

How did he exist?

By living with Mama Mikki, who scrambled his eggs and took out what he didn't want . . .

Right. How long did he stay at your place? Do you recall?

Long enough to feel guilty when I went to the hospital.

What do you mean? Explain that?

Several of the boys felt very guilty when I landed in the hospital. They felt they had driven me. You see, I didn't lock my door in those days, and they came and went whenever they pleased. I was up more than I slept, and I was being Mother Mikki to so many.

And also at this stage, you had a job, you were . . .

No. By that time I'd given up my job. We all just immersed ourselves in the folk scene. And it was too much and they felt they had driven me. You know, they nudged me all the time that I wasn't putting out enough effort on their behalf . . . yeah.

You mean you didn't have enough wine and booze around or something?

(*laughs*) No. They knew they wouldn't find booze. I never had booze ever in the house.

Why?

Because once in college I had two people come over and the men got drunk and one of them punched me in the eye.

Oh jeez.

And I decided never again. And besides, I couldn't afford it, certainly not all those freeloaders. I used to serve coffee and potato chips or something, and these people, they couldn't believe I could have a party without having booze. But I did.

You were talking before about how when Suze left, Bob started drinking.

When she went to Italy.

Yeah. Where did he get the money to buy the wine or whatever it was he was drinking?

Well, none of us knew. First of all, he was very good at freeloading. The Van Ronks were crazy about him and they had him around a lot, and Robert Shelton had him around a lot. By that time, we all knew he was going to be somebody . . . Oh, you know where he had a gig? At Columbia.

Oh really? When was this? Do you recall?

It was in the winter.

After Grossman? After the record contract, [the] Columbia contract? Do you recall?

I can't remember. And then he had a concert at Carnegie Hall, which I didn't see, where he made a mess of it, and then there was another concert at Town Hall, where he did *not* make a mess of it. He was very good.

That was a little later.

Yeah. That one I saw. He had a talent for getting people to take care of him. He would look helpless and bereft . . .

A "teenage sponge" somebody called him.

You never felt he was sponging. You felt he was somebody in terrible need and you wanted to help. You felt he was somebody in such need that you wanted to jump in and save him from drowning.

What about Carolyn Hester? Was she around at the time?

Yeah, and I don't remember how.

You don't recall any relationship Bob may have had with Carolyn? Was anybody aware that he was Robert Allen Zimmerman from . . .

No! And he was *very* closemouthed about that.

Tell me about some of that.

I remember the first time I asked him how to spell his name. I said, "Is it D-y-l-a-n as in Dylan Thomas?" He said, "No. It's D-y-l-a-n as in Bob Dylan."

Did he ever talk about Dylan Thomas.

That was as far as he'd go. I told you, he'd turn you off. He'd tune you out and you had to drop it because if . . .

Right.

If you went on with it, he'd just walk out. So, you either played it his way or you didn't play it any way at all.

Dave tells me he got the feeling all through this that he wasn't a "Bob Dylan,"

that he was something else and Dave said he even had the feeling that he was Jewish because of a couple of things he dropped and that he was a suburban kid who was pretending to be a southwestern vagabond or something. Did you get any of this feeling at that time? Did you make any judgments on what his background might have been?

(*pauses*) I'll tell you what. Occasionally I would let slip a few things not purposely but just because it's part of my way of life. I would make a remark in Yiddish here or there. And once or twice I saw a twitch at the corner of his mouth and I thought, hmmm. Jack Elliott was another one . . . by the time I knew Bobby Dylan I knew that Jack Elliott was Elliot Adnopoz.

Elliot Adnopoz of Eastern Parkway or something right?

If Jack can fool the public as much as he had and so on, then I figured Bobby could, too, but I didn't know what he was fooling us about.

Right.

But Jack played his part to the hilt and so did Bobby. He was sick at my apartment and I was nursing Jack. So, because of these names and everything—I mean Adnopoz sounded Greek to me. It didn't sound Jewish. But after I found out Levys and Goldsteins and whatnot, I began to realize that Jack was a *landsman*.

Were you around when it first became known publicly that he was Zimmerman?

You see, it didn't become known publicly. First it became known within our group.

How did that happen?

Somebody would say something like, "By the way, did you know that Bobby was really Zimmerman?" And I'd say, "You're kidding?" And they'd say, "No, really." And it would become . . .

You mean it became generally known?

Yeah.

What was your reaction? Did anybody really care about it or it was just this thing . . .

Nobody could have cared less. The main thing was that he was so incredible when he was in the mood. See, Bobby was a creature of "in the mood," just like Jack was. If Jack wasn't in the mood, you couldn't get a decent performance out of him no matter *what* you did.

Right.

And you had to work so hard to keep him up. And the same thing was true of Bobby. You had to work like a son-of-a-gun to keep up the level of his performance.

Yeah. You recall any other ways that you and Suze and some the others worked to keep up the level of his performance?

Well, as I say, we used to sit where he could see us. He had bad eyes and we would try to sit up close and . . .

Did he ever wear glasses?

He wore . . . let's see . . . he wore sunglasses. Anyway, we would sit up where he could see us and applaud and look enthusiastic and try to get everybody around us to shut up and stop talking.

Right.

So, we'd be busy shushing and busy clapping and busy beaming at him. A tremendous interplay was going on between the performer and us. And we'd get a whole clique involved in working in that direction. And if you worked hard enough you could get a decent performance out of him.

Did you have to do this with any of the others?

Just Jack.

What about with Dave?

Dave was always consistent. He always said he was lousy, but he was always consistent. He was *always* fine. Even when he said he stank, he was always good. And we'd be very enthusiastic in front of Dave too. But because we enjoyed what he was turning out. Not because we felt he needed it for his ego. And afterwards when you'd say, "Gee, Dave, that was a great performance." He'd say, "Oh it was god-awful."

Were you around when the thing with Suze started breaking up?

I think there was a, if I'm not mistaken, there was another apartment after the West Fourth Street apartment.

Yeah.

And I would meet Suze in the supermarket and she'd be going in that direction. Now whether she was living there alone, and he was courting her again there, or whether they were sharing it together, I don't think I ever really found out.

You remember where that apartment was?

Somewhere in the Village. Yeah, West Village. Yes, because she was shopping right across the street from my apartment at 1 Sheridan Square, at the supermarket there. And she looked troubled and she'd be disturbed, and she'd talk about her job and . . .

Where was she working at the time?

I can't remember. She was doing some artistic work for somebody and I can't remember who or what.

Did Bob ever talk about traveling on the road, hitching rides, bumming around, meeting Big Joe Williams?

Didn't talk about meeting people. Not specific people, but he'd talk to us, as Jack did, about, and—I'll tell you what I felt. They acted as though they had read Woody Guthrie's biography and were then planning to create a life for themselves that was a replica of Woody's.

Right.

And if there was anything phony about the way they were behaving, it was in being imitative, so strictly, religiously imitative of Woody, and singing his songs the way he would have sung them and putting down people who sang them differently, like maybe Phil Ochs or somebody who'd sing them differently. And they'd put them down immediately. And Jack Elliott took great pride in the fact that he looked like Woody, and as a matter of fact, what I said earlier, I'll correct it. He said, "Son of Woody Guthrie, Father of Bob Dylan" and later on he said, "Son of Bob Dylan" and he was so bitter.

Why was he bitter?

Because Bobby made it and he didn't. Bobby got the contract at Columbia and Jack didn't. And they were both so similar in temperament. They were both such prima donnas. And you had to kowtow to both of them so much. It was a very strange relationship I had with these guys.

Was there any more on Jack's part? Was it a feeling that Jack had taught Bob some of it?

Well, you see . . . now I know Jack pretty well, even better than I know Bobby, and I don't believe Jack taught Bobby anything—unless by simply sitting in the audience, Bobby picked up Jack's material.

Yeah. As Bobby seemed to pick up a lot of . . .

Yes. That's possible.

But not specifically saying, "Hey, try this chord. Hey, try that chord."

I don't think there was any of that. What I *did* think was that here was a guy with an almost identical personality, almost equally schizophrenic as Jack, equally uneven in performance, equally weak in character (*laughs*), and equally gifted in song, who was suddenly writing his own material and getting away with it. And everyone was lauding and praising him for it.

Right.

That was beyond Jack, to write his own material. Jack was marvelous with mimicry.

Yeah, well, this is what made Dylan, put Dylan a giant step ahead of the crowd.

That's absolutely true.

You said Bob talked about being on the road and bumming around the country. You remember anything he said about it? Hopping freights? Hitchhiking?

It came out in the choice of the song that he would sing of Woody's and other people. You *knew* somehow that he had had these experiences himself.

But nothing that he specifically said, for example, about Big Joe Williams. He told Dave Van Ronk that he hopped a freight with Big Joe Williams down into Mexico.

He had a different relationship with Dave than he had with me. Dave and Terri were like, what do you call it? Well, "substitute parents" is good enough. They were like parents to him. I was like a hotel where he came to make himself at home, and he could put me out as much as he pleased. He could get away with murder and take advantage. (*laughs*) And he did it. But I'll never forget when Robert Shelton gave me his first record album and I said, "Bobby, will you sign this?" and he said, "Sign it? I'll write the hell all over the whole thing." And he wrote over the typed part of it, from top to bottom, a poem which threw Shelton into a fit. And I was deeply touched.

Do you still have that album?

Of course! Of course, I've got that!

Do you remember his reaction to Shelton's rave notices in the *Times* that September?

No, but I'm sure he was thrilled.

Bob's been quoted in a couple of places recently as saying that he wrote some of those topical songs, the protest songs, only because he knew this was a way of getting himself heard. This was a way of —

Bullshit.

— making it.

I don't believe it. I don't believe it at all.

Why not?

I think he felt very deeply about the things he wrote about. I don't think he could have written that material unless he felt it. But he, even in those days he used to say, "Ahhhhggg, nah, forget it." You know. He used to put down his own material sometimes.

Why? What made him . . .

He didn't want to get drawn into . . . he was so inarticulate socially. It was incredible how infantile he was socially. He did not know how to carry on a conversation or argument or a discussion. And he didn't want to be drawn into any because he knew he wasn't good at it.

Right.

He'd sit like a bump on a log. He'd read a magazine while everybody else was singing and talking.

Or he would make an outrageous statement that what he just wrote was a lot of bullshit so that nobody would talk to him about it.

Yeah, he'd put down his own stuff. He'd do all kinds of kooky things just to avoid getting drawn into a discussion. Bobby was on a gig in the West, with Jack Elliott, and he said, "I'd perform with that man in a sewer." He happened to be a Jack Elliott fan, too, you see.

But you think he was . . .

Bobby couldn't write those songs as well as he'd written them unless he felt . . . unless in his schizophrenic way, he was being Woody Guthrie when he wrote them and then anti–Woody Guthrie when he discussed them. I'm not a psychiatrist, but it's possible that in his Woody Guthrie moods he would write a protest song and, in another mood, he would put down the side of him that was Woody Guthrie-ish.

Phil Ochs has been quoted as saying that there were meetings up at the *Broadside* offices where the folk singers and the people around would come and swap songs.

There were meetings everywhere. They happened at my house. They happened in the square [Washington Square]. They happened in Izzy Young's place.

Bob would come and say, "Hey, look what I just wrote. You want to hear it?" and play for some of the other folk singers around. Did he ever talk about influences on him, besides Woody Guthrie? I know he never shut up about Woody Guthrie.

He never said anything about Woody either.

He never talked about Guthrie?

But he would always sing a Woody Guthrie song, just like Jack did. And every performance they would pay homage to Woody by religiously singing one song of Woody's before they were through.

Did he ever talk about any other people who may have influenced [him], say, Charlie Chaplin? Some of his early routines were very Chaplinesque.

They certainly were. God, were they.

Describe some of the things he did.

Well, I told you he'd get up on the stage and tune his guitar and then get off the stage. And everybody would be rolling in the aisles.

You remember any others?

Oh, I'll never forget. His eyes were so bad. Nobody was sure whether it was a put-on, a joke or a serious situation. He began taking out of his pockets harmonicas and laying them on the table. And he'd look at one and he'd put it down and fish out from another pocket another one, and he would talk into the microphone very sotto voce and he'd say, "Now where is that E-flat?" or whatever. And he'd talk to himself and he'd be digging one out and he'd go over the bunch that were on the table already and he'd say, you know, "I've got that one . . . now where is the other one?" and he'd feel in his pockets and you'd have to laugh it was so funny.

What was your feeling? Was your feeling that he was doing this as part of a routine?

I didn't . . . I wasn't sure, but he was getting away with it as being terribly funny.

It's quite obvious on hindsight to a lot of people that it was part of his routine. That he was doing it deliberately.

You heard about this before?

Not this particular story, but I've heard of others where he'd pretend to be drunk and fall off the stage. And Terri said, "I thought he was drunk! It was not until later that I realized it was his act."

Well, Terri may be exaggerating. There were times when he was drunk.

Oh yeah. In fact, Terri says that it's possible that the first time it happened he was drunk and got a laugh and then kept doing it.

I see. Okay. Good. I'm glad she modified that.

Yeah. But what about things like Lenny Bruce, for example? Did he ever talk about Lenny Bruce, Lord Buckley, any other kind of . . . ?

Oh, he'd wanted a Lord Buckley record for . . . he had me typing . . . What did he want off that record? I don't know whether it was a lynching or a death . . . I can't . . .

Off a Lord Buckley album?

Yeah. And he had me type it. I took it down in shorthand and then I typed it up for him and he was going to do it. I typed everything he had scribbled.

Tell me about some of these things that you typed that he'd scribbled. Songs and routines?

Songs, poems, routines, not routines, songs. Poems . . . snatches of this and that, ideas . . .

Did he ever explain any of it to you? Like where he got it?

Hooohhh, lots of luck! Yeah, occasionally he'd say that he "actually leaked out. I've had this around for months and months. I don't even know where it came from, but type it up anyway." And then I would say, "What does it say?" and it would take him ten minutes to figure out what it said.

You recall some of it? What some of it was?

No.

That you later heard used in any way? In an act? On a record?

I never heard any of it used. And I was very frustrated and annoyed with him because he was getting me to knock myself out lying in the hospital in the end and chiding me I was too busy to sit and type for him. And yet whatever I did type he'd never use it and there was one, "My father was an engineer . . . ?" It was kind of a tongue twister. It was a very fast song and he did try to rehearse it with me.

That sounds like a Guthrie thing. Did he use that one?

I don't know.

Besides Elliott, who were other guys he was playing with?

Phil Ochs was one of them. And then another time I saw Bobby in a small room in Columbia. He and Mark Spoelstra, who was also a beginner at that point, and somebody else—I can't remember who—were on the bill. Oh, I know who it was it was! John Hammond, John . . .

John Hammond Junior?

Yeah. Junior. And I thought the three of them were very talented and gifted. But I was a little annoyed with Phil Ochs because I felt his chords were a little too, were a little too studied.

Did Dylan ever talk about running away from home, about his family, you know, after you found out he was Zimmerman? What did he say about it?

As a matter of fact, *before* I found out he was Zimmerman, it was obvious that he had run away from home because he was so young. I don't even think he was eighteen. He was so young looking that he looked like a runaway.

Did he ever talk about his family?

Just that he had run away from home and he had had enough of that stuff. I don't know whether I got this from Shelton or from Dylan. He was reading one of the German philosophers inside an English book or a math book or something and the teacher called him on it and he got in trouble.

Did he say which philosopher? Kant?

Kierkegaard or somebody. I don't know who. It might have been Kant. I don't remember *who* it was, but I just remember that he was reading philosophy in the wrong classroom inside the class book. And the teacher came and found him out and he got in trouble for it. And he would *never* admit to reading anything.

Why?

He didn't want to be taken for a highbrow. He wanted to be one of the kids. And he didn't want to be taken as an intellectual. But you always saw him with something, reading.

Did he ever talk about the things he was reading? What about poetry?

Never. Never one word.

Were you at that place on West Fourth?

Yes.

Do you remember seeing books around?

No. (*laughs*)

Dave Van Ronk says flatly that Dylan was basically pretending to be an American primitive and he would never let on that he was familiar with the French symbolists and . . . Rimbaud and the whole bit because he was this primitive boy from the Midwest or the Southwest.

That's what he was doing. Exactly.

And wasn't about to let anybody know that he had some brains.

Exactly. And even when his first songs began coming out, he still wasn't about to let anybody know he had brains. Even though the songs clearly indicated it.

Phil Ochs is quoted, somewhere, saying that when Dylan was writing the topical songs, the protest songs, he was, like everyone else around, he was very left wing, and that he talked a lot about civil rights.

He didn't talk. He just wrote songs. And they spoke for him. Because he was so inarticulate socially.

But even later?

Even later.

When was the last time you actually had any contact with that . . .

Well, I told you, '61, but it must have been, if Phil Ochs was coming up, in '63. I must have seen him in '63.

But you do remember Phil Ochs?

Yes.

What kind of contact did you have with Bob and some of the other people around? Any anecdotes that might explain Dylan.

Well, one time he went to a to a junk shop in Saratoga. And he came back with glasses with wire frames about the size of silver dollars. And he had them on and it was very chic. And really, he's the one that started that craze.

Before John Lennon started fooling around with—

Waaaaay before. It was back in, probably, '62. Oh, I do remember Carla, coming around to Sheridan Square, saying how worried she was about Suze and Bobby.

Why?

That their relationship was so intense, and that Suze was so young and that their mother was disapproving, and Carla kept saying, "But I know Bobby is going to make it." And I kept saying, "You better believe it." Carla and Suze and I were among the first people who knew. The others were so self-involved. We were listeners and we were so sure this kid was going to make it. We just *knew* it, and we were right.

Did Carla talk about her mother's attempt to break it up?

No. I don't know about that, but I met her and talked to her and tried to convey to her that Suze was perfectly safe as long as she was with me, and that they called me "Mother Mikki" and I was going to take care of her daughter and she shouldn't worry and after that there were no more phone calls and no more hanging around, so I guess she took my word for it.

This is after [Suze's] trip to Italy?

No, I think it was before the trip to Italy.

What about other people who were around, not necessarily professionals?

By the time he did his first gig at Gerde's, he knew Robert Shelton and then there's Jack Elliott and the Van Ronks. Even Bill Cosby was around in those days. Cosby was on the same gig as Jack at one point at the Gaslight and Jack introduced us.

Who else? See, Bobby would walk into a room and be in his own little world like he'd pick up a book and read it or at least leaf through it. He would not make contact with other people in the room. Somebody would say, "Bob, how about a song?" And if you coaxed him enough, he'd sing maybe for quite awhile even, and as soon as he was finished, he'd split.

Right.

He had the strangest approach. And then when he really wanted to get some serious work done, he wanted me to throw everybody else out and then just the two of us work together. I kept saying, "Bobby, I can't do that. I have loyalties to more than just you. You can't expect me to just devote myself entirely to you."

What was his reaction to this?

He would be teed off. He'd say, "You promised," and this and that. "You said" and "You told me that." I said, "I will when I can, Bobby, but I can't always."

What were some of the things he was asking you to do?

Well, type up all his material and then type up some of the stuff that was current that he was doing at the time. He then proceeded to throw it into the bottom of his guitar case, loose just as he had done with the written scribble, but at least these were typewritten pages.

What about Suze's trip to Italy, the first trip to Italy?

Oh, that was such a nightmare!

. . . with Mama? Was that in the summer of '61?

I don't remember just when.

Tell me about that nightmare.

All of us were trying the best way we knew how to keep Bobby together, and Bobby was falling apart at the seams. He looked awful and he just let himself go. He smelled awful. And he drank too much. And his performances were way below par. He was so depressed we were afraid he was going to do something to himself—to hurt himself. We really were frightened.

Did you ever talk about it amongst yourselves, the possibility of it?

Oh yes. And then he turned out all this poignant material. And that's when "Girl from the North Country" came out and it *couldn't* have been about anybody in Minnesota. He was all wrapped up in Suze.

No, it's not on the first album. See, there's a problem here. He was writing things and they wouldn't be released publicly until sometime a year later.

Well, we'd been hearing them all that time.

Yeah. At that time, he was writing "Boots of Spanish Leather." When was that being written? At this same time?

No, during the time Suze was away.

Towards the end of the relationship. But you recall that "Boots" was written in this first summer, this first trip that Suze made with the family?

I am almost certain that it was, yes. And then there was the one with the line "Only when my own true love is near me."

I don't recall the title of that song.

Neither do I. It was—I can hear the melody in my head, but I can't put the lyrics to the tune. (*hums tune*) "Only where my true love is near me" It pictures a naked woman and a naked man in bed. And it's the only time it happens.

Oh yeah.

It's beautiful, beautiful. It always made me cry.

Did Suze write to you when she was gone? Did she write to anyone?

I don't know. There was a great deal of effort on everybody's behalf to encourage Bob to hope for the best, that Suze had not left for good, that she would come back, and she would love him as she had. And he would always say, "No, she won't. It won't be the same." But some of his best songs came out of him at that time.

Yeah, out of that crisis stage in his life.

All of us were terribly concerned for him.

You started telling me something about Bob and Jack Elliott playing together. How did they work together?

Beautifully.

How did that work? Were they both being paid at the time? Or was this . . .

Well, when Jack had a gig, Bobby would get on the stage and when Bobby had a gig, Jack would get on the stage.

And how do they go together?

Like Siamese twins.

Tell me about the "Hansel and Gretel" thing.

There would be ten or fifteen of us going from my apartment over to Gerde's Folk City on hoot night. Bobby and Suze would walk apart from us, hand in hand or arm in arm and always with their heads together, talking so softly nobody could hear them, and they always seemed to be the two against the world.

Yeah, that's a great description of them.

You know, two little lost waifs. It was on their account that I used to call my apartment "Mikki's Home for Homeless Folk Waifs."

Do you recall anything else?

Well, they would come over to my house and they would automatically go to one corner and sit there, and you couldn't hear them. They'd be talking, or they'd be looking. Then one would be looking at a magazine. They both read the same magazine at the same time.

Right.

And everybody else would be busy talking and socializing, and these two would be off in a corner in their own little world, always.

Do you recall when Suze returned from Italy?

They got right back together again like glue. I just know one minute he was in the depths of despair—she was never coming back—and the next minute they were together again. And all of us had a big sigh of relief and said, "Well, thank God."

He wasn't staying at your place by this time?

No! He stayed away from everybody while she was gone. He didn't want anybody to touch him or to breathe on him. He was smoking pot and getting drunk, being irritable and oh, he was impossible!

Anything else?

No, nothing beyond "Hansel and Gretel," which was exactly what they were like.

JOHN HAMMOND SR.

*There are people who are originals, you know, and you don't mess
with originals. . . . You don't mess with a guy like Bobby. And Bobby
was feeling his way, and every instinct Bobby had was right.*

JOHN HAMMOND SR. was the great statesman producer at Columbia
Records. His background was patrician WASP—his mother was a
Vanderbilt. He began studying piano and violin when he was four and
saw his first jazz show on a family trip to London when he was thirteen.
It was an African American show that featured American jazz pioneer
Sidney Bechet. Hammond attended boarding school in Connecticut, but
spent his weekends in Harlem buying what were called at the time "race"
records and going to blues and jazz clubs to see singers such as Bessie
Smith.

He dropped out of Yale to write for the English music magazine *Melody Maker,* which led to a job in the early 1930s at Columbia Records,
where he arranged to have jazz artists Fletcher Henderson, Benny Carter,
Joe Venuti, and Benny Goodman recorded. He persuaded Goodman to
hire black musicians Teddy Wilson and Lionel Hampton, and in 1933
Hammond arranged the recording debut of the eighteen-year-old Billie
Holiday with Goodman. Later, when he became a producer at Columbia,
Hammond signed Billie Holiday and Count Basie to recording contracts,
not as "race" artists but as jazz musicians.

From the very beginning of his career in music, John Hammond Sr.
worked for an integrated music world and wrote regularly about the racial
divide. He stated in his memoirs, "I heard no color line in the music. . . .
To bring recognition to the Negro's supremacy in jazz was the most effective and constructive form of social protest I could think of." His interest in
social issues and social reform continued throughout his life. In the 1950s,

during the McCarthy era, he signed left-leaning Pete Seeger to Columbia Records.

Hammond's ability to sense talent never wavered. He discovered Aretha Franklin when she was an eighteen-year-old gospel singer, and he signed Bob Dylan in 1962 because he knew Dylan was "an original." Ten years later he could still spot talent and potential. He signed the emerging Bruce Springsteen.

Why did they call it Hammond's Folly? Let's start with that one phrase you kicked off.

Well, I brought Bob Dylan in—I guess it was early in 1961. I'd heard him first playing harmonica for Carolyn Hester at a rehearsal on Tenth Street—down in Mrs. Scott's apartment on Tenth Street.

And then I saw this kid in the peaked hat, playing not terribly good harmonica, but I was taken with him. And we did a session up at Studio A at 799, and I said to Bob, "Can you sing and do you write?" And he said, "Yeah." So, I said, "Why don't you come up here, you know, and—"

This is the Carolyn Hester session.

Yes. After the Hester session, and I said I'd like to do a demo session with him just to see how it is. So, Bob came up the morning that Bob Shelton had reviewed him at Folk City. It was that very morning.

Yeah. This was September when the review came out. You had been hooked into doing it even before.

Yeah. Before—or long before that. I asked him to come, you see, at the Carolyn Hester thing. This is before he had opened at Gerde's.

Let's get back to the Carolyn Hester thing, down at Tenth Street. You were down there watching Carolyn's rehearsal?

Yeah. I had come back to Columbia, you know, about a year before. And I was distressed at the fact that we weren't tuned in to kids.

Right.

You know, Mitch [Miller] was still running the show, and the first thing I did when I came here was sign Pete Seeger. We signed Pete when he was still under indictment, you know, for contempt of Congress. And we signed him at the time he was still being blacklisted by CBS.

We couldn't even get him down to Brooklyn College a couple years before that.

Yeah. So, that sort of gave Columbia a better image, I thought, anyway. Because we were willing to take a chance on obviously a great artist, but a controversial one. So, Bob came, and I was just waiting for somebody who had a message for kids, because we had nobody like that on the label. And practically nobody else had anybody like Bob Dylan on any other label.

Bob came in, I heard him, and I flipped. One of the first things was "Talkin' New York."

But back to Carolyn Hester's apartment: what did you think of him at that time?

At that time, I thought, what a wonderful character.

He was playing, rehearsing for Carolyn.

Playing guitar and blowing harp.

And I said, Jesus, I'm sure this guy—he's got to be an original, you know. It was just one of those flashes you occasionally have, Tony. So, I brought him up. And I said, "Bob, I'm going to talk contract right away. Because I've just had some success. I brought in an artist called Aretha Franklin here, and they may not know what to do with her, but she's great. I'm in fairly good shape right now, and I don't have too many artists, and I'd love to record you."

So, he did his thing, and I said, "Well, how old are you, Bob?" Bob said, "I'm twenty." And I said, "Well, you know, I've got to get the contract signed by your mother and father." He said, "I don't have any parents." You probably know this story.

Yeah. But I want more details. Tell me as much as you can.

You'll be discreet about it.

Yeah. In fact, there's a point here where you don't want yourself quoted on, or it attributed to you, just say "off the record." I'll be discreet later. I'll double-check back with you before I—

Well, he said, "I'm Bob Dylan, and I don't have any parents." I said, "Have you got any relatives that can sign for you?" And the classic line was "yes." He said, "I have an uncle who is a dealer in Las Vegas." I said, "Well, I suppose, Bobby, that I've got to trust you on this." He said, "John, don't worry. You can trust me." I said, "Well, who's your manager?" He said, "I don't have a manager."

Did he mention Terri Van Ronk?

No.

Because Terri was an unofficial manager at the time.

He didn't. I said, "Well, I'll get you the very best possible deal that I can. Now, they usually start new artists here at two percent, but I'm going to start you at four." And I said, "You're better off not getting an advance. Because that means your album will start to make money . . ."

Right.

". . . as soon as it's out. Whereas if there were a lot of costs, you know, you'll be in the red at the end of the year, and then they may not want to renew you." We could only sign Bob for three years, because he was a minor.

Why is that?

Well, in the state of New York you're allowed only two options—one-year contract with two option years.

On a minor.

On a minor, yeah. I mean, it's a very sound rule of law.

What was Bob's reaction about the no advance?

Oh, he didn't mind. He wasn't interested in money. So, I got Bob in the studio maybe five or six times, and we made an album. And the musical costs of the first album were $402. Because it was just Bob. (*laughs*) And it came out, and nobody liked it. The executive vice president of our company was furious because I had not signed Joan Baez. They said, "For Christ's sake, you missed Joan Baez."

How did you miss Joan Baez?

Well, Joan had come up, you see, and Grossman was representing her. But just before I was with Columbia, I was with Vanguard Records, and I got Vanguard to record the Newport Folk Festival. Vanguard's a very smart little company. Vanguard put a little card in every album they sent out: "Why did you buy this record, and what do you like on it?" So, all these cards came out—there were about twenty artists, you know, on these Newport Folk Festival albums, and it was the '59.

Yeah, that was the first year Vanguard started recording Newport.

And all the cards came back saying Joan Baez.

Oh my god. (*laughs*)

So, Joan came up—and I was at Newport, you know, when Joan was there. And I remember she arrived in a hearse. She was a real far-out girl. Albert was asking for a large advance for Joan. I said, "Well, you know, Albert, I think Joan's going to require a lot of work, because she's not that sure of herself. But I'll give you a $1,500 advance and, of course, top royalties."

Vanguard, I understand, offered a $3,000 advance. So, she signed with Vanguard. Now this is not for—just turn the machine off for a second. [Recording resumes.]

In any case, Bob accepted the no advance and the four percent. Was four percent rather high for a newcomer?

It was unprecedented. So, the album came out.

What was Seeger getting at that point? You had just signed Seeger—

Five percent. And no advance.

Right.

Because Seeger doesn't want an advance. For tax reasons.

So, Pete was getting five and Bob was getting four—

This was a good contract. Bob's first album came in, and a lot of people didn't want to put it out. And the same guy who was bitching that I hadn't signed Joan and signed this creep instead—he was the guy who dubbed Dylan "Hammond's Folly." And so, we had a wonderful publicity guy at that time called Billy James. And Billy and Bob really became very tight. And Billy got Bob full-page spreads in *Seventeen* and all the kid publications and made a real character out of Bob. Columbia did a good job in promotions.

But the first album was a dud. I think the first album sold about five thousand copies. And I was—

At that time? By now it must have sold—

Oh, it's sold half a million by now.

What was he like to work with in the studio?

Just a doll. Completely inexperienced. He popped every *p*. You know, he didn't play the greatest guitar, but so what? He was himself. He did what he does now.

Somewhere I read that Columbia at that time felt he was some freaky harmonica player and didn't know what the hell—except for you. But some of the brass around didn't know what the—

Well, they didn't know. One guy who worked here, the sales manager, thought he was sort of a far-out comic, because of "Talkin' New York," you know.

Well, he also had a Chaplinesque quality—

That's right. And we've always been lucky with Bob's covers. You know, we had an absolutely marvelous cover on that first album.

That corduroy cap—

Yeah, and the chick, you know. And all the rest.

What chick? You mean, the second cover?

Yeah, the second cover. Suze, yeah. So, it came out. Then Mitch became a great big artist, and then a guy called Dave Kapralik got him.

So, Dave called me one day. He said, "John, I think we're going to drop Bob Dylan." And I said, "Over my dead body. God, Dave, don't you see the potential in this guy?" And he said, "Well, all I can see, John, is that he sold five thousand albums and there's no money in that."

This was after the second or the first album?

After the first album.

Before you cut the second?

Before I cut the second album.

And Dave, as head of A&R, wants to drop him because he doesn't sell?

That's right, yeah. So, I said, "Dave—"

Excuse me. Let me ask you something. Five thousand at that time—what would be a break-even point?

A break-even point for Columbia would have been about five thousand at that time. But you know, it was no real money, because this was brought in for peanuts, $402. So then, we were working on the second album.

Wait. Did you fight Dave down on the—?

Of course. No question about it.

Dave sort of knew that I did have a little part of Columbia, that I had brought some important artists into Columbia originally, so he didn't fight me too much then. Then Bobby came into the office one day and he said, "John, do you know Albert Grossman?"

I said, "Sure, I know Albert Grossman. We've been on the board of the Newport Festival, you know, for the last three years." And he said, "Well, Albert has got a deal for me to go over to England and do a pilot for BBC." And he said, "There's a lot of loot involved"—it was two thousand bucks, which I could show you, because I've been lending Bob money, which he always paid back. And—

How much money you loan him?

Oh, you know, $75, $100—things like that, when he needed it. I also got him a publishing deal.

Which publisher?

Leeds. And I'd made the album. He didn't have a publisher, and so [to] Lou Levy, I said, "Lou, I got a real talented guy here." And he asked me, "Have you made an album, John?" I said, "Yeah." "Is it released?" "Yeah." He said, "Send him over. I'll give him a $500 advance." So, Bob signed with Duchess Music [an imprint of Leeds].

He said what do you think of Albert Grossman? And I said, "Well, I can work with Albert. He's not the grooviest guy in the world, but if you want to sign with Albert, go ahead."

This was after the first album had been released?

After the first album had been released, and we had just about completed the second album.

When did you complete the second album? Do you recall the date?

I don't recall the date, no. But it was, I would say, at least '62—something like that.

The first time you ever met Bob was at West Tenth Street with Carolyn—

Yeah—

You went into the studio the first time in November of '61.

The Albert Grossman thing—you're right—the Albert Grossman episode came about the following August, I'd say.

'62.

'62, yeah. No—turn the tape machine off.

[Recording resumes.]

Bobby had just written "Blowin' in the Wind," and Peter, Paul and Mary had heard [it], and Peter, Paul and Mary were, of course, the brightest stars at Warner Bros. recording, so—

They were about the only stars at Warner Bros.

Yeah. And so, when Artie Mogull at Witmark heard "Blowin' in the Wind," he said, "Bobby, I want to sign you right away." Bobby said, "Well, I'm sorry, Artie, I can't. I just signed a contract with Duchess Music." So, one of the smartest things that Artie Mogull—now, this is Artie Mogull's story—it's denied by Lou Levy, but Artie Mogull said, "Well, here, Bobby, here's a thousand. Why don't you go over and see if you can buy back your contract?"

And Bobby said, "Groovy." So, Bobby went over to Leeds, and as luck would have it, Lou Levy was out in Nevada someplace, and the guy called Hy Grill was running the office.

And so, the question is whether Hy took the money or not. Lou Levy insists that they gave Bobby back his contract, but Artie insisted Hy took the $1,000—and that's the most expensive thing that ever happened to Lou Levy (*laughs*) and—

Bobby got his contract back and he signed with Warner Bros. Which actually put ASCAP back in business. Because Bobby was the first young writer that ASCAP had come up with.

Yeah, everybody had gone to BMI.

Everybody was BMI at that time. So, it was a very important thing for

ASCAP. But anyway, we completed the second album, and this album started to take off, thanks to "Blowin' in the Wind," and thanks to the marvelous work Peter, Paul and Mary had done with [the song]. In fact, we put a special sticker on the second album saying, "Featuring Blowin' in the Wind."

Yeah, I remember that.

Then you can imagine that my relations with Albert Grossman were not the most pleasant. One of the reasons, of course, Albert was so uptight about all this was that Bob had signed a contract with Columbia before Albert was the manager, and he wasn't getting his ten percent. (*both laugh*)

Very clear.

And Albert and John Court insisted on coming up to all the sessions. And John Court was trying to tell Bobby what to do and telling me what to do, you know, and the rest and I ordered him out of the studio.

What was he trying to—?

You know, just saying, "This isn't good. I don't want him to do this" and all the rest. I said, "John, if you don't like it, you can leave." And he did. And Albert stayed around. And then Albert had a brilliant idea that Bobby ought to be recorded with a Dixieland band, and that was a disaster.

You mean, you actually tried it?

Oh, yes, a single was released, I think, in England.

What was the name of that?

I forget now.

Is that the "Confusion—

Yeah. "Mixed Up Confusion" on the other side.

I can't find it around. Was it released in England?

Yeah. And at this time, I was saying, "Bobby, you should be recording in Nashville."

Really? Back in those days?

Yeah. Back in those days. One night, we were recording "Oxford Town." And Don Law, who was the head of our Nashville operation, was in the building, and I said, "Don, you have got to come up and hear this kid. Because he's a genius, and he's got to work with Nashville musicians. We don't have the kind of guys around here who can play for him." And—

Even among the New York studio musicians?

Yeah. I said, "This isn't the right scene for Bobby." Don Law came in, listened to the lyrics of "Oxford Town" (*laughs*), and he said, "My god,

John. He could never do this kind of thing in Nashville. You're crazy." And walked out of the studio. (*laughs*) Don Law is my very good friend. I've never told this story before.

He was probably right at that time too.

Probably was. Anyway, I was being completely undercut by Dave Kapralik in this thing, because Dave was dealing directly with Albert, whom I wouldn't talk to. Because I insisted on talking to—to Bobby.

Was Dave dealing with Albert because you wouldn't talk to Albert?

No, no, no. I would deal with Bobby, but since Albert was not the manager at the time the contract was signed, I saw no reason to talk to Albert. Also, I felt that I understood Bobby a little bit better than Albert did, as to what Bobby was trying to say and what Bobby was trying to do. But Dave wanted to be a big man. So, I said, "Well, Dave, you know, if you're continuing to talk with Albert, I feel completely undercut." And I said, "There's a good new producer here in the company, Tom Wilson, and I think Bobby would love working with a good black guy who's aware and everything. Why don't you let Tom take over?" At this time, I was starting the third Dylan album. I said, "Why don't you let Tom record him now?"

But Dave tells me that you and Albert had a confrontation. And that you had an argument about Dylan and about Columbia and about the whole thing. Dave said part of the reason was the John Birch Society song, "Talkin' John Birch [Paranoid] Blues."

"Talkin' John Birch," that's right. Yeah.

Grossman charged that you didn't back them up sufficiently on the whole problem.

That's a lot of bullshit.

Wait a minute. Dave said—I made some notes—Dave said it was a huge confrontation between you and Albert, that Albert had come to him and said they didn't want you to produce Dylan any longer, and Dave said he later was sorry that he did put Tom Wilson on, because it was a great disservice to you, he felt. But he says he actually requested that you be taken off as producer, and that somebody else—

This is—Albert—obviously. I don't think Bobby ever did—but I also said to Dave—no, the "Talkin' John Birch" thing is very interesting. I had nothing to do with this.

Well, except in the sense that you were the producer and had some weight in the company. Grossman at least was using this as one of the reasons—

Oh, I screamed my head off. What happened with "Talkin' John [Birch]"—Ed Sullivan had Bob Dylan on a show, and this was the number Bobby wanted to do. And CBS lawyers said, "This is libelous. This libels every member of the John Birch Society." And CBS lawyers—and this has nothing to do with Columbia Record lawyers—

Yeah.

CBS lawyers came in and said it cannot be done.

I understand the irony of it is that Clive Davis was the attorney at the time for the CBS lawyers, who had to convey the message down here that CBS—

Oh no. Clive was a Columbia Record attorney, not the CBS attorney. On the contrary, Clive was very upset about this.

Clive was saying, "I disagreed with the CBS lawyers, but my hands were tied."

Yeah. Clive was very upset about it. Clive said to me, "John, what can I do? The network has taken a stand here, and after all, we are owned a hundred percent by the network. There's nothing I can do for them." I screamed. I don't think anybody else would have dared screamed as loud as I did on this. Because it was a funny song.

Yeah.

And they never could have sued on the song. Because it was in the spirit of satire. Anyway, they took it off the album. I was furious.

And Sullivan at the same time had to demand cuts in the song.

That's right, that's right. And so, by this time, I didn't have any more to do with Bobby. I requested that Bobby be turned over to Tom Wilson. Dave and I had an understanding on this, that Tom would be the right guy. Wilson had just joined the company about two months before. And I loved the idea of Tom doing something other than a black artist.

Dave tells me Grossman apparently was attempting to use all of the problems they were having with the Birch Society and a number of other problems as another attempt to get Dylan away from you. From the label.

I had made one terrible goof—I might as well confess this now—in the signing of Dylan. There's usually an automatic escalation clause on the contract. You know, you start at four percent, then you go right to five percent. Which is what I had requested in the requisition for the artist contract. But when the artist contract came through—and this was something I didn't notice, and Bob didn't notice—there was no escalation clause.

Bob probably wasn't even aware there should have been.

Yeah. Well, I knew there should be. And there was no escalation clause.

So, by the time Bob's contract was finished with Columbia, which was five years later—'66—there was a one percent thing there which amounted to hundreds of thousands of dollars, which was being held in escrow.

Yeah.

And, of course, would have been given back to Bobby as soon as he had re-signed with Columbia. But it was a wonderful bargaining point on Columbia's part. Because if this money was all going to be released at one time, Uncle Sam would have gotten ninety percent of it. (*laughs*) And this is what Columbia threatened. And then, of course it's— *

The end stage, when Bobby was threatening to move over to MGM.

MGM. Then, of course, Grossman negotiated this million-dollar deal at MGM and, well, my great friend Mort Nasatir was the president and was delighted because Morton knew what he had. And then the MGM board of directors turned it down. (*laughs*)

Why did they turn it down?

Because [it was] too much money. And they figure maybe that Dylan has shot his wad.

Yeah. This is '66 . . . this is after the accident.

Yeah.'66, '67. After the accident, and Bobby, you know, was very, very sick.

Yeah. There was some question whether he had broken his back—

Well, the neck was dislocated, you know. He was in bad shape. I don't know this personally. I do know it from my son, who was very close to Bob. Well, in any case, Bobby stayed with Columbia. Bobby got all his five percent, you know.

Retroactive.

Retroactive when he re-signed. And of course, the first thing he did after his accident was *Nashville Skyline,* which is the biggest—oh, excuse me— *Blonde on Blonde* was the first thing he did after the—

No, *Blonde on Blonde* was maybe released while Bobby was recuperating, but I think it was cut before that, wasn't it?

Yeah, yeah. It was released while he was recuperating—but, of course, it was the biggest album, and by this time, of course, the perfect man was producing Bob Dylan. It was Bob Johnston, who was ten times better a producer, I assure you, than I was.

Why do you say that?

He's a songwriter; he completely understood Bobby. He was irreverent—he was everything. He let Bobby have his head completely, and yet gave him direction when it was necessary, and it was just marvelous.

Phil Spector, in an interview in *Rolling Stone*, said, "They're handling Bobby all wrong. If I was to produce Bobby, I would have a great rock and roll star out of this boy."

What he didn't realize was that there are people who are originals, you know, and you don't mess with originals. You just don't mess with them. Don't think Phil isn't a bright boy. He is. But you don't mess with a guy like Bobby. And Bobby was feeling his way and every instinct Bobby had was right. Because you know, the big initial boost to Bob Dylan in this company was Johnny Cash.

Tell me how did Cash boost—

Well, Johnny is a rebel, you know. At least he was in those days. And Johnny loved me, because I brought Pete Seeger back into records, into respectable records. Pete's another person that Johnny respects. And also, Johnny knows I also have a certain amount of integrity. And so, whenever Bobby was appearing around, you know, Johnny would always come in; always come when my son [blues singer John Hammond Jr.] is appearing, and the rest.

And I think Johnny probably had as much to do as anybody getting Bob down to record in Nashville, and certainly Bob Johnston did too.

Yeah. But how—

Bob Johnston is just the most wonderful guy. He took two artists that I brought to the company—Bob Dylan and Leonard Cohen—and he—

Oh, was Johnston the Leonard Cohen producer too?

Oh sure. Yeah.

How did Cash push Dylan in the early days here at Columbia?

He was behind him every which way, and they all knew it. He made it known to Clive, to everybody involved, that Dylan was a giant.

Getting back to Grossman, you're quoted as saying that Grossman was trying to take Dylan away from Columbia. Obviously he was. What was the motivation?

I think ego. I think Albert really wanted to be a star-maker. If Bobby stayed at Columbia, he wasn't a creature of Grossman.

Is it true? I mean, I understand Bobby is suing Albert now.

I don't know if he's suing, but I know he's going around town asking if some people will recommend managers. The word is that he came back to the Village because he wanted to get out of the whole Grossman complex up there in Woodstock. Was just sick of the whole scene.

I could improvise a whole lot of other things about Bob Dylan and the rest, but I can tell you what Bob Dylan did for this company, Tony. Before we had Bobby, you know, we were a middle-age-oriented company. Bobby comes, Bobby hits, the next thing that happens is the Byrds make an album of Dylan's songs. Suddenly, we become the hottest thing in the underground. And—

Big, middle-aged company is the hottest company—

Yeah. And of course, Clive Davis, you know, takes over from Goddard [Lieberson], and Clive is almost the brightest man I've ever worked for. I mean, he's incredible. His antennae [are] such, and his work habits—I wish mine were one-tenth as good, because there isn't a product out of this company that Clive doesn't listen to, and doesn't know exactly. Whether it's in classical, in hillbilly, anything. I mean, Clive is there. Now, his decisions are not always right, but his instincts are great.

When you first met Dylan, or were working with him on those two albums, did Dylan ever talk about the influences on him?

Oh sure.

Like what?

Well, Woody, obviously. He followed Woody around for, you know—Pete was another. Jesse Fuller.

Did he talk about having met Jesse Fuller?

Oh sure.

What about rock? Was there any discussion of rock?

Well, Bobby wasn't that much—

As much as he was as a high school kid.

Yeah, but when he was here, he was thinking about roots more than anything else. And about injustice. And about, you know, a social scene he thought stunk. And Bobby, I think, really wanted to change things.

Did you talk about how he was disenchanted with our social system?

Yeah.

Did he talk about it in specific terms, outside of his songs?

Bobby was uptight about the whole setup in America. About the alienation of kids from their parents, and about the values. His instincts were superb. At least, from my leftist point of view, it was. I'm going to level with you where I was wrong, and I also want to tell you that I'm a guy who is tremendously classically oriented and jazz oriented and blues oriented. And I respect and value folk, but you know, it's not really my bag. It's not the bag that I know.

Let me run through a couple questions—on rock and roll, you are quoted as saying that Dylan and Robbie Robertson's group had gotten together rather early.

Yeah.

'62, '63.

That was wrong. I found out from my son John, who knows these things better than I do, that it was actually '65. And actually, they were working with John, I think, at a time when Bobby heard them and Bobby took them over—

Did he hear them up in Toronto?

Bob heard them up in Toronto. My son will give you the correct dope on the—I know one thing that when [the album] *Big Pink,* when the Band, was offered to us, [they were] turned down by Bill Gallagher. (*laughs*)

Did he really turn the Band down?

Yeah, he turned them down. Isn't that awful? Because by that time, I was out of the Dylan scene completely.

Dylan going into rock: the influences that created this. Why did he go into rock, in your opinion?

Well, partly growth, and partly his own ears. Partly Rolling Stones. Partly the Beatles. This is where the action was. Bobby always wanted to communicate with kids, and he wanted to communicate in an area they understood. I think Robbie Robertson had a lot to—

If they met somewhere in '65, Dylan was already into rock by then.

Yeah, but not really.

Well, August '65 was the Newport thing that they booed—

For him being electric. But he'd already met Robbie—I think he'd met Robbie a couple of months—

I'll check with your son.

I think it was in June. No, it was even earlier than that that he and Robbie had gotten together.

Right. There's [a] feeling around—Eric Andersen's feeling was, and he was close to Bob throughout the '63 to '65 period—that Dylan had always been heading towards rock. You know, it was the natural thing to do. And that Dylan, in fact, could have been the superstar, but the Beatles came along a little earlier and took the whole play away from him.

Well, this is possible, but don't forget one thing, and this again is just my own point of view: Bobby is not that heavy a guitar player. You know, Bobby's chord structure and Bobby's musical knowledge [are] much more limited than the guys that were really playing.

Yeah. So, it would be Bobby Dylan as a Mick Jagger, who doesn't play an in-strument, who is not heavy into any instrument, could have come off that way.

Bobby is not that kind of an exhibitionist. Bobby has always been so much more introverted. It's very doubtful Bobby could have been the super rock star, because Bobby is more reflective.

Yeah. You said Dylan's political strand was lost with Grossman, partly the money, partly Grossman made him a businessman and then *poof*—and changes.

Yeah. I would suspect—now, for instance, we're getting some pressure for reissuing "Talkin' John Birch Blues," which I would love to put out. But I don't know any longer whether Bob would want it out. I haven't checked with Bob on this. Because I respect Bob's privacy. I don't want to bother him about things like that.

Someone—I think it may have been Eric Andersen—tells me that another factor that got Dylan off the political track was the Kennedy assassination.

Oh I'm sure.

That Dylan was out front, and it's quite possible that Bobby was feeling I'm up front there and I could be next. Was this—

I wouldn't think this would have a thing to do with it. I wouldn't think so.

Why not? I don't mean necessarily consciously.

I think Bob probably is politically, pretty much the same as he always was.

Yeah. But the public posture is that he moved from the political thing to a more romantic, negative—

Intimate.

Personal.

Introverted thing, yeah. It's quite true. It's quite possible. I don't want to seem to be an authority on that. You know, Tony, I'm trying to be honest with you and not say things that I'm not sure about.

Dylan has become, from what people have told me, pretty much of a mature individual. Father and a family man.

I thought so very much. I mean, I just had maybe forty-five minutes with Bob that day. But I felt that it was a completely new person.

What effect is this having on his music? Do you have any idea where he's going now?

When you're involved with a genius like Bobby, it's much better not to prophesize. Because I have a feeling that everything Bobby does is going to be Bobby.

You clearly dislike Al Grossman—why?

Albert?

On or off the record.

I don't think he has ears and I don't think he has taste. That's off the record.

And he's—I respect Albert a lot for what he did with that club out in Chicago, for giving Bill Broonzy and other people I liked a shot. But I just don't think Albert is with it.

Right.

With all the long hair, with all the granny glasses and everything, I just don't think that—

He's still basically a businessman.

You said that, not I.

And of course, it was my son who originally told me that Bobby's name was Zimmerman, because John was doing a gig out in Minneapolis. He said, "Dad, did you know that Bob's real name is Zimmerman, Bob Zimmerman, and that he went to the University of Minnesota?" And I said no, I didn't.

Was this before he was signed?

Before he was signed. I said I couldn't care less what Bob's background is. It's his own business, but that was the first time, I thought—maybe there were parents.

Right.

You see, Bob had a romantic point of view about himself at this time. You know, when Bob told me he had no parents—as Bob Dylan, he didn't have any parents. Because, you know—he created a new person. At least he figured he did.

The big thing, according to people who knew him at that point, is a crisis of identity, but—

He didn't want to be the son of a—of a middle-class hardware dealer in Hibbing, Minnesota. Right?

And of course, the only really bad thing that Bob and Albert Grossman did that I'll never forgive them for, they tried to get Billy James fired here for the *Newsweek* piece. And that was miserable, because Billy did more for Bob than anybody you can conceive of.

But what response—how responsible was Billy James for that *Newsweek* piece?

He wasn't. *Newsweek* wanted to do a cover piece on Bob Dylan, and Grossman wouldn't allow Bob Dylan to be interviewed.

So, out of complete frustration and sheer rage, he did his own research then. And found out this whole story on the telephone. They asked a neighbor if they ever heard Bob sing before, and the neighbor said, "Don't you remember? We heard him at his bar mitzvah."

Who wrote that piece?

Hubert Saul, the music editor at *Newsweek,* who's a great guy. One of the best journalists in the business.

Yeah, that was lousy thing to do to Bob.

Well, this was not done to Dylan; this was done to Grossman. This was done very purposely to Grossman.

I always thought Dylan just shrugged off the whole thing. Because by then all his friends knew about it.

Yeah. Of course.

In that period when you first met him, he was telling people that he didn't want to let Joan Baez record some of his songs, because he didn't like Joan Baez at that time. Were you aware of any of this?

I'd heard about it, but I'm not aware of it. The other thing I always held against Bob was the treatment of Joan in that *Don't Look Back* picture. I think that was a disgrace, because it was Joan who made Bob in England.

Yeah.

And you know—he cut her right off. I thought that was unforgivable.

Yeah. Why did he do that? I wonder.

Oh, Grossman, obviously.

Dave Kapralik tells me—getting back to the Byrds singing—that you were so enthused about Bob at the beginning that Dave, who had writer veto on the contract, said to you, "Go ahead, sign him. You're so enthusiastic, I don't even have to hear the guy. Go right ahead."

That's true.

BRINGING IT ALL BACK HOME

CAROLYN HESTER

What was he as a man? Maybe he wanted to know.

CAROLYN HESTER was a warm, fresh-faced young folk singer from Texas. Called "the Texas Songbird," she had sung at festivals and folk clubs around the country, had made two records for small labels, and was then signed to Columbia by John Hammond Sr. She and her husband Richard Fariña met Dylan in Cambridge at Club 47, where she was regularly appearing all that summer of 1961. The interview begins with Tony and Carolyn discussing the early folk scene, and some of the artists who paved the way for her and Baez and Dylan.

———

Pete Seeger was, had always been, writing songs and the Weavers had their hits and so on. And Pete Seeger is kind of popular folk music. But I think because Dylan was so young, I think he gave that particular area a shove. And he had Grossman as a manager and he had the distribution of Columbia Records behind him.

He had everything going for him at that stage.

Yeah. At some point he goes over to England and I didn't see him in England.

He went to England around New Year's of '62, that is, January of '62.

No, February of '62. And I was singing two weeks at Gerde's right before I left, and I think I left on February 6, 1962, to England. It was my first trip. Now Dylan comes over there at some point, but I didn't see him. I believe he came—

Do you remember roughly when it might have been?

The summer of '62. And I think it may have been while I was here that Dylan had his concert. Now what impressed me was that I didn't know he was writing so much. But I didn't know how much until he unveiled onstage that night a host of songs.

"Blowin' in the Wind"?

"Blowin' in the Wind," "Boots of Spanish Leather," for Suze. A whole lot of things. I wrote down as he sang.

If you find your notes, maybe take a picture of it or something.

Anyway, Grossman's office must have a program of that concert. At any rate, I was bowled over by the concert. In fact, everybody was.

Did you see Bobby in London?

No. I don't think I did. I think I went in February of '62. I came back in May and June of '62. I was separated from Richard, except not officially. Everything was in an uproar. I had some gigs to do here, and I think while I was here, maybe in May or maybe in early—it might have been in May—Dylan made his debut concert. Now I may have that date all wrong. But that's my impression.

You're very close.

Now, in June anyway, I went back to England. In October I left England and I came back here. And I believe he came to England about that time. When he was in England, Ric [Eric von Schmidt] got to England and Ric and Richard and Dylan made a record. Do you know about this record?

No.

Dylan was under contract to Columbia Records, and of course they couldn't use his name. And he called himself Blind Boy Grunt.

Oh yeah. Was that in England?

Yes.

Yeah. I know the Blind Boy Grunt. I thought that was one of the Newport things. In which they used it on a lot of Folkways or one of the—

No.

Who made a record? Richard?

Richard. Ric.

You mean Eric [von Schmidt].

Yeah. And Bobby.

Remember what label it was?

No, it's a British label. And Ric did the cover for it. Yeah, it's a very well-known recording in England.

It's not well known here.

Izzy Young may be able to help you put your finger on the record. Well, anyway, Richard at this time had begun to play dulcimer, because a man made a dulcimer for me. And I gave it to Richard and Richard was playing it quite a bit. So, on the record I believe Richard plays dulcimer and sings and Blind Boy Grunt plays the harmonica. And maybe sings. And Ric sang.

Now, Richard wrote me a letter about that time and he said, "Ric tells me he's separated from his wife. Dylan is without Suze. And I'm without you. A fine threesome." That's how I placed the date. He may have been in England when I was here in May and June or—okay. I came back in October. In November of '62 I sang at the Blue Angel for a month. I had decided I was going to be divorced. In December I got an apartment on West Twelfth Street, 225 West Twelfth Street. I had the impression that Suze had come back. I can't remember exactly. But Bob was very upset about Suze. I think she had already come back and they were split up. And he was going to go to England and I said, "Look, Rory McEwen had helped Richard and [me] in England. He is the dearest friend to us. I want you to meet him. Rory is going to come to my house tonight and he wants to meet you and he would be a great help. If you want to get going in England, you know. I mean, this is one way you can do it, and he knows everyone and he likes your record."

What's Rory's background?

Rory McEwen is part of a very well-loved and very wealthy family from Scotland. His father was made a baronet by the queen because of work he had done, cultural activities and so on. And he was a folk singer. He and one of his brothers, Alex, sang together on a TV show called *Tonight*. It was a news program, and every night Alex and Rory would write a song about something that happened that day. Current-events songs. And they did it in the mold of the Jamaican songs. You know, those singsong, Calypso types.

Like Harry Belafonte.

That's right. So, they got very famous in England and Scotland and the British Isles for that. And they presented a program many years running at the Edinburgh Festival and they asked me to sing there. That's how I got to be known in England. Dylan was about to go to England. Maybe split up from Suze. I was very upset and split up from Richard. Rory and Romana McEwen came to my apartment, and I brought Dylan. They sat on the couch, and Dylan sat on the cover of the radiator. And I had the rug that Rory give me right in front of the radiator and Dylan's feet were very,

very muddy, and he muddied this new rug up. I was so shocked because the McEwens are very fastidious, and they had just given me this rug. And they would take their shoes off at the door or something rather than, you know, dirty the place. I loved Dylan and I didn't say anything to him, you know, but I definitely remember this meeting because of that happening.

Did Dylan finally go over and get a meeting with them?

Dylan finally did, and one of the reasons was that Richard was living in a house right behind them.

So Bobby goes over there and he's with—

He's with Richard and Ric. And the McEwens. I think they did meet him at the time. But I don't know what exactly happened.

How long did Bobby stay in London, do you know?

That I don't know, and I had seen Dylan a couple times right around then. And later, Richard told me that one of the reasons Dylan was coming around was that he had broken up with Suze. He was very upset and he said Suze and I were very much alike, and he knew I was broken up from Richard and he had eyes for me.

It was replacement for Suze, right?

Isn't that great? And, you know, I was wary of everyone at that point. I was very upset emotionally, and I wasn't ready for anybody. If Dylan was giving me those vibrations, I wasn't picking them up.

But isn't it possible it was because you were somewhat older than him and probably a hell of lot more sophisticated than this twenty-year-old kid?

Yeah, I was, you know, four years older, and I did feel that I shouldn't get involved with, someone that—I felt like his sister. That was all. He met McEwen. He was quite morose at the meeting. Rory sort of had to drag things out of him. Bob didn't really want to communicate.

I hear that this period, when Suze was in Italy and he was mooning over her, he was drinking a lot and maybe fooling around with some grass and such. You aware of that?

We did a TV show about that time. It was for the Westinghouse network. It was called *Folk Songs and More Folk Songs* or something like this. And John Henry [Faulk] was the narrator. And the Staples were on, Dylan and I were on it, and Barbara Dane. And it seems like he was drinking a lot of wine that day and maybe smoking. A combination of those two things.

When was this? Recall that?

I don't recall the date.

Was this before the McEwen meeting or around this period?

Maybe it was around then.

On the Westinghouse network.

Yeah. That was either at that time in late '62 or maybe it was early '63 that happened. It might have been early '63.

One show?

Yes, it was one show. I believe the producer of the show was Michael Saint Angelo.

Dylan and your rug . . .

And of course, the meeting was very awkward, and I was very embarrassed. And maybe Richard is right. Maybe he was thinking, why don't these people leave or something? You know what I mean? I don't know what it was. At any rate, I think Dylan left for England soon after that, and I—

You don't recall any overt act on Dylan's part that would make you think he was, you know . . .

No, I don't know. Maybe, you know, okay. Now, there is one other meeting, one other time I met with Dylan that I want to discuss. But I can't remember when it was. I still lived on Twelfth Street. I moved from Twelfth Street in '67. So it was some time maybe around '65. Now two things happened. One thing, in May of '64 there was an article, coverage of folk music done by the *Saturday Evening Post*. And Dylan at that time had achieved stardom, and, I mean, I remember in the article there is a photograph of Dylan and Baez together.

Was Dylan on the cover of this?

No. I was on the cover of this one.

Oh, yes, yes, yes. There was a piece done by Al Aronowitz, I think.

That's it. Okay. Now, they wanted to put a girl on the cover. Inside the article there were many pages devoted to folk musicians in New York. And there was a quote from me, there was a quote from Judy Collins, and the lead photograph in the article was a full page of Judy. And they photographed everyone. There were pictures of Bikel, Odetta, everyone. Then there were three pages or four pages done on Peter, Paul and Mary. Now Peter, Paul and Mary should have gotten the cover on that particular article. But I think they wanted a girl on the cover. And in the end they decided to put me on the cover and I don't know why. But it helped me very much, of course. And that issue, as a matter of fact, outsold many, many issues they subsequently had. And I didn't expect to get on the cover. I was told when they first took photographs, they said, "We think we want to use you on our cover." And of course then I wasn't aware of all the tremor that went through the field about me getting on the cover, and that Peter, Paul and Mary were particularly upset about it, and Al Grossman, I guess, was infuriated.

Now, a few weeks later, I saw Dylan and Al Grossman. They came into Gerde's, and I don't know if I was singing or if I just happened to see them at the Kettle of Fish or what. But we ended up over at Minetta's [restaurant]. And I was aware of the friction I had caused, and I don't know what month it was. It was sometime in '64. And I said, "Al—"

Sometime after the cover.

Yeah. I turned to Al and I said, "Al, I didn't deserve to get on the cover. Peter, Paul and Mary deserved the cover." I wanted him to know that I hadn't run after the cover. And he looked at me very curiously and he didn't say anything. He didn't really say a word. But later on that evening, I think he treated me and another girl and Dylan to dinner in Chinatown.

What was Dylan's reaction when you said this to Al?

Nothing. He didn't hear it.

By now did Dylan have another girlfriend?

I don't know. Dylan ended up coming, wanting to see me or something. And then maybe the next night he came over to my apartment again, to Twelfth Street. And I began to get this vibration that he had eyes maybe.

Had Richard said that about . . .

No. I don't think, no. Richard hadn't told me that, but I got this vibration from Dylan, and I was crazy about Dylan and I love him, I really do. I was on my way to work at the Gaslight, and I didn't have a boyfriend at the moment, and I was crazy about Dylan. But I was older than he was. And I did love him. I could love him. But I didn't think it was the right thing to do somehow.

Why?

Perhaps I was afraid he had a lot of girls. I think I was afraid he could love me and leave me or something, and I was still in emotional turmoil, and I had to protect myself, maybe. Maybe if I talked to him, he would have given me some time or something.

There was never a feeling that he might need you as a woman to—that he would want you to exclude everything else from your life except his need—

No, we never got into that.

Apparently this is what the problem was with Suze. Suze had wanted to be an artist or wanted to pursue her own career, even while possibly loving Dylan, but

Dylan, like, needed someone to support him. Morally support him, emotionally support him. Were you aware of any of this?

Well, not specifically. Basically, yes, but not specifically. Now I remember this night he came over. I got dressed up in a yellow wool dress—I remember the dress. And I sat down next to him and he was writing. He said, "Do you mind if I use your typewriter," and I said, "No, go right ahead." And I cleared away the table. My table was piled with papers and I had this little typewriter, the one I've got now. He started monkeying around with the typewriter while I got dressed and he came out and he had finished off a song. He said the song is about, "It's okay, Mom, I'm only bleeding."

Yeah, that's the title. "It's Alright, Ma."

"It's alright, Mom, only bleeding." And he was writing the song "if you don't now, go now, because if you don't go now, you're going to have to stay all night." Well, I thought that was written about me. And I thought, oh no. I don't know if he ever recorded the song. I understand later I believe the Rolling Stones recorded it, or Mick Jagger, I believe.

I have it on an unreleased tape. Dylan did record it, with the Band, I think.

And I have it. Dylan doing it. This is what happened. I said, "Dylan, sing this song for me," and he sang—

Did you call him Dylan? Or Bob?

Sometimes I'd call him Dylan or Bobby. When I'm with him I guess I call him Bobby. So yes, "Bobby, sing it for me, the one about 'I'm all right Ma.' I like that song." So he sang that for me. I knew he was writing "Go Now." Maybe it was that night that he wrote it. So, he told me while we were sitting there and talking, he said, "I don't have to go out and sing for a living now. You know, Peter, Paul and Mary and 'Blowin' in the Wind' really changed things for me." And I didn't know why he told me that, because he was very modest. And in other words, I got the idea that he was on his way to becoming a millionaire. And I told him I was going to meet my boyfriend and I was going to be with him tonight. So it turns out that Dylan slept on my couch all night and I don't know if he really thought I might come back or what, or if he just needed a place to stay, when he stayed and wrote all night. A lot of paper was gone. And I stayed that night with a friend who was running the Gaslight. I don't remember his name. But I told him, "Dylan's at my place, and I like him very much but I'm just not ready to get involved and I'm sorry—"

You didn't have a boyfriend at that time.

No.

You just used him for—

I had had a few boyfriends, but at this specific moment I didn't. I didn't have any excuse. I had to make up one. There's a room upstairs in the Gaslight and I stayed up there the night.

That's the back room that they used to play poker in a lot.

Terrible room. Just awful. I stayed all night in my old yellow dress on top of a heap of blankets. This guy slept in an adjoining room or something. And he and I laughed. He said, "Are you going to tell this story someday?" And I said, "I don't know. Maybe nobody'll ever ask me, but this is the honest truth." He said, "I was there. I shielded you from the great Bob Dylan." And the thing was, you see, I was in such a bad emotional state that at the same time I wanted to go right home to Dylan and on the other hand I was afraid of him.

You weren't afraid of Dylan as Dylan. You were afraid of him because of your problems at the time.

I was afraid of him as a man because of my own problems. Because I felt like I know everything about him as a person, as an artist, in a way, on one level. On the other level, as a man I know nothing about him. And you see, I suppose if he had been there when I got home, and spent a few weeks, you know, drawing me out or getting to know me, but I acted like his big sister. He probably didn't realize this other level. Maybe he thought I was, you know, rebuffing him. Maybe he thought I should at this point—he was Dylan. Why didn't I, you know, take care of him? I mean, I did not know him as a man.

People have said that throughout this period, Dylan seemed to have a great need for approval, a great need for people to approve of him and to be warm to him and open to him. Did you get this feeling, that he needed approval as a man, as an artist?

At that very moment, the only way I can answer the question is, I felt he needed approval as a man. As an artist he was—he was there.

Had gotten his public approval.

And I felt he needed approval as a man. Now, he may have been suffering from the lack of Suze, you know? What was he as a man? Maybe he wanted to know.

The relationship between Bobby and Richard.

Well, at some point I saw Dylan and it may have been part of this last meeting we had, where he was at my place. He told me that Richard and Mimi had been in Woodstock and that while he was gone someplace, either to California or to England, Richard came to his place and took the boards off the window. Dylan had boarded up the place, because curiosity seekers would come around. And Richard came into the house and brought people in and had a stay there or had a party or something and Bobby was very mad at Richard and he was furious and he didn't want to see Richard. The last thing I know about their relationship is that on Richard's last record, there is a song he writes about Sir Morgan the Pirate, and that's about Dylan.

Is it really?

Yes.

I'll have to go home and listen to that again.

In other words, there was some problem there and Grossman was managing Richard and Mimi at this point, at the time of his death.

Were there any problems before this incident at Woodstock? What was the relationship at the beginning, say—I mean, as far as you know?

Very friendly.

Did Richard have any influence over Bobby?

I don't think Richard had any influence on Bobby. I think also Richard, being an in-law of Joan Baez then, he felt Bobby had shafted Joan quite badly.

In what way?

I believe Joan and Bobby got involved at some point. And—

Oh yeah, I know they did. There's no doubt they did.

Yeah. And when they broke off, it was maybe Dylan giving the shaft to Joan. I don't know exactly. But this was an impression. See, I had a conversation with Mimi and Richard and we were quite friendly. We met in Cambridge at one point and right after Dylan and Joan had been together. There were lots of complaints raised or somehow Grossman got involved in it. They were being managed by Grossman, and Dylan was being managed by Grossman. And, of course, Joan's manager is [Manny Greenhill]. And the parents, Joan's parents, were involved in it. They blamed Grossman for something about Dylan and I don't know what it is. I mean, I didn't inquire. And that's about it. I haven't seen Dylan in a long time.

Yeah. When was the last time you saw him?

He came to Texas. I was in Austin, and he came to my hometown of Austin. Bobby [Neuwirth] was his road manager then, and Bobby and I talked on the phone. Dylan was being interviewed by a man I know, Rod Kennedy. And Rod mentioned to Dylan that I was in town at the moment, and Dylan said to [Bob Neuwirth], "Call Carolyn." So they called me and I was in touch with them, and I was going to meet them after the concert. It turned out that the concert went beautifully. Texas was the first state Dylan had where people didn't boo him for going electric. The kids loved him, and it was a great concert. It was in Palmer Auditorium in Austin, and he had to be rushed away to the private airplane [at the] airport in Austin, and I didn't get to see him. They wanted me to come to Dallas with him, but I couldn't. I was with my family. And at this point, I would have. I knew Bobby from a long time ago, and I knew Dylan and was very fond of Dylan. But I just couldn't do it. So, I missed seeing him that time and I haven't seen him since.

No correspondence? Dylan wasn't a person to write letters.

No, no. If I was in Woodstock, I suppose I could call up. I mean, if he wasn't involved in something. I have a good feeling about Dylan, and I would never approach him particularly. But I feel like I could.

I don't know. He must be swamped by people trying to approach him.

Yeah.

I get a feeling he's sitting down on MacDougal Street waiting for people to call him, from what some people tell me.

Really? Do you know what his phone number is? I heard he was back in New York.

He's at 94 MacDougal. He bought a house right off Bleecker. I don't have it in this notebook. I've got two numbers for him, and I'm not sure which is his number. One is definitely his. I'm not sure which. So I'll call you—

If you would. If you could. If he feels—I mean, if he wants people—if you get the impression he wants people to call, I will call.

That's what Terri Van Ronk tells me, that he seems to be lost and, like, searching for something and searching for some of his old—Terri tells me that he stopped by at her place a few months back and asked to see some of the mementos that Terri kept of those days, his corduroy cap that he used to wear at the beginning. And that he seems to be a person who's looking for something he lost when he split the Village scene and left all his friends behind.

It's funny. Someone who becomes world renowned and so on and an idol, as he is, you get the feeling they are larger than life and they don't have time, they're too busy with going on and on. At this point you think, well, he's probably writing a book and he is maybe preparing his next film or something, you know. He doesn't have time. He said to me one time that he owed kind of a debt to me because I was instrumental in his getting his start, that I was there and I really did help him. That was really extraordinary, to say something like that.

Especially from a guy like Dylan. How were you instrumental in his start? Tell me about that.

Oh, back in 1961, I invited Dylan to play on my third album, after I signed with Columbia and John Hammond Senior was my producer. I think Richard suggested Bobby play harmonica on my record so it would be a little different, different from Joan Baez and some of the other folk singers. And Bobby gave me a Guthrie song and a song Bobby wrote. It was "Come Back, Baby." Very bluesy and very, very different from anything else I had on the record. And John Hammond really liked him, which made us happy, Richard and me.

But the funny thing is that a lot of people are afraid to call him. [Eric Andersen] says, like, you know, even if he is lonely, I can't call him. Right, he's God practically. Eric is afraid of calling. Dave Blue [Dave Cohen] is afraid to call him. Even Terri says, you know, she's afraid to call him. But he is back and people do get the feeling that he is splitting from Grossman, for one thing. That's the big rumor.

I didn't know that.

Yeah. I mean it's a rumor. But he is talking in terms of needing a new manager. But it's so hard to figure out when he's putting people on and when he's serious. You know, that's one thing. Did you ever have that problem with him?

No. I never did. Maybe it's because of the special way our lives crossed.

Right. And also maybe he didn't really start putting people on until much later.

No. I knew he was doing that. But I sort of approached him very tenderly because I knew it was a possibility, the put-on, and yet I never saw it myself.

You were saying that Mimi called you when Richard was killed?

No, I was telling you that Patti Wilson, that Jack Elliott's wife, Patti Wilson Elliott—

Do you know whether Bobby went out to the coast or was he around at that time, when Richard was killed?

I don't think so.

Did [he] go to the funeral?

No. I don't believe Dylan was anywhere near.

By this time there had been this break between them.

Yeah, listen to the song and see what you think. I mean, that song was written around the time Richard died. So that may be one of the last clues. If you talk to Dylan, he may discuss it with you.

[Recording off/recording on] The following exchange is about the controversial boycott by several popular folk singers of the television show *Hootenanny* because Pete Seeger had been blacklisted by the show. Carolyn Hester spearheaded the boycott.

So you and Judy [Collins] [met] in Leventhal's office?
The meeting started at the Village Gate. Now, John Henry Faulk was from Austin, my hometown. And he had, of course, great problems with the blacklist. I called him up and I had to explain the situation. I said, "This is something I am very scared about. I am on uncertain ground." I said, "I don't think Seeger deserves that kind of treatment and he is the father of folk music. He deserves my respect, and there is developing a furor about this. There's going to be a meeting held, and I was part of getting it together and I just don't know what to do."

And he said, "Carolyn, do me a favor and protect yourself. Seeger has friends in high places. He will come through this, all right? I'm in the battle and I know what it is." I believe he came to this meeting to negotiate. My business manager [Sal Benoff] was there, Theodore Bikel and, of course, Harold Leventhal and Judy. We opened the meeting, and then we got off the stage and she and I never really did anything else. The thing just took off. And of course, we did boycott the show and the show failed. And I just felt terrible because I felt folk music needed the exposure. Of course, as a performer I could use the exposure. But I was so upset because I thought, this is just a knife down the middle of our folk community. It won't help us at all. It's going to hurt everyone. And it did. Of course, now Seeger came through it beautifully.

He always had that—
And folk music was hurt because all the good performers, and Dylan and all the rest of them would have gone on it probably.

Did Dylan play any role in this at all?
This I don't know. I do believe that that was a crisis for the field. And maybe part of why Newport won't bring rock performers in there. They

tried it a couple years back. I guess they had Janis Joplin there not long ago. They tried the jazz festival, with Blood, Sweat and Tears, and there was a near riot. And I just feel if there are a few of us who made it into "the music business," in quotes, through folk music, well, there are those of us who feel nostalgic because we have changed because the change was natural. But we have changed because folk music is a strange flower that has closed up on itself.

In what way has it closed up on itself?

Well, I just think there are one or two performers who are big in folk music today. Who are the new folk performers? There are no folk clubs. And in other words, folk music, as a way of life or as a business, is dead.

It's back where it was before the so-called folk revival.

And so, everybody wants to say folk was a fad. I'm sorry, that hurts me. I really don't like to think it was a fad. I think Bob Dylan, who was in our contemporary folk music, influenced pop music. He influenced the Beatles, and myself, and any number of people. And our birthplace was folk music. And it wasn't a fad, but now that's what it's labeled.

Yeah, But you think the whole Pete Seeger, the hootenanny thing had a great deal to do with the—

The show started out with a bang. We had thirty million viewers right off. It could have—

Could have opened up—

Could have definitely progressed, and now Dylan and Peter, Paul and Mary and a few of us, it was our responsibility. We gave birth to contemporary folk music. We—

You gave birth to contemporary pop music.

That too, yeah. But I mean, we are the ones that on our records, you find the Paxton songs, the Dylan songs, our songs; we became writers, we responded to the call. You know, we felt the need. We said we had new words. We did our bit. You know, if the generation now is thinking of revolution, ours was thinking of protest and of using our language.

And your use of that language has a lot to do with the generation that today has been your revolution.

Right. So we are now influencing popular music. That is my goal in life. This is why I write and that's what I'm doing. And that's what Dylan is doing. And—

Let's hope he still—

And we got scared off. Or maybe because we didn't get the chance. How many of us are on television even today? See, that TV show was a real important thing to us. If they hadn't blackballed Seeger, things would be different now, I think. Anyway, that is my opinion.

You were involved in some of the freedom scenes down in Mississippi, right?

Yeah.

Was Bobby involved in any of them? I know he went to Greenwood.

Yeah, that's all I know that he did.

You weren't together at any of them?

No. We weren't together.

What about the March on Washington?

I wasn't there. I went to Mississippi during Freedom Summer, which was '64.

Right. That's right after the March on Washington [in 1963]. The summer after the March on Washington.

Yeah, I was there, and I was with Gil Turner and Gil knows Dylan very well and—and I sang. And we hit Mississippi the week after the three boys had been murdered. And I wrote a song about that. Later I wrote a song called "Three Young Men."

The week after they were—

Yeah, and it was a terrifying experience. But then I later went down there in '67. I believe I went back because I was going to go to England and do some benefit concerts for Christian Aid Society to benefit Freedom City. It was outside Greenville, Mississippi. I visited Freedom City and sang songs for the kids and everything.

ERIC VON SCHMIDT AND
BARRY KORNFELD

*Whether it was his introduction or whether he was copping riffs from
Van Ronk or people that I didn't know, he did do some interesting
chordal things where he would take something that everyone else
would have been playing one way, or the folk idea was in a certain
direction, and somehow it would become a little lighter and a little
more complex and a little more somehow appealing, a little richer,
you know?*
—Eric von Schmidt
*But what made Dylan unique from any other single person I can
think of in the twentieth century is he's the only one who's had an
impact on lyrics. He's completely changed the possibility of what
one can do lyrically in popular song.*
—Barry Kornfeld

Eric von Schmidt, folk singer, songwriter, illustrator, children's book
author, became close to Dylan in his early professional years. Von
Schmidt went on to mentor and inspire Dylan, as well as Tom Rush and
Joan Baez. In the interview von Schmidt meanders all over the folk and
blues music map of the 1960s scene. He is joined by friend and fellow
musician Barry Kornfeld. Toward the end of the interview Eric and Barry
get into a lively discussion—they riff along—about Dylan's songs and his
musicianship.

I've got a lot of correspondence from Dick Fariña—about forty-five letters.
Do any of them refer to Bobby?
Yeah, he wrote a thing on Bobby. As far as I know, it's never been published. It's just a little sketch, a little verbal sketch of him. And we were
planning or plotting to put a book out on folk singers. And I was going
to do an illustration which would be the facing page to his little sketch.

The one on Bob is a beautiful description of Bob at that time. In fact, it was written shortly after we did the record.

I wonder if it would be possible for you to read any of that to me. You know, any of the letters.

Yeah, sure. I really feel that all of these things should be out where people can see them.

I'll tell you what. Why don't we do this phone interview, and then when you do get up to New York, we can just sit down and rap again. I'm sure after I've gone through the tapes and made a transcript of my discussion with you, a lot of other questions will pop into my head and we can just fill in some of the holes.

Right.

Jack Elliott was telling me that he heard that when Bobby was in London, somebody took him to see Robert Graves. Do you know about that?

No. If that happened, he didn't mention it.

In fact, Jack Elliott and Carolyn both mentioned it. They didn't have any details but just that it was a bad scene. Graves apparently was turned off by this freaky young poet type.

Yeah. That's interesting. I don't remember any mention of that. Bob first met Dick [Fariña], as I understand it, to have him in at Carolyn's session, when Hammond spotted him. Dylan at first seemed to pretend that he couldn't remember any of that.

Oh really?

And yeah, it was a little bit, these two young hotshots and they were very cautious with each other at first. Especially Bob towards Dick.

Joan describes them as a couple of young lion cubs feeling each other out.

That's right. It was weird. It was almost like you could see the back hairs on his neck standing up, you know, very animal.

But that poster that you did of Bob and Joan—

There's a funny story to that—

Why don't I call you, you know, roughly eight o'clock.

Okay, swell.

[The following part of the interview was done in person at Eric's brother's Midtown Manhattan apartment.]

Let's start with how you first met Bobby.

I think it was the second Indian Neck Folk Festival. I don't know if you remember that thing.

I remember the Indian Neck Folk Festival.

It was the first year I was asked. It probably was about maybe '59 or '60. I'm not sure. But I was very happy to be asked. I'd been singing in Cambridge a year, or maybe two years. And Joan was singing there then. I'm getting off the subject. Okay, Geno Foreman and Gary Davis were there. Fariña was there that year, too, with Carolyn. And it was the next year, I think I was asked again—and I hope you don't mind—

No, no.

A lot of digressing.

Fine. Some of the digressing produces wonderful results for me.

Okay. And it might lead to other people's thing. Bob Jones said, "Hey, there's this guy down there you really got to hear. He sounds just like Woody Guthrie."

This would be '61. Would have been the same year you met him that summer. In Cambridge—

Yeah. I think it's that year. I'm pretty sure it's '61. Yeah, it would have had to have been.

But Joan told you about Dylan.

Yeah. So Bob Jones said, "There's this guy and he sounds like Woody Guthrie and he sings these funny songs." And the song that had caught him was the "Bear Mountain Picnic" song.

No, but it's on some of the underground tapes.

Right and so later on that summer, Bob Jones showed up with Bob Dylan. And you know, he was young and puppylike and sweet and just real live—

Was he open and warm?

I felt that very much. It's possible that he had the feeling—I've heard this expressed so many times—the difference between the Cambridge folk scene and the New York folk scene. The Cambridge folk scene was kind of loose and goosey and, you know, whereas New York, everyone was kind of ready to shoot down the other guy because—

Also, you were pretty young up in the Cambridge area. Down in New York you had the Lomaxes shooting down the younger kids.

There was no Lomax figure up there. There were guys, most of them old thirties Commies, you know, who had always kind of dug folk music and—

Somebody expressed to me it's high folk versus low folk. And the kids were considered low folk, because they were experimenting.

Maybe. This must have been about '59 or so. And Jack Elliott had done a record, *The Bad Men Ballads* [*Badmen, Heroes and Pirate Songs and Ballads*].

I had come back from Italy, and I knew Jack from quite a bit earlier. He says that we met around 1950. And you know, he was—his nickname was Xerxes. And everyone thought Adnopoz was Greek. And it was really before he officially switched his name around a bit.

Before he became Jack Elliott.

Before he became Jack, yeah, right. Buck Elliott was [his] first [name]. But at that time it was Xerxes. And Bob came up with—and I can't remember who the other guy was.

I have an impression it may have been Ian and Sylvia who brought him up.

No, no. Not the time I saw him. It was another young guy. We were passing the guitar around, and I think maybe Bob might have played something. But I do remember just Bob and me, Dylan and me, driving around East Cambridge. We were playing harmonica. Both of us were kind of pleased that we could play harmonicas together in a duet and have it sound pretty good. And our big number, as I remember it was "Jump Jack, turn around, pick a bale of cotton." You know, very nice, simple thing to play on the harp. I remember driving and playing the thing with one hand. And he was playing the other part. And then I think maybe we would switch. You know, he would play cross and I'd play straight. And we drove out to West Roxbury, where Bob Jones was living at the time. And he had a croquet set, set up in the back yard. And you know, Bob was gung-ho for anything. He'd really try anything. And I still have visual flashes of that croquet game. I mean, he was one of the most uncoordinated guys I have ever seen. He couldn't hit the ball. You know, and he wasn't stoned. We'd been drinking a little bit. But anyway, it's kind of a delightful game. We never got through it because he just could never seem to make the mallet come in contact with the ball. I don't remember what happened after that. But that was the first time I ever met him.

Did you see him when he worked the 47 unofficially?

Oh yeah. I was at that concert. I played at it too. Yeah, that was arranged by Jones again.

This was during Carolyn's gig.

No, Carolyn—well, you know how he got signed with CBS, at least the way I understand it. Playing harp at Carolyn's recording session. Right. Okay, but it may have been two separate times, but there was the hootenanny, which was the big term right then. And one night, they had everybody there. Dylan, Joan, Carolyn, Fariña, me, Jones, I think the Charles River Valley Boys. It was a folk concert for free, really. Now, when Carolyn was there on her own, appearing with Fariña backing her up and just being there, that was when I met Fariña.

But you had met Bob.

I'd met him before that. Before that, right.

So that this would have preceded Carolyn's gig, which was in July.

Yeah, and I don't think he played anyplace that time he was up. But I do remember the first time he did play at the club, he did the "Bear Mountain Picnic" and he did maybe a couple more of his own songs. Maybe some folk songs. But I can't remember whether it was that time or the time, you know, when Fariña and Carolyn were around. And we did go out on the beach. That was the first I had heard about Dick's novel. Dick said, "I'm doing this novel. I want you to do the cover, I want you to do the illustrations." And then about a year later, I got a letter from Fariña saying here's the first chapter of the novel. You know, because he wanted me to illustrate it. Not just do the cover. It was going to be an illustrated novel. And I've lost that chapter. Then I saw Bob, I think, two times in New York.

As I get it from Carolyn, his attitude towards you to a great extent was, hey, wow, teach me things. You know a lot, show me.

Well, I think it was probably his attitude towards Van Ronk and towards anybody that knew a little bit more than he did in terms of chords. He wasn't looking for ideas. He was really looking for a kind of folk musical instrumental chops, I think. And I think both Van Ronk and I represented a coming together of a black expression. And you know, we were into that, and that was kind of what he wanted at that time. And that it was Van Ronk's and my connection with, you know, the concept of a black funky thing that was at least first appealing to him, you know, like I could have sung "Brave Wolf" or something like that. And I think he would have said, "Hey, play, you know, 'Ain't no grave can hold my body down,' " or something like that. He was probably already into the Jimmy Rogers things and I've never read any of the stuff about, in fact, the guys, Turner and those guys knew him out in—they knew him way back when they called him a "little fat Jewish boy." And I think he was very much into country stuff.

Yeah, he was very much into country stuff before he arrived here.

Right. And Guthrie was a natural. He got funkier and funkier, and Guthrie was one of the funkier country guys. But it was that amalgamation with the black sound that I think made Van Ronk and me momentarily important to him. And I do remember playing "He Was a Friend of Mine," which is a nice song. I had gotten it from the Library of Congress and, you know, his being very impressed by that and just the concept of taking that kind of song and being able to sing it. He wasn't at that time quite able to handle material that related to blues and he was still feeling around for a way to do that. And it really wasn't till—he was getting to it with ["Corrina"] on the second album. And he had Bruce Langhorne to help him along with those guitar licks that he put down. So, I think the "Baby, Let Me Follow You Down" business—I played it that day for him. I had learned it from Geno Foreman. Geno was a Joe Cocker without somehow ever having learned it consciously. He could sing in the most beautiful, uninhibited, raucous way. When they did the Elektra album, *The Blues Project*, the guys that particular night that were recording were Geno, Van Ronk, me, [Geoff] Muldaur was down, and John Sebastian came by the session and Dylan came by the session too.

This is the first Blues Project probably.

This is the blues, yeah, right. Not the group but the record that Elektra put out. Yeah. Dylan's on that.

Is he really? I wasn't aware of that.

Yeah, yeah. He plays piano on "Downtown Blues."

Dylan was on that piano?

He was playing—we got to playing a version of Guthrie's song, you know, "Was in the Valley" and we were doing that, "Stoned on the mountain, stoned in the valley. And you're going to smash just what you stone," was the final thing. Yeah, Dylan at that time was turning it around the other way. It became "and all the little martyrs like there," and so after the session, everyone kind of got their—

Do you remember when that session was, roughly?

I think it's maybe '63 or '64.

It had already been happening for Dylan.

Yeah, right, right. He—yeah, he still came around.

He came around to see what everybody else was doing, most of the time.

But this, I think, was not just that he was there to cop what you were putting down. It was that he loved to be, he liked to bounce back and forth, you know. He really was one of the best guys that I've ever played with who you could fool around with, throwing a verse out, and he'd do the answer verse and back and forth. He's a master at it. And I'm sure a great many of his songs have started off and probably even been concluded in this sense, of just let it happen right now. And I remember Dylan was working on a film too. They had some shots of him shaking hands with John Wayne out in Hawaii or something. You know anything about that?

No. I know he was doing something with a guy from Second City in Chicago. They did a film together of some kind. I don't know how much—

When was that? Do you remember?

'64, '65?

That sounds right. They were just mostly grab shots and going up. Sort of jive. I never saw a single thing of it. He just mentioned it and—

But Neuwirth is apparently pretty much full-time into that now. Neuwirth is the only guy who refuses to talk to me.

Yeah. Well, he probably is a lot closer to Dylan than most people. Like, I don't consider myself to be that close. I mean, I feel close to him, but I didn't go on the road with him. I didn't live with him and I didn't schlep for him. And we've always kind of come together on a nice basis of let's have a party and then you go to your home and I go to mine. It's that other thing that can bring the pain and the—the time in England probably—

Wait. Before you get to that, let me—I interrupted you about the Blues Project thing. You were starting to talk about after the session.

Oh, yeah, right. After the session everyone had done their solo things. Let's all jam. It was a jam that seemed to us very spontaneous. And it was. Sebastian was just busting to play some wild blues harp. And I ended the session with this pretty good version of "Alligator Holler." And everybody was just going out of their minds, wanting to wail. So we all drifted over to the piano, and Dylan played the bottom part of the piano. We used to do that when we'd get together and he played the bass parts and I'd play the top part, or vice versa. In this case I was playing the top part and actually blew a lot of notes. And on the record they call him Bob Landy. And they said I was playing the bottom and he was playing the top, where it was the other way around. It was very bad. But the song itself had great spirit. You know, Muldaur by this time just went baaaah singing, "Come downtown, Daddy."

I remember that. So exuberant.

Yeah, it just blasts through. And they use it as the last cut on the record.

Jeez, I haven't listened to that record in years.

He's the one playing the bass part. Then we just all kind of split from there. I don't remember too much other than that. I was staying with Sam Charters. Sam always put him down. Dylan at that time was starting to be hailed as a poet, where Sam's criterion for poetry was a whole different thing, much more academic and much more tuned in to some traditional thing. I think there's certain truth in what he says. I don't think Bob is, you know, a great poet. I think he may be as close to a genius as I've ever met. But I wouldn't say he's a genius of poetry. His songs seem to be so singable. He worked very closely and he's not innovative in the music, at least never struck [me] as being terribly—

No, I think he's always considered the music as unimportant to what he was trying to say, for one thing.

But he did introduce certain—and whether it was his introduction or whether he was copping riffs from Van Ronk or people that I didn't know, he did do some interesting chordal things where he would take something that everyone else would have been playing one way, or the folk idea was in a certain direction, and somehow it would become a little lighter and a little more complex and a little more somehow appealing, a little richer, you know? But his own musical innovations, I think, were very minor. However, in terms of what he said, the way he said it, I think maybe he kind of wished he was named on the record. He could have done it even as Dylan, I think. Elektra seemed to have a pretty good thing going with other companies. I think Albert was one of the forces that kept Bob out of being a part of other people's things, with using his own name. I think Albert sensed a potential and he wanted to keep it totally in a controlled area. Because when I first met Bob, I think Grossman had signed him by that time.

That early.

Yeah. If he hadn't signed him, say, that summer, he did within months. He also wanted to sign Joan Baez.

Wasn't he Joan's manager for a while?

As far as I know, never. But she sang out at his club in Chicago. And he wanted to be her manager.

Well, he was acting as her manager at one point where John Hammond tells me he tried to sign Joan at Columbia. Grossman represented her.

Albert has a way of bringing the aesthetic together with the good business head, you know.

Like getting Peter, Paul and Mary to record "Blowin' in the Wind," for one thing.

I don't put them down, you know? I think Albert has been really maligned a great deal. He's difficult to deal with, but to his artists he's usually very good. And as somebody in the business myself, frankly I feel if he's going to be hard on somebody, I'd rather he be hard on them, you know, than us.

I hear he and Bob have broken up.

I guess they have. Yeah, I don't know where Bobby is at right now. The last I talked to him was about, well, maybe fourteen months ago, when it was about notes for my last album.

How did the liner notes thing come about?

I asked him to do it, you know. And he did it, which was pretty damn nice. And I think a lot of the people that were going through what we were going through at that time have a kind of feeling about each other. You know, if he asked me to do something, I'd do it.

And I think that was one of the major things that made that scene good, that even though Bobby was making it a lot bigger than—funny, I'm calling him Bobby. I never called him Bobby in my life, you know.

Really?

Yeah. I never have called him anything other than Bob. But I'm just hearing other people—

Why is that?

Just like "Joan" and "Joanie." I've always called her "Joan," but she herself, you know, will send me a letter and she's apt to sign it "Joanie." I don't think it makes that much difference. If you're friendly, you can call somebody "Ass Face" or something.

Tell me about the last time you saw him, fourteen months ago.

Well, I didn't see him. I only talked to him on the phone.

How did that come about?

As I say, I did the record and it's been five years since I've done a record. My first album, Bob had on the cover of his—the *Bringing It All Back Home* album. The picture has some albums spread around on the [chair], and mine is one of them. Yeah.

And one is yours.

And one is mine, right. There was a song on there called the "Gulf Coast Blues" that I think is probably my only original blues in terms of a melody line. And Bob dug it. And he kind of used it as like a folk source too. It entered his head and he liked it and he used it. And put the album down there too. When this thing came up I thought, well, I will do it like that first album, even though it's all going to be my own songs. So, I thought, maybe Bob, because he liked that first album, would dig this. I called him up and I asked him if he would do it, and he said, "Oh yeah, sure."

Was he living here in town by then?

No, at that time I think he was still in Woodstock. And he said, "Okay, right." We talked a little bit and I mentioned I'd send him the tape as soon as I could. I sent him the tapes and later I did get hold of Bob, and by that time he had heard an acetate of the session, and he really didn't like it. But he's still willing to write the notes. And the one song on the album he liked was "The Wooden Man," and he said, "Look, that's a really nice song and why don't you get out there and do it again and kind of work it in that direction." I said, "Bob, this is the first record I've done in five years. They ain't gonna let me back into that studio, you know, unless I sell my car. And so, it's just going to have to go the way it is. And I still sure would like you to do the notes." I kind of stayed on him, you know. I'm sure he wanted to write the notes, but he would have liked to have written them for an album that he really liked. And what he did in the notes was not really mention the album at all. I think at that moment he was more interested in the idea of putting down music than of putting down an intellectual concept.

Yeah, he's starting to consider himself a musician now. More than a poet. You know, quote unquote.

Yeah, maybe. Another thing I want to talk a little bit about, too, is that the historic '65 [Newport Folk Festival] where he was playing with Butterfield's band, which I think has been totally misconstrued by everybody, including Dylan.

In what way?

Well, it all happened in a bizarre fashion. And, like, this was his first year Butterfield was at one of these things, and they were really gung-ho to make a big statement. And they played Sunday afternoon, but that was the "new faces" kind of thing, you know?

Almost an amateur—

Yeah, right. Which it really wasn't.

Hootenanny. Yeah—

You kind of have that feeling that as a performer, if you really had it, you should be on the Sunday night bill. So, Butterfield had played last at the blues workshop, which I was running that year. And it took maybe three-quarters of an hour for them to get the blues band set up and I got incredible shit from one, two, or three people who said, you're letting these kids play this music and you're running that thing. And I sang a couple things myself. You know, it was that kind of thing where everyone sang something. It was supposed to have been a workshop, but it was getting away from that already. But anyway, Butterfield finally got set up and they were great, and it was obvious that they should get some kind of a spot in the Sunday performance other than—

The kiddie show.

There was some talk of putting them on. But you know, that was the Lomax/Grossman fight that year. It pissed Lomax off so much that they were bringing electric instruments here that he was just furious with Grossman, and Grossman was saying, "Well, fuck you, you know, we've got to go on. There's got to be a progression to this. They're playing blues. Does everybody got to swing an ax to qualify? And chop cotton?" And they apparently started calling each other fags and fat assholes and one thing and another. And Fariña was there. And he dashed in to break this thing up. And they both kind of went off in their opposite directions, as firmly convinced of their positions as ever. But I must say, it was the first time I really thought, well, hey, Albert, you're all right. I think most of the other folk performers thought Grossman was going to stifle Bob because he wouldn't, in the early stages, let him play at, say, at the 47. And we just all thought, well, here's this magnificent talent developing, and this son of a bitch who won't let anybody use him. He wants top dollars, and we thought it was terrible, you know? Turns out he was very smart. But what he had to do was—everything was turned down through Grossman's office and then Bob would just show up.

Yeah and do it for free. Because he wanted to be in there.

He was just getting started and he was loving it all and wanting to do what he knew he could do.

After he started working for him, he would come back and play the hoots on Monday night at Gerde's. You know, even after he was becoming big.

Yup. Right. I heard him at Gerde's one night when I was down there. There was Jack Elliott and Peter La Farge and Bob showed up at that. And I played and Cisco Houston was there. Maybe six or seven months before he died.

But anyway, getting back to Newport, the electric—

My theory, the von Schmidt theory of what happened that night. *Bringing*

It All Back Home had already been out then. I don't remember who all was on there. Al Cooper maybe. Yeah, right. It was very electric and, you know, very rock.

It was half-rock. One side was rock and the other—

Yeah. But the best side was rock, right. In fact, it always disappointed me that as far as I know, his only recorded version of "Tambourine Man" is so inferior to what I've heard him do because it's one of my favorite songs. I think I was in the audience the first time he ever did it at a concert. And he—

The Town Hall—

No. It was up in Boston. It was when he and Joan were kind of popping back and forth. Now, maybe he had done it before. But it was just so, so beautiful, and I was always amazed that it became a big hit. I think this was kind of a turning point, in fact, because that a song like that could become a popular hit, widely accepted and talked about and, I hesitate to say, understood. You know, I mean, everyone understands it their own way.

The main reason is the Byrds' version was a good, slick rock version. Just came at the right time. Perfect Top 40 stuff.

But at the same time they were singing those words, and the words were not Top 40 at that time by any means. So anyway, he had made the record and he was—I saw him two or three times that year. That was '65. During the performance, he came out and I went out in front to hear it. And it was remarkable in that Bob, who always seemed to know when to make the moves, whether it was him, or how much of it was Grossman, was always impossible to tell. But this was one time where he got taken advantage of. It was like the Butterfield band were so excited to be on that stage, and they also knew that there were certain people who didn't think they should be there.

Who invited them on that stage for that night?

Dylan.

Oh.

He had heard them. I don't remember when the blues workshop was. It was maybe Friday. And he had heard them and realizes this is a great blues band. And so, he thought, I want to do "Maggie's Farm" and I want to do it with them. He only did four songs, as I remember it. The first one was "Maggie's Farm."

He had done a couple of his own with acoustic guitar first.

No. He came out with the band. He had a polka dot shirt on. He looked a little bit like a jockey. And he was very worried before the performance. He seemed very withdrawn and I went in to see him and just bullshit a little bit. Because I was getting my usual rum high on, and thinking, oh, wow, this isn't the place for me, you know. Old Happy Eric, seems to be something going on here that I don't know anything about. So I better just, you know, get out of here.

You're saying then that Bob didn't decide to use Paul Butterfield until he was actually up there?

Oh no. He had decided—up there, you mean up at Newport?

I mean he didn't bring a—

As far as I know. As far as I know. Absolutely. I don't think he had ever even heard of Butterfield before that. Because Grossman hadn't signed them.

Apparently, he was with Robbie Robertson at this time.

Right. They had done—

If he's going to bring anyone around, he would have brought Robbie.

He didn't bring the group that they had done the tour with—he had already done the tour by this time, the worldwide tour, I think, right?

No, no. '66 was the worldwide tour.

So it was before—

But he knew Robbie and—

Levon [Helm] and the Hawks and that.

Yeah, he had been working with Robbie and [Rick] Danko and the whole crew.

Right. But, as far as I knew, he was going to do acoustic guitar, but he heard Butterfield and he realized these guys had a good sound.

This makes a great deal of sense, because I've been sitting trying to figure why he used Paul Butterfield when he already was hooked up with Robbie.

Well, none of them were there and he heard this band. As I understand, they had rehearsed for a couple nights—at least one night would rehearse stuff, the songs they were going to do. Just jam but also a little rehearsal.

You mean blues—Thursday afternoon.

I think it was maybe Friday. I think maybe Friday night and then Saturday night, he jammed with these guys. Because I know he wasn't at the main jam. But he was somewhere else practicing with Butterfield. So it was a calculated thing. But you know, a surprise thing, unannounced—

I have a press release in which Butterfield was not even scheduled for that Sunday night.

No, no. They weren't at all. They showed up onstage. And so what happened, the mics, whoever was working the sound system, had a lot of to do with all of this. And Albert was in control of all the sound shit on this. And what happened was, he came out and he played "Maggie's Farm," which I thought was, I still think, is a great song, and I was so delighted that he was going to sing it. Came out with an electric guitar, and it looked like he was singing the song with the volume turned off on his voice. You could not hear anything, any words to the song. You could barely hear him. So he got finished with that song. And you know, Butterfield was pulling all the stops out. And Sam Lay was beating the shit out of the drums. And after it was all over, you know, we kind of dug the music, not just me but a number of people were saying, "Hey, we can't hear ya"—and we were sitting in the press section, well, probably thirty yards away, right? "We can't hear ya." You know, "Put the band down." You know, and about four or five people were hollering. And then they did the next song, and I can't even remember what the next song was. But no one changed any dials. It was just like a solo of Butterfield's band but with, you know, the voice not being there.

That's strange, because Albert is always so careful with the sound system with Bobby.

Well, yeah, I—of course he wasn't out in front. You know, he couldn't really hear how it was sounding. And so, after that, more people started saying, you know, "We can't hear Bobby."

At the same point, weren't people screaming about the electric instruments?

No. We're now getting to the crux of the von Schmidt theory that the whole thing was a mistake, that people were not putting Bobby down for playing electric. It was that we couldn't hear him. The balance was fucked up. And I didn't hear anybody at all in the press section or anywhere say, "Go get your acoustic guitar" or "We want the old Bobby." But the thing is, that rant did start, but I think it was a misunderstanding of the people in the back.

The people in the back, the people in the front—

Were saying that.

And they picked up on that—

But I think this is where it's a very interesting thing. Like, the people who were in front and could really hear much better than anyone else were not opposed to this change or this direction or anything else. It was people in the back who probably wouldn't have started hollering if there hadn't been hollering in the front, which was for a whole different reason. I'm convinced of it and I was there, and I never heard any of the stuff that got reported. I remember what people were hollering and it was just, like, "Shut up the band, less sound on the band." "Bring up the voice." "We can't hear you, we can't hear you."

They weren't able to hear what was being said.

I think there was too much confusion. I think Bob was aware that somehow this charisma that had always turned Newport audiences on had left. But I don't think he understood why. He just knew that people out there were hollering things. And I think he was confused. I think he probably heard what being said. But he really wasn't in a position to do anything about it anyway. Like, what surprised me was that they didn't do anything between the first and the second number, between "Maggie's Farm" and whatever the second one was. Because by the time the second one was there, it was obvious that if it went on the way it did, you might as well just have him go home, because you couldn't hear him, and this is supposed to be Dylan playing. These guys were totally drowning him out. And the cries [got] a little more pissed off and I was more pissed off.

So, basically they're saying, "Get rid of the goddamn band because we can't hear the singer."

Yeah, right. It was, "We can't hear you." Not, "We don't like the songs." So what became this big moment really grew out of, I think, massive, confused currents flooding back and forth.

How do you account for the fact that at Forest Hills they were—

Oh, by that time they had read the reviews and they—it was like—self-fulfillment.

Everybody was telling him—

Everyone had their part. Everyone by that time knew what part they were playing in this drama. In other words, it was like redoing it. But I think this first thing was honestly a great confusion and whoever was working the sound system, you know, created a legend.

But in any case, he did come out again and do—

Everyone was kind of shocked. He'd walked offstage, and, you know, there was some calling and no one knew what was going to happen. It was like a Fellini movie there for a bit. And then he came back out onstage with the acoustic guitar, with, I think, tears in his eyes, and he sang "Tambourine Man" and "Baby Blue" as well as I've ever heard him sing. He was incredibly good. And walked off and everyone, of course, "Yah! Yay! Yah!"

and he didn't come back on again. It was just about as good as I've heard him play those two songs.

Now, after he walked off, when did you see him again?

Oh, after that whole thing? I think he split. I don't really remember. But I was at a party afterwards. Fariña was there. So I guess Dylan, I think he packed up and left after that. I'm sure I heard that he was rehearsing with Butterfield. That was a planned thing. But when they got out on the stage, they really—there was no cohesion whatsoever. They were doing their Butterfield boogie, and this is where Bob—he was obviously a little bit shocked by that too.

Oh, really?

It seemed like one of the few times when he knew he was not in control, you know, and I've never talked to him about it. He did seem to look kind of stricken. But you just go on. You can't stop.

That's what you do, right?

Yeah, right. Now, I don't think they were trying to do him in, but they just did because of the way the mix was. And they were—

Just trying to show their stuff.

"Hey, Ma, look at me. Yeah, right. I'm playing behind Dylan."

And if his voice wasn't coming over, that's—

Right.

I can't just see Paul Butterfield pulling the plug on Bob's mic.

But the weird thing was, essentially it was Albert pulling the plug on Bob's mic. Yeah, I think he really was hurt by it. And I think he did leave that night. There was a party afterwards and—

Yeah, I can't imagine him sticking around after that kind of reception. Especially if he really did indeed think they were yelling at him, you know, that they were calling him a traitor.

And then the repeat at Forest Hills, like an instant replay when everyone knows what to do. This was the start of the scene, at a concert. Before that they were concerts. And then it really was the beginning of the tribe taking over, whereas before, the performer was it. You were there as a kind of negative space. And then this negative space gets more active. I keep getting flashes of things to talk about. One is the trip over in England with Dick [Fariña].

Right. I wanted to bring it back to London.

And I think he was over there. I know he was over there with Grossman, although I don't remember ever seeing Grossman at that time. He was with Grossman and Odetta.

Oh really?

Yeah, Odetta was the main—Bob didn't have any singing engagements.

Well, he had a TV show.

On the BBC or something?

Yeah, and he played in a young beatnik folk singer kind of thing. The play got badly reviewed. But the couple of reviews said—

You mean he was in a play or something?

He was in a TV play, and apparently all he did was sing. He may have had a couple of lines. But from what I can gather from the reviews that I've read, all he did was sing. You know, he wandered around like a minstrel. And he got $1,000 was what he told Izzy Young. And his idea was, hey, I'm going to go and I can look for Suze in Italy while I'm there.

Yeah, he was in Italy. But this is after he had come back from Italy, I think, when we were there.

Right. As I get it from the liner notes, he apparently went to Italy first. He went early to look for Suze, before going to London and doing the TV show. He never talked about the TV show?

Never mentioned. I don't remember anything about the TV show at all. I was over there doing a specific project. So, I didn't see him a lot. I was staying with Dick the whole time. I went over there for two reasons and one was to get away. The other was to finish up the soundtrack for this movie that I mentioned earlier. And also there was a record to do, just a whole lot of little things. Bob came one night—we just smoked a lot of dope, and Dylan and Fariña did the most lovely two-way free association kind of thing that night. I was a bit of a spectator to it all.

But that first time I met Bob again—after the time with the croquet and all that, the early summer—was in England. There was one time in New York with Suze but I can't remember when that was—I just remember drinking a lot of wine and being in their apartment.

Not the place on Fourth Street.

Yeah, I guess. But this was the first time Bob had seen Fariña since Carolyn's recording session. They were so funny, especially Bob. They were both talking and it was like I was the interpreter, like they were both talking some foreign language and they were both looking and talking at me, and I would kind of relate to what he was saying.

And then I would say it to Dylan and Bob seemed to be pretending that he had never seen Fariña before. I do vividly remember that little session with the two guys.

Bob had come from Rome. Did he talk about Suze at all, about trying to find her or missing her? Anything like that?

No. No. He knew I had been in Italy and mentioned it, but he didn't seem to have had a very good time there, and you know, couldn't quite understand what the hell was going on. And they couldn't figure him out and he was happy to be with us, it seemed, to get the hell out of there.

Was he in Rome, in Italy, with Grossman?

I think so. I think he was. But at this time, Bob had the most incredible way of changing shape, changing size, changing looks. Like the whole time we were there, he wore the same thing, all the times I saw him. He had that brown jacket and the blue jeans and a cap. But sometimes he was very big and muscular and the next day he'd be like a little gnome. And one day he would be very handsome and kind of virile. And the following day he would look like, you know, a thirteen-year-old child. It was really strange. I've never seen it so markedly apparent as Bob during that period. You never knew what he was going to look like. Like he could have gone all the way from small to large.

That's amazing. Was it his moods that were affecting this, or was he playing a role at various stages?

I haven't the slightest idea. I think he was searching for an identity at that time, but I don't think it was conscious. I mean, if it was conscious, it had nothing to do with attitude, as I think back on it. It was physical, is what I'm talking about. He physically looked different every time. He just seemed like Bob Dylan but a whole different version. But all the same clothes, like Plastic Man. It was incredible. And yet, you know, we had a really lovely time.

Did he talk about Guthrie at all?

No—maybe he did some—

I ask because it's around this time that he decided the identity of Woody Guthrie was not Bobby Dylan anymore. I gather from Suze and a few other people that Woody Guthrie was a role he could play in Minneapolis and his first days in New York, but he was finished with that. And I'm wondering if he indeed was searching for an identity.

Very possibly, very possibly. What was his age at the time? He probably was about nineteen or something.

He was already twenty-one. Or twenty-two, right.

Yeah, so he wasn't as young as I thought because he's already put out the first album and I don't—

It wasn't released till March.

I guess I had heard that he had [done] "Baby, Let Me Follow You Down," which I was very pleased about. But someone also told me that he had done "He Was a Friend of Mine." And you know, I'd played "He Was a Friend of Mine," which was kind of my song at that time. And I picked it up from the Library of Congress. And someone told me that Bob had told some people he had written the song. And someone said, "Hey, you know, Dylan's doing one of your songs." And I thought, well . . . In fact, I've never heard it on any album.

Oh, I know. I have a tape that he cut at somebody's house.

Yeah, it's not on any albums at all that I know of.

And in fact he did in effect rewrite the song, because the version that he sings on the tape I have, the lyrics are his version.

Right, yeah. This is, in a business sense, one I let get away. You know, because what I did, I was the first guy to really pick it up in the Library of Congress and say, hey, this a great song and good idea. And I sang exactly the same words that the guy who wrote it sang on the Library of Congress [recording]. I never even considered copyrighting it. I thought that along with doing the words, I was also doing the tune [by] the Library of Congress guy and because of my faulty musical memory, I really had created a whole new tune. And so it was—it's not the tune in the Library of Congress. So, all the following things really derive from my tune, not the—

Was Dylan aware that it's your tune?

I wasn't aware of it at that time. And as you say, the lyrics and by that time even the tune got changed around. I never felt bad about that because somebody gets the credit for an arrangement and it's kind of nice if it's the guy that had something to do with finding the song.

I've heard your version and I've heard Dylan doing it.

Mine is the simplest. It's very simple.

Anyway, getting back to London, how did Bobby get involved—first of all, how did the record session come about?

Well, Fariña had already worked this out with a guy called Tom Costner, or Coster.

His name is on the album.

It's on there somewhere. And he had the idea that he was going to make it big in recording folk singers, and so he set up the session, which was to be held in the basement of a record shop there. And this was tied in with doing the soundtrack for *The Young Man Who Wouldn't Hoe Corn,* which was the movie I was working on. And Dylan, having shown up, we invited him to the session. We did it twice and he came in and just rapped in the background, you know, carried on—

Yeah, do you recall what cuts he's on? On some he's playing the harp, it's obvious where he's singing.

I don't think he plays the harp at all.

Somebody's playing the harp, sounds like Dylan.

Well, both Fariña and I played harp. And—

And at that time Dylan was copying some of your harp riffs.

I'm not so sure about that. Because I think he plays harp in the strangest kind of way. I admire it more than I can say I like it.

How is that? How is it strange?

In such a way that I can't tell whether he's playing in front or back. It's kind of a free floating—it's like he's making a statement with the harmonica instead of playing the harmonica. It's basically less musical than you would normally think a harmonica should be or any instrument. But he's saying something with that thing that is original in his overall musical sense. Very simple but very unexpected.

As Van Ronk put it one night after drinking a lot of Irish whiskey, a prince breaks all the rules, but he does it beautifully.

He does it a little bit on the guitar, in the changing around of the patterns. Like still using only the three or four basic folk chords, but he stacked them up in a new order.

And he probably does it with piano too. Al Cooper finds that he does something marvelous with the piano. Have you heard Dylan's new album?

I've only heard one cut and it was on the radio. *New Morning?*

Yeah. He plays piano on about seven cuts.

Because I was kind of disappointed with *Self-Portrait.*

Obviously he put out *New Morning* because everybody was disappointed with *Self-Portrait.*

Yeah. What surprised me is that he would have put it out. And I don't quite understand the rationale for putting out, especially a double album. Like they could have—

They could have taken the best eleven pieces, that's right.

But to stretch it out over a double album.

Two "Albertas" and two—

Yeah, right. You think of all the other stuff, and my God, he's putting things on them. Two "Little [Sadies]" and—I mean, it gets to be kind of an esoteric thing. Like it's interesting to see various ways of doing the same song, but he was getting a little academic about it all. And I don't think they were that great, the two versions.

I know he went into the studio and he was cutting a lot of Simon and Garfunkel songs and a lot of Eric Andersen numbers, and a lot of old folk stuff from back in '61 and '62. He laid down maybe fifty or sixty tracks. And they selected these for some reason. Apparently, some of the other stuff just didn't work. But I can't get anyone to tell me, you know, precisely what happened and why these were selected.

It's amazing when you put that many down, that that was the best they can come up with.

Anyway, getting back to London and to that album, that record. How did it come about that Bobby—

Yeah. We just invited him to the session, right. There were a couple other things that happened with Bob on that particular—

Because you said something about "he makes the strange jumps like electricity."

Well, I think his mind is the instantaneous kind of a calypso mind. It relates seemingly unrelated things to form a whole.

It's insight, is what he seems to be able to pull in—by relating seemingly unrelatable notions and putting them together . . . it's like those chords, those three basic chords, he can put together in a way that makes them seem fresh again. And he seems to work in his ideas the same way. He doesn't go from A to B to C to D. He can jump from A to G. At the same time, he will occasionally do something like "Hollis Brown"—a narrative song—and he does it as good as anybody that's working today. I really think he's a folk song writer. But with this incredible, wild, creative head.

He always used to say, "I don't know what the business is about, all this, you know, Albert talk." I think that was true in the sense that he didn't want to be involved in that. But he was too bright not to know what was going on. And then the whole "Baby, Let Me Follow You Down" thing, he heard it from me, and his version of it, the chords are very different from what I play. And Bob heard it and liked it. In fact, that's what he says on the record. He says, "I first heard this from Ric von Schmidt." He doesn't say, "I learned it from him."

I didn't feel it was really my song. I was delighted the way he did it, the little introduction and all that. It's unique to say, the least. And then the next time he was up in Cambridge—I guess it must have been about a year, he said, you know, "Hey, we'll copyright this thing. You know, you should be getting—are you getting anything from that?," I guess is the way he probably phrased it.

Like "Hey, are you getting any money from that?" And I said, "No, I don't know anything about it." He said, "I'll talk to Albert about it." And so, they sent me a contract and—this is a little painful because I don't put it on Bob—this is something I may not want to have you use. But he said, "I don't know what's going with this. But let me talk to Albert about it."

So, I got the contract from Witmark and it was copyrighted in Dylan's name and my name, which was fine with me, because I didn't really feel like I'd done that much. I'd sung him a song that—

[Door buzzer]

Must be Barry. Barry's a good guy to get in on this conversation.

Anyway, before Barry gets up, finish that story, which you won't let me print anyway.

I didn't get a nickel, but I probably didn't deserve a nickel either. Bob felt that it would be nice that I got something. So, they sent me a contract and it said I get 50 percent and Bob gets 50 percent and his 50 percent starts on the day the album was made and my 50 percent starts the day I signed the contract. I wrote back and said I didn't understand that. Anyway, here's Barry [Kornfeld, a friend and fellow musician].

BARRY: As a matter of fact, I was still living in Boston when Dylan first hit New York. I lived up there in '60, '61. And I met Bobby just shortly after I returned, or even perhaps on one of my little weeklong returns.

You know, I've been meaning to call you for, like, a year now. So, here we are.

ERIC: So, what happened was, I said, I don't know what the hell this is really all about. But they said you should get it, Eric, and so what did happen was they sent me this thing and Bob's thing started when the album was made and mine was a year later. So I did a pretty dumb thing. Barry, this is about "Baby, Let Me Follow You Down."

BARRY: Oh yes.

ERIC: I finally wrote back and I said, "Look, I'd be delighted to be part of this royalty agreement, but, you know, I can't see why—if in truth Bob and I do have the rights to this—it should start when he recorded it, for him, and when I'm signing the contract, for me. And furthermore, I learned the song from Blind Boy Fuller through another guy, Geno Foreman, and—I was really trying to see maybe Blind Boy Fuller had some wife or sister or something out there that should really be getting this, you know?"

BARRY: Also, I think what you may be forgetting is the temper of the times. At the time this was getting very scandalous, putting your name on something you didn't write.

Yeah, but Lomax had been doing it for years.

ERIC: I don't think too many people were hip to that.

BARRY: That's right.

ERIC: Lomax was the guy that was telling everybody, you know, be a straight arrow, and if it wasn't copyrighted, nobody got it. But it gets back to somebody—this gets back to somebody's going to get it.

That's right. In other words, if Lomax didn't do it or you didn't do it, Joe Schmo's going to come along five years later and copyright it.

BARRY: Or the record company gets to keep it.

ERIC: But the crux of why this is a little painful, we change the name or change the tune, change the chords. So, we probably should be getting it. Then I didn't hear anything for a long time. After a while I got the letter from Witmark saying, "You're quite right, Mr. von Schmidt. You don't have any claims to the composition on this song and in fact we are honoring a prior copyright." I thought, well, okay, I lost that. But Blind Boy Fuller is or his daughter or whatever.

After I signed with Robbins, we got talking about this particular song, and I mentioned this prior copyright that they had alluded to. They looked up the prior copyright and the prior copyright was Bob Dylan. I'm sure he would not have done that, but the thing is, if I didn't know him, and didn't feel the way I do feel about him, I would say he's a motherfucker of the first—

You really feel he didn't know what was happening?

ERIC: No, not in this case. I don't think—

Because I find so many people defending Bob for—

BARRY: For this kind of thing.

For this kind of thing and blaming Grossman or the company.

ERIC: Well, in this case it was Witmark. I think I was kind of getting the lawyers' hackles up.

Well, you were in effect telling them to go look up Blind Boy Fuller, and they were saying who's this guy to tell us our business.

ERIC: They just figured, well, here's this guy giving us a hard time. Well, fuck him, you know. We offered him—he's already admitted that he really didn't do much to deserve it, and—but at the same time he's asking for the extra year's worth. So fuck him.

BARRY: There are other cases, I think, where Bobby could have headed off a legal hassle over copyrights.

Well, Paul Clayton for one, for Dylan stealing words—

BARRY: Right.

Yeah, where Paul actually sued him. I don't know if it ever got to court but—

BARRY: I know what the outcome of that one is. My attorney, who was one of Witmark's attorneys at the time, told me they found the guy that Paul got the song from, some college professor. A folklorist. And it seems that the part of the song that Dylan had copped, Paul had written exactly one word in.

Oh really?

BARRY: The melody was a folk tune in toto. It was called "Who's Gonna Buy Your Chickens When I'm Gone."

ERIC: I knew this was going to be a good night.

Who recorded for?

BARRY: Monument, I think. And there's no question that Dylan got the song from him.

Is that '65?

ERIC: Much earlier than that. '63.

That's when he had the bullwhip.

ERIC: He was snapping a bullwhip pretty good by the time. He was going with Joan and they were staying up at the Minute Man Motel or some ridiculous joint there. And he came by and we all went down by the river. Mimi was there and they were dancing on the riverbank and he was doing very well with this bullwhip.

BARRY: You have to be very careful about Bob Dylan as far as his talents and abilities. Because he would always profess inability. Standard patter. Like with chess. We used to play chess all the time and he always professed that he didn't know anything about chess, and he always beat the shit out of me. He would always profess that he wasn't even that good, right? And then somehow miraculously these incredible moves would appear.

He professed not to know anything about the French symbolists and then Van Ronk would walk to Fourth Street and see all the French symbolists, well thumbed and notes in the margins.

ERIC: Well, at the same time, I think a lot of it had to do with just the fact he was able to make these connections we were talking about before, that it was not something that he studies, it's more of a visceral thing that combines with intellect.

The question I wanted to toss out—

ERIC: And all of a sudden, pop, pop, he's doing very creative chess. You know, it's creative chess. It isn't chess by the book.

BARRY: Nonetheless, he knew he was a better chess player than he let on.

I was kicking something around with Suze. Bob had always said that even back in Hibbing, he saw things other people didn't see, and heard things other people didn't hear. And that he was so lonely. And Suze's feeling is that Bob is one of these rare people, and a lot of artists and musicians and poets have it, who's able to, in effect, tap the subconscious that is in some way—

BARRY: Yeah, but every artist does that. The essence of art is subconscious. In some cases, it's more so than for others. And I think the less disciplined the art form, the more so it has to be. Like writing things without really being too sure of what they mean. And they do mean something. Or they sort of evoke an image and they sound good. You know the song "Whiter Shade of Pale"?

Yeah.

BARRY: A song that really has no real meaning.

Except it's copped from Bach. You mean the lyrics.

BARRY: Yeah, I'm talking about it lyrically. At first I said, "Where the hell is that song at?" And I listen to it, and I can feel it. It was just a bunch of images and they felt good and it wasn't a joke. There was a meaning there that transcended and defended literal meaning. I mean, there's some fantastic images in there, even if they don't connect. There's an overall mood that is evoked. It really is a sort of a musical poetry. You know, it's the sound of it and the feeling of it, as opposed to any literal meaning.

And you feel Dylan's lyrics work on this basic musical mood—

BARRY: Oh, a great deal. You know, somebody who is basically a primitive—

Well, he makes himself out to be a primitive. All right, basically he's a primitive, you're right.

ERIC: Yeah, I think so. I put myself in the same category. You know, you can tell the primitives from the people who have a very broad and concrete understanding of the form.

The structure.

ERIC: I think Bob did catch a direction and helped to create it. He flowed with it, and you know, moved it. And he's one of the most long-lived guys in the pot.

BARRY: There are other people as long-lived, but none who've been able to go through the changes he has gone through.

ERIC: The thing is, he is an innovator.

BARRY: I'm not saying anything new, but Bob Dylan has had one of the greatest effects on popular music of any single person in the twentieth century. A colleague of mine says the two people in the last decade he felt had the greatest impact were Elvis Presley and the Beatles.

Yeah, except the Beatles are saying that the guy who had the greatest impact on them is Bob Dylan.

BARRY: Well, the Beatles, as it happens, like Dylan, have copped from everybody. But what made Dylan unique from any other single person I can think of in the twentieth century is he's the only one who's had an impact on lyrics. He's completely changed the possibility of what one can do lyrically in popular song.

ERIC: And this is his contribution to the Beatles.

And he made "Whiter Shade of Pale" possible, for that matter.

BARRY: Also, I think he did this without himself achieving comparable success, without himself becoming a mass craze, while he had a fantastically strong following. I don't think you could compare his popularity with the Beatles, even today. But his impact was—when he was selling, you know, a third of a million records on an album which is good but nothing compared to the people he was influencing. He hadn't had a hit single yet. People who are imitating him, like Sonny and Cher, had a hit before he did.

Right. Or the Byrds.

BARRY: I don't remember whether the Byrds preceded—

They had a number one record before Dylan ever did, with "Tambourine Man."

ERIC: In fact, I think they, more than anybody else, turned the pop culture and the kids, on to Dylan.

BARRY: Peter, Paul and Mary.

ERIC: You think more than the Byrds?

BARRY: Sure, because they were the first ones to have hits with Dylan songs. They were huge and they brought—

ERIC: Maybe you're right. You're always right.

BARRY: I'm not always right.

Then again, we get back to Grossman getting Peter, Paul and Mary to record "Blowin' in the Wind," and others to record some of the Dylan numbers.

ERIC: Of course, this makes sense. Because they also happened to be good songs. Like "Blowin' in the Wind."

BARRY: It's not [that] he twisted their arms. I don't think that was the case. Grossman didn't have the world's hugest smarts, but I think those people were in touch with each other, and by far, the greatest way of getting your songs recorded, when you're in this bag, is not through a publisher or through a businessman. It's through personal contact. And sometimes lesser songwriters get greater recognition because of their personal relationships, and the artists they know personally are favorably recording their songs, as opposed to a lesser—

ERIC: Like Judy Collins calls up and says, "Eric, what you got new? I need material for my next album." And I say, "What do you mean, what do I got new? Why don't you do some of the old ones that are good? You know, no one has done them. What the fuck you talk about?"

BARRY: Right. I've run around and hustled songs. I hustled songs for Paul Simon. I hustled Eric's songs. I ran around with "Sounds of Silence" for two years.

Did you really?

BARRY: And nobody—it's the first song I ever published. Nobody would hear it. Everybody said, "Oh, it's just another Dylan copy." Even after "Sounds" was a hit, I got that tossed at me about Paul's songs, you know.

ERIC: I was a little slow on Paul Simon's stuff.

BARRY: And of course his writing did mature and so on and so forth. But it was never fair to say he was a Dylan imitator. Dylan made what Simon did possible, yes. No question about it. There's a genre. But that's not the same. Here's an example of how a song happens. Judy Collins is at a party or a hootenanny and everybody's stoned, the mood is just right, and somebody sings a song and it's all right. With the right treatment it could be a hit, which probably covers about 50 percent of all the songs written. And the mood is just right, and she hears it. Groovy, you know, and she records it. Whereas when you see sheet music and the demo, you know, sometimes it just doesn't make it.

ERIC: My problem is that everybody likes my funny songs, which are great for performances, but no one wants to put a funny song on a record.

BARRY: Depends on the depth of it, Ric. Because I think your funny songs—it's unfair to call them just funny. First of all, they're witty and very often people do like witty songs. But I—you know, my single favorite song, I still call "Grey Dawn."

ERIC: Yeah, but that one's very personal. That's what scares everyone off that one. It's too personal, which I think is bullshit because the reason these things have a life is that there is that personal quality to them.

BARRY: Yeah.

ERIC: You know, it would be interesting to know how much the producer adds. Like the Columbia producer Tom Wilson, and people like that, what they had to say about these things.

BARRY: Well, I can tell you certain things if you won't quote me.

I won't quote you.

BARRY: Tom Wilson, I think, had certain things to say. I've worked with Tom on several things, including Simon and Garfunkel and various other things. And I think he was very influential in getting Dylan to go electric. And a few other things like that.

ERIC: Yeah, but that was the black Tom Wilson, right? With the glasses?

You're thinking of Bob Johnston now. Johnston took over.

BARRY: After Dylan had cut, for instance, "Like a Rolling Stone," which Tom Wilson produced.

Oh, that's right. Wilson produced—

ERIC: Which was the first Dylan album he took over? *Bringing It All Back Home?*

BARRY: I think so, yeah.

ERIC: Because that laughing on *Bringing It Back Home* is Tom Wilson, that wonderful—Dylan and Wilson.

BARRY: The question is whether or not Wilson carried over into the next album. But Johnston, you know, of course now I'm going to get into personal stuff. I didn't really care for what Dylan got into thereafter. Certainly not in terms of his performances. And it went through the

"Don't Look Back" period, where success has really kind of fucked him up a lot, and he's insulated himself a lot and surrounded himself with the sycophants who told him that his every fart was art.

ERIC: But he also, well, he creamed himself on the motorcycle right around in there.

Highway 61 Revisited. No, Blonde on Blonde, then the accident.

ERIC: *Highway 61* is the one where he's wearing the motorcycle thing and somebody standing behind him. He wrote some very good songs. And he had some incredible moments in a lot of songs—

Phil Ochs says it's still the best album that's ever been made.

ERIC: Which one?

Highway 61.

ERIC: Phil Ochs judging, you know, a total musical thing is, is like me judging, you know, a kind of tea-drinking contest. I don't think Phil Ochs knows that much about music.

BARRY: I'm glad you said that.

ERIC: I didn't want to say it.

BARRY: But anyway. I found that, the singing, as far as singing, I absolutely cannot listen to that whole period. That whining style that he developed I found to be so annoying, really like a fingernail on glass.

I don't know, I personally find that the whine, and that kind of effect he has, lends some force to it all.

ERIC: Well, that particular song—"Highway 61," with the, you know, just surreal bullshit kind of imagery. It's like a carnival. He's was into a carnival thing—

BARRY: There were a lot of songs prior to that I could listen to and really get into. And you know, once he got into that—

ERIC: I love that he was riffing on Albert and, you know, get all the stuff out under the sun and hold it out on Highway 61. You know—

BARRY: I found a lot of it to be word salads. They did not become a "Whiter Shade of Pale" for me. That's an opinion. But at all times there is at least a certain amount of genius showing.

ERIC: I think this is what you get back to finally. I was very turned off by *Blonde on Blonde* when it first came out, but since then I've gone back and listened to it, and realized the validity and the beauty of some of those songs. And there's always something there.

BARRY: No matter how varied the moves are, you know, I can always feel the same person coming through. People either change with the times in order to not go out of favor, which is sort of the very weaselly reason, or people change with the times because they're just fascinated with the changes the times seem to call for.

ERIC: Okay, now my feeling about that chameleon thing was that Dylan is continually inventing himself and I think that London experience was as physical as what he has done ever since, and even before in his art. He was doing it before your very eyes. When I was over there, Barry—

BARRY: Is this the "Don't Look Back" London tour?

No, this is much earlier. This goes back to his seeking his identity that we were talking about.

ERIC: We were hanging out—it was only a couple weeks. Some of the time we were together, it struck me, because I had only seen him three or four times before—I began to realize that he was different every time I saw him. He always wore the same stuff. You know, I think he only had a coat and a pair of blue jeans and that hat. But one day he would be very massive and strong and virile looking, and the next day he looked like a little dwarf, a crumpled-up kind of thing. And the next day he would look handsome and aesthetic and poetic. Every day he was a different size. Like one day he was three feet eight. And the next day he was eight feet three. Even Fariña said, "I cannot understand this guy. Every day, when we get together, he's a different shape."

That was Fariña's reaction?

ERIC: I mean, Fariña was a great absorber, and he got turned on when the third party was there. Then he'd get into the real competition of language or ideas. Dick was always writing—he stayed out of a lot of things and tried to get other people to make the moves.

BARRY: The objective third person.

ERIC: Yeah, Dick—more than most artists—was seeing himself with that third eye. And you know, Dylan does it, but I think Dylan is much farther out than Dick. Fariña could have been the chronicler of all of this, because he was right in the middle of it and a very good writer.

BARRY: You know, it's one thing you said that really strikes me. You can never get to who Dylan really is. He's always—

I don't know whether Dylan knows who he really is.

BARRY: I would say that, in the few times I've spoken to Dylan recently, I've gotten more of a feeling there's a person there than ever before. And less a feeling of a character playing a part. I got a much closer sense of the human being there.

What role was the accident and his withdrawal, his period of introspection, his chance to rest and figure out who the hell he is—

BARRY: I can only assume—I take a look at a guy who goes into an accident and what I consider a very fucked-up, paranoid, frantic period, and comes out what seems to be someone who's a lot saner.

ERIC: And he also, you know, he got Sara and the children—I think, you know, it's meant more after he was wasted, and had to get back with the help of, you know, her and other people.

BARRY: You know, I was not in touch with him since that funny, fateful night that Suze and Carla had the blowup—

You're talking about the second breakdown? The oven thing or the one after it? Was it West Fourth Street or Avenue B?

BARRY: Avenue B.

Okay.

BARRY: Avenue B, yes. For a long time, Dylan and I were not on speaking terms after that thing. Not that I did anything to him. I think it's just a very embarrassing situation for him, and I more or less took Carla's side, not directly, but you know, I'll go into that later. And you know, I really had virtually no contact with him until after the accident. And there is Robert Dylan. This was after—no, it was before the *Nashville Skyline* album. I remember he was very cordial, serious, going to see how Dave and Terri were doing. It was nice to see him and he was just, you know, much more cordial and relaxed. And I subsequently ran into him here and there, a party at Clive Davis's and Manny's Music and so on.

He just seemed very different, like he was when he was at his most relaxed and at his best, when he'd just come into New York and was kind of bumming around and being very loose and relaxed. Only, I think, a little easier to communicate with, a little less of that constant obfuscation that he always had going on. And he just seemed to be a hell of a lot straighter. Odds are that lying flat on your back for a year or whatever—I really know very little of the details, the whole accident, or his recuperation or anything. I just assume, you know, it gave him a lot to think about. Or look at the huge change if somebody decided, I'm going to be a family man, which is a very sane decision to make, especially for someone who can afford to make that decision.

Yeah, what made him decide to make it?

BARRY: I don't know. Maybe he just decided he didn't like being onstage anymore. I did.

Well, it's not only a question of being onstage—

BARRY: What else did he do?

Well, there's a complete change lyrically, in the kind of songs—

BARRY: Yeah—

In effect he's saying, you know, I don't want to be this freaky cat who you're holding up to be a god or a Christ.

BARRY: There have been four albums and four changes since. Okay?

Like he's deliberately going through changes as changes?

ERIC: To me his most interesting album is *John Wesley Harding*. I think that has got some ballbreakers in that. Maybe because it has, you know, my kind of imagery, my love of a kind of contact with the past and thoughts about the now and where we might be going. To me, *Nashville Skyline*—there's nothing earth shattering about it. It's just saying that it's nice to have kids and that simple things can be nice. It's just that generalizations can be true.

BARRY: I think you're a little bit wrong on that, Ric. Because there are some things that sort of defy deeper meanings, and you know, when the Beatles first came around, there was nothing earth shattering about what they were doing. But there was. You know, you couldn't really quite put your finger on it. Interesting tunes, interesting chords. Simple lyrics. And yet he made it unique, very different. But you would not sit and say, "Wow, ain't that heavy?" But you could sit down and say, "Man, that's really nice and it is different. And I can't put my finger on it, but it just isn't quite like anything I've heard in that bag."

ERIC: I like *Nashville Skyline*, but it doesn't turn me around. I have a feeling that maybe a lot of people who were on that other trip along with him weren't aware of this other, little green pasture. And you know, he had gotten kind of intellectualized. But in other words, I like a little bit of both. And I think that in *John Wesley Harding* he was doing a little bit of both. I really got into *Nashville Skyline* out west. The first cut with Johnny Cash threw me, I've got to admit. I broke up laughing and couldn't believe it.

BARRY: To me that's what *Self-Portrait* might have tried to be, but didn't. I find that Dylan is a human being, a complex guy, but he's no more complex than any number of people I know. It's just that his work happens to make him transcend.

He's also a phenomenon.

BARRY: Yeah, he is. But the fact that he is a phenomenon also leads one to very much superintellectualize a whole lot of things and to start, you know, reading incredible meanings into a whole lot of things.

ERIC: There's very few reflex actions in Dylan's makeup. In fact, he fights against that. That's where I think his whole career is, you know. I think if there's one thing he fears, it might be a reflex action. Because then he's out of control.

BARRY: I think *Blonde on Blonde* was a reflex action.

A reflex to what?

BARRY: It's sort of this direct subconscious expression without anything intellectual going on.

ERIC: I was thinking of it more in a visceral kind of way instead of that phrase you used earlier, "word salad," which is a really good word. I think Bob has some fear of being out of control. And I think that—let me for as long as we're doing this thing, this was after that session in the jazz record shop.

We all went down to a club. Some British folk place. We were all smashed, and this is the session that Dylan was on. And we thought, well, it would be great just to carry the recording session right down to the club.

Dick had intimated that we could just walk in and do like we did at 47, and so alternate with whoever was onstage, because we were feeling pretty important, and full of music. We got there and there was this Israeli chick who, you know, had her boots on and tambourine—

And she says, "I've been hired here for the night and the fucking hell you guys are going to get up on the stage. This is my show." You know, this was her evening and we were interlopers and we looked kind of Egyptian, and fat. And so, we went backstage and we said, "Look, can we just get out in between your sets?"

Obviously, we were trying to figure a way to get hold of the stage. She had a watch on. She said, "All right. You can have seven and a half minutes."

So, we all went backstage, Fariña, Dylan, me. And the guy backstage, I can't remember his name, but he had some very nice grass. And so, we had a bottle of gin and we were drinking and smoking and just getting outrageously high.

And this poor Israeli chick was out there doing, you know, her act and as soon as she got off the stage it was all over, because there were so many of us and so few of her. So we went out, and at the same time there was as many of us as there was of the audience. This great performance was for about eight people.

We all went out individually, and then we'd do some stuff together, and finally, you know, I can't remember what happened to the chick. But she realized there was just no way to regain the podium, and Dylan was smoking very, very heavy. He seemed so wasted that you had a feeling he wouldn't be able to even gain the stage and like he'd fall down or fall off the front.

He was playing back and forth between control and uncontrol, coordination, uncoordination—here I am, macho cat, and here I am a little wizened-up petal of a poet. And, you know, all this stuff going around. So anyway, he ended up, he had everyone amazed.

They were really used to just sitting and hearing someone sing "McPherson's Lament" or something like that. And we were all doing stuff that nobody had ever heard. And finally, Dylan ended up going out and he didn't even play. He had his guitar and he was kind of weaving around the apron of this little tiny stage, making kind of dopey remarks about—"it's like we're underwater, you know."

These people are wondering, what, what? Doesn't look like it's underwater to me, mate. I mean I started sobering up and I started worrying.

About what?

ERIC: And he's just weaving around, this mad young man weaving around the stage. And there was a little stool almost at the very apron of the stage. And he was out there with his guitar and just doing this kind of a thing and talking. And then somehow, it was like Chaplin. It began to get this connection between ballet and Dylan, you know. He did start to play a little bit. But the English audience was sitting there in near total shock. A guy in kilts came down—a guy who used to be a regular musician at this club. And everyone kind of went "ooh" when he came in. You know, and he sat down at the side of the stage—

Like wondering what the hell he was going to do.

ERIC: Here was this guy weaving around the stage, singing things. They didn't have the slightest idea of what was going on.

And as I say, getting into a ballet, this Chaplin thing, always staggering and falling, landing on the chair. At first it horrified me. And then

I started thinking, this is one of the greatest things I've ever seen in my life. You know? He's doing it. He's got all these people totally buffaloed, totally confused, and yet he's doing a great thing.

And finally, you know, when the guy who was sitting there, wanting to get up on the stage, he kind of lit a cigarette, and he's smoking a cigarette and looking at Dylan, and I've never seen anyone do it other than in the movies.

Smoking this thing, and he starting talking to Dylan. You know, putting him down, trying to put him down.

To heckle?

ERIC: At first it was obvious Dylan was pretending to ignore him, and of course he always was. But after a while, Dylan just went on talking and playing and wheeling around and falling back on the chair, this guy was smoking his cigarettes, they were disappearing on a single inhale.

And finally, you know, the guy realized that even though he had all the people there that were really his audience, little by little it was like this guy was disappearing, until finally he didn't exist. The last thing he did before he stalked out of the club, I mean, he threw the cigarette down on the floor. I remember the shower of ashes. And he went out of the club and Dylan just kept right on staggering around the stage and it was one of the most total wipeouts I've ever seen.

And I learned a little bit about what can happen to you if no one will let you exist, you know?

BARRY: I have a question and I'm really curious about it. Was Dylan singing or talking?

ERIC: Both.

BARRY: Was he funny?

ERIC: Oh yeah. No false moves.

BARRY: I remember the funny Dylan, yeah. That second Gerde's gig, the Huck Finn cap peeping over the harmonica holder; he would get up there and start running a rap, and it was cute, but he'd back himself into some corner and you'd say, how is he going to get out of that now? And he'd come with some mindblower, right? And he'd be frightened, you know, and he's, like, oh my God, what am I going to do now? And everybody's saying, my God, what is gonna happen now? But he had it up his sleeve all the time. Because you'd hear him run the same riff the next night.

I wanted to ask you, how much control did he have over what he's doing?

ERIC: I think he had much more than I—

Than you imagined—

ERIC: Believed.

BARRY: Certainly is a funny story. That this guy with his cigarette was just—he was not allowed to exist.

ERIC: I think he was not so wasted that he wasn't aware that this guy was talking to him. It's just that he had the incredible sense and instinct maybe, and this goes against what I was saying further back about his fear of being out of control. I think in this case he was letting the instincts go for it. And you know, they must be good instincts.

BARRY: They got to be mighty good to keep him landing on that chair every time.

ERIC: One of the things I've always liked about Dylan is that combination of control and lack of control or seeming lack of control. You never think he's going to quite hit the note, but he never embarrasses you. Even if he misses it, he somehow misses it in a way that it doesn't matter.

There is a thing that you can pull out of yourself by that tightrope walk—which can be a disaster if you fall. But first of all, it's got everybody uptight and on edge and if you get out of these things, if you pull it off, it sweeps an audience along with you like nothing else in the world can do. You know it isn't an act. Sometimes it is. In other words, you're a performer working with a sophisticated audience. The only way to create a performance tension is to go way beyond your capabilities and hope somehow you'll pull it off. And then, of course, Dylan is at a stage now that everyone is going to love it no matter what—just the fact that they're seeing him in the flesh.

BARRY: He got out of trying to be a performer per se shortly thereafter. People started to take him seriously. And he just stopped worrying about being the cheerful cherub.

ERIC: And I think the cheerful cherub was most endearing—in other words, that was a stage where he couldn't do wrong. Everybody had to love him. But I'm talking about going beyond that into more dangerous waters than the cheerful cherub. I'm talking about the one about the— not "Masters of War" but the—

BARRY: Yeah, the one we used to call "War and Peace."

ERIC: You know, the sound, bells of something are chiming or something—I saw him backstage at Symphony Hall. And he got out there and sang "Sounds of Freedom Flashing."

BARRY: "Chimes."

ERIC: "Chimes of Freedom Flashing."

That's not the war and peace song.

ERIC: No. Maybe "Masters of War."

BARRY: No, it's not "Masters of War." It's a very extraordinarily long thing that's based on "Everett, My Son."

"Where have you been, my blue-eyed . . ."

ERIC: Yeah. [That] is his [magnum] opus. "Hard Rain's A-Gonna Fall." Yeah, that's what it is.

"Hard Rain," the one that he says he wrote each line as a song in itself because he didn't know if the war was going to end tomorrow.

ERIC: Right.

"Hard Rain." Is that the one you call "War and Peace"?

BARRY: Yes. Listen. It was one of the first times we ever heard a song that long that didn't come out of a child.

Oh, yeah, that's "Hard Rain."

BARRY: But I think the beginning of that whole thing was "Hollis Brown." Remember that one?

ERIC: You mentioned that earlier. I think that's one of his greatest songs.

BARRY: Yeah, great song.

ERIC: Very traditional.

BARRY: I've got a Dylan story. It's not really a Dylan story, but Dylan happened to trigger it off. There's a studio guitarist by the name of Jay Berliner, who has no soul whatsoever, the most incredible chops that ever came down the pike. And it's sort of, you know, classical jazz technique. And he reads. He's got perfect pitch and perfect timing. And plays anything faster and, just, you name it. He is a sensational musician and if he'd ever get out of being so fucking blasé and phlegmatic, he might make some music. Jay was sort of a folk studio player. And there was a show, a folk show, that the Westinghouse network did at the time, which actually is one of the best specials done on folk music at that time. John Henry Faulk narrated and did a very good job.

Yeah, Carolyn told me about that. Carolyn was on it, yeah.

BARRY: And Jay and Bill Lee and I were the musicians. And we'd just broken for lunch and Jay was sitting there with his ninety-dollar guitar, which he couldn't decide if it was the greatest guitar in the world. And

Dylan comes over and he says, "Hey, man, can you play that there Warsaw Concerto song?" Which is not really a guitar piece, you have to admit. But Jay, along with being very phlegmatic and having fantastic chops, also has no sense of humor.

ERIC: So he plays.

BARRY: The Warsaw Concerto. He played it classical. He had those chops and those ears. He played about halfway through and couldn't remember any more. So he went back to the top and played another third, ending with two jazz chords. And that was the one time Dylan shrank into the woodwork, with egg on his face because he put somebody on and they—

Throw it back at you.

BARRY: Not only does he accept it and throw it back at you, but he's straight.

ERIC: Never caught on.

BARRY: It's like saying, "Hey, man, why don't you levitate for me?" And he does.

ERIC: I was talking about the '65 Newport thing where Butterfield's group kind of stomped all over Dylan on those first songs where no one could hear Dylan. You know, it's one of the few times I've ever seen Dylan being used. And in this case, this goes beyond being put down by your own jive ass remarks by somebody who's so straight they don't even know you're being jived. But I think Butterfield was doing that. It wasn't so much Butterfield. I think it was that he was out there wailing with his guitar and he wanted everybody to hear it way up in the back seats.

Were you at the '65 Newport?

BARRY: I don't think I was. The last Newport festival I went to was the one that Van Ronk ragged on—

ERIC: Is that the one where Jack Elliott threw his hat up on the stage and fucked up "The Alabama Song"?

BARRY: I think so, yes. I believe so.

ERIC: Terri Van Ronk was ready to kill him.

Wait a minute. The theory that Butterfield, the basic theory is that Dylan did not plan when he went up to Newport to bring the electric instruments up. But that he saw Paul Butterfield and his band up there and decided—

ERIC: Use them. You know, play "Maggie's Farm," and it was kind of like the record and all that.

BARRY: I wasn't there.

No opinion? I did want to ask you—

BARRY: All I know is, he sold out.

ERIC: I sold out.

BARRY: I sold out.

ERIC: We all have our price.

Hey, there is one thing we didn't cover. The poster. The funny story of the poster that Bobby didn't want to use. I have it hanging up on—

ERIC: The poster I did that you're speaking of, the Baez/Dylan poster, the Toulouse-Lautrec direction, I got after Manny and Albert realized these guys were, you know, Bob and Joan were going with each other at the time and they always popped out of the wings about two-thirds of the way through the concert and sang five songs, you know? And it really was a duet, and our dual concert. You know, getting Dylan and Baez, either way you did it. If you hired Baez, Dylan would show up. And if you hired Dylan, Baez would.

BARRY: Best thing was to hire the cheaper act at that time.

ERIC: Right. But then they decided, well, we'll just do it like this in front, you know? So Manny—I did the thing through Manny and he claims he paid for the whole thing and it's possible. But I had a shot of Bob and a shot of Joan and I knew them both and so I knew pretty much what they looked like. And somehow or other this Toulouse-Lautrec thing seemed to work pretty good. So they used it once in New Haven. And this was before the San Francisco, the West Coast poster craze. And you know, they just threw them away afterwards. And I was trying to tell Manny to stick them in the lobby or give them away or something. But when you do a poster like that, it's done in overlay, so there really is no original of that. The original is the print of the thing.

What I have hanging up in my office at home is an original?

ERIC: It's as original as there is.

Right.

ERIC: It's like a lithograph. It's made from the plates. And what I did was to make the plates. This is the way most separated, color-separated stuff is done. But when I sent it out, after it was printed, they couldn't tell what the hell it looked like before it was printed. Just strange black squiggles. And Manny objected to it because he said that you can hardly see Joan, you know? And you know, there she is, right in the forefront. And at the same time Albert was saying the poster sucks, you know? You can't see Bob and when you finally do see him, look at that nose on him. You know?

That's his Sioux Indian nose, right?

ERIC: And so both of them thought it was terrible. Manny thought all you could see was Dylan, and Grossman thought all you can see was Baez. And it shows where agents are at.

Manny is now telling me that Albert and Dylan both objected because you had the cap on Dylan's head and he was past that stage.

ERIC: Oh, nobody ever told me that. And it didn't really matter that much because they split up at that time and they never—

I think it's a marvelous poster.

BARRY: Did you use that as one of your—

ERIC: Flyers. It was only used once, and Manny had it printed up in two sizes. One was the flyer size. So he gave me about a hundred of the large ones with the heavier stock, and I use it as a flyer. I overprinted a little message, like, "Use Eric for your graphic needs." In fact, I did a Toulouse-Lautrec riff on it, I think. There's that little man, nearsighted man with those funny glasses and the little beard. And some say Toulouse, some say Eric von Schmidt. And I never got a fucking job from the whole mailing.

LIKE A ROLLING STONE

IZZY YOUNG

*Bob Dylan was, he was the first one for my money that broke up
the ballad standard, and not only broke it up, he put in the music
to fill in. And he used the contemporary ideas. So, it would sound
natural. It sounded like it had always been in the ballad form. . . .
He broke out of the ballad standard completely. . . . That was his
contribution. . . . That can't ever be taken away from him. In fact, I
feel in some ways that a monument should be raised to him for what
he did.*

SRAEL (IZZY) YOUNG ran the Folklore Center, a combination record and
music shop, folk library, folkie booking center, and general hangout.
Young produced folk concerts and was a member of the board of *Sing
Out!* Dylan wandered into the Folklore Center in 1961 and joined the
regulars listening to Young's vast record collection and reading folk song
lyrics in back issues of *Sing Out!*

Young kept journals and read entries to Tony during the interview:
"I'm very excited by Bob Dylan. I'm producing a concert so I can hear him
entire. Purely from the way he talks he seems to have greatness in him,
an ability to stand on his own." Izzy Young was instrumental in launching
the young Bob Dylan, but when he talked to Scaduto, Young clearly felt
some bitterness. Young spoke to Tony about Dylan's scathing, hateful
"Positively 4th Street" that had everybody in the Village asking if it was
about them. Said Young, "It's unfair, and I'll explain why. I'm living in the
Village . . . twenty-five years now. . . . He comes in and uses my resources
and everybody else's resources . . . and then he leaves. . . . He writes the
bitter song. . . . He's the one that's complaining. He's the one that left. And
it's really his problem."

Midway through the interview photographer David Gahr dropped in
and joined the conversation. Gahr documented the Newport Folk Festivals
of the 1960s, '70s, and '80s. He created iconic images of the folk, jazz, and

blues songwriters, artists, and writers of the second half of the twentieth century.

.

—————

Let's start with how you first became aware of Bobby.
I had a store on MacDougal Street and he came into the store in '61. And he almost immediately just took over.
How so? What did he do?
Well, he would come in with songs every day, singing new songs. And singing the old songs then. And so something about him, that's—I'm still trying to figure out how he came to New York, where he got his folk music from; everybody accepted him completely, especially myself, as something that fell out of the sky.
That's amazing, because even the people out where Woody Guthrie was staying at the Gleasons', out in New Jersey, those kinds of people—
Well, it's connected with a lot of things. One day I'm going to write an essay on why Bob Dylan changed his name from a Jewish name and why Jack Elliott changed his name from a Jewish name. And it's, like, why Jack Elliott is a failure according to American ideas and why Bob Dylan is a success. Because Jack Elliott tried to re-create another idea and you can't be an interpreter anymore, but Bob Dylan is an interpreter again on the record. I'm going around in circles.
Yeah, go ahead. I find my greatest stuff is when people ramble.
So in the beginning, for example, he was telling us how he knew Woody and Jack Elliott, as if he were the center of this thing, and nobody thought to call up Paul Nelson in Minneapolis and say, "Hey, who's this Bob Dylan?" So anyway, he came in, and no one asked a question, including myself, as to where this guy came from, how he came.
What did he say? Do you recall the first day? Did you lend him money? Did he say he was broke?
No, he never asked for money. Well, not from me anyway.
Because Manny Ross at the Cafe Wha? remembers the first night that he came into town. And he came in and he said, "Hey, can I sing?"
I'll read what he said. He told me this story, which is—
Why don't you read it now before we forget. Break the chronology of it and read it.
All right. So, well, this was written October 20, 1961.

Ten days before the concert.

[Reads from his notes:] "I always thought that Jack Elliott for my money was the best folk singer in America. And now has decided to be a song-writer and sorry to say, he's not. He really is an interpreter. There's no room for the interpreter anymore. And I feel bad about Jack because he should have stuck to his guns."

His attitude now is that, "Shit, I could have done what Bobby did and I think I'm going to start doing it now." No, he meant, "I could have written a song for Woody," is what he's saying. "I should have done that."

He couldn't have done it. And he should have stuck to what he was. He would have been the best American singer still. And that's what happened to so many people, and Bob Dylan was smarter. But I'll come back to that. But after being a fan of Jack Elliott's—I put him on his first concert in '57 also. I'm writing this: "After listening to Jack Elliott two nights last week, I think he will not make it." Grossman, you see, I talked to Al Gross-man—he let it be known that he was the manager at the time.

Really? Why did he let it be known that he was a manager?

He was managing Odetta, but everybody thought Bob Dylan was a free agent.

Oh yeah. He apparently signed Bobby just around the time of that Shelton re-view. Because as I get it, he came into Gerde's a couple of nights after Shel-ton's review, which was September 29, and he told Bobby, "Come on up to the office next week and we'll talk." And Bobby signed—within a couple of weeks.

He had his fingers on him much earlier than that. [Reads from his notes:] "Well, you can see that Grossman thinks that Bob Dylan has a much better chance of making it. He thinks Peter, Paul and Mary will be one of the top commercial groups. Grossman also thinks that Belafonte stole in his earlier success, all the material by Bob Gibson. That was a scandal. I just made arrangements with Bob Dylan; it was . . . early in November. Al Grossman spurred me to do it." So anyway, Friday, October 20, Dylan comes in and this is really the first interview of his. [reads:] "Bob Dylan, born Duluth, Minnesota, 1941, moved to Gallatin, Mexico." Incredible. You know, no questions.

[reads:] "He says he lives in Iowa, South Dakota, Kansas, North Dakota for a little bit. Started playing carnivals when he was 14 with guitar and piano. He's been practicing piano at Bob Shelton's house, which he was living there for a quite a while. Started playing harmonica two years ago, always interested in singers. I didn't know the term folk music until he came to New York City. Bullshit. I've been in New York City since January '61."

I heard that he was in music the summer before, but I didn't meet him at that point. I heard that he was here in the summer of '60.

In the summer of '60 is when he was doing that thing—when he was down in Colorado City. Do you know that city?

I have that written down. He talks about that. [quotes Dylan:] "I got a scholarship to the University of Minnesota, went there for five months, went to classes for five days and left. Hung out with a blues singer, maybe four or five years ago."

What's the name?

Bella Gray. Chicago street singer, blues singer. And it's interesting. The names he drops are always famous names. It's never—he never met a guy, you know, who no one heard of—

A name he recognizes—says he recognizes in Minneapolis.

[Dylan:] "Used to know a guy from Navasota, Texas. Listened to him a lot."

Is this pretty much a direct quote from Bobby? Your reconstruction of it? Or was Bobby talking to you as you wrote it?

Bobby was talking to me as I wrote it.

Okay, yeah, continue. That's beautiful.

So, in a way it was much easier to just write it down even with repetition and things. But he was talking very slowly. He wanted me to get every word down. In a sense this is better than a tape even:

> [Dylan:] Met him through his grandson, a rock and roller. He'd heard Woody Guthrie records in South Dakota, dustbowl album.

Current folk music is inane. Seems a lot of jazz songs, sentimental cowboy songs, Top 40 Hit Parade stuff. See, that was one of my arguments, was that he should have started out that way, right away, rather than be a folk singer, then have to deny it later on. And that's my big argument. People have to name it something, so they call it folk music. Now very few people singing that way. It's being taken over by people who don't sing that way. It's all right, but don't call it folk music. The stuff I do is nearer to folk music. Now singing old blues and Texas songs, I don't want to make a lot of money, I just want to get along. The more people I reach and have the chance to sing the kind of music I sing, they have to be ready before people understand it.

People often say the first time, this isn't folk music. My songs aren't easy to listen to. Favorite singers are Dave Van Ronk, Jack Elliott, Peter Stampfel, Jim Kweskin, and Ric von Schmidt. Her voice goes through me. She's okay. [Joan Baez he's talking about.] Wherever I go, I go, I guess. Like a matchbox. Too many matches in a tiny box. Not a planned concert. I sing songs that tell something, is this America. No foreign songs. The songs of the land of the free. TV or radio and very few records, offering a chance to hear them.

I start recording for Columbia next week and, out probably the first of the year. Groups are easy to be in. I've always learned the hard way. I will now too. When you fail in a group, you can blame each other. When you fail, you yourself fail. Just the way he does, just because I want to dress this way.

Carl Perkins from Nashville, Tennessee, sings them. I never checked that out, but I don't think. Talking blues and topical things. "California Brown Eyed Baby" has caught on. "Bear Mountain" song, wrote it because Noel Stookey working at the Gaslight asked me if I wanted to hear this story about people stranded waiting for a ferry ride. Sang it on night it is open mic night. Never sing it the same way twice. Never saw it, just heard about it. No one really is an influence for me now. Actually, everything does. Can't think of anyone in particular now.

Who is Noel Stookey?

Well, that's from Peter, Paul and Mary. Paul Stookey. His name is really Noel.

I didn't realize that. That goes way back.

From my notes: Monday, October 23. I am very excited by Bob Dylan. I'm producing a concert so I can hear him entire. Purely from the way he talks, he seems to have greatness in him, and ability to stand on his own. On the other hand I believe I've been sadly mistaken when I took Jack Elliott for a legend. You can see how Bob's really influenced my thinking. Jack, poor Jack, may even reach a reasonable success but his road goes down from now on, a failure caused by his character; his friends have helped as much as they could. The thing is, like Jack Elliott was supposed to be at the Philadelphia Folk Festival last week. He just didn't show up.

He didn't make it? I was going to go down just to talk to him. I've got two more questions—

You know, not one person asked about him. And he always does this to his friends. Like he didn't show up to two concerts for me. He always thinks, really, that all of us are too small. Like he'll tell me, "Izzy, I don't want to do concerts for you, I want to do concerts in Carnegie Hall." I say, "Well, it doesn't work that way." And so he always fucks his friends.

He struck me as being very hungry when I talked to him, very hungry.

[reads:] "Bob Dylan played piano with Bobby V, would have been a millionaire if he'd stayed with him; played piano northwest of Montana, one day Cafe Wha? playing harmonica with Fred Neil. Bob was bored stiff. That's okay. It was warm and Bob stayed the whole winter. Went to see 'Raisin in the Sun.' Lou Gossett was in it."

That was the dollar-a-night gig at the Wha? behind Freddie Neil.

Right, yeah. I think he mentions that somewhere.

> [Dylan:] He believes in cards, plays a lot of cards. It's time to cash when you get aces and 8s. The other things I believe in are logical, the lengths of his hair, less hair on the head, more hair inside the head. And vice versa.
>
> Let mine grow long to be wise and free to think. There's no religion, tried a bunch of different religions. Churches are divided. Can't make up their minds, neither can I. Never seen a god. Can't say till I see one. Got a free ride to New York. Came to see Woody Guthrie. Came to the Folklore Center and there was girl playing with banjo, Toni Mendell. Oh God, this is it, this is New York. Everyone's playing banjo. And playing faster than I'm playing guitar. Couldn't really play with them.
>
> Used to see Woody at Greystone whenever we had enough money. Met him once before in California, before I was really playing. I think Jack Elliott was with him.

In other words, at the age of twelve he was the center of the whole folk music movement.

That's right. That's pure bullshit. Because Jack Elliott was in Europe, for one thing, at the age that Dylan says, okay—

Nobody questions it.

Isn't that wild?

Everybody accepted it. Did you hit Dave Van Ronk?

Had a couple of long raps with Dave. The only trouble with Dave is, he gets drunk rather quickly and you have to keep going back. Okay, continue—

> [Dylan:] I think Billy Faier was there too. I was in Carmel doing nothing. During the summer Woody impressed me, always made a point to see him again. Wrote a song to Woody in February of this year, was going to sing all Woody's songs.

Jack and Cisco came out. Woody carried the paper Bob wrote the song on. Woody liked to hear his own songs. Woody liked Bob's songs. Haven't seen anything really funny. Woody doesn't like Joan Baez or the Kingston Trio. Baez, for her voice is too pretty; and Trio because they can't be understood.

I like to walk around, just walk around. Like to ride motorcycles. Was a racer in North and South Dakota, Minnesota. First guitar I had, strings were two inches away from the board. Had a classic but couldn't play it. No one ever taught me to play guitar or harmonica or piano. Used to play sort of boogie woogie type of stuff, play with rock and roll songs, never knew the names of the songs; the Twelve Bar Blues played along with them. Two coffeehouses refused to let me play when I came to New York. Bob Shelton helped by writing an article, talked around; someone from Electra came down but nothing happened. Bob Shelton has been like a friend for a long time.

Now around this time, I started peddling him—

Why? What made you decide to do this? I know a lot of people around were impressed by him.

Well, every once in a while, you hear someone I think is really great. I tell everybody. No one does anything about it. So, I brought him up to Vanguard Records and they said no. And a year later I brought him up to Jac Holzman, Elektra, and he passed.

Terri Van Ronk was telling me that she brought him up to Solomon, too, at Elektra. She called Solomon and he said, "No, I've heard this kid. He's no good."

Well, he told me that he doesn't want to put out freaks, only important things. Then Bob went out to *Sing Out!* magazine and they threw him out too.

[Dylan:] Yeah. Friends are pretty hard to come by in New York. Dave Van Ronk has helped me along in card games because he is always losing. I've been with Jack. We have an island in upstate New York. We saw the island out in the lake. We named the island Elliott Isle and swam back.

Now this, I really think, is dirty.

[Dylan:] "Jack hasn't taught me any songs. Jack doesn't know that many songs. He's had lots of chances."

He has a killer instinct right away at the beginning. But at the time that he was doing this, he was imitating Jack Elliott. His great concert was a Jack Elliott concert, it wasn't him.

Your concert, the one that you put on.

I was very disappointed with that concert.

Bob did mostly Jack Elliott stuff—

It was all Jack Elliott stuff. So, for him then to say he learned nothing from Jack Elliott is really wrong.

Yeah, Manny Greenhill says when he first met Bobby, Bobby was sitting there at the feet of the master, Jack Elliott. That's the impression he says he got when he walked in the room, that Bobby was sucking up to Elliott.

But did you see the way he—

That's right. The killer instinct that early.

> [Dylan:] I went out to the Gleasons and stayed out there for a while in East Orange. They have a lot of tapes of Woody's VD songs. Learned a bunch of those, sung them to Woody. Came down to Denver two summers ago. Dezi was playing downstairs. Upstairs was Don Korpin. Oh, he's living in Canada now. Learned the way he does songs. Mixed his style with mine at the time. Before that there was a farm hand in Sioux Falls, South Dakota, who played autoharp, picked up his way of singing. Wilbur, never knew his last name. Cowboy style, I learned from real cowboys. There's been no one around to cut records like the old Lead Belly and Guthrie.

I'm really enjoying reading this to you.

It's great. It fills in a lot of holes. You know what's great about this? Pieces of it I've gotten from, like, Spider John Koerner in Minneapolis. Yeah, he said some of this. I started trying to reach you back in April and I finally said, "Well, look, let me grab Jack Elliott and Joanie and everybody else. And then after I've done it all, I'll come back to Izzy and see what he says."

I never got the message. Well, we're here, we're here.

> [Dylan:] So young people that are singing like that, but are being held back by commercial singers, people radio programs don't play.
>
> Jim Kweskin, Luke Faust aren't appreciated by enough people. Folkways is the only company that would record such stuff. Went up to Folkways. I had written some songs. I said, Howdy, I've written some songs. Would you publish some songs? We need to look at them.
>
> I heard folk music was good. True, but they wouldn't even talk to me. Never got to see anybody. Saw Sing Out on the door but it must have been the wrong place.
>
> It seems ironic I'm on a big label. The article came out on Thursday night. Bruce and I backed up Carolyn Hester.

Bruce Langhorne, right.

> [Dylan:] Showed the article to John Hammond.

So, you can see Bob Shelton's article's very important. Like, at that point I was one of the people who was advising him. He said, "Izzy, should I write this thing on Dylan." I said you gotta.

> [Dylan:] Anyway, I showed the article, the Times article, to John Hammond. Come in and see me. I did, and he's been courting me. He asked me what I do. I've got about 20 songs I want to record. Some stuff I've written, some stuff I've discovered, and some stuff I've sold. That's about it. Used to see girls in the Bronx, in Chicago, with their Guthrie string guitars, singing "Pastures of Plenty," "No Lipstick," "Brotherhood Song."
>
> Opened up a whole new world of people. I like the New York kind of girl now. Can't remember what the old kind was like. Can always tell a New Yorker out of town, wants everyone to know they're from New York. I've seen it happen. First four or five days, people just stare at me. Down south was different from New York City. Beatniks.
>
> Ten years ago a guy would get on a bus with a beard and long sideburns and hat and people would say look at the rabbi. Some guy gets on the bus today, the same people say, look at the beatnik. Played the 5th Avenue Hotel for the Kiwanis Club for Kevin Crown for no money. All kinds of big people want to be there, had to do it.
>
> Okay, never got back 75 cents he owed me but stayed at his place. Okay, but don't care for classical music, don't go for any foreign music. I really like Irish music and Scottish music too. Colleges are the best audiences. Much better than nightclubs. New York is the best place for music. School was too. Lived on the Mississippi River about 10 feet under a great bridge.

Imagine everyone in New York accepting this. The idea of living like Mark Twain. You know, it never occurred to me that he was Jewish. Or anybody. Not that it makes a difference anyway, in general.

Well, it makes a difference. It's a clue to the guy's character, he's hiding his background.

He's hiding it. I'm working on an article [about] why people like Jack Elliott and Dylan are forced to change their names. It really means that minority people are still oppressed in America and are ashamed of their background. But I feel, though, they've got to reckon with that one day. Because the older he gets, the more Jewish he's going to look. There's no way out of it.

> [Dylan:] About ten feet way under a great bridge. I took some theater courses, said I had to take science.

You know, you should really put all these papers in some archives some-where.

Well, I do when I go home. I take this and I put it on a big tape. You know, a good tape recorder. And I'm going to store them in a vault someplace. I'm going to make a note in my book, if anybody wants to see them, give me a call.

> *[Dylan:] Carnivals and fraternities, so much crap. So much phooey stuff. You might as well get out and live with some other people. Big hoax. Walked out of anthropology, read a little, went to see the movies. One time I flunked out of English. The teacher said I couldn't talk. Poetry you had to read, hard to think about it for one time.*
>
> *Poems should reach as many people as possible. I spent more time in Kansas City, about 400 miles away. A girlfriend was there. Went to high school in upper Minnesota, Hibbing, a nothing little town. Fargo, North Dakota, a lumberjack and mining town. Used to hop trains, big open pits, lots of strikes there, lots of political stuff, a real mining town.*
>
> *It's easy to criticize big moneymakers like Belafonte and the Kingston Trio, Belafonte is really like a popular singer; criticized by jazz folk and calypso, always talking about Belafonte here. And he's making all the money. Won't criticize him until he sings one of my songs, but he'll make a lot of money for me. I liked Belafonte on a TV show. Odetta, frustrated show singer, folk music is wide open for good voice. Instead of starting at the bottom in opera or show or jazz, they start at the top of folk music.*
>
> *Logan English is one guy—I can't figure out the word—every time I see him it's failure, singing folk music. But there he is, still trying. Logan's singing is one big batch of phooey, he's terrible. Lots of people sing simple but Logan dwells on this. But he doesn't have it. Even when he sings Jimmy Rogers.*

Logan English did a lot for him at the beginning.

Yeah, he did. He was the MC at Gerde's and he was around the whole night, and he was giving Bobby a big hand there. And he was helping him out at the Gleasons'. The Gleasons told me Logan English helped get Bobby friendly with Seeger and with everybody out there.

> *[Dylan:] Oh, Peter La Farge is a great songwriter. Bruce Langhorne is great. Was at a party once, playing. Let me have a guitar, didn't have much fingers. Read "Bound for Glory" twice. Book should be taught to college kids. His poetry should be taught in English classes. McKinley's Bar in Kansas to the 5th Avenue Hotel in New York City.*

What's the date on that?

October 23.

John Hammond records him almost immediately after this. Within a week or so after.

Oh, Oscar Brandt walked in and I got Bob Dylan on his program on Sunday. That's the end of October '61.

[Dylan:] Izzy called up, Westinghouse called up.

What did he say about Westinghouse? I'm trying to track down the date on that TV show he did.

[Dylan:] Westinghouse called me and asked me to come down and spoke to me about doing a show on folk music, something educational.

Bob Shelton has been very helpful with giving me information on who to reach. He felt he was out on a limb with the September 29 article on Dylan in the *New York Times*. It feels more justified now.

I think this is for Dylan's concert:

He will be in Nashville at the time of the concert, but he will review the tape, which is really unusual. Like Jack Elliott showed up three days late for his appearance at the Ashgrove, Friday instead of Tuesday; that's when he called at midnight to say he was sorry.

You know, he was always doing that kind of thing. Actually, I kept these notes all the time—

That's wild. You sit down and do this.

Once in a while. February 1, 1962. Okay, so this is the middle of the winter. Bob Dylan wrote a song: "The Ballad of Emmett Till."

[Dylan:] After I wrote a song, said another was written but not like it. I wrote the chords. I'm playing it February 23. I think it's the best thing I've ever written. Only song I've played with the capo. I stole the melody from Len Chandler, a song he wrote about a Colorado bus driver.

The song is in true American ballad style. "Born a black skin boy, and he was born to die." A narrative that is strong but still not getting its full power. You can still see what's coming.

I'm writing this as I'm listening to him playing it. Just a reminder to you that this kind of thing still lives today in the dormant Ku Klux Klan. And the quote again. But the song is better than any similar song in the last ten years. It is a tremendous song.

That's you saying that.

Yeah.

[Dylan:] I bought an apartment, it cost $350. Rent is $80; 161 West 4th Street.

I'm getting some money from Columbia. I'm supposed to be making all kinds of money. One thousand dollars in checks, $300, $400, $150. All adds up to $1,000. No one would cash them. Lee's gave me money.

Who's that?

Lee's Music.

He got $500 from Lee's.

[Dylan:] I sing, I don't play guitar if I don't feel like playing. I'd rather get drunk. I hate coffeehouses to play at. People come down to see freaks. Sometimes I'm in a bad mood. I don't like the idea too much.

Well, that is true about the whole Village scene. People don't come to hear the music. They come to laugh at the people, really.

[Dylan:] Carnival was different. I was with the same people. Entertaining in coffeehouses just doesn't have the togetherness. Have to stay in New York for a while. Might go down to New Orleans for Mardi Gras. I like New York. At one time I said if it wasn't for New York I'd move there. But I sort of like the town. 42nd Street, that's about all. I went to Brooklyn Hospital, seeing Woody, studying for a year.

Still has the story set in his mind. He liked my songs. You have to see the notes by Bob Shelton. I never figured I'd play with Belafonte. I practiced piano at Bob's house. Next album I'll play piano, guitar and harmonica. Writing a song called "The Death of Robert Johnson."

"The Death of Robert Johnson"?

He did a blues thing. I don't know if he ever wrote the song.

No, I don't recall. I know who you mean. I know who Robert Johnson is. I don't think he ever wrote the song. Or it's never been—

I never heard it.

Terri Van Ronk showed me a lot of lead sheets she's gotten.

Actually, that could be a thing to check out. But I don't think he did.

[Dylan:] Don't like to go up to John Hammond's. Ivy League kids treat me like a king. At first, I liked it. It gets sickening after a while. I took Lee Chandler just to see what would happen. He couldn't believe it. Lee's book comes out in April, with thirteen songs and three arrangements. Hammond isn't a manager, more an adviser.

I'm sort of disconnecting myself from the folk music scene. Too many guys want to make a big entertainment out of it, with jazz and comedians. Thirty-year-old guy Buffalo Bill, looks older. Why isn't he recorded? Gil Turner brought the tape there. Curious to know how long the New Lost City Ramblers stayed at the Blue Angel.

Can't see the future. I hate to think about it. It's a drag to think about it. How could anyone know who I am? I'm inconspicuous. February 7, 1962. "Strange Rain," written while Gil and I were in Toronto, December '61. I set out to say something about fallout and bomb testing, but I didn't want it to be a slogan song. Too many of the protest songs are bad music, exceptions being "Which Side Are You On?" Most of the mining songs are good.

Came to New York City 1960, back to Oklahoma several times. Disaster trip to California. No one liked me. Felt pretty low and I left, more than twenty songs.

What's "Strange Rain"?

A song that he wrote.

I'm not familiar with "Strange Rain."

Is it called "Strange Rain" or "Hard Rain."

Oh, "Hard Rain"? He recorded it as "Strange Rain" then?

I wrote down "Strange Rain" because Tom Paxton's song was popular at the time. He wrote a song, "Strange Rain."

[reads:] February 22, 1962. Bob Dylan just rolled in and wants to sing a new song, a song about fallout shelters, the meaning of life has been lost in the wind. Learning to live there, burned out, whatever it is. Let me die in my footsteps before I die on the ground.

There's more elegant poetry in Dylan than in Woody Guthrie. "Rambling Gambling Willie"—I'm saying this is as good as any folk song coming out of America. I don't think he ever put that on a record.

No, it was going to be on the *Freewheelin'* album, and he pulled it off at the last minute because his head was changing and he was going more into the protest.

Well, I'll tell you. That song is fantastic. It's a great dead-man ballad. As good as any dead-man ballad. He considers his song of Emmett Till his best.

[Dylan:] April 20, 21, 22 in Ann Arbor. Just me and Jesse Fuller, concert at Goddard College. Billy Jay from Columbia Records doesn't want me to sign too many things, so as not to interfere [with] their plans until the record comes out. Love my—

Is he saying there that he's going to play with Jesse Fuller in Ann Arbor?

Yeah, April 20, 21, 22.

And the concert at Goddard College never came off as far as I know, according to—

He was talking about it.

And the Jesse Fuller thing apparently was set. He did do it. As far as you remember.

I don't even remember anymore.

[Dylan:] Loved my life there. Waiting for my book to came out. More than a record. "Gambling Willy" is in the book. "Bear Mountain," "Reminiscence Blues," "Stood on a Highway," "Poor Boy Blues," "Talkin New York," song to Woody Guthrie. Paxton's songs, they're good, I guess. Broadside. I think it's a good magazine. Can't hardly tell from one issue. Who needs songs like that?

Carolyn's record will be out in May or next September. Mine is coming out in two weeks. And she recorded two months before me.

Haven't called Mitch Miller to hear some of Bob's songs. Mitch wanted them for Frankie Laine. What happened? Ernie Miles is writing songs all over the place. I've never even looked at them. To tell you truth, except for a few, they're pretty good, I guess.

I like Johnny Cash's songs. He writes a lot of songs. I think Woody Guthrie wrote better songs. I've seen some songs that were never recorded. Woody Guthrie songs, "Jackhammer John," "Hard Travelin'." I like them all, really, except some of them seem absurd. Oh, "Your Dirty Overalls," that's really good.

Lomax, I like him, I really like him. He stuck around one night to hear me sing at the Bitter End. MC said there was no time. I was at his house, we were sitting around, something, eating apples.

But Lomax, at the beginning said that Bob Dylan was a bad buck. And then quickly changed his mind later on.

Yeah, at the beginning Dylan rubbed a lot of the more traditional people wrong, because of his style and his interpretation and his gritty voice.

As far as I know, I don't think there's one person in the Village that didn't dig him right away.

Well, Carla, who was working for Lomax, told me at the very beginning, Lomax and the people around him were anti-Dylan.

Oh, those people. But that has nothing to do with the Village, really. Oh no—

I'm talking about the traditionalists.

The traditionalists, yeah, right.

[Dylan:] Sure wish Cisco was still alive. I really didn't know him. I liked him because he was real, just a singer. Heard Bonnie [Dobson] last night. She's okay, I guess. I [met] Big Joe Williams . . . in Chicago. I really didn't play too much. I just followed him around. I sung then. I've got a cousin who lives in Chicago. He lives on the South Side. Funny thing, Big Joe Williams remembers it.

4:30 p.m.; playing around on harmonica, sitting by the fire. I'm going to finish—"Talking Folklore Center."

He wrote a song for me. I have to reprint it now. It's called "Talking Folk-lore Center."

I'm not aware of that.

It's actually the only song of his that's not owned by him.

You own it?

I own it. I never let anyone use it. I published it. I reprinted it. I've done everything with it.

> [Dylan:] I think Paul Anka is the worst songwriter. Saw some of his songs in the Hit Parade book. I think Johnny Cash is the best songwriter. Can't think of anyone else. Len Chandler, he and Sylvia, have picked up some songs of his.
>
> He drew a picture of a block head with an umbrella. "Strange Rain," Tom Paxton—I don't understand it, umbrella? Why can't he say how they shoot off the bombs? You ought to go to Valley where all the stuff is going on. Go out there, you'll find some strange rains. I think the scientists and politicians are together in this thing. How can you like a song you can't understand?

It couldn't be any more simple, the song.

> [Dylan:] It's like in a foreign language, but this is our language, I should be able to understand it.

Your notes start from October.

October.

Dylan shows up in town in February.

Yeah.

You started making notes because you were making notes on the concert thing.

Right. Otherwise it might not have been done.

What was your impression of him at the very beginning?

That he was very powerful right away. He took over the room right away. And that he was—this is in retrospect—he was very competitive. He really didn't look at anybody else. And he would just sort of wait his turn, you know, to sing and sing and then go out.

Is that what the setup was like at that point? The kids would come in and wait their turn?

Yeah, back of the store [Folklore Center]. Everyone would be playing.

But the attitude was not that they were performing for people as such, but it was more like a group of people together.

Bob Dylan was performing—all the time.

The thing I get from people back in Minneapolis even, when Bobby came into

the room with his guitar, he wanted to be the center of attention. Anyway, he
was competitive.

Yeah, except, as I said, it was so transparent that nobody noticed it at the
time. I'm sure everyone's telling you pretty much the same thing about
him. In '61 he was very competitive about the other singers. Especially not
singing foreign stuff and, you know, not caring for money.

Putting down Paxton.

Describing him like Walt Disney almost. I never really was a close friend
to him the way Dave was or Bob Shelton. Now I feel that he came to the
store more as a place to be heard than as a close friend of mine.

He was using it more as a showcase kind of thing.

Yeah, I'm not complaining about it. I never was invited to his home or
anything like that. And I think by the time he has a recording session, I
didn't even feel like going anymore.

**Apparently, in the very beginning he was a kid who seemed to want to learn
from others, like from Dave.**

He would listen to anybody all hours of the day and night. He knew exactly
what he wanted.

Yeah, he knew how to use people.

He knew how to use people. And when the point came not to use them
anymore, he dropped them, whether it was Jack Elliott or Allen Ginsberg.
And he always was making it like it was never for him to say, for other
people to say it. He was associated with the Beatles. He never said he was
associated with the Beatles. He was a poet. But he never said he was a poet.
Just the PR people say he was a poet. He never said anything. And so he
would go along with what people said.

**How did he get people to say this? Not only the flacks but friends like Dave
Van Ronk.**

Everybody believed it. Even though there was evidence coming up all
along that he wasn't that way. Like, for example, it was around this time,
maybe a little later, that the blacklist letter about Pete Seeger—

I think it was late '62.

I was the secretary of that group, and we had a big meeting, Judy Collins
and Billy Faier and me. In fact, there was a little question about me; people
saying Izzy's not a folk singer, so Carolyn said I was a folk singer. And
everybody signed [the letter]. Except Bob Dylan.

Really?

He said, "It doesn't mean anything what I say."

When I asked Carolyn, "Was Bob involved in this whole thing?," she said, "No, gee, that's funny. I don't remember what happened with Bobby."

No, he was there. He was at the big meeting at the Village Gate.

Did he sign?

No. He didn't sign. That I can say definitely. Then the second point, where he was supposed to record "Talking John Birch Society Blues."

Oh really? On the *Freewheelin'* album where they threw it out after the—

Over his dead body. That song had to go on the album. And it did go on the album. And then I have the original downstairs.

Because I'm not clear which songs were dropped. I know "Rambling, Gambling Willie" is one of them and—the liberal line he wasn't dropping songs—over my dead body—

First you do the shit, then you can do what you really want to do when you get more famous. And then—so that's the album and then the attack on the Civil Liberties Union. But that came later.

Yeah, that was the end of '63. Right after the Kennedy assassination.

And still people accepted him as a revolutionary, as the person changing things. Well, because in my mind now I see the pattern. And there comes a point where you can chart—there's no such thing as a person not knowing when he sells out. In other words, Bob Dylan says, I think on the second album, "I don't trust anybody over twenty-one who sees what's happening and doesn't say what's happening." He says that. There's no such thing as a person consciously changing, unconsciously changing. And that's the problem with the protest song in general. From my viewpoint I begin to see it, the protesters, like the voice of the middle class, [don't] really want to change things very much. They want to have a little mea culpa.

They want to get rid of their guilt feelings by singing along with Pete Seeger.

Because you only see beautiful white people at these concerts. You don't see the ghetto kids there. You don't see the Indian kids or the Chicano kids there. And there's something about protest, it's [so] middle class. They don't understand how they're oppressing.

Right.

There comes a point at which you have to say what's wrong. So, Tom Paxton took a full-page ad in *Rolling Stone*. I think it's Paxton. He says I'm not on the soapbox anymore, but I wanted you to know I still care. Why does he have to say that? Well, Judy Collins in *Life* magazine last year says it's not interesting to sing and demonstrate and sing the same songs all the time.

Your basic feeling, then, is that Bobby came in deliberately wanting to make it as a star of some kind, and using people.

Well, here's the way it works—

Let me say this. Bobby comes out of Hibbing, right, where he had been play-ing rock and roll. He also had been playing hillbilly. He got hooked into it with some friends who were into hillbilly and some of the country stuff, right? And some of the folk stuff. And he comes down to Minneapolis and it's all folk. The crowd he falls into is a folk radical crowd.

And he says to an old girlfriend from Hibbing, "I'm going into folk because that's the way to make it." He comes here to New York and gets involved im-mediately in the younger folk scene.

Yeah.

And again, "This is how I'm going to make it." Is this your basic feeling? This is my feeling.

Yeah, this is how it works. So, the artist has to start from a point. Eventu-ally they accept you, and keep accepting you forever. All you got to do is tickle a few nerves and pat them on the head, and we're with you forever. But the instant you make it into the mass thing, then you have to say goodbye to the starting group no matter what it is. And that's what the sellout is, really. People think I'm bitter about Dylan. Now every song is a production, every song has a lot of money riding on the song. It's the same thing with Dylan.

They're all reaching for that brass ring, for that gold ring.

And there's no end to that. Now the kids are seventeen, eighteen, nineteen, and they start with that idea and they forget it very quickly. Because Joni Mitchell wrote a song last year she sang at Newport, "The Fiddle and the Drum." Sort of saying, look, America, you know, you don't have to kill people. You know, I'd like to make $1,000,000 a year, but why do you have to have wars?

And she doesn't understand that making $1,000,000 is what's killing everybody, what's making the wars necessary, that sense of competition with the whole world. So a lot of things are in this position. And then they're saying life is beautiful, which it is to them. Same thing with Joan Baez. You know, you wonder why the Black Panthers don't say life is a circle, you can do anything you want. Incredible String Band, you know, telling that to the audience.

Dylan didn't start it, but it really comes after him, like in Woodstock. On one side they're getting, grabbing, grubbing all the money. On the other side they're the sensitive artists. Now with Dylan what I found is—to this day the kids will not accept the fact that that he's a sellout. I do not understand this—

Oh yeah. You know Carl Oglesby of SDS, one of the founding presidents of SDS. He said after the last album, "I know as we talk he's a sellout." But up to this point he didn't think so. And I said, "Well, geez, Carl, you know, it was so obvious years ago, even when he was writing the things that you were calling radical, they were just rock-and-roll songs to make the million bucks. They were hit singles he was looking for." And Carl says, "No, they weren't."

Now with Dylan, what's happened, the kids refuse to believe that Dylan was a cop-out, and what Dylan really is, is a kind of evolution in a way. I spoke to five hundred kids at Rutgers. They booed me when I explained how the movie *Don't Look Back* is a cop-out. The only person that he's attacked so far in America is the American Civil Liberties Union. That's the only thing he's been angry about.

But I always come back to William Blake, you know. They have all kinds of names for him today. Mysticism, you know, all that kind of thing. But still, when Tom Paine was in England, he hid out in William Blake's house. So I say the more power, the more money you have, the more responsibility you have. America does the opposite. The more money, the less responsibility.

Then it became—and he started it, a situation where the interpretation was lost. It was just a song. And then they have to invent these crazy words, singer-songwriter, these long dramatic words. And it came to a point, a few years ago I ran a folk song workshop at the Philly Folk Festival, and I said anybody that sings his own songs exclusively is a businessman. Then comes a point you're supposed to sing only your own songs, so that it became unstylish to be an imitator, like the New Lost City Ramblers with traditional material.

Well, there's nothing wrong with Dylan stealing the melodies from the old songs and making his new—

Yeah, but you can't steal from him.

Right, right. But the point is, he's making the threat.

Suddenly it became bad to be an interpreter, to be an imitator. So now you ask them, what do you do? Original material. What do you do? Do my own songs. What do you do? My own thing. I mean—so I say, Jesus Christ, I'm doing my own thing, you're not telling me what you're doing.

Now the point is Dylan is back doing other people's stuff.

Dylan was very creative, he worked very hard, he knew what he wanted, he knew what the people wanted, but once you make it to the top, to this imaginary area, you never know what's going on anymore. America won't listen to the poor people who write songs or the black people or the Indians. It's always got to be translated—white middle-class ideas. And that's exactly what Bob Dylan does. So the latest cop-out of Bob Dylan is accepting a doctorate from Princeton, after somehow allowing himself to be the one to say, drop out of college, drop out of school, it's not important, you know, an attack on middle-class parents.

He said college is bullshit—who needs college? I dropped out after four months and, you know, learned that the road teaches you more than college.

Yeah, but now he accepted the doctorate. Oh, when he wrote "Positively 4th Street," at least five hundred people in a few months' time asked me if I was the one in the song.

Actually, people like Dave and Tom are saying that it's everybody. You know, everybody around the Village that Dylan knew in the early days is the guy in the song. You know, the song was written to put you all down, every one of you.

But it's unfair, and I'll explain why. I'm living in the Village twenty years, twenty-five years now, and I'm in business about fifteen years in the Village. I was here yesterday, I'm here today, I'll be here tomorrow. Dave Van Ronk is still in the Village. I'm one of the representatives of the Village because I've been here.

But he comes in and uses my resources and everyone else's resources in the Village, and you know, the bars and the clubs, and then he leaves. He gets bitter, he writes the bitter song. Dave Van Ronk never wrote something saying what a cocksucker Bob Dylan was. You never heard me say what a son of a bitch Dylan was. No one has ever said anything about Dylan. He's the one that's complaining. He's the one that left. And it's really his problem.

A few years ago Bob came in. I'll tell you, I didn't recognize him.

Why didn't you recognize him?

Well, because I hadn't seen him for two or three years. And his hair was cut differently. And he had a quiet look about him. Anyway, he had a much more somber look than I remembered. Very serious. And, oh my God, that's Bob Dylan. I was thinking, schmuck. So, he says, "Well, I walked into Izzy's store. I got ignored." I wrote to him. I said, "Look, Sixth Avenue is busy. If I don't see you, you know, we're old friends, you could have seen me. You could have said hello to me."

What was his response?

He came into the store and he said, "What's troubling you? Is something on your mind?" And I said, "Well, no."

He says, "Well . . ." He came up with a great line.

Okay, so Bob Dylan, I was really happy that he came in because it meant that I still have my place in the field. You know, whatever it is, you can't fuck around with that. But he's smart because he doesn't put it in writing. You can't—

You can never pin him down.

There's no tracks. He's never left any tracks, really. A lot of that stuff in that *Rolling Stone* interview, if you recall it—I didn't like the interview, I mean, but it was right.

Yeah, but everyone was saying, oh, he was just putting Jann Wenner on.

Oh, that's the other story, that he's putting on people. And I think there's a time in which you stop putting on people and say what you mean. Like, the guy can write fabulous songs. He can also say what he thinks as far as an interview. And it's a cop-out to say that you can't talk about the song.

Oh, that's pure bullshit. Yeah, he tried to leave the impression that he was to-tally inarticulate and that he couldn't talk about anything. But Van Ronk said he can sit for hours bullshitting and arguing. Why did you decide to put Bobby on? When did you decide to let him sing?

Well, because I thought he was fabulous. I thought he was tremendous. Bob Dylan was the first one for my money that broke up the ballad stan-dard, and not only broke it up, he put in the music to fill in. And he used contemporary ideas. So it would sound natural. It sounded like it had always been in the ballad form. As opposed to someone like Phil Ochs, who's imprisoned by the ballad. It's A-B-A-B-A-B. He doesn't know how to break out of that. He's never been able to break out of it. A very clear example is the way each of them [sang about] Medgar Evers. The way Phil did the ballad standard, and Bob did "Only a Pawn in Their Game," in which he broke out of the ballad standard completely.

So that was his contribution. For popular literature, really. That can't ever be taken away from him. In fact, I feel in some ways that a monu-ment should be raised to him for what he did. And he should be executed for what he's doing now. But there's no contradiction between the two. In other words, Bob Dylan is in exactly the same position now that Carl Sandburg was, except thirty years, forty years younger. In other words, Carl Sandburg's poetry was in the protest magazines of the time, the '20s.

You know, "I Am the People, the Mob"—that appeared in the communist literature of the '20s and '30s. And then when he died, he didn't know anything about Vietnam.

How much effect did Al Grossman have on what happened to Bobby?

Unbelievable. In fact, without Grossman I don't think Bob Dylan would exist.

No, no. I mean, what happened to Bobby and his sellout. I'm not talking about in terms of fame. I'm talking about the sellout.

The sellout is completely engineered by Al Grossman. In other words, Al Grossman is actually smarter than Bob Dylan.

Could he have accomplished the sellout if there wasn't fertile ground there for it? If Bobby wasn't prepared for it from way back when he wanted to be a rock-and-roll star back in high school?

Oh yeah. Like we're knocking him for doing rock and roll suddenly. That was his original issue.

Anyway, getting back to Grossman.

Grossman was the pure engineer of this. Because nobody in New York—I don't even think he realized he was a manager until after the record came out. I wanted to manage him. But he was actually being managed already by Grossman.

Really?

This way Grossman was managing for years, and nobody knew about it.

All you knew about Al was that he had Odetta and Peter, Paul and Mary.

Yeah. But he was doing that with everybody.

Getting back to the concert now. Tell me your impressions—first of all—

I put on this concert—just the way I put on other ones—like I put on Jack Elliott in his first concert, Peggy Seeger, another one, you know, I felt it was an important concert.

You paid seventy-five bucks for the chapter hall.

Yeah, I paid—I was supposed to split the profit with him, after my cost. This is the way I worked in those days. The hall cost me $75, expenses another thirty, thirty-five. And I printed up tickets, which I never printed for any other concert. And the word really was all around. Al Grossman was supposed to help and he never showed, which is—

By this time he apparently had been signed to Grossman.

I think fifty-two people showed up.

Fifty-three with Dylan. Dylan made fifty-three.

Oh yeah. About fifty show up. Paid $2. So, I'm really losing money on the whole thing. And—not including my time, and I made a mailing, postage. You know, but something told me—this is incredible. I printed more copies of this than I did of anything else.

How many people can sit in the hall?

Maybe 150, maybe 200 you could squeeze in. Something told me at the time, you know, print a lot, and I still have the leftover tickets. And now kids come from all over, they want a copy—I didn't make anything but it's not right not to pay a singer. So, I gave him $20.

But the original agreement was you'd split fifty/fifty on any profits? And because there were no profits, you gave him twenty bucks. What was the audience reaction to Dylan at the first concert?

The general reaction, I remember, was pretty blah. I don't remember anybody saying it was a great concert.

Did he discuss with you beforehand what he was going to do?

No. I never discuss with any artist—I mean, it's their evening.

What was Bob's reaction?

He thought it was a failure, the concert. He wasn't happy about the concert. He thought it was a flop.

Right. As did pretty much everyone else.

Is that what people said about it?

Yeah, some people had the feeling that he was doing too much other people's songs. And Mikki Isaacson, you know, said too much Jack Elliott and then he screwed it all up, that he should have done the stuff that he was writing by now.

I don't think he sang any of his own songs.

By then at Gerde's he was doing "Talking Bear Mountain," he was doing "Talking New York," he was doing all the stuff on the album. He was cutting the album.

Yeah.

What about during the period where he was—where the fame was really building. Maybe Newport '63, where it really started to work.

He was still coming in—

What was happening to his head? Because everybody I've talked to is talking about the changes.

Well, at this time already I wasn't so close to him anymore. I mean, he would come in once in a while with Joan Baez or something. The last time I saw him, I think it was in '65, really, came in with Joan Baez one day and sang for an hour or two.

With Joanie?

With Joanie in the store. In other words, I'm out of the picture, actually, after '63. So I mean, I've seen him maybe a half dozen times since that point.

The reason I asked about Joanie is because '65 is around the time they were breaking up—just before the "Don't Look Back" tour, which was in May. They were breaking up at that point.

I'm the only one that's pointed out the mechanics of Bob Dylan. Oh, that's the most beautiful example of Bob Dylan's mechanics.

What's that?

He sang with Joan Baez for two years all around America. And all the stories grew up and people always knew that Bob Dylan would be brought in from the side. And then she goes to England with him. And she doesn't appear at any of the stages. In *other* words, the moment he realizes, he sang by himself. You can see in the movie. I'm the only one that wrote about it, hey, you know. Like, he says, "I'm bigger than you, fuck you." She actually realized that she was out?

Oh sure.

Oh good. I was wondering.

I asked her. I said, "Look, I know there must be a thousand feet of film on the cutting room floor of you. You must be in some of it. What happened?"

No. I don't think she appeared on the concert at all.

She said, "He wouldn't let me sing with him."

You can see that in the movie, very pathetically, how she's trying to show that she's part of him.

Yeah. She said he was just destroying her. He was totally vicious. Anyway, what else? Did I miss anything? I think we've covered pretty much. Why don't you think about this? Let me glance through this and your scrapbooks and other questions will pop into my head. And then we'll sit down and talk again.

[Recording off/recording on. David Gahr, Dylan photographer and friend, joins the interview.]

Again, let's see here. The basic question is about Grossman again. What's your basic feeling about Al Grossman? Some of your experiences with him? You started with telling me—

IZZY: Grossman, I met Grossman through Chicago, through the Gated Horn, originally, in '57. Or maybe earlier. He had Odetta. I don't know if he was involved yet with Richie Havens at that time.

No.

IZZY: No? He was the one who arranged my first concert, actually, Peggy

Seeger. He called me from the Gated Horn one night and arranged for
me to have her so he actually started me on my concert career.

What kind of guy was he when you first met him?

IZZY: He was very sharp.

Guillotine sharp, businessman?

IZZY: No, he didn't come on like guillotine sharp—he came on like he was
very concerned, you know, for the artist as a human being, as a person.

Oh really?

IZZY: And so I went to some folk festival with him and he was talking
about a concert for Ian and Sylvia, I think at the time, and a person said
some figure, and he said, "Well, I don't know if they could really live on
that. And after all, they have to work hard for their money and I'm very
concerned with that." So they were all having lunch at some big club
there, and talking how he was concerned about the artist.

So, it's a joke already. But he says, "Look, Izzy, I've done more for the
artist than any person has. I made the artist have respect for himself,
because I got more money for the artist than anyone else did before.
Nobody's going to work for $500 a night anymore, not after me."

**Yeah, but the charge has been made that Grossman came along and commer-
cialized what had been quote pure folk unquote.**

IZZY: Well, he did it—nobody died because of it.

Yeah, but everybody bitched because of it.

IZZY: The only people that bitched were the people that he didn't sign up.

Right.

IZZY: The complaint about him is actually that he owns too much of the
artist. And he made it very clear that the artist made more money with
him than they could on their own.

The fact that he owned part of the recording company or that he
owned the music, that he owned the recording studio, the way Grossman was a genius, better than anyone before him. He owned Peter,
Paul and Mary. He owns Bob Dylan. Bob doesn't write the songs and
that's it. Al set it up so every time a song or property goes back and
forth, he gets a slice, a slice this way, a piece of the recording studio, a
piece of the company, a piece of the production deal.

**The only thing I know is that John Hammond says Dylan told him back in the
very beginning that Grossman was only getting 10 percent. Well, what has happened since then? If anything—**

DAVID: Dylan's no fool on money either.

IZZY: That was, like, one of the biggest-kept secrets.

Yeah, and I do know that Dylan went around asking advice of everybody he could find before signing up with Grossman. He just didn't jump in and sign up.

IZZY: But I understand when he signed him in '61, they had some kind of agreement already.

Yeah, that's right. Grossman is earlier promoting Dylan, but not admitting that he's his manager.

IZZY: He really operates behind the scenes, you know, then he works out deals with music publishing holding corporations. Now I understand Dylan's not with him at any level, but I don't know.

The contract ran out last June 30. And they split. I know he was running around town talking to some of his old friends about having to find a new manager.

IZZY: But the point is, that it was a partnership outside of money.

Right.

IZZY: I think Grossman knew more about how to push him in the public eye than Dylan did. In other words, Dylan was in no sense cheated by Grossman.

Right. But Dylan apparently today has the feeling that Grossman cheated him emotionally, that Grossman forced him into certain things that he shouldn't have done.

IZZY: He wasn't an innocent lamb. I want to insist that it was an absolute equal partnership except Grossman was probably the only man in all those years that was smarter than Dylan. He's the only man that wasn't conned by Dylan.

Some people who were around them at that time say the feeling they got was that Dylan would be very flip and very hip when talking to somebody like you, or talking to Terri Van Ronk or people around, but came on to Grossman like a little kid begging his father for something. Did you see any of this?

IZZY: I wasn't—no.

DAVID: No, I don't think so.

IZZY: Not that I'm aware of. I really feel it was a smoothly operating business. Somebody else maybe saw a father/son thing.

You would have—right, you would have had to be at a party with them or up in, you know, Grossman's apartment or something like that, to get hipped into this. Okay, the charge has been made by everyone. That Dylan sold out unquote. That Grossman made him a businessman.

IZZY: Oh, that's not true. If anything, it's the other way around. I have to insist again that was a meeting of minds. I mean it's wrong to say that Grossman was able to corrupt Dylan.

Why would you say that?

IZZY: Dylan knew all the time what he was doing. I may not have realized what he was doing at the time. And I explained to you, in some detail, how I was taken in by him.

But I just wanted, you know, to pull out some of your own words.

IZZY: Dylan wanted to get where Grossman was taking him. And that is a point that Grossman has made with every artist. "Izzy, I don't want to work with artists that don't want to go someplace. Any artist that I took someplace wanted to get to that place." I think Grossman's absolutely correct on that.

I have stuff from back in high school and back in Minneapolis where Bobby Dylan is saying to his friends, "I am going to be as big as Elvis Presley. That's where I'm going." I mean, I agree with you. I just want to hear, you know, you say it. I want to hear it in your words.

IZZY: Okay, let me say because I'm remembering Grossman's saying he got more for the artists, he made the artists have self-respect for him, more than anyone before him. I remember when he negotiated a deal for Ian and Sylvia with Vanguard Records for $175,000.

Right. Unheard of amount of money.

DAVID: Unbelievable, unbelievable. Frank Sinatra prices.

IZZY: And you know, for folk music, he got prices nobody ever dreamed of, whereas people are getting now, you know, for rock groups and stuff, but back then getting $175,000 for Ian and Sylvia—

DAVID: Unbelievable amount.

IZZY: Then another deal he wanted from Vanguard. He wanted $250,000 and he got it somewhere else. Then he got a deal from Capitol because he did a favor for them. So again, anyone signing up with Grossman understands his rules.

Those are the precise words said by Manny Greenhill. Anybody who signs up with Grossman knows the rules.

IZZY: They could never do it without Grossman. No, I suspect Grossman's power is waning now. I think there are a lot of giants around, I mean, that are as big as him.

DAVID: Well, his relationship with the Band is pretty strong. It's stronger than ever. As a matter of fact—

IZZY: Yeah, well, with the Band—it's just as clever as anyone else. He creates this air of mystery that the Band is somehow—he helped them get to the top so they can dream and think all day long. What life is.

DAVID: No, no. The Band, I think they appreciate the old man.

IZZY: Well, in the underground press where they say they really don't want to have to do the commercial stuff—

DAVID: That's untrue—

They're talking for the underground press. Saying what the underground press wants to hear.

IZZY: In other words, the lie of being an artist in America and making millions of dollars on one side and pretending you don't know where it came from, you know, that you're just a sensitive artist on the other side, the Band is part of that.

And I'll tell you what, when he first told me about the Band, they had no jobs yet. The record wasn't out, he played a demonstration record for me.

Grossman did?

IZZY: Yeah. Well, he did for everybody. And I said, "Well, gee, let me put on a concert in the church because this sounds really great and I really like it." He said, "Well, they got a lot of jobs and stuff." They didn't do their first job for a year or something after that. In other words, he very carefully builds up—he does his homework. Little underground papers are just as important as the *New York Times* for him. And the Band, you only saw, like, partially revelatory things about them in *Rolling Stone*. "Hey, I got a good article for you. You're going to be in on a new big thing." And those things are inculcated, you know, very carefully. But he does that work terrifically.

DAVID: Remember, he had Peter, Paul and Mary for at least a year before Dylan, didn't he?

IZZY: Yeah.

DAVID: And they were powerful then.

IZZY: Well, Peter, Paul and Mary are really important, you know, in the career of Bob Dylan. They got him "Blowin' in the Wind."

Oh, sure, sure. A hit single is one of the biggest factors—that and Joanie Baez, taking him up on her tour, sure. Those two factors.

DAVID: This was the—that's some of the free Grossman network.

IZZY: You're not doing this with any part of his songs. I'm sure you don't have permission.

No, I don't have permission at all. I can paraphrase the songs. You know, my assumption is, anybody who buys a book on Bob Dylan damn well knows his songs and will know what I'm talking about. I recall by paraphrasing, recall what the song is about.

DAVID: Here's the funny thing. I'm still very fond of Dylan. Despite all the shit—

Anything else about Grossman?

IZZY: Well, all I can say is that I felt very close to him. I always felt he was extremely special. That we were really pals. Now I realize he was giving me the information he wanted to give me. He never gave me the complete information.

Telling you what he wanted you to know.

IZZY: Yeah, and there was—actually, I realize now that not for a moment was he a friend of mine. I can tell you a story, meeting him in Newport two years ago. I met him in Newport—He says, "Oh, I haven't seen you in so long. You represent light, I represent darkness, you're good and I'm evil."

Oh, he's been reading Hermann Hesse.

IZZY: He doesn't respect me for not making money. But one day he may need me again.

Dave Van Ronk, when I made a particularly nasty crack about Grossman, Dave Van Ronk said you can't be hard on Grossman. He was programmed to do what he's doing.

IZZY: That's true. I mean, no one is a lamb led to the slaughter.

And anybody—and you're a failure and I'm a failure. We're all failures because we haven't made it. But Al Grossman—

IZZY: Except I can still go to his office now to talk, go for an hour privately.

DAVID: Because you have power. A certain underground power.

But you're not totally a failure.

DAVID: That's right.

But your basic feeling is—John Hammond says Grossman made Bobby Dylan a businessman and he screwed up the whole protest thing because he made him a businessman. My impression has always been that Dylan knew exactly where he wanted to go, from the very beginning, and that if Al Grossman made him a businessman, it's because Bobby wanted to be a businessman.

IZZY: John Hammond is not innocent in this.

DAVID: Exactly.

How so?

IZZY: When he put out the record, he cut out "Talking John Birch Society Blues."

He claims he couldn't do it.

IZZY: He was only the president of the company.

Who, Hammond?

IZZY: Yes.

No, he was just a producer. He was the head of artists—

IZZY: He's not just a producer.

Head of talent acquisitions.

DAVID: Not just a producer. A socialite bigwig in this fucking country.

All right, he—

IZZY: I can't tell you that John Hammond was—a little side issue. John Hammond is no little lamb. It's incredible. A guy making $400,000 a year out of Columbia has no say.

He admits he was a power in the company. But he says Clive Davis came and said, "Look, the lawyers insist, CBS, the parent organization, insists it must be killed." And that's the word from the lawyers. David Kapralik told me the same.

IZZY: And what about—but John Hammond made no fuss about it.

Hammond says he fought. Kapralik said he fought too. John and Dave insist they fought.

IZZY: Because John Hammond dumped the record even at one point. The second record.

Oh no. The second record had advance sales.

IZZY: What I'm telling you, at one time there was a point—I think they thought it was just something that didn't work. That was the feeling at Columbia.

The first record. The first record only sold five thousand copies, and Kapralik wanted to drop Bob Dylan. And John Hammond claims, and Kapralik says it's true, he said, "Over my dead body" and fought Kapralik on it—

DAVID: He seemed over his body there, but he didn't fight over his dead body on "Talking John Birch Society."

Well, he claims he was powerless, and Dave says the same thing.

IZZY: That's always the talk of rich people, that they're powerless—

Oh, of course, that's the liberals' out.

IZZY: You have stuff about the demonstration at CBS? That we actually had a demonstration—

You planned it and he never showed up. He and Suze never showed up.

IZZY: Or Grossman. And I think that's a very telling, important thing.

Getting back to the concert now, you were going to try to remember, if you could, what Dylan's reaction had been.

IZZY: He was very unhappy about the concert. He was very shaky. He thought people didn't like it. I was alone with him backstage. There was nobody—I remember one person coming back stage to congratulate him on the concert.

That's strange. That's unusual.

IZZY: Especially a concert that's supposed to be—I don't remember one person coming up and saying it was good.

Did you like it?

IZZY: Oh no, I told him—I told him it wasn't bad, but I mean—I can't tell him it was terrible.

Can you recall what he said about it? He obviously knew he screwed it up.

IZZY: He may not have said anything. I mean, you could see he was visibly shook by it. He knew that he flopped. There wasn't any big excitement. There wasn't any big applause. Nobody—everybody felt let down. I'm not aware of one person feeling that they'd gotten—

DAVID: I remember about a week before the concert, Izzy caught a hold of me on MacDougal Street. He says, "Dave, you've got to come hear this kid. I'm putting on this concert—he's going to be great." I remember that. I didn't make it. I mean, I didn't make the concert.

IZZY: Well, that's why you're starving, why you have to work for *Time* magazine.

DAVID: Were you at the first *Sing Out!* concert, a hootenanny put on by *Sing Out!*? You have to find out about that. I called my wife today. It's the first time I heard Dylan live.

Was this after the November 4 concert?

DAVID: Oh sure, oh sure. I have never—my wife looked at me. My wife hates folk music, hates folk country. Never laughed so much. He sang that song about going around the island—

"Bear Mountain."

IZZY: "Bear Mountain," yeah.

DAVID: He was fantastic.

IZZY: It was really good.

DAVID: My wife looked at me. I looked at her. I didn't believe it. We didn't know he was that good. But he was great. Because he had a sense of humor. And it caught.

CARL OGLESBY

The best thing Dylan's got going for him is his hype, his con, or his whatever—his Sphinx-like ambiguity. You can never be quite sure the guy's not putting you on, no matter what he does. That means the interpretation of his songs becomes an interpretation of oneself. Consequently, his songs remain permanently contemporary.

CARL OGLESBY, radical theoretician, writer, folk singer, and songwriter. He was a former president of Students for a Democratic Society, a progressive protest movement of the 1960s until it was splintered and destroyed by the more radical Weathermen group. Oglesby discusses Dylan's songs as a response to the failures of the old left, the liberals and other one-time radical groups and as anthems for his generation.

There's a point there where Dylan was traveling, you know, hanging with important people. You were in the movement at that point, and Dylan came on strong. What effect did he have on you personally, and what effect did he actually have on the movement?

Well, I don't know if it was anything so explicit and direct as that.

I wouldn't think there was, but still, there had to be.

I think basically what Dylan does is establish the horizons of a radical sensibility that feels right to people. That means two things: one, getting rid of something, and the other is setting some new ideas up.

Okay, two things.

Well, one thing that was a lot clearer about political activism in the middle of the 1960s, or the early part of the 1960s—seems to be that you couldn't explain yourself to yourself or anybody else by use of the old Marxist vocabulary, or even the old left-liberal vocabulary of the Roosevelt New Dealer types.

There was a different sense that people were operating with about what they were doing and the old definitions didn't hold. The old vocabulary wasn't useful. Politics was, in a funny kind of way, romanticized again. The movement then proceeded to define as political life the kind of life it was into living, which included the life of singing songs and dancing dances.

Somehow it was perceived that to dance in a certain way was a very political gesture, because it had something to say about how you related to your body and how through your body you related to other people. So all this stuff that comes out of Chubby Checker—the whole music thing—is important for the movement. And then within that are not only Dylan's early songs whose political importance is kind of clear—I mean, the anthems are—

Left anthems.

Well, of the civil rights movement, in any case. And the fact that they appeared so promptly as to seem absolutely contemporaneous with the civil rights movement, so that there wasn't any lag—it wasn't as if a songwriter was coming into an already established political room.

Oh, it wasn't like that? Were the records saying, okay, boys, let's get the Edwin Hawkins Singers to do something else?

. He seemed to be part of it, and the songs were as informative to the movement in some peculiar way as the movement seemed to be informative to the songwriter. So there was that relationship of reciprocal dependency and cross-fertilization. I mean by that to indicate something that's always puzzled me and has been kind of a problem lately.

Dylan doesn't seem to me to have fulfilled the responsibilities that he has to the movement. He's been quite willing to let the movement define him just as he's willing to let anybody define him—to be a Proteus for everybody—and there was a time when the content of his songs was explicit enough even after the anthem-writing period, even after "Desolation Row." I guess it's *Highway 61 Revisited,* the album.

A new kind of literary ethic started operating. He became more political precisely in those kinds of moves than he had been before and it's reflected in the songs that show up on *Highway 61*—the emergence of a distinctive self-consciousness in the movement that didn't refer itself to simple old battle cries as the movement matured from civil rights to a genuine, radical picture of America. So, Dylan moved from a liberal kind of song to a radical kind of song—a liberal critique to a radical critique—it became more radical simply by being suppressed more—linguistically suppressed.

Well, the critics call it negative. The critics who were thinking in terms of the folk idiom call it his negative period. Although it's really not. The older critics—let's put it that way.

Yeah. I guess what happened is that at a certain period in a young man's life, he will say, "How many years?" What is that song? How many men, how many years, how many this, that, and the other thing will it take? ["Blowin' in the Wind"] And a little bit later on, having been around, seen what happens, and cased the joint—got a better sense of the immensity of the forces in play—he knows it would take a damn long time.

What were some of those immensities of forces?

I mean, just recall how everybody thought in the [early '60s], when the Freedom Rides began, there was some kind of assumption—very rootedly American, I think—that reality corresponded in some important way to laws that were written and passed by legislatures. So, if the legislatures could be gotten to pass certain kinds of laws, then reality would come into life.

You can still affect your world by getting certain good acts passed.

The whole attack on Jim Crow. Probably it was necessary to do that to produce real results or not. It still was a matter of a self-education of an American left which had no background—no legacy at all—because all of that had been wiped out.

In any case, what we can see as an important change involves the understanding that laws are not written out of the scruples of the humanistic assumptions of liberal politicians. That's not how laws get made, and the making of laws is not how social reality gets shaped. The laws, if anything, are very dim reflections of realities of power—who has it and who doesn't. So, if in the late '50s and early '60s the movement operated with a very naive set of assumptions about power in America and could sing songs such as Dylan was writing of simple, uncomplex outrage, it couldn't do so for long.

With the undertone that if we sing them loud enough, things will be changed.

Sure. Like, Dylan orchestrates "We Shall Overcome" and provides a poetry for "We Shall Overcome" that goes beyond that song, but without going beyond its assumptions. Dylan rewrites "We Shall Overcome" over and over and over again—you know, a dozen times—in really powerful ways. You know, the stuff about the miner and the stuff about the killed cook?

Killed cook?

You know, Hattie Carroll. He couldn't do them now, because everybody is so sophisticated. Everybody knows how much crime there is in the world, how many criminals there are, and above all how powerful these criminals are. They understand the world to be run by these criminals. So, I promise it's no surprise to hear about those lamentable deaths to people who have seen lamentable death close up and often—and if not death, then at least betrayal, the scrubbing of dreams, and the losing of hope. So Dylan was, I think, important for the way in which he gave character to the sensibility of the movement—you know, to the contents of the mind, the furniture.

Somewhere along the line, Dylan discovered, or it was made clear to Dylan, that these songs—"Blowin' in the Wind"—weren't working, and he goes into what the older folk crowd is calling his negative period, which is more a radical period actually. But since then, something has happened to the guy's head, and he has totally deserted all of it, including _Nashville Skyline_. I mean, what is it? It's a bunch of pretty little songs. Dave Van Ronk's feeling is in the beginning, Dylan was afraid of the monstrosities within America. Now he's afraid of the monstrosities within himself, and he's let his own hang-ups take over.

Hmm. Well, I don't know. It's an interpretation. The thing Dylan—the best thing Dylan's got going for him is his hype, his con, or his whatever—his Sphinx-like ambiguity. You can never be quite sure the guy's not putting you on, no matter what he does. That means the interpretation of his songs becomes an interpretation of oneself. Consequently, his songs remain permanently contemporary.

Right. The fact is that up until _Nashville Skyline_ there was really no need to interpret Dylan's songs as such. You got the feeling. The emotion of it came through. You knew the cat was saying something to you.

Right, but I think you can say the same thing for _Nashville Skyline_. It's not a record I happen to like, and I think in fact it's a cop-out.

But is it a cop-out or a put-on?

Well, I thought it was neither one until the interview in _Rolling Stone_, which I thought was just a disgrace. I mean, that ends it so far as I'm concerned. I have no further responsibility to listen to Dylan. He's not kicking with the rhythms of this period anymore. But you see, that lamentable interview fixed for me the dimensions of his intelligence. Before, I could read his songs in the freest possible way. The interview fixed the meanings of those songs too much, and it would be better for everybody if the interview had never been published or taken place—or at least it should be recorded, so we could tell from the tone of voice maybe—

That's right. In fact, I'm trying to get Dylan to let me hear the tapes of it.

Well, it'd be good to know, because the thing is so flat and banal, and his intelligence so trivialized. I mean, he comes out with this gosh, gee whiz kind of bullshit.

And yet people who have seen Dylan around the period that the interview took place say that this is where his head is at. This is him.

But until the interview, you could look on—at least I could look on *Nashville Skyline* as being interesting, if for no other reason than Dylan got interested in the working class; that the white movement did. And *Nashville Skyline* could very plausibly be seen as an effort to establish another constituency. And on those terms, it's a very valid political act, in the broadest meaning of political. But it was remarkable that at the same time the movement was getting turned on to the displaced and alienated white hillbillies in the northern cities—and more and more convinced that if it didn't find some way to reach the young kids in the working classes, it wasn't going to have any political future at all.

At that same time, Dylan comes on with a kind of one-two punch—the *John Wesley Harding* record, which I thought was a very handsome repudiation of that god-awful "can you top this" ego game the companies and superstars had got into. He comes right after that, and in another way just unfolding another elaborate way of seeing the world. It's great. I think it's his best album.

Yeah.

He comes right after that with *Nashville Skyline,* which says in so many words, from now on the problem is, how do we talk to America? We know generally what's the matter and what to say, and we don't need to explain the problem to ourselves anymore. That's what, say, all his records up to now had been doing: a critique of the culture. The critique is established and in-depth. *John Wesley Harding* is kind of a résumé of the whole career from the early folk ballad kinds of protest songs—which you can hear all kinds of echoes of in *John Wesley Harding*—through the surrealistic kind of language that he developed later on.

It's a very controlled statement as to the necessary electricity of contemporary music, the relationship between that electricity and the acoustical sound, and the simple—transparently simple but, on the inside, very complicated—melodic unit of the folk song. I mean, musically that's hard stuff. It's really advanced, I think—and *Nashville Skyline* too. You just don't pick up a guitar and strum those songs out with three chords. It's very subtle stuff, yet it sounds simple. And that's a very high degree of artistry.

Yeah, Eric Andersen said he tried to do a couple things from *Nashville Skyline*, and he couldn't handle it. (*laughs*)

I mean, the guy has clearly been spending his time doing something—thinking about music. That's good. That's cool. By the way, if I sounded hard before about Dylan, I'd like to qualify that by saying I have immense respect for his sense of craft. In that way he's got an integrity that's just—

You're basically hard on his sense of his place in the world or in our society as such.

Yeah, but I guess I want to soften that, too, because—

Even that depends on what he meant by that *Rolling Stone* interview.

If it hadn't been for that interview, I'd still be holding out the—well, look. I'm waiting like everybody else for the next record. I'm wondering what the bastard will say.

I'm disappointed in what he's trying for the next record.

Why? Have you heard it?

Yeah. He threw it all out. He went to the studio and did a bunch of old Eric Andersen songs and a lot of Simon and Garfunkel stuff.

Dylan did? Why?

There were twenty-six sides, and they all came out shitty. And he threw it away.

Why was he suddenly doing somebody else's songs?

I don't know. He spent the summer with—last summer with Paul Simon out on Fire Island, and apparently he's been grooving on Paul Simon's craft or something.

Oh horrible.

Yeah. God. I've talked to people in the studio.

Is he drying up?

I don't know. I just can't get to him yet. I really don't know. It may have just been, you know, "What a gas. We'll blow everybody's mind if I come out with all these stupid Simon and Garfunkel songs."

Maybe, but that's a very destructive kind of arrogance, you know?

Yeah.

Almost better to shut up.

Yeah.

He could afford to do that. He could afford to shut up for two years, at least—three, maybe—and that would only heighten the suspense.

Sure.

I think maybe it's a piece of bad luck or good luck that interview showed up, you know, at the time it did. But anyway, if it hadn't been for that interview, one could still hold out all kinds of hope. I really want to emphasize that the importance of that move to working-class language—you can hear any old place. On any place on the bayou, if you turn the car radio on, you can hear somebody say it's only love that makes the world go round. And you know, you just don't even hear it.

Like Gleason [critic-columnist Ralph Gleason] pointed out, when that kind of language is being used by the guy who wrote "the ghost of electricity howls in the bones of her face." Then you know something's up. That then becomes a very conscious manipulation of verbal stereotype, and you have to raise the question, what's it for? It becomes an intentional gesture, defining a strategy of sensibility and not a limit of intelligence. So to the extent that in *Nashville Skyline* Dylan could be seen as a strategist, one had to raise the question, for what objective was the strategy being conceived? There was no other way to understand those particular moves.

Musically or poetically, you couldn't understand *Nashville Skyline* unless you presuppose that he had something on his mind, and that he had decided on the necessity to reach another constituency and that that was something like a political decision and that it had something to do with decisions that the movement was reaching about the necessity to go to the working class. You know, you just couldn't keep on saying that the rednecks were fascists, are going to elect Wallace, and kill us all.

If your interpretation of *Nashville Skyline* is correct, and I have no reason to doubt it, it seems to me rather weird that Dylan has been so totally in step with the thinking of the movement all along the line, yet denying that he's political in any way or a part of any movement.

But we who were political and who listened to Dylan always understood and smiled when he said he wasn't political. What he meant was that he was not going to be the mayor of the town or president of the empire.

Well, no. Also, he said very specifically in one of the interviews, "I ain't no leader of any movement." I forget the line precisely.

Well, you know how it is with a movement. The movement says anybody crazy enough to want to be a leader of us is going to lose fast, and the movement has had that sense of itself from the beginning. And Dylan has, in that respect, been exactly in the spirit of the movement—he refuses to be a leader. He even refused to be a kind of a cultural leader of critics.

You know, there are other left-wing songwriters around who don't have any of Dylan's panache, his verve, his credibility, or his legitimacy, like Phil [Ochs], for example. One suspects that he wouldn't be that sorry to be a leader—you know, to be the musician by appointment to the people's revolution.

Oh sure, oh sure. I don't doubt it. I've sat and rapped with Phil a number of times, and Phil still has the feeling that he could possibly become the leader if Dylan would drop dead, basically. (*laughs*)

Well, he couldn't. Because nobody could.

Yeah.

And the way to guarantee that you won't is to try.

Yeah, and he's been trying. That's it. He has been trying so damn hard. The unfortunate thing about the *Rolling Stone* interview is that Dylan is not a verbal cat at all. Dylan's lyrics are something that come out of his head and then come out of his fingertips on a typewriter. But he just can't sit and rap with people, and I think this is one of his basic problems. He's a banal cat verbally.

Do you know him?

No. No. But everyone I talk to says Dylan just doesn't talk. Dylan cannot talk. He's just not a verbal cat at all. You know, I guess I get the same feeling. I respond to hearing this, because I'm not a verbal cat, and I can see some of the problems that Dylan is going through. And that *Rolling Stone* interview may have been very, very unfortunate if it leaves that effect—that he definitely is filled with banalities, but I think this is basically Dylan's problem with verbalizing.

Yeah. You know, it was a bad interviewer too. I mean, the guy was in a way profiling himself. Who did it? What was the guy's name?

Jann Wenner, who owns *Rolling Stone*.

I thought his questions in a way produced the Dylan of the interview. I hope Dylan responds to questions and says whatever needs to be said, but there's the extenuating circumstance that the cat who did the interviewing was fairly stupid and didn't know what was happening. He didn't know what was happening politically and had some kind of personal interest in seeing Dylan in a sort of a political apostasy.

If Dylan commits himself to a political stance in a ragingly political world, then that means other people have got to commit themselves or else abandon whatever claim they have of living in the same moral universe Dylan lives in. So, he does turns out to be important to other people, and therefore other people will do whatever they can to kind of remake Dylan in the image of their own fears, the image of their own choices, and so on. The *Rolling Stone* interview reflected, as much as it did Dylan's position, the position of the guy who did the interview, the magazine, and the whole Woodstock trip.

Yeah, Wenner is totally on the defensive for being the kind of guy who is attempting to use the Woodstock Aquarian bullshit for his own ends—you know, to make himself a millionaire. And I can see that if he gets Bobby Dylan in his corner, the banalities and all of it just bolsters him. And I think basically he did it because, "Hey, wow, I'm the first guy to talk to Dylan in a couple years. Groovy."

I wonder why Dylan let the interview happen?

I don't know. That's something I do not understand.

I mean, it couldn't be money. He doesn't need money, does he?

No. I don't know why he did it. Wenner won't tell me why Dylan finally consented to see him. He would only say it took six months to get Dylan to agree, because he worked like a son of a bitch and pushed every which way he could possibly push him.

I wonder if Dylan read the final, edited typescript of the interview.

I very much doubt it. I really don't know, but I've got to sit down and talk to Wenner about it. There's really no reason to hide. He's just being a prick. Wenner is a strange cat. He said to me, "You'll never get through Grossman. You'll never get through Dylan. You'll never have any luck getting anything you really need." And I said, "Why don't you lay off?" He's supposed to be one of the spokesmen of the so-called Aquarian revolution. You'd think he would be in favor of—

[*laughs*] Why didn't you tell him that you'd give him a couple of chapters and see what he would do then?

That would have been a little too bald-faced. Actually, I was slightly stoned at the time, and I just walked away from him.

Boy, that's really bad about what Dylan's been doing. That's sad news.

Yeah. I don't understand it. I haven't gotten close enough to anyone to know what he's thinking or was thinking at the time. I'm trying to get Simon to talk to me, but he won't.

Shit, if he just has time on his hands, I could think of a lot of things that he could do musically that would be fun.

That's one of the thoughts I had: that he just had time on his hands, wanted to lay down a couple things and see what might come of it. But if I could find out what cuts he laid down—you know, exactly what he did—it might be some sort of tip-off to what he's thinking. Some of the Eric Andersen songs were pretty much in step with the movement. But there are a couple of things that are that schlock rock kind of bullshit.

Yeah, too close to the Kingston Trio.

Well, okay. This has been a very interesting rap.

Well, my pleasure. I don't know if—

I never became involved in the movement. I've only been an observer over the years. And you were there, know what the thinking was, and know what was going down at the time. You're an authority. I'm not. Obviously, there are no specific areas in which Dylan affected the movement—you know, as specifics. Obviously, it had to be a psychological thing more than anything else.

Yeah, the thing was, the guy just read all the sails and let it all hang out. You know, he took the three buttons off politics, put politics in a work shirt, and gave political cadence to the most intimate associations a person could make about the world he lived in, the world he was trying to make—and he gave voice to the despair that cheered us up and voice to the enthusiasm that chastised us—and was all in all just a good person to have around in that time.

Well, the one thing he made clear was there is no place else in the world for a thinking person but within the movement. I think this is one of the roles he played. He just led so many people to realize that nothing else existed, really— that if you were a human being, this is the only place to be.

How is his marriage? You know anything about that?

No. He married a model who at one point was a very mystical kind of chick and was into a lot of Eastern religion and then became a mother. One of the fears of a lot of people is that Dylan has become a father and a suburbanite, worried about—

Suburbanite?

Well, he's living back on MacDougal Street in the Village—you know, worried about the schools his kids are going to do and what to do with his investments.

He lives on MacDougal Street?

Yeah, 94 MacDougal. I haven't gone and knocked on his door yet. I've been trying—rather than intrude directly on him—to go through intermediaries to get to him. I sent a long note to Naomi Saltzman, who I was told is an intermediary, so I gave her a call. Then I sent a long letter to her explaining why I thought he should talk to me—the benefits and then, of course, the drawbacks, and she passed it along. She called me back a couple days later. "Bob read your note. His reaction is as long as Tony has talked to so many people about me and about my background, he doesn't really need me to write a book about me, right?" Then Naomi says, "However, he's very interested in knowing what everybody said about him, and maybe we could get together and rap about that sometime."

Tell him that you're available for an interview.

Yeah. (*laughs*) That's what I told her. My tape recorder or yours? (*laughs*) I said, "Fine, I'd love to." But then as I started going over the notes of what people have said to me, I realized that there's so much nastiness there that I really can't show him a lot of the things. I love that people I talk to open up on the basis that I will show them exactly how I'm quoting them. So, they'll have a choice of how they get attributed if they do it.

Well, that's a graceful thing to do.

I think that's the only way I've gotten people to open up and be totally honest with me—you know, have people trust me. I haven't been turned down by anyone except Dylan himself.

VISIONS OF JOHANNA

JOAN BAEZ

Some of it was just really beautiful. I remember days when . . . we'd
stop on the highway and get out and dance and we'd horse around
and be crazy. And then Bobby and I would fall asleep in the back of
the station wagon. I mean, that was really, really nice.

JOAN FIRST SAW BOB DYLAN PERFORM at his debut gig at Gerde's Folk City in 1961. She remembered, "I was amazed and I was happy that there was somebody with that kind of talent." By 1962 rumors began swirling about a Dylan–Baez romance, but although they were occasionally together, they were still primarily a couple of professionals with music in common.

Dylan made his first West Coast appearance performing with Joan at the 1963 Monterey Folk Festival. She told Scaduto, "I wanted people to hear him. . . . I wanted to have as many hear him as possible." Bob was her unannounced guest during her concert tour in the summer of 1963. Joan provided him with a ready-made audience, the kind of audience that would appreciate Dylan and spread the word about him. Of all those promoting him, Joan was probably the most important and the most effective.

Joan shared gigs with him, helped Dylan get exposure, was happy to help his career. Normally she never worked two nights in a row, but she did for Bob. She played several successive gigs with him, helping to pack in audiences. They were friends and then lovers for at least a year, spending as much time together as they could manage considering they lived on opposite coasts. They were the king and queen of folk.

Joan told Scaduto that she had seldom talked about Bob in the past "out of loyalty to Bobby." She explained, "There are so many people who live vicariously off Bobby. And I hate it." As she reminisced with Scaduto about what it was like being with Dylan, she said, "I realized that everybody who talks about him must really like it because in all our lives there's so few things that ring real."

Scaduto's description of the setting for his interview with Baez around June 1970: "Joan sat in a Scandinavian modern chair in a New York City hotel room, her arms hugging her knees to her chin, in blue denims, blue-striped polo shirt, her hair cut a lot shorter than it's ever been, and you're caught once again thinking she's so much more enchanting than her photographs. Her black eyes sparkle, she laughs often, her smile is lightning quick. She turns serious as she recalls something painful from those days. Then the smile comes again as she remembers something funny, or as Gabriel, Joan and David Harris's son, age six months, gurgles in his playpen."

Why don't we start [with] how you first met Bobby—your first meeting with Bobby, your first reaction to him?

I guess it was in the Village. I'd heard his name whispered around. And it was in that place, used to be Gerde's Folk City?

Gerde's Folk City.

I remember seeing Bob, singing about Woody.

"Hey, hey Woody Guthrie"?

I think so. He knocked me out completely. As I remember him, it seems that he was about five feet tall. He seemed tiny, just tiny, had that goofy little hat on. And he tried to put the make on my sister. He really liked her. I think she was sitting nearby. It was either that night or the next. I think I went back a couple times to hear him. I can't remember. It's all kind of fuzzy. And he just was astounding.

So, your impression at the time . . .

I was knocked out. It was very curious. I was with a boy I'd been with for about two years, this terrifically jealous type. And I had to sit there and drum my fingers on the table, pretend I was half listening to Dylan. And I was totally absorbed. And I thought, God, you know? And his style and his eyes—just his whole mystical whatever it was. I just thought about him for days. I was amazed.

I was happy. You know, he really made me happy, that there was somebody, you know, with that kind of talent. I mean, I love genius. I'm really hooked on genius. Anytime it happens along, I really get excited.

Your first meeting with him. Did you meet him that night?

He came over that night. Somebody said, you've got to meet Joan or something, and he came over. And there wasn't anything I could say, you know.

I said, far out or beautiful or something. And Bobby mumbled something;
I don't know what he said. Something equally dumb, and that was all.

**Tell me more about these early days with Dylan. The first time you got together
and traded songs in any way, anything like that. Was Dick [Fariña] around at
the time?**

I think a couple times Dick was there. I don't remember very well. Bobby
was always just out of reach, the way he probably is for most people. I
can't remember the order of how he—I remember vaguely once being at
a party and he had just sung, and I was in that state of disbelief again that
anybody was turning out something like that.

And he was very, a lot of mystique about him, you know, hiding—but
sweet and funny. You know, the really wonderful thing about him is that
sense of humor. It's really terribly funny, cynical. And forming, you know,
he was forming. And I don't remember time order at all. I remember
vaguely being at, I think, one party is all, because I'm not a partygoer and
I don't think he was either. And then somewhere in there came "Blowin'
in the Wind." I guess that was a year later or something?

**Yeah, that was after he returned from London. He was in London with Dick
and—**

Oh, I see.

And Eric [von Schmidt].

Yeah, right, that's right. Yeah, yeah. I remember Dick talking about it.

What did Dick say about it?

Well, Dick was hung up on fame. I mean, he just found it absolutely
irresistible. And I love Dick and he had the kind of ego that just thrives on
that. And he was so cute because he would talk about it. He'd tell these outrageous stories of what they did. And Bobby was busy writing his songs
and stealing all these English tunes, which I don't think he recognizes he's
done. A lot of times I think he just forgets.

He's stealing songs from some of his close friends too.

Right. And you know, Dick would just speak about it with twinkling eyes
and obviously he loved it. I gather that he and Eric and Bobby did have a
good time. But I didn't know anything about that, really.

**Tell me about when you first started working with Bobby. You brought him up
as a guest on a number of your concerts.**

I don't remember the first one where I asked him up as a guest.

How did that come about? Had you drawn close by that period?

Not really. I think we liked each other, and I think I wanted people to hear him. I mean, I really loved him. The funny thing was, he was almost like a pet, you know. I wanted to take care of him and have him sing.

Really?

Yeah, I mean, brush his hair and brush his teeth—

I get that from most girls and women who knew him in the old days. There was this great maternal—

Yeah, and then I wanted to have as many hear him as possible.

Because most of the people I get the maternal stuff from are those who are not in show business, quote unquote. And I got the feeling that maybe it was possibly the fact that he was going to be a star in their eyes and that kind of thing. But that wouldn't be the same in your case.

Well, I thought of him as a—I don't like the expression "star."

I use "star" in a general sense of being known and appreciated and bought, the records people bought and the concerts—

Yeah, maybe.

By that time, you were kind of gobbled up.

Yeah, but I never considered myself gobbled up. You know, I was, like, treading water to stay up there.

Really?

Yeah. Oh no, I mean, I know people knew me. You know, [I was] well known.

Yeah, but by '61 you were more than "well known."

I once had a doctor who helped me considerably through some rough years and I once said something about being famous. And he said, "Nuh-uh, you're well known." And it was really a good thing to say, you know, because there's a difference between being Elizabeth Taylor and being well known. Elizabeth Taylor is famous. You know, she's paid the price and considers herself famous and does all the things a famous person does.

The trappings and stuff.

Yeah. Wears all those shitty coats and that shitty jewelry. And if you don't fall into that life, then I think it's helpful. I remember a couple of concerts when it started to be the fame. One was the tennis courts. Was that Long Island?

Forest Hills?

Forest Hills. Yup. I was a little bit afraid for Bobby. He didn't show stage fright kind of fear. He seemed to submerge that, but it came out in paranoia about people afterwards or, like, coming at him for autographs and stuff. He's so terrified. And I remember times later when we sang together officially, you know, like those concerts where nobody could decide how to arrange the names so his wouldn't be higher than mine and all that crap, you know.

But afterwards the getaways were all planned.

What was planned?

Getaways. Bobby always had big getaways planned. And I think that in a way he needs that—people pounding on the car and breaking the car antenna and climbing onto the hood and everything and he'd say—

A real scene.

I can't stand that shit. Anyway, it's obvious that there were other ways to get out of the building, you know, and then one time we hired a limousine somewhere. This is later too. It was when we were doing concerts together. And two girls came screaming at him. "Bobby!" And he said, "Oh wow, let's run." I said, "You dumbass. Just stand here." And he said, "What, what?" And I took his hand. He was like a little kid, and the girls came up to us all teary.

And I said to them, "Now stop acting so stupid and he'll give you his autograph." And then he calmed down, they calmed down. And he was embarrassed.

Really? Must have been a marvelous sight.

It was beautiful. And I said, "Just talk to them a minute, Bobby." So he did, and you know, he—I mean, he gets control the minute he sees he can have it. But I think he genuinely was terrified of people like that. But you have to be human first or they'll just go on with that dumb scene. If he had run, they would have gone crazy.

That's right. The craziness.

And I've never been able to understand that. I mean it's very flattering. You've got to admit. You know, flattery will get you anywhere.

You handled it well the other night in Philadelphia. There were women who were in the audience booing you, and then came out, asked for your autograph, and asked you to pose with them. That was a funny—

But it's hard.

They're ready to tear you apart when you're up there.

But they're really torn because they—I mean, fame to them, it's something that's just irresistible. You could see all their little pasty faces in the Midwest, and they couldn't resist getting an autograph or a picture, whatever it was.

One time we were on the way in, had gotten out of the car, and somebody said, "Who's that? Who's that? No way that's Joan Baez." And the first one says, "Yuck." I went and patted her on the back and said, "Yuck, you better keep your voice down." And she was mortified. The more barriers you can break down, obviously, the better.

Did Bobby have an idea he could break down some of these barriers? Or that he could calm down these kids who were ready to tear his clothes off?

I think he eventually learned some of that. But certainly, at the beginning, when we did concerts together, he didn't understand it. Because it's a conflict. I mean, you want the people to scream and holler and love you and climb up on the stage and pull out your hair. You want that because it's irresistible to an ego, because ego doesn't understand it. It has nothing to do with love. It has nothing to do with anything genuine. It's just hysteria. And so, you feed on it in a way, and then the other half of you recognizes that it's bullshit, but then Bobby had the added thing of genuine fear of being hurt, I think, of being trampled. Because you can see yourself getting trampled.

Did he have a fear of the audience before the big getaway scene? That is, I'm told by people who knew him back in '61 at Gerde's that they had to put drinks into him, a lot of wine into him to get him to get up and perform again.

I have heard things like that too. But I saw it come out in very different ways. I mean, he never had traditional stage fright the way I did. I sit down and have diarrhea and feel nauseated for forty-five minutes before a concert. He was always bopping around writing songs. But it would come out in another way, a sudden furious tantrum because, oh, like his coat was stolen one time, but you've probably heard about—

No, I haven't. Tell me about it.

It's unbelievable. It's horrible, the coat, which I'm sure to this day he thinks I must have stolen it because I saw him throw up all over it. He got drunk and threw up on it. And it was this shitty-looking, horrible little brown thing, and it smelled horrible and it was too short, short in the sleeves. He looked like a poverty-stricken little Welsh schoolboy.

And I was really working on him to get rid of that jacket. Well, one night we showed up backstage and I guess he must have left for a while and then gone back to the dressing room. His jacket was gone. And he had a tantrum. I mean, like a five-year-old. And he screamed at the policeman and the policeman scurried out. And he screamed at whoever else was there, and they all scurried out. And it was that kind of tension that I would always think would have something to do with, you know, how he had to perform.

That night was amazing, though, because I didn't scurry out. He was really wild-eyed with fury. "That fucking jacket, somebody took my fucking jacket, and all you fucking cops get out of here and fuck, fuck, fuck." I said, "Oh Bobby, take it easy" or something. And he started to blow up. Because nobody was supposed to talk to him like that. And I said, "Do you want to practice, or do you want to have a tantrum?" Or some equally dumb maternal thing like that.

And then he calmed down. He said, "I'm not mad." I mean, I've seen that in people before, and I don't know what you call it. He refused to admit he was mad, and he calmed down, switched roles. We practiced; he gave a brilliant performance in the first half. In the intermission I said, "Gee, you ought to get pissed off more often," and he had another tantrum. He said, "I was not mad." And I said, "No, you were furious." So the turnaround was amazing.

This thing was his form of stage fright basically.

I have no idea, but it seemed it was all built up around performing—I mean, it happened at times when he wasn't performing. But it seemed like a tension from having to perform and having to be who he would have to be and all that.

Did he ever react to reviews? Bob Shelton in the *Times*, for one, who put Bobby down, said he detracted from the program. Like the August '64 Forest Hills [concert] and complaints from people about the Hollywood Bowl in '63.

Yeah. I think he was drunk or high or something. And he went on much too long. He could never resist singing what he had just written, and he had just written "Lay Down Your Weary Tune" and it was about forty-five minutes long, you know.

Somebody called that "War and Peace" because of the length of it.

Right. And it was just endless. I was perfectly happy except I was concerned. I've always had audience sensibility. I mean I'm always worried about them and whether they're getting tired and whatever. And he wasn't.

About his "War and Peace" song and being drunk and going on.

I don't know if he was drunk. Yeah, he used to get drunk a lot. Audiences got sore at him and I should have known better because it wasn't good for him, people getting mad, this little punk who came out of nowhere singing these forty-minute-long songs.

Well, by this time, in '63, not so many in LA knew who Bobby was.
Well, the Hollywood Bowl is a weird venue.
This isn't Berkeley. That's right.

No, see, at different places he was received differently. In Boston he was received well. He was drunk there, though. That's another thing I think is stage fright. His getting loaded so he doesn't feel anything. He did beautifully, no matter how he was. He'd stand up and sing whether he was smashed or straight. When we used to perform together, and he'd started getting keyed up by that coat thing and start, always start screaming about who was in charge of the getaway car and who was this and who was that. So I slipped a Librium in his coffee.

I don't think he ever knew that. Sometimes I slipped two of them. And a couple of times it helped. I mean, I could just see him sag a little bit, and whew, you know, because he was just a bundle of nerves.

And he was never aware of you drugging him?
The Librium? I don't think so. I think he would have been pretty pissed off.
This was after a concert.
No, this was before.
Before he went on. Oh really?
Uh-huh.
And did that improve his—
He didn't need improving. It just improved my nerves a little.
Well, did it improve his stage presence?
He did relax a little bit.
You're concerned with your audience. He's concerned with his material and himself more than the audience.

I could never figure out what he was concerned with. I mean, the most real conversation I ever had with him, which is the beginning of Bobby and me going in different directions, was after the last concert we did together. I can't remember when or where, somewhere on the East Coast. But we were having fun. There were a lot of people up in the hotel, taking goofy pictures, him ironing my hair and stuff. We were really, you know, we felt good together.

And it had been fun and everything. And then, you know, we had to have these private talks. We had to go hide under a couch somewhere and talk, or he'd drag me off to the bathroom and talk. At Madison Square Garden, I had a really funny feeling, and I said, "What are we going to do

with Madison Square Garden? How do we do Madison Square Garden?"
And I thought about it and I said, "I'm scared. You be the rock-and-roll
king. I'll be the peace queen." And he always put down whatever sounded
like a theme as bullshit. But the fact was, that night the kids had been
pleading for "Masters of War," ["With God on Our Side"], any song that
he'd ever written that meant something, that he's going to be a social
conscience for them.

And he knew immediately what I meant when I said I'd be peace queen
and he'd be rock-and-roll king. He said, "Hey, hey man, I heard those kids.
I heard them, right. I can't be responsible for those kids' lives." I said,
"Bobby, you rat. You're going to leave them all with me." He said, "Hey,
hey, take them if you want them, but man, you can't be responsible." It
didn't mean he didn't love them, you know, I think he was just afraid. And
he meant it and that's the last time we ever sang together.

Why was it the last time you ever sang together?

Because of that.

Because of that?

I think so. That was the end of that tour. We didn't continue it. After that
he came with me a couple of places where I was singing. That's all.

**My impression was that the whole *Don't Look Back* was the last time you sang
together.**

I never sang with him. He wouldn't let me sing, to put it bluntly.

**That's right. He didn't. Well, I'm not even sure of that because I know he cut
you out of the film drastically.**

Bobby cut me.

**Tell me about that. Why did the film end up that way? I know there's lots of foot-
age of you in that tour.**

I was going to go to England and sing and have a concert tour. And then
in the middle of that, Bobby's rise to fame came so fast, and a few months
later we said, well, we'll go together, and we'll do split concerts. By the
time it got around to England, Bobby was much more famous in England
than I was.

And so, Bobby just took England. I mean, I didn't even bother with the
tour. But I thought he would do what I had done with him, that he would
introduce me. You know, and it would be very nice for me because I had
never sung in England before. That's what I had in my mind. And then
by the time we got to England, something happened in Bobby's mind. I've
never seen him less healthy than he was in England. He was a wreck. And

he wouldn't ask me onstage to sing. And I was really surprised, and very, very hurt, and I was miserable, and then I was a complete ass. I should have left. I should have left after the first concert.

But there's something about situations like that, you hang around. I stayed for two weeks, I guess, and then when I finally walked out the door, I went to France and stayed with my parents. They lived in France then. But it was one of the two, you know, really most painful weeks of my life, because I couldn't understand what the hell was going on.

I'm going to toss out a personal question, and if you don't want to answer it or want to think about it, okay, but I understand that there was a proposal of marriage on Bobby's part at one point, which was around the time you last were singing together.

I wouldn't put it that formally. We joked about it, you know. You see, Bobby's and my coming together was inevitable. I mean, "crown prince of Newport" and all that stuff. It was inevitable. I was involved with other people, and he was involved with other people. And when we finally finished with the other people, we were together. You know, it's as though it had to happen in the course of our lives.

Yeah, there's a whole king and queen thing, as pop journalists were putting it. It was inevitable.

Yeah, right. And then I think we were both halfway kidding about it and got scared and backed off. I wouldn't say Bobby proposed to me, no. But we talked about it. We talked about getting married and we kidded about it because we knew that in a sense, we almost felt that it was inevitable too. But luckily, we both had enough sense to realize—

It would be a disaster.

It would have been a complete disaster, you know. But I think what happened was that I expressed it before he did.

Expressed what?

I don't know. That it would be a disaster because—

Well, the stress factor wouldn't work in the relationship.

Something like that. That's probably the way to put it. He would have probably eventually, but he was still, like, in the joking stage and I said, "You know it won't work," and after that was the switch and after that he never—after that he was always trying to get back at me forever and ever.

He's got a highly developed sense, a need for approval.

And pride.

And pride. And fear of rejection in one form or the other.

Yeah, I think that's what happened. And so, he was on the East Coast and I was on the West when that came about. And ever after. Then it was the Europe thing. It was as though he was playing around, you know, with my soul.

Was this before Europe?
Yeah.

So that Europe thing was possibly—
But I didn't figure out what was the thing about Europe, which is really dumb on my part because I should have put together his kind of psyche, you know, and how he was going to feel. "Hey sure, yeah, sure, come to Europe. You can help me out," is what he said. And I thought he meant that I'd sing with him. And I think probably, originally, he planned on it, and then decided against it.

Were you aware at the time, before he got to Europe, that he was—
Hostile.

No, no. That he was bigger than you, so to speak?
Oh yeah, yeah. I knew that perfectly well, which is why I wasn't singing, why I canceled my tour. And was perfectly happy in that position.

Yeah.
When we landed in England, I think Bobby was torn, because I think in a way he was scared and wanted me by his side. I couldn't tell for sure, so I stayed back because I didn't want to impose on his scene. It was Bobby's tour. And I literally was not noticed by anybody. And that was fine. A couple of times, as I think back, he gave a look; it was, like, "Help." And I couldn't decide whether it's more important to go and help him or stay back.

When was that?
It was just coming out of the airport after a press conference. And he went like this, like, "Come here." But I didn't want to jump into his scene, and maybe it was stupid modesty, because maybe he needed something then. But I didn't jump in. And that happened a couple times, and after that he never asked again.

And so, then I never saw him. I mean, I was, like, never allowed. Oh, I went into the room and stuff, but it was that stupid revolting scene. Bobby would get a record player, put on his record, sit with his back to everybody and type and everybody would sit around and eat. You know, it's really revolting. The most human he got was that night in the film, when we sang some stuff, or I sang a song he'd written and he'd forgotten. And then I kissed him on the head and left. It was grueling for me. It was horrible.

And that was the last real contact you had?

No. I saw him once after a concert in San Jose. I went to see him in San Francisco and in San Jose. I think. Two nights in a row, I think, in San Francisco, and I spent late into the night with him at San Jose. But he was not being real. I mean, he was getting into arguments with people about—I remember him saying, "Fucking bums. I mean, I don't give a fuck." He couldn't say anything more real than that. And that was when he was married, and he didn't tell me he was married, so I didn't know.

Oh really?

Yeah, so that was very confusing too. And I feel now that I really imposed myself and should have gone home. When you're around somebody like Bobby, you do impose. I mean, you stay around until everybody's kicked out.

Why is that? What is it about him?

Charisma probably.

What's charisma all about?

I've never understood charisma. Not many people have as much as Bobby has. I've never met anybody that has as much. My husband has a different style of it when he speaks. But it isn't as glamorous as Bobby's because David's telling people to do something.

I get the feeling that David is not manic the way Bobby is manic.

Yeah, and there's a charm about Bobby's being maniacal. I mean, you can't resist watching it to see which way it's going to go next, even if you stand there and get hit over the head with it.

Did you feel the maniacal charisma at the very beginning?

Oh yeah. The charisma was obvious. He was on the edge of something. See, I think Bobby is closer to being psychotic than neurotic. I say that because a couple times he got drunk and turned on friends, just turned on them. I couldn't believe it. I would never buy it. I mean I would stand there and fight him.

Yeah, but apparently the friends did. Even people like Phil Ochs took it from Bobby.

Yeah, it's insane.

Yeah. Phil has told me a lot of stories about when Bobby was very hostile to everybody.

I guess the most I did take it was in England, and I'm amazed, you know, as I look back, that I did that. But I loved him, and I couldn't believe he was being so hurtful. And even when he was sick at the end of that tour—and he got so sick. God, I was just in agony because I didn't know how sick he was, and I wasn't allowed in his room.

What was he sick from?

Hell, I don't know. I think he overate in Sweden or something. They all went off—I mean you live with Grossman and you're going to eat, you know, so everybody said let's go somewhere where there's a good restaurant. I thought they went to India or somewhere. But everybody took off and came back sick. And I didn't know whether Bobby had tonsillitis, syphilis, you know, stomach poison, or what, but he was pretty sick.

And that's when he called in Sara. He would see my mother. He'd see everybody, but he wouldn't see me. And I don't think it was conscious, but somehow, the one concert I did in England to pay for my tour, he managed—

You did the Albert Hall.

Uh-huh. He managed to have everybody up in his room. I was having a little party, a little gathering in my room afterwards, and one by one they were all called to Bobby's room. Albert had to go, they all had to go. He called my mother up there. But I wasn't allowed to see him.

Really?

Yeah. And I went out and bought him a shirt, something. I wanted to tell him, I wanted to tell him that I loved him, that I cared for him and it didn't matter what was going on. And I was glad Sara was there because she seemed to care for him and somebody was there to take care of him. And I bought him a shirt and went to the door.

I had never met her, but I guess that's who came to the door. She took it and I never heard anything after that. It was the closest I got to seeing him. Then I left England.

That was '65. In the very beginning Bobby came up on some of your programs, your concerts. How did that come about?

I asked him.

Why?

Because he was brilliant. And he is brilliant. I loved him, I loved his music. I wanted people to hear him. I mean, I wanted to share him. And he dug it. I mean, he was so scared and everything, but I know he dug it.

Oh sure. At one point, the impression has been left that Bobby turned you on to the protests, quote unquote protest songs.

Not in my spirit, but in songs, yes. Because there weren't any I could sing until he wrote them.

Tell me how—

Well, I think he wrote songs that hadn't been written yet. There aren't very many good protest songs. They're usually overdone. They're overstated. The beauty of Bobby's stuff, aside from the fact that he's a genius, or maybe because of it, is they're understatements. You don't have to hit anybody over the head with it. Even in his most blatant stuff, when he was really young, it's still clever enough that it's not dull or heavy or—

Yeah, there's a stamp of genius even on—

On absolutely everything he ever wrote. Even the crummy—I mean some of it's crummy. Crummy.

Manny [Greenhill, Baez's manager] told me that he had to play you some demos of Bobby because you weren't really listening to anybody's stuff. That he had to get you into the habit of listening to things.

I don't think that's true. I think he had a demo with the white label, which I still have, and he brought a record player over.

You remember he played that?

Very vaguely. Again, I was stricken with the genius of it all. And I think I learned a couple of songs off that. I don't remember what's on that record. But it's true. I'm really lazy.

This again has nothing to do with Bobby, but do you get much material sent to you from songwriters?

Yeah, and 99 percent of it is unusable. That's what's so sad. I write medium well, and I very seldom write anything.

Why don't you write?

Because I'm not good. I don't like not being a genius. I can write nice tunes, but the words come very slowly and they're very mediocre. Writing in prose is very different for me. It's a different story trying to fit words into a tune. I look at my writing sort of the way Grandma Moses painted pictures. It's very simple.

Primitive—

Yeah, exactly.

But there are wonderful examples of primitive poetry, you know.

Yeah . . .

Anyway, getting back to Bobby. My basic feeling about Bobby was that he wasn't a revolutionary, that in the beginning he was writing basic protest topical songs that were understated. And somewhere along the line he moved from writing "anthems" to the more personal songs. The personal stuff was truly more radical.

Did Bobby ever talk about where he was going? Did he ever talk about the writing? Did he ever talk about the movement?

No. He just denied everything he'd ever done. Didn't mean any of it.

Even personally?

It would take me sometimes four hours to get something out of him that I knew was the truth. One night he shouted at Victor [Maymudes]. Bobby was in one of his psychotic frenzies. I don't know what it was about, but it was at my house. Victor was nothing but a road manager. I said, "Bobby, what a way to talk to someone." I didn't want to hear him talk like that in my house. And then it all simmered down and later on he made light of it. I said, "Bobby, why did you talk that way? And then why were you rude to me?" He said, "Hey, don't look hurt." I said, "You think I looked hurt? That's all it's about to you? I did not look hurt. I wasn't hurt, I was mad. I wasn't hurt and you know it." I can't believe he does that to people all the time.

Did you ever pin him down on his writing? Ever talk about his writing protest songs?

It became this law. I said something about "God on My Side." "What were you thinking when you wrote that stuff?" He said he wasn't saying anything political. And I said, "Oh Bobby, you don't think I'm going to buy that, do you?" He said, "You know, it's not what people make it," and he denied it all. And I said, "Well, you can deny it, but I believe it.

He never talked about [how] it was radical thinking or the radicalization of politics?

No, because he'd never admit to anything like that.

Well, I think Bobby was saying that it's in the air and he just translates it onto paper, you know, that kind of thing. In your book you call him the "Dada King." Can you verbalize some of that?

Well, he was so busy saying he was being Dada. You know, everything's crazy, a sort of comical cynic or however you want to put it. And avoiding being real with anybody by doing that. He had weird stuff going on. He'd just written "Visions of Johanna," which I believe had images of me in it. I can't ever say that publicly. But he'd been talking to Ginsberg about it.

Oh really?

It was very odd. And I loved the song and really wanted to feel flattered but was wondering whether, I mean, everybody in the world thinks Bobby's written songs about them, and I consider myself in the same bag. So I would never claim a song. But it did sound, you know, sort of images in there sounded very strange. And then Ginsberg came up at one point and he said, "What do you think 'Johanna' is about?" "I don't know, Ginsberg. Your guess is as good as mine."

He says, "No, no. What do you think it's about? I mean, Bobby says . . ." and then he reeled off this pile of crap that had nothing to do with anything, and I said, "Did Bobby say that or did you make that up, Allen?" And I had a feeling the two of them were in a sort of cahoots, you know, to make sure that I never thought the song was about me, that the song had nothing to do with me. I've had that feeling a lot, you know, and I wouldn't say any of that. I mean, Ginsberg was trying to get me to say I thought the song was written about me. And I would never say that about any of Bobby's songs.

So, Ginsberg was acting as Bobby's front man.

Yeah. Bobby had been hanging around Ginsberg. That's another funny story, of how I met Ginsberg. And by the way, I dig Allen. He's crazy but I dig him. It was at a party.

How you met Ginsberg for the first time.

It was at a party, and I guess Bobby must have given a concert. But I was feeling great that night. Bobby was getting very drunk at this party and he was flirty, flirty, flirty, talk, talk, talk with this redhead. And so I started talking with Bobby Neuwirth and hanging out with Neuwirth. I think Neuwirth had on a blue velvet jacket.

Anyway, Ginsberg came up and introduced himself and announced that he wanted to talk to Bob. And I said, "What's holding you back?" He said, "I'm shy." I can't remember much more about that meeting except that's all Ginsberg wanted to talk about. I was a little insulted myself. I had realized he had no interest in me at all.

Oh, you didn't know Ginsberg.

No, I didn't. And then Bobby was completely and totally drunk, got all maudlin. I don't remember what he was saying, but I told him, "Ginsberg wants to go to bed with you." He probably threw up on that horrible little jacket. That was the first time. When people fall in love with Bobby, they do it all the way. Ginsberg was just "Bobby, Bobby, Bobby."

Paul Clayton had the same thing for a while there.

Probably, yeah.

What was the thing, the song and dance that Ginsberg was giving you about "Visions of Johanna"? Do you recall?

Oh no. I don't recall, but it was absolutely insane. I heard people do that, somebody wrote an article. I didn't see it. It was "Sad-Eyed Lady," an intricate explanation of everything in "Sad-Eyed Lady." Somebody told me about it.

Was that recently, the thing in *Saturday Review*?

I haven't read it, so I don't know.

A friend of mine who teaches at City College told me about it.

That's amazing.

Intricate interpretations of what Dylan really means when he said it.

God, how funny. See, that's the first thing. When you said you were doing a book on Bobby, I'm always nervous because there's so many people who live vicariously off Bobby. And I hate it when it happens. A guy started talking to me in a cafeteria. Asked would I mind if he talked about Bobby because he's doing a paper on Bobby. And I said, "No, go right ahead."

And he said Bobby's whole thing, his Oedipus complex, he's hung up with his mother, and I said, "Well, I'm glad you figured it out because a lot of us are trying." Then he starts trying to pin me down. He said, "Well, what about homosexuality with Dylan?" And I said, "I'm finished with my tomato soup, thanks." And left.

Wow. And the Dada King, getting back to that. You said, "He put us all on but mostly he put himself on, a bizarre liar, a huge, transparent liar. He almost drowned and you heard the pleadings."

That does seem like a huge ego problem. I mean frantic. And lost. And so wrapped up in ego that he couldn't see more than four feet in front of him. Well, can't anyway without his glasses. I'd written him a note. I think that's the one where I'd written him a note on Ralph Gleason's typewriter, which has that old-fashioned print, saying could I come back and see him, because it would make it easier for me.

I still felt terrible from London. And something in me was still in love with Bobby. I mean, it's hard to get over because when somebody ignores you, you know, you always wonder where you missed out and you want to get back to where it's okay.

It's like you ask, "You still like me? You still like me? Am I still okay in your books?" And that's what the note was really saying. And apparently, he got the note and he didn't even look inside. "Oh yeah, yeah," or something. And was very vague about it and said, "Oh yeah, sure, come on back and say hi." So, I went back and said hi. And I felt he was just completely unreal. You know, "Hi, I hear you're running a school."

You know, this is another time Ginsberg said, "Bobby says you're running a school. No, Bobby says you've got a great school." He says, "It's very nice," or some horrible thing like that. I mean, yeah, he said very nice. And I said, "Oh, Ginsberg." I said, "Bobby, did you really say it was nice?" And Bobby said, "Yeah."

And later on, I was talking to Ginsberg and Ginsberg said something about one of Bobby's new songs. And I said, "Yeah, it's very nice." He said, "What?" I was fairly relentless. I still like him. I mean, I think that's a phase in his life.

Oh, very much so. Getting back to, you heard the words, the pleadings, the denials, hearing the music live.

It's just the music has such range, full circle, hard gutsy stuff, highway blues, you know, and he sounded like Presley for a couple of minutes. And I was wiped out by it.

And then I watched Bobby do that thing. I was moved by it, you know, and I made fun of it to my sister. She made some wisecrack because he was just terrible.

When was this?

I can't remember. It was one of two concerts. It hadn't been advertised, so it wasn't a full house and Bobby said it was just for my friends. So if only two thousand people showed up, he wouldn't feel bad. I know the performer's mind well enough.

This is before the *Don't Look Back* tour?

No, no. This is was way after that. In fact, I think I saw him twice after that, but I can't remember.

But in the book, getting back to what you wrote, it makes it sound a lot more personal than you're just seeing him in a concert.

Oh, it was personal. I still wonder what Bobby thinks about me. And you're bound to do that with somebody you were very close to once the person turned on you.

But he would never talk about it, I mean superficially, like in high school. You know, but inside you're wondering, "What does Bobby really think?" People want to be loved. They want to be accepted. And when you feel as though somebody's slapped you in the face, you always want them to just explain and so that's what I was feeling. But it's mixed up. I can't remember which concert is which. And which night I stayed on. And so afterwards, I just went home.

And that one was the time I went back home. And I did have a wonderful feeling afterwards. You know, at this point I've stopped wondering why Bobby didn't spend time with me and what's he doing in his life. I just thought, I hope someone takes care of that.

What was Bobby Neuwirth's effect on Bob?

I don't know.

I think some people claim that he had a very big influence.

I know he made Bobby laugh. A lot of times I felt as though I was imposing when I was around them. I couldn't ever interpret that shit. I don't know. I think partly because Neuwirth was there to keep Bobby from me. I think Neuwirth was on the spot, and nobody had a handle on Bobby, certainly in England; Neuwirth was with Bobby, I don't know, first thing comes to my mind is Neuwirth was there to protect Bobby from me. I don't know beyond that because I wasn't around enough.

Someone said that he encouraged Bobby to be cruel with others, you know.

I really don't know any of that.

So, it's not something you saw.

I think you get into that role, protecting, when you're close to somebody like Bobby. I think it was unconscious, but I do think he was testing me and I'm sure I did the same thing, you know, partly knowing him and partly not knowing him.

Tell me about spending time with Bob in Woodstock.

The house in Woodstock. I spent, well, one night there.

Yeah. Tell me about your night there and about the house.

I feel like it was all about the motorcycle, me and Bobby. We went out for a ride. I think he was driving. And maybe he was on acid. He was talking about acid all morning long. We were on the motorcycle and we came to this fork in the road and I was terrified. It was one of those things where it hangs over through the whole next day. But anyway, we were near the antique stores. There were lots in Woodstock.

You and Bobby alone?

He used to go out a lot. I mean he used to go places in Woodstock.

Really?

Yeah. It would be different for him now. But he used to go to that little coffee shop in town. I wanted to say something about his memory, his fantastic memory, right. He says he never forgets anything. And I think it's probably true. I mean, he forgets what he wants to forget, but if he wants to remember something, he'll remember forever.

I used to drive his motorcycle around. And I prefer to drive because he's a terrible driver. Just terrible. I mean I figured there was a better chance we'll stay alive if I drive. He was so sloppy. He was, like, unconscious. I always had the feeling it was driving him, and if we were lucky, we'd lean the right way and the motorcycle would turn the corner. If not, it would be the end of both of us.

So, when we got out of the store, I said, "Let me drive." He said okay, so he got on the back and I drove, and I went over a bump. He said, "Hey, watch it, waddaja think I am, a fucking can of tomatoes?," and I laughed. Sometimes if he'd say something like that, I'd laugh for an hour. I laughed all the way home and then later at the house, I'd be looking out the window and I'd thinking about it and I'd start laughing again. It was really funny, riding around with him.

Did he ever talk about learning to drive the motorcycle in the early days?
No. What I said once, we were turning a corner and every time we turned, if there was like a hill and someone was walking by the side, you'd slow down. And I get the feeling he's been in an accident. So he was doing that once, and I said, "Were you in some kind of accident?" And he made another wisecrack, brushing it off.

Oh, and another thing. He wanted to be the best driver in the world. That's what he wanted us to think. Bobby insisted on driving the car one night in Woodstock. And he was driving horrendously, it's all terrifying. And I was thinking that would do it.

So, he's driving and then we had to go the bathroom, so he had to pull in and we all got out of the car and he got out of the car and somebody else got in the driver's seat. And he laughed. He started complaining and I said, "Oh, shut up." And he got in the back seat and put his head in my lap.

After that, what effect did Grossman [Dylan's manager] or anyone else have on Bobby? By that time—
I have absolutely no idea.

You had no contact.
I didn't by then. I guess I never saw Bobby after England or that time in Woodstock.

Not even flowers, or anything like that? I mean, does Bobby ever do something like that?
I don't know if he does now. I don't think he acts like that. But I think with Bobby anything's possible.

Grossman and Bobby had a falling-out.

Bobby has a falling-out with everyone.

Bob wrote that song about him. It had something to do with the house in Wood-stock. Grossman was up there, and Bobby wasn't around.

I think it's probably something like that.

Tell a little more about being together in Woodstock, in Carmel. Or let me ask you this. The journalists were calling you the king and queen at one point. Bobby was going around saying it. You know, "Hey wow, I'm the king, Joan's the queen." Tell me about some of that.

I never heard him say that, but he was probably so relieved to get that crown off his head. But he also wanted the world to know about it.

Had you gone down south long before Bobby ever did?

I'm not so sure. There's that picture in *Don't Look Back* that shows he was down there pretty early.

Was there ever any discussion between you and him about working on the marches in the South?

Not that I remember. I don't remember. I'm also inarticulate, was inarticulate politically in the early days. Bobby did do some political stuff, stuff he thought was political. You know, like he accepted that Tom Paine Award, that big fiasco acceptance speech. Things like that, though—

That was a funny speech. I heard a tape of it.

It was a disaster, I knew from their end, because they were friends of mine and how terrible I was to them. They loved Bobby and he stood up and just damned them all to hell. I mean, they saw the humor in it, too, but it was very hard, because they were responsible for that evening.

But Bobby was just scared. I remember one time, when I was talking to Bobby, I think it was after the discussion about Madison Square Garden. And I said, "Bobby, we were alive up to a point and then we just split." You know, and I said, "We both agree that the world is totally fucked. You know, it's really a mess. But I think there's something we can do about it, and you don't." And he went into a long rap, a very cynical rap, which a good deal of was true, talking about, oh, the American white liberal mostly, who, you know, goes campaigning into the South.

And he said, "Hey, how many people do you know who are willing to die for the cause? How many do you know?" And I named a couple of people.

White people?

Yeah. I mean, not necessarily just that cause but willing to put their body really where their words were. And I considered myself one of them, I thought. That may not be true. Because you never know till the last minute. But I feel that way now and I felt that way then.

I said, "Why do I think there's something that can be done?" And he said, "Maybe it's because you're a chick," and that's all he said.

What was his reaction to the civil liberties fuss? Did you hear about that?

He was sort of, like, oh well, fuck, I mean, oh God. He'd really been awful but he didn't—he was torn because Albert on the one hand was telling him, "You don't have to worry about that, you're a star. You don't owe them anything," you know, and Bobby's inner conscience was saying you really screwed up a bunch of people, until he wrote them that apology. And then after—

It was sort of an apology.

Yeah right.

He went to great lengths to put him down again.

Yeah right. But to somehow get it in his mind he tried to get it straightened out. But I think the whole Albert thing was so destructive for him. And it's sad because Albert used to think he was doing right by people . . . money and fame. I mean, Albert used to say to me, "Like, what do you want, who do you want to meet? Hey, you're a star, you can meet anybody you want to meet. What do you want? I mean, I'll get it for you." That's Albert. I'd say, "Don't talk to me that way. It makes me nauseated."

Like, "You want to meet Marlon Brando, I'll get—"

Exactly. In fact, it was probably Marlon they were talking about. And then I could see how Dylan's mind was—

Albert screwing up his mind—

Well, see, first of all, everybody who's around Bobby, because he's so powerful, automatically feeds that. Because he, in his childish way, is demanding. And in England, the biggest fantasy I had was of smacking Bobby in the face and saying, "Stop it," you know, and sending everybody out of the room and saying to them, "You want to just completely destroy him or you want to just halfway destroy him?"

I mean, it was impossible. But I thought he was completely blind, and he was acting absolutely foul, and everybody there was feeding it. Including Neuwirth, which was sad.

Yeah, this is what I meant before when I was talking about the less pretty things in Bobby's head.

Neuwirth must have been very close to Bobby because I think—whereas I won't talk about stuff that might have been written about me. I'm happy to talk about what was written about somebody else. And I think that song—what's the name of it? "Like a Rolling Stone"—was about Neuwirth.

Really?

Uh-huh. Because that was when Neuwirth left Dylan.

Why did Neuwirth leave?

Because he couldn't stand it anymore. I mean eventually you can't stand it. Because Bobby treats you—Dylan treats you terrible when he's fed up.

You started to say earlier that you, you at that point weren't politically articulate.

I had all the feelings and the urges, but no clear direction.

Was Bobby saying to you at that point, "Hey, you don't know where it's at," as Richard Fariña quoted him?

Bobby had some faint respect for me, I think. I think he recognized that I was real, and even if I hadn't put it together yet, I think he gave me credit for—

No, was he attempting to get you to see that it was time to put it together?

No, we talked about Madison Square Garden. He didn't try to convince me I shouldn't be responsible for the kids. I'm just commenting on what was a vague semblance of respect that he didn't put me down for. Sometimes, but I don't think he did much of it.

No, not necessarily even putting down, but an attempt then to guide you. Maybe along those lines.

I don't think so. I don't remember. But I don't think so. Sometimes it came through Neuwirth, and I had a feeling that Bobby and Neuwirth had talked about it. Saying that I didn't really know what I was doing. Or the nonviolence that meant absolutely nothing to them. They figured I didn't understand it well enough to be preaching about it.

Fariña quotes you at one point: "I don't like the word bomb in a song. People don't listen to words like bombs. I don't like the word bomb." That was around the time that Dylan was moving away from explicit protest.

Yeah. Right.

Was there any discussion or feeling on your part about what Bobby was doing? What was in your head and his head at that point?

Well, at that point I wasn't talking about his music. I was talking about the people who wrote crummy protest songs.

Yeah, I realize that. But it was in that period that he was moving away from the more beautiful protest songs.

See, I'm still sort of puritanical and stiff. I can never enjoy the things he did that weren't protest until a year later. I mean, I'm still like that with a lot of this stuff.

Really?

Yeah, because I felt so abandoned by him, you know, by him saying I won't be responsible for those kids, in his music and in his words, that I just felt sad. And so I was determined not to listen to the other stuff. Like I didn't really like "Highway [61]" until three years after it was written. I was mad at it. You know, I was furious.

Why?

I thought it was a bunch of crap. I didn't really listen to the words. But I felt as though he was inching away from being committed. He was. It's hard to figure out exactly what I feel about that. Because Bobby did what he had to do, and he did leave a lot of us in the lurch. But he wasn't made to do the other things. You can't push him. You feel sad about it. But why bother feeling sad? You know, just go ahead and dig what he does. A lot of what he does, a lot of the music is, to me, wrapped up in nostalgia. I mean, I cannot figure whether it's a life force or a death force. Let's put it this way, some of his songs, even like "Lay Lady Lay," you know, it's beautiful, but it makes people reminisce. It makes people nostalgic.

There is a theory among the thinkers in the movement that the *Nashville Skyline* album is Bobby's way of reaching out to the lower middle class, the lower-class, white working men who the movement is trying to reach now. And Bobby has kept in step with the movement.

That's because they still love Bobby.

Yeah. What's your reaction to it?

Bullshit. I mean, see, Bobby might be writing to those people, because whoever is currently left out—Bobby's on the side of the downtrodden. Bobby plays to the underdog, you know, and whoever's the underdog, you're for.

Is he consciously playing underdog?

I don't know that.

I mean, was he consciously playing it back at that point when you were close to him?

Oh, I think so. Yeah. I don't think he knew it. I mean, then you couldn't call it conscious.

It wouldn't be conscious. But at least intuitively—

Intuitively he did it. I mean he did it in every single phase of his life. Like if he gets sixty-two million fan letters, he says, "I can't handle all this shit."

And then somebody will hand him one and it's written by, you know, some kid, and he sudden gets stricken with that thing of, oh, you know, he has a picture of the kid in his mind, he can see this poor kid.

Did he ever try to draw on that feeling?

Yeah, he did.

Yeah, could he consciously be writing for the downtrodden now?

It sure doesn't sound it to me. I don't think so. You see, if somewhere it came together in his life, then it would make sense to me. What does make sense to me, though, is that he cannot bear to be stale. I mean he's got to move faster than anybody in the field, which he has.

Wouldn't you think he would realize that possibly doing "standards" would be an indication he's stale.

No, not the way he'll do it. He won't be stale when he does it. I mean, I wish he were doing something other than "Blue Moon," but I'll probably enjoy the album. I think the problem is that he's so charismatic and a genius to the point where it doesn't really matter what he does. In a sense he can get away with it, whatever he wants.

Yeah. Except so many of the kids who feel he was writing to them now feel he's deserted them. Especially those political kids.

That's because he has.

Yeah. But he deserts them now even more than he deserted them back at Madison Square Garden. You were telling me about it. Those concerts from '63, '64, '65.

It was fun. I'd look forward to them. The most fun part in the concert would be when I'd ask him up on the stage and we'd sing almost all his stuff, a couple things we did, I guess we did "Butcher Boy." But he'd just come up and sing and, you know, in the hipper places people just went wild. I mean, they just loved him. He'd sing some stuff alone and then we'd sing some stuff together.

What about the Hollywood Bowl? Tell me about that.

I knew they were furious. He had gone on too long.

Was he aware that the crowd was hostile? What was his reaction?

He just seemed very young when that happened. He seemed young and smaller than usual, and I just wanted to protect him all the more, you know? He said something like, oh, he'd never talk about it. But if you brought it up, then he'd admit, wow—

Did you ever bring it up? Was it ever brought up?

I don't remember. No, that would be real touchy then.

No, not then but even later.

I don't remember either.

Describe the hostility of some parts of the crowd.

I think that was part of the whole style. Playing underdog. He wanted to be loved.

Yeah, but why not realize the audience wasn't with him?

He sang the eight songs he'd written that morning. That's what he wanted to do. You know when he wrote "[When] the Ship Comes In"? That is amazing, the history of that little song. We were driving around the East Coast. We were up in the boondocks somewhere, and I had a concert and I don't even know if he was singing with me at that point. But we got to the hotel and I said, "Run in and check and see if this is the right place." He ran in and came out and said, "There's no reservations here." And I said, "Are you sure?" So, I went in and checked. "Oh, Miss Baez, we've been waiting for you." And I said, "Hold on a minute. I want an extra room, please." And then Bobby walked in. He's all innocent and looking shitty as hell. And I said, "Give this gentlemen a room." "Oh, certainly." But they wouldn't talk to him because he had asked, "Does Joan Baez have a room here?" Of course they said no.

And so then he went to his room and he wrote "[When] the Ship Comes In." "And they raise their hands and shout from the bow, your days are numbered." He goes out that night, took him exactly one evening to write it. I'm so pissed he had written something. I couldn't believe it, to get back at those idiots so fast.

Did he often get revenge in his songs? Like "Positively 4th Street," for example.

I think so.

Did he do a lot of writing out at your place in Carmel?

Yeah.

Sit in the corner with a Coke and a typewriter.

Well, he was writing his book then. I still have a big hunk of it. If he wants it back, he can have it.

I think he's about given up on that.

I think so too. He just wrote like a ticker tape machine. He'd just stand there with knees going back and forth.

Still banging them out—

He's standing, and he'd smoke all day and drink wine and I—the only way I could get him to eat was to go over and eat right next to him. You know, get over his shoulder and chew. And then he'd start to pick at it, whatever

I had in my hand. I'd make him "pick" food, so he'd eat. Because otherwise you say, "You want something?" "No, no, no." And he just wrote. He
wrote. One time when he was visiting, he wrote "Four-Letter Word," and a
couple other things. But mostly, the second time he was writing the book.
**Did he ever talk about the different names—the people in the book, what he
was trying to do?**
No. He just said, "Met a girl named Mona, right?" So, he wrote fifteen
pages about Mona. He said, "You know, I've got these fifteen pages about
Mona."
**I always wondered about Echo and Carol and all the other girls back in child-
hood.**
I don't know if Mona existed or not. He wrote some beautiful things about
running up to the house and trying to get in. He had to pee and there was
Mona behind the screen door. He's bouncing up and down and had to pee.
They were beautiful. He never edited anything. So that's probably why the
book never came out. He couldn't take anything out of his "masterpiece."
**You were saying that Bobby would sit in the corner with the typewriter and dash
off hundreds and hundreds of pages and move the typewriter to the next corner
because that was loaded. And then forget it all. You know, you would retrieve
songs and manuscripts.**
I'd pick up stuff.
Wasn't "Treble" one of those songs?
No. "Treble" was an improvisation.
Wasn't it on one of those?
No. He and I were singing at Gerde's one night, and he said, "Hey, I was
thinking of this song." I said, "Well, sing it." "I haven't finished it." "Well,
finish it while you're singing it." So, he got up and made it up.
**Was he in the habit of writing songs and then just discarding them? Did he
leave things like that?**
No, he usually took at least one copy. But the way I remember "Treble" . . .
there was only one written copy anywhere. A friend of mine has it. And
she wrote it down again for him. But there was a verse missing, so the
song I sing on the record I had to make up a bunch of it.
Oh really?
Yeah. But I knew from England that he didn't remember it as it was. We
were at my house and he was floored because we went down to Cannery
Row. There was nothing happening in town. I mean, he's from New York,
right? So we were looking for somewhere to go.

He's from Minnesota, remember. He's not from New York.

Well, but I mean he'd been in New York and the only place you would possibly go in that whole Carmel area was Monterey or Cannery Row. There's one place in Cannery Row. And for some reason that night everything happened in that place. People were jumping up and down on tables. There was this huge guy, sort of a big black giant guy from Big Sur. And Bobby just flipped, holy shit, you know, he'd never seen anything like this in the Village for years. Far out. And he was sitting on my lap and then I'd sit on his lap, and we just walked around, and he was just absolutely amazed. We had fun there.

Did he ever talk about Steinbeck and *Cannery Row*?

Nuh-uh.

Because apparently that was what led him to Woody Guthrie. Steinbeck and the Okies and then Guthrie from there. According to his high school friend, he never grooved on reading *Cannery Row*, but did he mention *Cannery Row*?

No. I was thinking of how, at first, I didn't want to talk about Bobby because I have a loyalty to Bobby. Then when you get started, I realized that everybody talks about him and they like it, because in all of our lives there's so few things that ring real and powerful. No, most people are half-dead, you know, and Bobby may be on a death trip but he's got more life, you know, more something, or zonk, or something to him. So you start talking about him and, it's fun.

What makes you think he's on a death trip? I think I know what you mean, but expand on it.

I always pictured Bobby with a skull and crossbones on his forehead. I guess it's because I've seen him be destructive to himself and to other people. I've seen him not take care of himself. But see, I haven't seen him in years.

I mean back at the point when you were close.

Back then, I was sure he was on something of a death trip and a withdrawal from life. To me it always seemed like that. I mean a withdrawal from commitments. Whenever somebody's mystical, I mean you'd have to be a mystic to be a saint, but you don't have to be a saint to be a mystic. And Bobby's a mystic. He may be more devil than he is saint. I don't know. But he gave us a lot.

You don't have any idea where he might be at now?

No. I think he would like to be somewhere comfortable, and I don't know if that's possible for somebody with a mind like that. I think he's attempting that, from everything I've heard about him. He's attempting it with his wife and children. I mean I hope he finds something there. Maybe he has. Some people say he's happier.

And others say he seems to be searching for something he lost.

Well, Bobby will always search.

For something he lost along the way.

Maybe. But, I mean, I can't imagine Bobby sitting back and saying, "Oh, hi," or "I've finally found peace," but then who the hell would say that, except some moron? I think he's going to try to be isolated. And I don't think you find anything that way. I think you always feel guilty enough in that isolation that you can't find peace. But I do think he's calmed down, and maybe some of the worst times of his life may be over. I mean England was hell. I think it was as much hell for him as anybody else.

In what way was it hell for him?

He was just tied up in knots. I thought so anyway. He was treating everybody like shit and screaming, hollering, and having fits and pasting stuff all over the room in the hotel and breaking things.

When he moved into that hotel room, he cut things out of magazines, took all the pictures off the wall and put this crap up all over the walls. You know, ordered forty-two pounds of food to keep his manager happy. And the room just looked like, you know, the end of the Civil War. It looked like the end of Woodstock. Yeah. I mean it was this picture of total restlessness.

Earlier you talked in terms of loving Bobby. Do you stand on that? You know, I don't [know] how personal we're going to get here.

I think it's hard not to love somebody like Bobby. I'm really drawn to people who are exceptional. But also with him there's that maternal thing we talked about. But you know somebody's got to take of him because he sure as hell doesn't know how to take care of himself. And then just really loving his music. I mean, you love it. You want to hear it over and over and over again, most of the stuff he's done.

Were you able to separate loving his music and loving the man?

Oh, I don't know. That's a hard question to answer because, I mean, how can you ever imagine Bobby not having written that stuff? You know, it wouldn't be Bobby if he didn't write that, and if he weren't a genius. It's a hypothetical question you can't deal with. It was everything. You know, it was the whole combination that makes up Bobby that made him irresistible. And his humor. His warehouse eyes.

Warehouse eyes?

That's his term: "My warehouse eyes, my Arabian dreams . . ." One time—
these just were stupid grubby days. We were traveling somewhere and
I looked through his glasses, and I said, "Jesus, Bobby." And I took his
glasses off and cleaned them. "Oh, hey, wow. Now you can see." And I
said, "How do you like what you see here?" It was pretty low. It made him
laugh.

He was really grubby. He threw up out the window that night. He got
drunk on wine. In a tunnel somewhere he threw up. And just kind of
hollered at whoever's in the back seat to shut their window.

Say a little bit more about what those grubby days were like.

Grubby. They were fun. I remember one time in Newport, Bobby was out
cavorting all night, I guess, and Mimi was with me. And it was when he
was the prince [that] year, you know, Dylan was the prince. And he had
been kind of hanging around me.

That was the '63 Newport.

I guess so.

Prince year, yeah right.

He knocked on the door around six in the morning. In Newport you'd
never go to sleep. Mimi and I were just pooped. So, there's this knocking
on the hotel door and Bobby comes in and he's wiped out. Mimi scolded
him and I can't remember what she said, but he always loved Mimi. She
always loved him, but she always picked on him, and, you know, she had
the knack. She said, "Oh, naughty Bobby, out screwing around all night
and then comes to Joanie's room at six in the morning. Get in," she says.
There was one bed there, and we all got in together. But then he would
seem like this itty-bitty little boy. Naughty Bobby, you know?

What about some of the traveling. Tell me about some of it.

Some of it was just really beautiful. I remember days when I guess we
were with Victor and Dick and Mimi and Bobby and me, and we'd stop on
the highway and get out and dance and we'd horse around and be crazy.
And then Bobby and I would fall asleep in the back of the station wagon. I
mean, that was really, really nice. Because I mean, if you're with somebody
for long periods of time, they're bound to have to calm down. You know?

Once he bought me a beautiful coat, a blue green corduroy thing. I wore
it with a silk scarf and I bought him a black jacket and some weird lav-
ender cufflinks and a white shirt. I remember it was winter and we were

staying at the Earle in the Village. We were leaning out the window one morning watching the kids. I felt as if I'd been with Bobby for a hundred years and all those kids wandering around out there were our children, you know? This couple looked up once and I know they recognized us. They were beautiful.

ANOTHER SIDE OF BOB DYLAN

BOB DYLAN

*Scaduto: Why did you decide to tell me things I don't know about
you?*
*Dylan: Because you wrote a good book and I want to help you make
it better. . . . You know, some of it is pretty straight. And some of it is
very straight. Some of it is exactly the way it happened.*

T ONY INTERVIEWED BOB DYLAN over the course of several phone calls
and in-person meetings. This interview incorporates recorded material
and Tony's notes written during and immediately after their meetings at
Dylan's studio. The manuscript they discussed was published in 1972 as
Bob Dylan: An Intimate Biography.

---

*Dylan told me to come to his Village studio at three o'clock. I arrived as agreed
on a January afternoon, rang the bell and waited at the door for a few minutes. Another door opened several feet from the one at which I was standing.
Dylan was peering out from a second door to his studio. The door opened out-
ward, toward me, and only Dylan's head showed around it. It suddenly flashed
on me, the image of the Bob Dylan hiding behind those huge title cards in the
opening frames of* Don't Look Back." *My reaction was, "He's trying to screw
around with my head."*

*"Got your copy of the book?" Bob asked, pointing to a carbon of the man-
uscript I had sent him two weeks earlier. (This was the old days of typewriters
and carbon copies, before computers and printers.) And then we sat down at
his desk, shoved against the front window of his street level studio—a heavily
traveled West Village street. We got right to the business at hand, which turned
out to be a freewheeling interview/rap session about Bob Dylan—book and
man—in which Dylan talked about his life, his fears, some of the forces that
drove him, his pain at feeling alienated in his world.*

Dylan, dressed in blue denims, with a wool pullover shirt under a denim jacket, boots, and a gray fur-lined hunter's hat he didn't remove in the three and a half hours we talked, was soft spoken, gentle, warm and very open and talkative.

He looked a little chubbier and a great deal less nervous and manic than he had ever appeared in concerts, press conferences, or films. He was a man chatting amiably with a snoop and intruder, and being . . . well, charming is the only word to describe him. He sat next to the window, smack against bamboo blinds that offered no protection from a pedestrian-filled street.

Don't you have any problems with people gawking in at you?

No, man, not at all. If you're uptight about it, we can move to the back.

So, your thoughts . . .

I thought it was great. It ran smooth and true until I got to the interview with Joan Baez, and right after that it began to change for me. Some stuff is untrue. It's cruel.

I'll definitely look at it again and if it's untrue, I'll cut it.

And this is changing drastically now. You get the impression there's some kind of gross spirit in the air. The book was changin' on me right around here. I like the book. That's the weird thing about it. I start as a lad from the Midwest, wanting to make it, and you described all that happened to me. And then it gets to Albert. . .

Okay, and what bothers you about what I say about Albert Grossman?

This here: "Grossman appeared to be more than a manager at this point. He had become almost a substitute father." That's not true. You shouldn't put that in the book 'cause it's just not true.

That's what I got from all the people I talked to—people who were around and seemed to know. That's why I wanted to talk to you. To get your side.

Yeah, yeah. But I never said he was like my father.

But you told Bob Shelton, "If it wasn't for Albert, I could be on the Bowery now. Albert's the greatest manager that ever lived in the whole century of the world." He certainly guided you in a big way.

Yeah, well, I haven't seen him in years. And this thing you wrote about my manipulating others—why can't you say I've been used as much as I've used others? Why don't you show how much I've been used by other people?

Fair enough. I gotta ask you, how did you pick the name Dylan?

I needed a name in a hurry and I picked that one. It just came to me as I was standing there in the Scholar [one of his first gigs in Minneapolis]. The owner asked me how he should bill me, and the name just came to me.
It wasn't [from] Dylan Thomas?
No, not at all. It just came to me. I knew about Dylan Thomas, of course, but I didn't deliberately pick his name.
From lots of comments from old friends in Minnesota, I get the feeling there was some influence from Charlie Chaplin. Of course, Woody Guthrie was a big—
No, I wasn't into Chaplin. If Brando had been into Chaplin, I might have got it secondhand from Brando because I was diggin' him. But I didn't even see Chaplin movies. They didn't have any of his movies there in Hibbing. You should see some pictures of me from back then. I look like Marlon Brando, James Dean, or somebody.

———————

I'm thinking so far the interview was going well. I had been requesting this interview for over a year and had been told again and again by Dylan's personal assistant, Naomi Saltzman, "Bob doesn't give interviews." And finally, "Tell Scaduto as long as he's talked to everybody who knows everything about me, he doesn't need me to tell him about me." So why was he finally agreeing to talk to me? Self-described "Dylanologist" and "garbologist"—he often rummaged in Dylan's garbage pail searching for secrets about him—A. J. Weberman told Dylan, "Scaduto is doing a book that will expose what you really are, a vicious exposé filled with your dark secrets." Dylan had screamed at Weberman and tried to chase him away from going through Dylan's trash. Angry words led to an actual fistfight that ended with Weberman telling Dylan, "You think the things I say about you are rough. Wait and see what Scaduto wrote about you."
    Dylan called me the next morning.
    My son, Larry (or maybe my daughter, Teri—they argue about who it was to this day), woke me New Year's Day morning. My wife and I had partied late the night before, so I was groggy and a bit hung over. I instantly came awake when I was told Bob Dylan was on the phone. I grabbed the pad and pencil I kept by the phone from my many years of working as a journalist, and madly took notes during our conversation.

———————

Do I have your firm promise that after you see the book, you'll sit down and talk to me?

I don't know if I'll sit down and talk to you. I mean, I might sit down and talk to you. It might have nothing to do with the book.

All right.

I'll be glad to give you back the book and sit and talk with you for a minute. I'll tell you what I think of the book.

I don't know if that's going to be enough.

Well, I can't give you a promise I'm going to sit down and talk with you about the book.

Yeah.

I know all the people that you've been talking to. And I can pretty much visualize what they're going to say. I know who they all are. And I know the book is going to be mainly about them.

Well, of course. Unless it's an autobiography, it's got to be about them.

I'm writing an autobiography now.

I know that. But I'm saying, unless it is an autobiography, even if I were doing a book on Napoleon, it has to be primarily about the people who have left memoirs about Napoleon, who have left documents about Napoleon. That kind of thing, especially since I don't have access to you or your papers, so-called, right?

I guess so. I'll read the book and then I'll it give it back to you and I'll tell you what I think of the book. That's about the best I can do.

Okay. I don't know, Bob. I still feel that in return . . . you know, it's a big deal to let somebody see an unauthorized book that's being written about them, to let them see it in advance. And I think the least you should do is let me tell you the basic thesis of my book, and just kick it around with you in advance.

Well, I'll be glad to do that with you. Let me see the book first.

No, no. I'll be glad to do it with you if you let me talk to you first. Even as an informal kind of interview. I just want to let you know who I am and what I am before I let you see the book. Or sit down and talk to me about what you're doing today.

I'll see you after I see the book. I promise you that.

All right . . .

I don't know what to talk about, but I'll see you after I see the book. I would like to see the book. You see, because—

Yes—

I was going to say because I'm working on some things now, and if it goes on too much longer, I'm not going to want to see the book.

What do you mean?

I mean, the book will be in press and I'll be doing some other things and stuff like that. I'm interested in the book now, in this time. I wasn't interested in the book before. I really didn't have any interest in the book.

Okay. Are you doing an autobiography?

Yeah, and it's big. I mean it's really big. I never thought of the past. Now I sometimes do. I think back sometimes to all those people I once did know. It's an incredible story, putting together the pieces. It's like a puzzle as far as stories go. I meditate on it sometimes, all that craziness. I really like to work on it. So I'm trying to do the best I can.

Yeah, but are you ready with it?

No, I'm not ready with it at all, but I'm just getting the stuff together. And I'm sort of keeping my mind on that for a while. And it's a big project. But I figure I should do it, you know? I think it's important for me to do it.

Part of your return to the Village, searching for a piece of the past?

Actually, searching for myself.

Right. How far along are you?

I've been doing it now for about six months. Plus, you know, I've got records to do and different other things which come about. So like I say, I want to see the book. I don't know if I'm going to lose interest in wanting to see it where I just won't care about the book anymore, because I get that way. I can run hot and cold.

If you're doing an autobiography, you're liable to be killing that year of my life if you get your autobiography out before my book comes out.

No, I don't think that's possible.

Why?

Oh, because mine's not even ready to be typed up. So, you . . . Get the book on over—

In any case, wait a minute. If you're going to see my book and know what I've done and you've got an autobiography that—

No, mine's not going to have anything to do with your book. I just want to see what these people have said. Because I know all the people. And I want to see, like, if they're bullshitting you or what they're saying, you know, because I heard a couple rumors.

Like what?

Weberman told me that your book is all like some kind of exposé. And I ain't never done nothing to be exposed about. He said it's all homosexuality, dope smoking, name it. Right? You know.

You know, Weberman is a guy who made you roll up your sleeves. I mean you know where his head is at.

Yeah, he—I did that for him. I offered him a job—working as my chauffeur, drive me around. I said he could hang around me and see I'm clean. Weberman told me, "I won't let you bribe me." He turned me down.

He turned you down? That's crazy.

Yeah, I know. I don't know where his head's at, to tell you the truth.

I mean, you know basically what kind of a freak he is.

Yeah, I do.

Yeah. I mean, obviously. And one of the reasons, you know, again, one of the reasons I told Naomi that I want to talk to you first is my basic feeling that, you know, you're supposed to be shy as all hell and you don't like to meet people. But if you can sit down with a freak like Weberman, then you can sit down with a straight guy like me.

I totally agree with you, and I'm looking forward to meeting with you.

No, and really, Bob, about the homosexuality and the dope thing, of course I discuss that only in terms of what you have talked about in terms of how it's affected your head. There is some dope stuff in the book, definitely, because you made it plain through the years that you were into dope. But it's not an exposé as such. And the homosexuality thing, hell, you know, a lot of people have told me things, but I wouldn't print something like that. I mean that's the kind of thing, you know, you've got to be cruel to use something like that, in my eyes anyway.

Okay, so look, Tony, I'm looking forward to seeing you. I really am.

Listen, I just—you've got to give me a promise that we're going to meet after I've let you see the book.

Yeah. I'll hand you the book back in person.

But you're not going to say, "Thanks, fella, goodbye."

No, no, I wouldn't do that.

You know, I really would like if we can just sit down and you tell me what you're doing today. You know, is it true that you're working on the Broadway show? That kind of jazz.

Okay, I'll tell you all that.

Yeah. Straight and legitimate. All right. I'll get the book to Naomi. It's a pretty long book, and I have to edit it. I have to tighten it up. You know, basically as it reads now, it's a book of interviews.

Okay.

I'll get it to Naomi within a day or two.

Well, that sounds fine to me. And we can meet sometime.

Okay, Bob, thanks . . .

And a few weeks later, at my West Village apartment, Bob seemed a little on edge. He wasn't carrying the copy of my manuscript, but he had a small note-pad.

What did you think? Everybody bullshit me?

What?

Everybody bullshit me?

Well, I don't think it's cut-and-dry like that.

Yeah?

I made notes, like you said.

Oh, that's great.

You know, some of it is pretty straight. And some of it is very straight. Some of it is exactly the way it happened.

Right. Frankly, I think I probably got, you know, closer to the truth than anybody's ever done before. I'm sure a lot of people bullshit me because everybody sees things from their own viewpoint. You know, there are so many people around who are kind of pissed at you. And of course, they're going to be seeing it from that viewpoint. But I do think I've got as close to it as anybody has ever done—any writer on the outside has ever done.

Uh-huh. Well, here's what I want to do. I want to tell you straight out, you know, I'll point it all out to you, who's telling the truth and who's really bullshitting. You can take it from there. I mean, you can print whatever you want. I've got nothing against the book, really, but I'll tell you the truth about the book if you like.

Great, great.

Well, how flexible are you now in the book? Are you going to be willing to change it or—

I'm flexible. I can do almost anything because the book has just been turned into my editors and nobody's doing any editing job until I tell them to do so. So in my own editing job I can certainly make changes. You know, any decision is going to be mine finally, but I'd be very, very happy to give you a chance to refute some of these things.

Well, let me tell you. I mean, I don't care. You could publish that book.

Oh, hell no. I'd rather have it straighter. If you say that somewhere along the line somebody's bullshitting me, I'd much rather have it straight from you.

It's not necessarily a question, though, of somebody bullshitting. It's a question of—

Also my interpretation you might object to.

No, not necessarily. I don't object to any of it really. But the only thing that really comes to mind right now is—all the stuff that Van Ronk said was great. I thought that was great. And Eric too.

Did you? Both—well, Van Ronk especially is pretty uptight over what your reaction might be to what he said.

Yeah, no. Well, that's fine with me. Everybody in there sounds pretty good except a couple of the early stories, which I disagreed with you in the letter there when you said you were going to tighten up the early part. I thought the later part should have been tightened up. One thing was that—I've got it all noted, actually. But let's see, the things which come roughly off the top would be the Jules Siegel thing. Jules Siegel—not to say that he lied or anything, but he did present a very distorted picture.

Which—you mean Jules Siegel in talking about meeting you in California? At the house?

At the house and at the concert. In the motel. And this—we can go over this in detail.

Okay.

But I wanted to tell you that right now, that I didn't dig him even being in the book. He just wasn't always around.

Wasn't he?

He just followed us. I think he even came on the airplane. But I never knew what he wanted. Anyway, I thought it would be a good idea if he just wasn't even in the book. I didn't even see the need for him. But—and the other thing was the Australian actress, who I do remember.

Rosemary—

And she is just bullshitting.

Is she?

Oh, she is really bullshitting, man. I couldn't believe that. I mean that's the stuff which really gets to me because none of it was fucking true. You know, like the part on explaining my songs to her. It's nonsense. I remember kind of what went down, and she's really out of line in saying that stuff. I don't know where she is now, but she's really off the wall. I thought I would tell you that.

Okay. I'd like to talk to you about what did go down.

Well, I can't remember what did go down, but I know what she said went down didn't go down. I'm not about to, you know, resurrect what did go down. I don't want to do that.

I was turned on to her by a close friend who swore that she's an honest chick, and you know, the whole bit, that she's legitimate

Oh, she's just telling a story.

Okay, but the thing that was important to me was, number one, that she was saying in effect what I had always felt about your music from that period.

Well . . .

And again, as you see through the book, I try to avoid as much as possible interpreting you, because I think that's bullshit.

Well, you did do the "John Wesley Harding" thing.

Well, the "John Wesley Harding" thing, I think, was necessary because in my eyes it was a reflection of where your head was at after the accident. I don't know if I'm overboard on . . . the God stuff.

Yeah. Well, all that stuff, I mean, has been written before. Like I said before, "John Wesley Harding" was a silly little song.

Yeah. Maybe I'm overboard and other people are overboard on that, but what I wrote is my honest basic feeling about what that's all about. I may be wrong. People are wrong about what Edgar Allan Poe was saying and what Yeats is saying.

The thing is, I discovered something about all the songs I wrote earlier. I discovered that when I used words like "he" and "it" and "they" and talking about other people, I was really talking about nobody but me. I went into "John Wesley Harding" with that knowledge in my head. You see, I hadn't really known that before, that I was writing about myself in all those songs. I don't know if it's "God," but that's what I figured out.

Let me ask you something. Why did you decide to tell me things I don't know about you?

Because you wrote a good book and I want to help you make it better. I copied down a lot of these things and I can give you a lot of information which you don't have.

Can we talk a little about the music, like if I'm really overboard. You said about "Blowin' in the Wind," the idea came to you that you were betrayed by your silence. That all of us that didn't speak out were betrayed by our silence. Betrayed by the people in power. And you went on to say people don't know. They don't even care.

That's true about "Blowin' in the Wind." I say that to you because it means a lot to me, that song. It means a whole lot to me.

Usually you refuse to talk about your songs, to explain them.

They speak for themselves.

"Blowin' in the Wind" and the songs on your first album—you're not silent. You said "They refuse to look at what is happening." Not you—

There was a violent, angry emotion running through me then. I just played guitar and harmonica and sang those songs and that was it. Mr. Hammond asked me if I wanted to sing any of them over again and I said no. I can't see myself singing the same song twice in a row. That's terrible. And when you talk about me talking about John Hammond, I'd like you to insert "Mr. Hammond" because I do respect that man. If I was talking about him I would have said "Mr. Hammond."

"Boots of Spanish Leather" is a little angry . . . it's about Suze Rotolo?

I was in Italy with Odetta. Suze had gone back to the States and that's when I worked up the melodies of "Boots of Spanish Leather" and "Girl from the North Country."

Echo was the girl from the north country?

Yeah. Of "Spanish Leather"—this is girl leaves boy.

Before we get to your notes and it looks like you have lots, a little more about your songs, feelings about your songs.

I make songs out of what I know and what I'm feeling. A song is an experience. You know, you don't have to understand the words to understand the experience.

There's a lot bitterness in *Another Side of Bob Dylan*. Who were you talking to? Talking about?

I was really talking about no one but me.

Blonde on Blonde—you seem to be coming down hard on people, specific or maybe in general. "Leopard-Skin Pill-Box Hat"—is that a specific person?

I was coming down hard on all the people. The straitjacket—we all gotta break out of society's straitjacket.

Again, talking about you?

Yeah.

Your feelings about _Highway 61_.

I'm not gonna be able to make a record better than that one. *Highway 61* is just too good. There's a lot of stuff in there that I would listen to.

Okay, the Beatles. I know you met them, John Lennon and Paul McCartney. Did you dig their music?

The Beatles. Man, I had heard the Beatles in New York when they first hit.

Then when we were driving through Colorado we had the radio on and the top ten songs were Beatle songs. In Colorado! "I Want to Hold Your Hand." All those early ones.

The words were a little silly.

Yeah, but they were doing things nobody was doing. Their chords were outrageous, and their harmonies made it all valid. You could only do that with other musicians. Even if you're playing your own chords, you have to have other people playing with you. That was obvious and it started me thinking about other people.

Like working with other musicians—a band.

Yeah, but I just kept it to myself that I really dug them. Everybody else thought they were teenyboppers, that they were gonna pass right away. But it was obvious to me that they had staying power. I knew they were pointing the direction of where it all had to go. But I was not about to put up with other musicians. In my head, the Beatles were it.

You're thinking this driving around in Colorado?

In Colorado I started thinking it was so far out, I couldn't deal with it. I mean, eight in the top ten. It seemed to me a definite line was being drawn. This was something that never happened before. It was outrageous and I kept it in my mind. You see, there was a lot of hypocrisy all around, people saying it had to be folk or rock. But I knew it didn't have to be like that. I dug what the Beatles were doing, and I always kept it in my mind from back then.

You are a musician, as well as a songwriter and a singer. What about training, music lessons, learning from somebody?

I can remember traveling through town and if somebody played the guitar, that's who you went to see. Not necessarily to go meet them, but to watch them, listen to them, and if possible, learn how to do something— whatever he was doing. And it was quite a selfish type of thing. You could see the people and if you knew you could do what they were doing, with a little practice, and you were looking for something else, then you could just move on. But when you knew they knew more than you, well, you just had to listen to everybody. It wasn't necessarily a song, it was technique and style, and tricks and all those combinations which go together—which I certainly spent a lot of hours just trying to do what other people have been doing. I guess that was my training.

Okay. Your notes about my book.

Like I say, I read the entire book, and—opened it up and closed it. And frankly, it didn't make a dent. You see? So I don't care if the book is out or not.

What do you mean it didn't make a dent?

Well, I mean it didn't cause me—

It didn't cause you—

I used to pick up these magazines and see articles about me or stories and things like that, and they used to—sometimes they used to hurt.

This one didn't cause you any pain?

No, this one didn't cause me any pain at all. In fact, I rather enjoyed it.

I'm glad to hear it.

And—but I just wanted to clear you up on the information, which I thought if I could do, because it's in my power to do, and the book is going to be out. My book isn't necessarily like this book. Although a lot of the facts you have in the early years, I do—I've got a lot of people in the book which you don't have in the book.

Right. Yeah.

But in any case, I'm willing to go over it. I made a lot of notes, an awful lot. And we can sit and talk about these notes, if nothing else.

Yeah. Also you have not seen the last chapter, and at this stage—

I'd love to read that too.

I haven't even done it yet because frankly, at this stage I'm trying to see how I can sum you up. Basically, the problem is that everybody around town, all the cats in the movement, are running around calling you a capitalistic pig who's ripping off the youth culture and say you should be giving your millions to Jerry Rubin or Alan J. Weberman, or bullshit like that. While others are saying, basically, leave you alone. And my basic feeling at this point is, shit, you're entitled to do whatever the hell you want to do, and why should you support Alan J. Weberman and the rest of the so-called revolutionaries? So, my basic problem with the last chapter is precisely how I feel about this bullshit at this stage, and how I'm going to sum it up.

So, I'd like to rap with you a little bit about that if, you know, if you see clear to discuss your feelings on that kind of crap.

Well, I'm doing something else, you know, so I'm not really too much into that.

Music? Writing?

Producing. Been doing my own producing for a while now. I'm doing everything. Jacket photos. The whole thing.

So *The Basement Tapes*, the bootleg stuff . . .

You should hear the originals—I mean, the originals of *The Basement Tapes*. They're just fantastic. The crap they're putting out doesn't even sound like me. And they're sure not in the order I'd put them on an album.

Before *The Basement Tapes*, before that, the touring was intense, lots of pressures and then you had the accident. You disappeared. What was going on?

You were right on it in your book, when you described all those pressures. But you only touched the surface. The pressures were unbelievable. They were just something you can't imagine unless you go through them yourself. Man, they hurt so much. I had to let things slide.

You stopped touring, you stopped writing your book . . .

Yeah, the book was meaningless. But I plan to release it now—*Tarantula*—because I dig it now. It's a good book. I didn't dig it back then, but I dig it now.

So, Weberman and the so-called radicals. You don't give a shit what people—

You can talk to some radicals who are up on me, right? I hope you don't paint me on just one side of the radical thing.

Do you think people want you to give them answers? Is that what it's about?

Yeah, the times are tough. Everybody wants a leader. Everybody wants a father. They only want somebody to lead them out of their troubles. I don't want to be out front. I have to keep something in reserve. I'm just trying to be as good a musician and songwriter as I can be. I play music, man. I write songs. I try to have some balance about things. Everything else is bullshit.

Like Weberman and others pushing you, saying you're not writing good stuff.

I still have a lot of talent left. I can still do it. None of it has left me. All of those people who are down on me—they'll understand someday. They've got a surprise coming.

What about why you left electric and went country, *John Wesley Harding*? I mean, it's a big shift from electric. The Beatles had just come out with *Sergeant Pepper*, and *John Wesley Harding* is almost acoustic.

It's the best album I could have done at that time. It's a great album. I didn't intentionally come out with some kind of mellow sound. I would have liked a more musical sound, a good sound with more steel guitar, more piano, more music. At that time so many people were into electronics, and I didn't know anything about that. I didn't even know anybody who knew it. I didn't sit down and plan that sound. It wasn't a question of this is what I'm doing and come over here.

So, less sound, more focus on the words?

Something like that.

***Nashville Skyline* is the least angry of your albums. And it's country. It's also a hit. Are you reaching out beyond college kids—to the working class?**

There's no attempt there to reach anybody but me. And it's good singing, really good playing and really good singing. *Nashville Skyline* is the best record I've ever done. So, Weberman, you can talk to him again if you want to, you know.

No, I want to stay away from him. Weberman's too freaky for my taste.

But I mean that kind of thing is, that's pretty, that's pretty New York-y. That type of, that whole type of attitude, you know? That's just a New York type of attitude.

Well, it's pretty much of a campus attitude too, among, at least among the people who are still involved in SDS and, you know, the rest of that revolutionary kind of nonsense.

Well, I really don't have any comments on it, because I'm not, you know, when I was out on the scene, those things didn't even exist. And . . . it's all bullshit. People shouldn't look to me for answers. I don't know what's going down on the campuses, what's in their heads. I have no contact with them, and I'm sorry they think I can give them answers. Because I can't. I got enough to keep me busy without looking for other people's problems.

It seems with "My Back Pages" you're pretty much done with politics and causes.

You can't change the world by protesting against the criminals and their crimes. I can't wage false battles. I have no answers and no truths.

Like what you said in 1965: "I can't be expected to carry the world on my shoulders."

Yeah. I felt it then and I still feel it. You know, I told them not to follow leaders, to watch parking meters. I wasn't going to fall for that, for being any kind of a leader.

Yeah but, you know, it's obvious that you have affected the lives of these people and they now feel you deserted them. It's in effect as if, as if Jesus had come down off the cross and said, "Sorry, fellas, I made a mistake. It was all bullshit. I'm going to do my own thing." This is what they feel about you now.

Yeah. Well, see, I can't talk about that as much. I know people who can. I know some people—I could have somebody come along who could answer all those questions for you.

How so?

Well, he could articulate what I really can't articulate. Because I just don't give a shit, you know what I mean? And I can't even get myself to think about it.

I'd love that opportunity to meet whoever you think could articulate it for us.

Yeah, but I'm sure someone—I could get probably someone who could answer a few of these questions. I don't think you want to spend all day, you know, talking about it.

No, no. It would just be enough to—

Okay, well, when can we meet again?

Well, how about sometime tomorrow?

Tomorrow would be good. Let's say around three?

Yeah. Yeah, all right, tomorrow. Around three.

Yeah. 124 Houston Street.

That's where you have your studio.

Right.

Okay, I'll see you at three over there. Listen, I'm bringing a tape recorder. We'll work out how we're going to—

No, let's not use a tape recorder.

Well, for accuracy, for one thing.

Yeah, it's accuracy, but—

All right, let me—

I was told not to use one.

Why?

Well, because usually the tape can get out of hand and they sell the tape, and—or the tapes usually find a way of getting all over. And I just don't want to . . .

Well, can we do something—

Yeah, we'll write it down exactly verbatim.

All right. I was thinking, let me just toss out an idea. Put it on tape. You keep the tapes and have somebody transcribe it, and then you own the tapes and I would just have a typewritten paper. Something like that. You know, you can get one of your girls just to type it, transcribe it from the tapes. Just for the greater accuracy.

I prefer to do it . . . I prefer just to talk about it first.

Okay. All right, let's see. I'll tell you. I'm going to bring the tape recorder. It'll be in my briefcase. I won't hook it up. And we'll just rap on how we're going to handle it when I get there. But I'll have a tape recorder with me.

Okay. I've got a big list of things we'll go over first, and we'll see how you feel about them.

Yeah, okay.

Okay.

We'll just, you know, do it pretty freewheeling kind of thing and see how it works.

Okay.

———————

So, here I was at Dylan's studio. We were finally going through our copies of my manuscript. Bob was flipping through the pages and checking his notes. So far so good, I thought.

———————

I'll definitely look at the section about Grossman and the story about Joan. Why I wrote it and I'll think about that and if it's untrue, I'll cut it. So where do we stand on other stuff? And the outline of the last chapter?

Yeah, because the concert tour with Joan was a great concert tour. I have nothing but fond memories of it because it really worked so well. Okay, I'm really concerned about those changes that we were talking about before.

But the thing about, the thing about your wife and kids. You know, we've got to get down to hard solid ground.

Sure, like what about yours? What about your wife and kids?

My wife and kids? Nobody's writing a book about me.

Well, I wish somebody would.

Look, Bob, in your autobiography you're going to have to mention Sara and the children, aren't you?

Not in that way.

Well, in what way?

In my poetic way I do. In my style, not yours. But certainly not in your way. What about your wife and kids?

It's really not relevant.

It is relevant, because you know, it could happen to you.

Yeah, and if and when and it does, I guess I would be disturbed over it too. I told you that. I told you my basic feeling has always been that I wouldn't ever talk to a writer.

You know, you can mention that I have children if you want. And—

Okay, Bob, the thing is that I cannot write a biography of Bob Dylan without mentioning the fact that he has a wife and five children. I mean, it's totally relevant to your life, to your way of being in the world. I have kept it down to a minimum. I think I have in the part that you saw, I mentioned that you got married

and I had people discussing—discussing what Sara meant to you at that time and it was maybe two or three paragraphs, tops. And I think she comes in at the accident, which again is one paragraph mentioning her.

Well, why don't you finish up the last chapter and we can talk about that part.

Yeah. But the thing is, I want to make it clear that I cannot in any way take Sara and the children out of the book. I have cut it to a minimum. And that's what I intended to do from the beginning, and if I find you object to any specific points on the way I mention it, I can change it. But I have to have them in the book. Now you've got to understand that. I know that if somebody was doing something like this on me, I'd be pissed too. But I'd understand that it's necessary.

Well, I'm known to retaliate, you know.

I know you are. But first of all, you can't scare me.

I'm playing in the big league and I'm sorry, you know . . .

Come on, man, I'm not any kind of bullshit artist. I'm not. I'm doing a job and I think you recognize that I've tried to do as honest a job as possible, under the circumstances, and I think I've . . .

I hear you did a book on the Mafia.

No, I wrote a number of magazine articles on organized crime and I guess I was the "Mafia expert" for the *New York Post* for over a dozen years.

Oh, I was wondering why anyone would want to do a book like that. It's like doing a book on Bob Dylan—you can't ever get to the truth of the subject.

I've written other books.

Yeah, I know all about them.

I've tried to be as fair and as honest as possible on you.

Well, okay.

But you know, talking in terms of retaliation, that's being a little . . . okay, retaliate, man. No, seriously. I must mention Sara and the children. We can kick it around, we can talk it around, and if you've got ideas . . .

No, I just want to see what capacity you're going to do it, and I'll tell you if I don't approve of it or not.

Okay.

And if I don't approve of it, I'm past playing games too.

Okay.

But I'm serious about it. And I'm just not going to stand for it anymore.

I don't know why you're getting tough.

I'm just not going to stand for it. That's all.

Yeah. But I don't really think there's anything you can do. Really.

Are you kidding?

You can create some problems, but nothing that's going to be, that will be insurmountable. But I don't even want it to reach that stage. I approached you, and when we talked from the very beginning I laid it all on the line.

Everything's cool except on that. In that area.

All right.

And I'm serious now about this. I mean, you should know that.

Yeah. But my feeling still is that I cannot do a book on you without mentioning your wife and children.

Well, I would just want to see how you're going to do it.

All right. I've let you see everything I've done. I mean, I've been straight with you completely, Bob.

I know you have.

I've taken a large step by letting you see the book in advance, and I don't think I can be straighter or more upfront than that. And by sitting down with you and saying, sure, I'll knock out Rosemary McCarty. If you object to that, to what that chick told me, I'm knocking it out. Now, you know, how much fairer can a guy be?

Well, that sounds pretty fair. Now this last part here about my wife and my children, I would like to see what you're going to write about my wife and my children in a book about me.

You've seen what I've written so far. You have it there. In the outline, I just have a sentence saying that I'm going to say something about Bob Dylan at home with wife and children. I don't even know what the hell I have, but it's not going to be a lot. Okay, I'll show it to you when I write it.

Okay. How many nights a week do you figure I go home?

I figure you go home every night in the week when you're not really busy working somewhere.

All right, okay.

But if I mention the fact that you were married, you know, back in '65, I just cannot ignore your wife and your children later on in the book. I feel that I must have them in the book. I'm not in any way going into any great detail. I'm not discussing the fact that they go to school around the corner from you or any jazz like that. I'm just bringing up to date the fact that the stage where the book is ending, you've got five kids.

Okay, I'm sure it'll be all right.

Yeah. Okay. Were there any other, besides the DeVito thing [Don DeVito, A&R

executive at Columbia Records] was there anything else that, in that outline I sent you, that creates any kind of pain?

No, it wasn't painful at all. It was—no, it wasn't painful. It was . . . nauseating. No, that was mainly it. Just the DeVito thing.

Don DeVito called me this morning. Not this morning. Late this afternoon, just after I got home. And told me that you had talked to him and you were a little upset over the quote about how you handled your kids.

No, I wasn't upset with him. I read the thing with Don DeVito, and frankly those things that he's talking about, I mean he, he said a lot of stuff. He didn't say anything bad, I know.

No, not at all.

He said a lot of stuff which I don't know where he could have got it, unless it just came out of his imagination or something. Because he just came over every day to bring tape from my A&R man and he dropped it off and he left. There was a thing in *Rolling Stone* that quoted him. And you know, and it just wasn't true. He said a lot of stuff which wasn't true. And the story about the kids and the Kent State thing, I think he just imagined that.

I can't see how he could imagine it.

Yeah, well, I mean, it didn't happen. But he did imagine something else before, which he wrote in *Rolling Stone,* and he did imagine that. And that's on the record, because there were a lot of people there when he was there. And I don't know if you ever saw this.

Oh, come on. Quoted him on you?

Yeah. In *Rolling Stone.* It all came down to, to find out what was going on, and the only person they could find was him. Who had been there and who had come, again, to drop some Everly Brothers records off for Bob Johnston. And he came to do that, and from being there for about a minute or two, he told his incredible story to *Rolling Stone.*

So I don't, you know, I don't suspect him of lying or something. I just think that he may imagine things. It doesn't ring true, that's all. It doesn't ring true.

You saying, "They never listen?" Your reaction to Kent State?

Well, I mean I didn't react that way to Kent State, I'm sure.

Then how did you react to Kent State?

Well, I don't know. But certainly not like that. I don't even think that it happened when he came over. It couldn't have happened.

That kind of, that's a reaction I would expect of you. "They never listen."

Yeah, I know you would expect it of me. I mean, I think that's something you would have expected me to say too. In fact, I'm pretty sure he must have imagined me saying it. But I couldn't have said it in a million years. It's just not me. That's all. I wasn't into politics. I didn't want any part of that.

Okay, but now are you into some form of politics?

I was talking to Louis Abolafia [West Village radical, political organizer] last night, the guy who ran for president. Told him he should run for president again. He was ahead of his time and should run again. Maybe I should run. Maybe you should run.

That's no answer. You're being vague.

That's because I'm a vague kind of guy.

You haven't answered the question.

Man, just use the quote. Let the quote stand. You see, my thing has to do with feelings, not politics, organized religion, or social activity. My thing is a feeling thing. Those other things will blow away. They'll not stand the test of time.

Okay. So, you're backing off political commitment. What about the radicals who are angry because you gave up your crown of leadership?

A lot of kings throw their crowns around. You know, what's so sacred about a crown?

Afterword

NEW MORNING

STEPHANIE TRUDEAU

I N AN AFTERWORD for the Kindle publication of his Dylan biography in 2008, Tony Scaduto updated Dylan's discography, discussed his exploration of his Jewish roots, his interest in evangelical Christianity, the end of his marriage to Sara, and his subsequent marriage to Carolyn Dennis in 1986. That marriage produced a daughter and ended in 1992. In 2016 Scaduto also reported on Dylan's movies and tours—the Rolling Thunder Revue filmed by Martin Scorsese and his Never Ending Tour that continues today.

In 2016 a friend who is a hard-core Dylan fan and I caught a Dylan concert in Rhode Island at the Providence Performing Arts Center, a 1928 deco movie palace restored to its former glory. The audience was a diverse mix of young and old, their kids and grandkids. Dylan sang from his extensive songbook, and everyone was rocking. I even loved his version of "Stormy Weather." The next year we saw him at the Beacon Theatre, a somewhat seedy former movie theater in New York City. I was moved to tears by Dylan's rendition of "Blowin' in the Wind," which was accompanied by electric violin. A year later, in 2018, I thought he was terribly boring when we saw him again at the Beacon, and we left before the end of the show. Dylan indeed blows hot and cold, but he remains a force to be reckoned with.

The pressure to be a prophet, to be more than what he has always been—a charismatic, ambitious, driving poet/singer/songwriter—has been enormous. Dylan might back away, even disappear for a while, but he always returned to writing, recording, and touring. He told Jonathan

Cott in a 1978 *Rolling Stone* interview, "I have to get back to playing music because unless I do, I don't really feel alive."

In the 1973 paperback edition of his Dylan biography, Scaduto summed up Dylan's journey:

> Attempting to freeze Dylan into a statue of Tom Paine or a wood carving of a latter-day Moses, blowing us the newest version of the Ten Commandments on a mouth harp, is absolute nonsense. Dylan's songs are a search for his salvation, for his solution and no one else's. They may touch a universal chord but that was not his intention.

"Songs—that's my religion," Dylan explained. "I don't adhere to rabbis, preachers, evangelists, all of that. I've learned more from the songs than I've learned from any of this kind of entity. The songs are my lexicon. I believe the songs." Dylan elaborated during a conversation with Scaduto: "You see, my thing has to do with feelings, not politics, organized religion, or social activity. My thing is a feeling thing. Those other things will blow away. They'll not stand the test of time."

Dylan was inspired by potent American vernacular music: folk, blues, and hillbilly—the voices of Woody Guthrie, Robert Johnson, and Hank Williams. In his Nobel Prize speech, Dylan said his first musical influence was Buddy Holly. "Buddy played the music that I loved—the music I grew up on: country western, rock 'n' roll, and rhythm and blues. Three separate strands of music that he intertwined and infused into one genre. One brand." Dylan said Lead Belly was his other major influence. "Somebody . . . handed me a Leadbelly record. . . . And that record changed my life right then and there. . . . Like I'd been walking in darkness and all of a sudden the darkness was illuminated. . . . I had a natural feeling for the ancient ballads and country blues, but everything else I had to learn from scratch."

Dylan embraced the blues and folk. He infused his songwriting with their fundamental themes and created a lyrical language of haunting imagery that is penetrating and universal. Dylan's lyrics occupy the interstice between feeling and knowing. Your mind might not grab and hold all the tumbling words and images, but you feel something is happening.

In his Nobel Prize speech Dylan said, "If a song moves you, that's all that's important. I don't have to know what a song means. I've written all kinds of things into my songs. And I'm not going to worry about it—what it all means. . . . But it sounds good. And you want your songs to sound good."

When Dylan was inducted into the Rock and Roll Hall of Fame in 1988, Bruce Springsteen said, "The way that Elvis freed your body, Bob freed your mind. . . . He showed us that just because the music was innately physical, it did not mean that it was anti-intellect. . . . 'Like a Rolling Stone' posed a question that has not stopped ringing over American life: How does it feel / To be on your own, with no direction home."

From the mid-1960s onward, after he went electric and conquered rock and roll, Dylan veered into country, produced some tracks that almost sounded like easy-listening Mantovani music, hinted at gospel, and covered the American Songbook standards. As Dylan told Scaduto, "They're all just songs. Songs that are transparent so you can see every bit through them. They're just songs to me, that's all. Seriously, I'm just writing songs. With a capital *S*." And singing with a capital *S*. Dylan said singing was as important to him as being a musician and a songwriter.

Todd Haynes said he was unable to find an approach for his film about Dylan, *I'm Not There*, until he read Tony Scaduto's Dylan biography. It made him realize Bob "created a new identity every step of the way in order to create identity." In a *New York Times Magazine* interview, Haynes said, "The minute you try to grab hold of Dylan, he's no longer where he was. He's like a flame. If you try to hold him in your hand you'll surely get burned. Dylan's life of change and constant disappearances and constant transformations makes you yearn to hold him and to nail him down. . . . Dylan is difficult and mysterious and evasive and frustrating, and it only makes you identify with him all the more as he skirts identity."

In his 2016 *New Yorker Radio Hour* podcast interview with David Remnick, Springsteen explained how both Dylan and Scaduto's Dylan biography jump-started his recording career:

> I had just read Anthony Scaduto's biography of Dylan and there was so much about John Hammond Sr. in the book, I knew I had to get an audition with Hammond. I borrowed an acoustic guitar—didn't have a case—and got on a bus from New Jersey with the guitar over my shoulder. I figured I had nothing, nothing to lose. I got the audition. I was in a small room with John Hammond. He was wearing a suit and tie, gray flat-top haircut, horn-rimmed glasses. I sang my song and Hammond said, "You gotta be on Columbia Records."

In 2016 the poet laureate of rock was awarded the Nobel Prize in Literature. The press release announcing the award stated that Bob Dylan "created new poetic expressions within the great American song tradition." Dylan responded in a letter read by the American ambassador to Sweden at the Nobel Banquet in December 2016: "Not once have I ever had the time to ask myself, 'Are my songs *literature*?' So, I do thank the Swedish Academy, both for taking the time to consider that very question, and, ultimately, for providing such a wonderful answer."

In early 1964 Dylan showed up at the Kentucky home of Pulitzer Prize–winning poet Carl Sandburg. Dylan introduced himself by saying, "I'm a poet, like you." Izzy Young, Folklore Center owner, stated in his interview for this book, "Carl Sandburg's poetry was in the protest magazines of the time, the '20s. You know, 'I Am the People, the Mob'—that appeared in the communist literature of the '20s and '30s." Pete Karman, friend and tour assistant for Dylan on that particular trip, told Tony that Dylan was writing all the time. Tony asked, "He was writing lyrics at that time?" Karman answered, "He was writing poetry. The feeling you got was that he was writing poetry and he just happened to be a singer."

Listen to Dylan's Nobel Prize speech because it is one of his best performances ever. He says he learned everything he knows about literature from books he read in grammar school: *Don Quixote, Moby Dick, All Quiet on the Western Front, The Odyssey, A Tale of Two Cities.* Dylan said, "[They informed my] view of the world . . . and the themes from those books worked their way into many of my songs. . . . Quotable poetic phrases that can't be beat." Dylan gives examples: "Somebody asks [Ishmael] where he's from, and he says, 'It's not down on any map. True places never are.'" Dylan says *All Quiet on the Western Front* is a book that makes you lose your childhood. War "is the lower region of hell." And this is his seemingly offhand comment on Odysseus: "He's a travelin' man, but he's making a lot of stops."

Dylan heard the music in the themes and phrases of those books and turned them into lyrics because "songs are unlike literature [because lyrics in songs are] meant to be sung, not read." Thus Dylan brings us to the primacy of the voice, of singing, and the song as one of our earliest art forms with this invocation: "I return once again to Homer, who says, 'Sing in me, O Muse, and through me tell the story.'"

ACKNOWLEDGMENTS

STEPHANIE TRUDEAU

WHY DID TONY OPEN A DUSTY BOX in our basement? He found a treasure: the reel-to-reel tapes of his interviews for his Dylan biography. This discovery came toward the end of his life, and when he died the task of completing his project—this book of interviews—was left to me.

I would like to thank the people who helped bring this book to fruition. I am so grateful to Erik Anderson, my editor at the University of Minnesota Press. His encouragement gave this "baby author" the courage to carry on. I thank my friend and my "one-girl rewrite desk," Sharon Avery-Fahlström, who held my hand along the way, gave so much of her time, offered advice, and read and edited my written contributions to this book. Thank you to Terri Thal for friendship and the willingness to go back in time to add recollections and corrections.

It started with the tapes. My thanks to Joe Lizzi and Ben Young of Triple Point Records, who digitized the old reel-to-reel tapes to create a workable format for transcription. Lisa Hann and Allison Davies carefully transcribed the sounds to written words, brilliantly capturing the lively conversations that these interviews memorialize.

Finally, I thank Sue Hagedorn, documentary filmmaker and utmost Dylan fan, who took me to Dylan concerts, offered encouragement, and always wanted to know how the book was coming along.

ANTHONY SCADUTO (1932–2017) was a journalist and biographer of rock musicians who also wrote under the name Tony Sciacca. His most famous work is *Dylan,* the landmark biography first published in 1971; this influential book was one of the first biographies to take an investigative journalist's approach to the subject. In 1976, he wrote *Scapegoat,* an investigation into the kidnapping and death of Charles Lindbergh's son. He also wrote biographies of Mick Jagger, Frank Sinatra, Marilyn Monroe, and John F. Kennedy.

STEPHANIE TRUDEAU has been an actress, singer, and writer, and she was a research assistant to authors Anthony Scaduto and Ludovic Kennedy. She lives in Brooklyn, New York.